Human Communication Technology

Scrivener Publishing
100 Cummings Center, Suite 541J
Beverly, MA 01915-6106

Artificial Intelligence and Soft Computing for Industrial Transformation

Series Editor: Dr S. Balamurugan (sbnbala@gmail.com)

Scope: Artificial Intelligence and Soft Computing Techniques play an impeccable role in industrial transformation. The topics to be covered in this book series include Artificial Intelligence, Machine Learning, Deep Learning, Neural Networks, Fuzzy Logic, Genetic Algorithms, Particle Swarm Optimization, Evolutionary Algorithms, Nature Inspired Algorithms, Simulated Annealing, Metaheuristics, Cuckoo Search, Firefly Optimization, Bio-inspired Algorithms, Ant Colony Optimization, Heuristic Search Techniques, Reinforcement Learning, Inductive Learning, Statistical Learning, Supervised and Unsupervised Learning, Association Learning and Clustering, Reasoning, Support Vector Machine, Differential Evolution Algorithms, Expert Systems, Neuro Fuzzy Hybrid Systems, Genetic Neuro Hybrid Systems, Genetic Fuzzy Hybrid Systems and other Hybridized Soft Computing Techniques and their applications for Industrial Transformation. The book series is aimed to provide comprehensive handbooks and reference books for the benefit of scientists, research scholars, students and industry professional working towards next generation industrial transformation.

Publishers at Scrivener
Martin Scrivener (martin@scrivenerpublishing.com)
Phillip Carmical (pcarmical@scrivenerpublishing.com)

Human Communication Technology

Internet of Robotic Things and Ubiquitous Computing

Edited by

R. Anandan
G. Suseendran
S. Balamurugan
Ashish Mishra
and
D. Balaganesh

Scrivener
Publishing

WILEY

This edition first published 2022 by John Wiley & Sons, Inc., 111 River Street, Hoboken, NJ 07030, USA and Scrivener Publishing LLC, 100 Cummings Center, Suite 541J, Beverly, MA 01915, USA
© 2022 Scrivener Publishing LLC
For more information about Scrivener publications please visit www.scrivenerpublishing.com.

Wiley Global Headquarters
111 River Street, Hoboken, NJ 07030, USA

For details of our global editorial offices, customer services, and more information about Wiley products visit us at www.wiley.com.

Limit of Liability/Disclaimer of Warranty
While the publisher and authors have used their best efforts in preparing this work, they make no representations or warranties with respect to the accuracy or completeness of the contents of this work and specifically disclaim all warranties, including without limitation any implied warranties of merchantability or fitness for a particular purpose. No warranty may be created or extended by sales representatives, written sales materials, or promotional statements for this work. The fact that an organization, website, or product is referred to in this work as a citation and/or potential source of further information does not mean that the publisher and authors endorse the information or services the organization, website, or product may provide or recommendations it may make. This work is sold with the understanding that the publisher is not engaged in rendering professional services. The advice and strategies contained herein may not be suitable for your situation. You should consult with a specialist where appropriate. Neither the publisher nor authors shall be liable for any loss of profit or any other commercial damages, including but not limited to special, incidental, consequential, or other damages. Further, readers should be aware that websites listed in this work may have changed or disappeared between when this work was written and when it is read.

Library of Congress Cataloging-in-Publication Data

ISBN 978-1-119-75059-8

Cover image: Pixabay.Com
Cover design by Russell Richardson

Set in size of 11pt and Minion Pro by Manila Typesetting Company, Makati, Philippines

10 9 8 7 6 5 4 3 2 1

Contents

Preface

It is with great pleasure that we introduce this book on "Human Communication Technology: Internet of Robotic Thing and Ubiquitous Computing". Our objective in writing it was to adopt advancements in the field and help disseminate results that cover a broad cross section of technical disciplines concerning recent applications and case studies in the areas of human communication technology, robotic intelligent systems, and ubiquitous computing among working professionals, academics and researchers. The book is also designed to provide students with a platform for exploring knowledge relating to human communication technology that will enable them to produce serviceable innocuous and purposeful systems using cutting-edge technology to yield computer systems with decent usability. In order to achieve these goals, developers must first attempt to understand the factors that determine how people use technology.

These new architectures, networking paradigms, trustworthy structures, and platforms for the integration of applications across various business and industrial domains are needed for the emergence of' intelligent things (static or mobile) in collaborative autonomous fleets. These new apps speed up the progress of paradigms of autonomous system design and the proliferation of the Internet of Robotic Things (IoRT). Collaborative robotic things can communicate with other things in the IoRT, learn independently, interact securely with the world, people and other things, and acquire characteristics that make them self-maintaining, self-aware, self-healing and fail-operational. Due to the ubiquitous nature of collaborative robotic things, the IoRT, which binds together the sensors and the objects of robotic things, is gaining popularity. Therefore, the information contained in the sixteen chapters of this book, as briefly described below, was chosen to provide readers with a better understanding of this interdisciplinary field.

– Chapter 1 describes how robots share information and operate in a common environment.

– Chapter 2 defines the BCI-based headsets developed with the architecture of the IoRT to analyze incoming EEG signals for the corresponding actions of human beings.

– Chapter 3 explains why automated verification and validation of IoRT systems warrant the functional safety and reliability characteristics of software using appropriate program verification techniques. These include automated model checking and theorem proving in combination with automated test frameworks for establishing independent testing in ubiquitous software environments using reduced manual resources and timelines to verify and validate systems with a higher degree of operational efficacy.

– Chapter 4 explains the sequential pattern mining process and fuzzy time interval sequential pattern mining using genetic algorithm (GA), pattern matching using similarity computation index (SCI), classification based on SCI value, and significant pattern evaluation process. The second part of the chapter shows how patients are assessed using a belief network automated via the IoRT.

– Chapter 5 describes the various Li-Fi technology applications used for man-to-machine and machine-to-machine communication. Li-Fi will be the future technology for short-range wireless communication.

– Chapter 6 highlights the computation process for monitoring human activity using human-centered computing. It focuses on the design, implementation, and evaluation of interactive information gathered from the technological system in relation to usable and accessible information gathering. The multimodal human communication interaction system is premeditated to receive communication from humans to provide improved results and an operative communication process.

– Chapter 7 showcases the automatic robotic systems designed and developed with a combination of computing, intelligence and the internet of things (IoT).

– Chapter 8 outlines the general layered architecture of an IoRT system with an emphasis on the various communication protocol choices available for each layer. The initial subsections summarize the latest developments in communication standards and data exchange protocols that tie robotics and the IoT together. There is a discussion of some of the prominent communication challenges in realizing an IoRT system along with the latest research solutions. A later subsection provides details about the open platforms available for developing IoRT solutions and also highlights the developments in the industrial sector that could bring such solutions to everyday life.

– Chapter 9 describes a real-time hazardous gas classification and management system using neural networks. The chapter begins by giving a detailed view of the preparation of an input dataset from a sensor for an artificial neural network model that helps to classify and measure the concentration of gases and ends with network training using the dataset.

– Chapter 10 focuses on medical imaging research that uses a noninvasive diagnostic technique and many effective algorithms, such as gravitational search algorithms (GSAs), for optimization of modular neural networks (MNNs) in pattern recognition. In this chapter, a novel method known as the hierarchical elitism gene gravitational search algorithm is proposed.

– Chapter 11 proposes a machine learning algorithm that combines the IoT application areas. A basic aim of this chapter is to also analyze the different uses of machine learning in the IoT for healthcare, logistics, transportation and agriculture among others.

– Chapter 12 describes the time-variant adaptive techniques for feedback cancellation in hearing aids. The IoT-based bias analysis provides a statistical evaluation of the steady-state performance of an acoustic system and offers significant and robust feedback cancellation in the presence of varying environmental conditions.

– Chapter 13 applies the concepts of Industry 4.0 and Smart Cities Mission to pave the way to the concepts of Agriculture 4.0 and Smart Farming through the use of the IoT. With the evolution of the IoT, we have the ability to totally change the different phases of agriculture.

– Chapter 14 mainly focuses on the green computing practices used in combating COVID-19 in a study by the Institute of Health Sciences in Gaborone. This study investigated different literature reviews concerning green computing practices assisted by several theoretical models, such as the technology acceptance model, utilized to present an economical explanation of the components that define the adaptations, which are generally applicable to many utilization behaviors from different computing innovations.

– Chapter 15 lists the available technology of sensor, pervasive computing, and intelligent information processing widely used in body sensor networks (BSNs), which are a branch of wireless sensor networks (WSNs). These BSNs play an increasingly important role in the fields of medical treatment, social welfare and sports, and are changing the way humans use computers.

– Chapter 16 explains how the IoT, assisted by advanced electronic tools, offers the best ways of experiencing and responding to the outside world. However, at the same time, with the help of sensor information, new problems and obstacles will emerge as new application scenarios are envisaged. Therefore, this chapter investigates further developments, such as the interoperability between heterogeneous devices and confidence in smart devices, to meet business and technical requirements such as validity, safety, and trust.

To conclude, we would like to extend our appreciation to our many colleagues. We also extend our sincere thanks to all the experts for providing preparatory comments on the book that will surely motivate the reader to read the topic. We also wish to thank the reviewers who took time to review this book, and are also very grateful to our family members for their patience, encouragement and understanding. Special thanks are also due to many individuals at Scrivener Publishing, whose talents and efforts made the publication of this book possible. Finally, any suggestions or feedback from readers to improve the text will be highly appreciated.

R. Anandan
G. Suseendran
S. Balamurugan
Ashish Mishra
D. Balaganesh
August 2021

Internet of Robotic Things: A New Architecture and Platform

V. Vijayalakshmi[1], S. Vimal[2]* and M. Saravanan[1†]

[1]Department of Information Technology, School of Computing, SRM Institute of Science and Technology, Kattankulathur, India
[2]Department of Information Technology, Vel Tech Multitech Dr. Rangarajan Dr. Sakunthala Engineering College, Avadi, Chennai, India

Abstract

IoT is an interconnection of internet-enhancing devices that increases the usage of internet. It provides a stable base for users to form communication with other devices. The linked devices will share data among themselves through network protocols. Internet of Things is a technological change among the Blockchain, AI, Cloud Computing, Machine Learning technologies with increasing speed to solve the problems.

The area of Cloud robotics includes cloud computing, Internet technologies and cloud storage. It enables robots to benefit from quick increases in online data transfer rates and reduces the maintenance, updates. By using cloud robotics, operation durations can be reduced and costs increased. Cloud robotics is used in a variety of areas, for example cloud computing, big data, distributed computing-Human and robotic constraints, such as service quality (QoS), physical infrastructure, privacy, jitter, multi-robotic management, etc.

In order to avoid limitations in cloud robotics we combine the Internet of Things with Cloud Robotics to provide smart, high performance, reliability, stability, cost-effectiveness and collaborative multi-robot networks. This paper describes how robots will share the information and operating in common environment. IoRT can make a solid base for implementing robotics in diverse applications. This work discusses about the architecture and platform of IoRT.

Keywords: Amazon web services, real-time processing, robot operating system, cloud services, internet of robotic things, robotics

*Corresponding author: vimalshan@gmail.com
†Corresponding author: saravanm7@srmist.edu.in

R. Anandan, G. Suseendran, S. Balamurugan, Ashish Mishra and D. Balaganesh (eds.) Human Communication Technology: Internet of Robotic Things and Ubiquitous Computing, (1–26)

1.1   Introduction

Internet of Things (IoT) is an integrated system of computers with special identifiers that is capable of transmitting data across a network without human interference. Smart home is a traditional control center, usually a handheld monitor of home appliances. A basic function is to switch the computer near or remotely on and off. In recent years the use of cellular networks has increased and is increasing rapidly.

A global data society system enables advanced automated administrations by interconnecting mechanical items that create, interoperable data and communications developments in distributed computing, distributed storage, etc. which is based on the benefits of hybrid cloud and joint administration. Internet creativity is focused on the advantages of hybrid cloud and public willingness to allow robots to take advantage of the tremendous processing, storage and exchange capabilities of today's cloud providers. At the same time spelling maintenance and refreshment overheads and improves flexibility on Custom Domain dependent middleware levels.

A robot is basically a machine which utilizes a mechanical stage that joins distinctive interconnected sensors, PCs and actuators to complete an activity. An automated stage encourages equipment deliberation, encourages programming, mechanical gadgets and electronic frameworks interface the executives. The multifaceted nature of the created conduct is limited by the handling intensity of the robot, which diminishes the first versatility of the robot, contingent upon the nearby equipment. The remote relocation of robot computation encourages robots to diminish weight, equipment expenses and battery use. Furthermore, it makes it simpler to access and store the information created. Distributed storage is one method of remotely getting to and putting away information.

Distributed computing alludes to a brought together cloud-based database of adaptable assets. The virtual machine, gadget or various cloud highlights, for example small scale administrations, is utilized as a cloud administration. Small scale administrations are cloud administrations running serverless from outsider providers, for example, Amazon, etc which abstracts the designer's equipment. Distributed computing empowers a wide scope of versatile preparing force and capacity ability to be utilized as focal usefulness for robots through conceptual equipment. An idea named cloud robotics [1] is developed by consolidating the two regions of mechanical autonomy with distributed computing.

Cloud apply autonomy is a cloud-based robot that utilizes the common pool of cloud assets. Cloud applies autonomy present incorporated highlights, designate capacity assets and procedure capacity to numerous

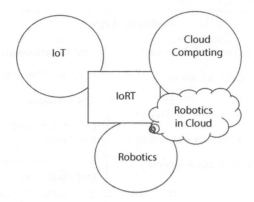

Figure 1.1 Description of the IoRT innovations.

robots. Anyway one significant element of cloud apply autonomy is the capacity of the robot to convey over the Internet utilizing normal correspondence innovation with different robots and devices. One answer for a worldwide system for availability is IoT.

IoT is an overall system that can connection and move information over the web to a group of gadgets known as things. This permits all members to convey utilizing [1] a typical correspondence innovation.

Subsequently, we intend to build up a novel idea, "Internet of Robotic Things" (IoRT) which is joined using these networks, as appeared in Figure 1.1. Internet of Robotic Things includes IoT, mechanical autonomy and distributed computing. Internet of Robotic Things attempts to interface propelled robots, utilizing existing and developing correspondences innovations, to trade interoperable information, as a general foundation.

1.1.1 Architecture

The architecture of IoRT is divided into five groups and each layer is represented in Figure 1.2. The protocol stack for each layer is represented in Figure 1.3.

    (i)   The hardware/robotic things layer,
    (ii)   The network layer,
    (iii) The internet layer,
    (iv) Infrastructure layer, and
    (v)   The application layer

i. Hardware Layer
The layer comprises robots, like vehicles, sensors, railings, submersible equipment, home equipment and mechanical sensors. The hardware layer

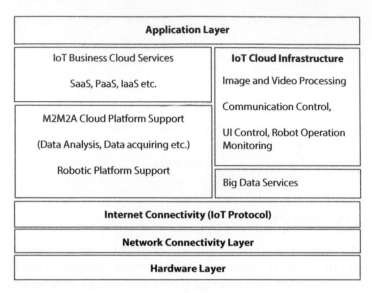

Figure 1.2 Conceptual model of IoRT Architecture.

is concealed in physical matters for using data in the layer above, namely the network layer.

ii. Network Layer

The second-base layer with system configurations is the network layer. This layer transmits data segments between frameworks as groups. Right when you message your buddy, this layer gives out source and objective IP conveys to the data parts. Your IP address is the source, and your partner's is the objective. Layer 3 similarly chooses the most ideal ways for data movement. Cell availability including 3G [3] and LTE/4G [4] are empowered in this layer, which enables smooth direct of transmission of data in the mechanical system [5–7] foundation in wider separation.

Application Layer	**CoAP**
Transport Layer	**UDP**
Network Layer/Routing	**IPv6, RPL**
Adaptation Layer	**6LoWPAN**
Datalink Layer	**MAC 802.15.4**
Physical Layer	**PHY 802.15.4**

Figure 1.3 Protocol stacks of IoT.

iii. Internet Layer

This layer excludes the shows that fulfill the inspiration driving keeping up interface states between the close by center points and that commonly use shows that rely upon the encompassing of bundles express to the association types. Such shows have a spot with the association layer. Web layer shows use IP-based groups. Distribute/purchase in training, multicast support, forward communications, products distributed structures, scatter the layout sorted out, provide protection for data chart displays, middleware lining, lightweight quarter-based computerization, and direct buying depends on the constantly embedded systems.

iv. Infrastructure Layer

IoT-based mechanical cloud stack is the most critical (cloud managerial, middleware, business process and information-oriented methodology) component of all network holding. The IoT-based mechanical cloud stack is a mix of five separate, but linked entities such as automated cloud storage, M2M2A cloud storage, IoT cloud management, Big Data and the technical base of the IoT cloud. Let us address each of them.

Cloud M2M2A is ready to use the worldview of MachineToMachine ToActuator as a robotic powered machine that anticipates being a basic machine to contribute to IoRT. M2M can be visualized as a variety of machines linked to a system that transfer data in and out without human interference and provides ideal computerized control. In order to bring real and virtual world together MachineToMachineToActuator [9] method uses helpful structures, where various sensors and mechanical inventions can be combined. In such sort of arrangements, pictured data administrations created by the sensors are between connected among themselves while figuring particular chain of activities/responses made to be performed by the robots. Out of many, information assortment, investigation, gadget the board, map cum climate information coordination and sensor information aggregation are of most significance. To lay it out simply, business fogs do serve the IoRT by allowing affiliations and makers of computerized structures to reduce their overhead of operational (business related) practices through an average layered technique where a wide scope of fundamental backings are given.

"A model intended to encourage the data society, empowering propelled benefits by interconnecting (physical and virtual) things dependent on, existing and developing, interoperable data and correspondence advancements through ennoblement of omnipresent, advantageous, on-request arrange access to a mutual pool of configurable figuring assets (e.g., systems, servers, stockpiling, applications, and administrations) that can be quickly provisioned and discharged with insignificant administration exertion or specialist co-op collaboration that influence the need and heterogeneous availability issues of the client driven things in all around characterized style" [10].

In such situation, IoT cloud empowers automated frameworks to be enabled with a few administrations of which not many have been introduced, for example, picture handling, video preparing, area recognizable proof, correspondence control, organizing with SNS, mechanical conduct situations, and UI control as uncommon consideration.

v. The Application Layer

The application layer is the first most layers in the IoRT engineering which scatters the client experience by finding the tests performance over utilizing the mechanical autonomy. This layer lies over the organization divulgence layer. It is most vital layer in the designing loosening up from the client closes. It is the interface between the end devices and the framework. This layer is realized through a committed application at the contraption end. Like for a PC, application layer is executed by the program. It is the program which completes application layer shows like SMTP, FTP and HTTP. Same way, there is application layer shows demonstrated in setting to IoT as well.

1.1.1.1   Achievability of the Proposed Architecture

Let us first present the center attributes of IoRT engineering which is trailed by the highlights of the most diffused robots (automated framework), at that point IoT handling units, and cloud mechanical technology stages. IoT and mechanical technology are mutually embraced to oversee upgraded benefits in everyday human way of life.

1.1.1.2   Qualities of IoRT Architecture

Internet of Robotic Things gives a few notable highlights that are not quite the same as conventional mechanical technologies administrations, for example, cloud apply autonomy and arranged apply autonomy, which are summed up as underneath?

i. Similarity

The proposed IoRT engineering utilizes the interface named Web Service Description Language (WSDL), it endeavors to normalize a few correspondence interfaces conveyed for the design of IoRT. WSDL is incorporated to encourage some general correspondence between the independent robots (or automated frameworks) and along with different fragments of the IoRT.

Administration index will store the data of all the sent administrations for mechanical frameworks. All the administrations are distributed as a web benefits along these lines make IoRT simpler to form the intricate applications by utilizing fundamental online parts.

ii. Context Awareness

With regard to the physical and natural parameters detected, the IoRT biologic system connected sensor hubs obtain information on the overall environment. The decisions made at this time by the mechanical frameworks are well informed.

iii. Diversification Virtualized

The current IoRT design utilizes a devoted framework segment containing area ID mapping based layer answerable for virtual mapping robot articles with robots which is physically present. In this manner producer and individual just demands wanted administrations without thinking of robots physically present are doled out for with their prerequisites. The design would bolster and approve the dissimilar mechanical technology; every separate robot (or automated framework) may have totally extraordinary equipment engineering and programming. For instance, a portion of the sent robots could be adjusting in medical clinics, some others in cafés, not many for amusement reason, and some as robot-cops or in salvage activities and so forth. Thus, the IoRT design is really virtualized and differentiated by its trademark.

iv. Elasticity

Increased IoRT engineering by new robotics type, e.g. rambles, steward robot and so on, is the existing mechanical administrations. With cloud MachineToMachineToActuator or new administrations in the IoRT, the framework is empowered and distributed as it was purchased on the web interface.

v. Compatibility

IoT gadgets can support a few interoperable communications protocols in conjunction with the network and government, so they can speak to various kinds of gadgets so foundations. The IoRT is now compatible with its own ethical character.

vi. Dynamic Self Adaptive

IoT hardware and systems should be able to slowly adapt to the various environments and carry on tasks that depend on the operating situations, the individual circumstances of the robot or the situation detected [11].

vii. Geographical Distribution and Ubiquitous Networking

Necklaces are usually available via the internet and use the internet as a transport aid. Any Internet gadget, whether an electronic frame, a mobile phone, a PDA or any other equipment, can also be reached by distributed cloud administrations. Moreover, a large number of current robots consist of cloud-enabled server farms in many remote geographical regions around the world to achieve high system performance and limitation. A technical group can produce the most exceptional support without a very impressive geo-organized set of ranges. This makes IoRT an unavoidable impact geo-passed.

1.1.1.3   Reasonable Existing Robots for IoRT Architecture

All things considered, mechanical independence is requested by dual groupings: Robotics Service and Robotics Field [8]. Robotics Service says to Domestic and Humanoid robots that run the human arranged consistent assignments. Model incorporates household, office work, individual portability associates, room cleaning, and conveyance and so forth. The Robotics field then again makes the difference between robots that function in uncontrolled and unstructured conditions, especially externally [31].

Type	Model	Technologies description
Humanoid & Domestic Robot	Adept Mobile Robot	Encouragement of human computer interface practices and other robot vision, travel, security and control and education tasks
REEM Robotics	REEM_Robotics	Promoting human activities in a broad range (i.e. hotels, the industry and the airports) indoor environments
Robosoft Robulab	Family of Robosoft Robulab	It control entire home related communications and used for urgent calls and social uses.
Fly-robot	AscTec Quadrotor	Control and monitoring of the environment

(Continued)

Networked Robot	Tele-operated robot	Supports research, awareness to public and education
Autonomous robot	Autonomous robot	Exchange data with minimum human intervention
Robot of Marine	Robotics Clear path_ Kingfisher	Used in Marine transportation

Extra equipment might, for example, be used with the above robots to gather additional data, such as sensors, RFID, weather forecasts, meteorological and cameras.

i. IoT Processing Devices

IoT's importance for smart agribusiness was mentioned [12] as the significance of 5 essential keys of IoT systems, including physical layers, data-connected layers, routing layers, transport layers and applications layers [13]. Related to IoT correspondence innovations incorporate conventions, cloud administrations, and the board issues are as of now introduced in IoRT design. Here, this sub segment would bring up the proper gadgets (preparing modules) that are generally appropriate for mix of IoT with apply autonomy.

Arduino Uno, Arduino Yun, ARM mbed NXP LPC1768, Intel Galileo Gen 2, Intel Edison, Electric Imp 003 Raspberry Pi B+ and Beagle Bone Black are among the numerous IoT preparation systems. ARM mbed is also available. It is classified dependent on like the arguments voltage, transport, memory, situation advancement, clock speed, voltage, Input/Output availability, types of processor used. These preparing units are generally reasonable for improvement of IoRT. It is deals with asset obliged situations effortlessly of consistent heterogeneous availability as needed for the IoT.

1.2   Platforms

1.2.1   Cloud Robotics Platforms

As we discuss about Internet of Things empowered technology, stages of cloud assume an essential job require for information driven, machine driven, condition driven, and framework driven important data in a problem free condition where most extreme part of calculation, correspondence, and dynamic exercises are utilized. As distributed computing are improving it has assists with starting a couple of cloud-based mechanical stages among worldwide market. The existence of mechanical phases gives attention to the possibility of IoRT building in the coming years. Different cloud mechanical stages being utilized for genuine and inquire about purposes. Most of the phases will certainly provide the Software as a Service (SaaS) model, while the Platform as a service is only recommended by Artoo and FIWARE. From the data we can claim that most of the mechanical autonomy stages that are allowed by cloud are still at their beginnings. Rapyuta, FIWARE and Artoo are encouraging to go further in areas such as IoT and related fields, while others struggle to achieve this goal yet, IoT is planned to be added as a significant change to the other stages in the project.

The fundamental segments incorporates, progressed automated frameworks, extra sensor/actuator based gadgets, asset compelled however suitable preparing units, and existing cloud upheld mechanical stages, might be aggregated to build up the IoRT. Internet of Robotic things has been established by combining Internet of things and cloud robotics which is expected to evolve in the new automated creations in the world.

1.2.2   IoRT Platform

The IoRT stage, robotics, IoT and distributed computing can be done in the context of three improvements. The additional capacities required by the system are important to fabricate a stage that characterizes IoRT attributes.

- Interoperable data dissemination among different robots utilizing existing and advancing correspondence advances.
- Modern server farms give unified distributed computing administrations which permit information preparing, stockpiling and correspondence assets.

The IoRT platform can be built by combining the following as shown in Figure 1.4:

i. Distributed Network
The main capacity is named as dispersed system in which correspondence innovation supporting numerous end gadgets to speak with one another.

It arranges various robots to impart data to one another over a typical correspondence innovation empowering all the robots associated with build up associations with one another.

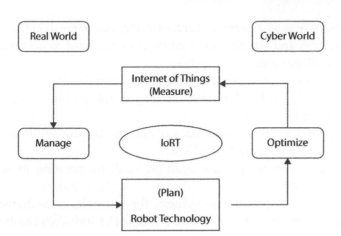

Figure 1.4 Platform of IoRT.

ii. Centralized Cloud Processing
The subsequent capacity has a place with this and it bolsters the distributed computing functionalities. This helps robotics to use highly oriented features, making it easier for robotics to exchange data, use data which can be deleted and unload their local appliances.

iii. Combining These Empowers an all the While Unified and Dispersed System
We expect to build up an IoRT stage by consolidating existing advances for example a blend of administrations comprising of an automated stage, an IoT stage and cloud administrations.

1.2.3 Design a Platform

To plan a stage to empower no concurrently share data utilizing disseminated system of robots notwithstanding empower perception, stockpiling and preparing power utilizing incorporated cloud benefits progressively.

1.2.4 The Main Components of the Proposed Approach

- Robot Operating System (ROS): It is a structure and Open source mechanical stage with huge programming libraries and apparatuses to create automated applications.
- Amazon Web Service (AWS) IoT center: A stage wherein Internet transport conventions is mindful to interface distinctive IoT gadgets.

- Function as a Service (FaaS): Collection, elimination, evaluation and simulation of cloud features, used as serverless administration.
- DynamoDB: A FaaS database giving stockpiling.
- AWS Lambda: Compute service for calculation condition giving handling power.
- Serverless: A common pool of equipment powerfully oversaw by an outsider cloud seller.
- Micro-administrations: Multiple FaaS cooperating to play out an errand.
- Service: A product usefulness, for example, a mechanical stage, an IoT stage, Amazon DynamoDB and AWS Lambda.

1.2.5   IoRT Platform Design

The IoRT phase structure consists of a mechanical stage, an IoT phase, cloud administration and related links. Figure 1.5 shows the Service Oriented Test Platform to show how the connection is made from ROS to AWS.

i. Robot Operating System
ROS is a mechanical open-sourced system regularly utilized for structuring apply autonomy. It utilizes a distribute buy in informing design. There is an ace hub in each RO system to start a correspondence among distribute and buy in, empowering hubs to distribute and buy in to the themes/channels to which they are set. A hub in the system is a members, is capable to impart its data to different hubs utilizing depicted points/channels.

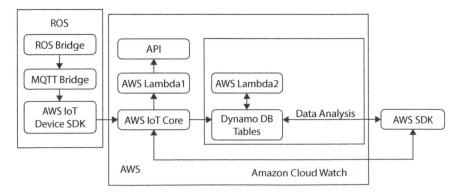

Figure 1.5 Service oriented test platform.

In Figure 1.6, the ROS Master builds up a shared association among the distributing and buying in hubs upon commencement, and persistently focuses for fresh out of the plastic new promotions. The association between the hubs is arrangement with concurred conveyance conventions, for example, TCPROS [14] or UDPROS [15].

ii. AWS IoT Core

AWS IoT Core [16] is an AWS IoT serverless interface that enables two-way interconnection between one to another gadget secure. As indicated by AWS [16] the stage can scale trillions of messages on request supporting billions of gadgets. AWS IoT center backings distribute/buy in informing design. MQTT is utilized as the correspondence convention. MQTT is given over Web Sockets, permitting any assistance to associate with the web of straps utilizing Web Sockets. IoT center additionally bolsters HTTP when clients present information on any point/channel and when the solicitation message incorporate data, the post utilizes demand/reaction message pattern [17].

But AWS IoT Core can easily be used to set up AWS, Amazon Lambda, Amazon Kinesis, Amazon S3, Amazon DynamoDB, Amazon CloudWatch, AWS CloudTrail, Amazon QuickSight or Alexa Voice Service, which assemble, process, disrupt, and monitor IoT applications built into your computers without a framework to which AWS IoT Core can be assigned.

iii. AWS Lambda

AWS Lambda [2, 18, 19] is a backend database framework for object transfer, with Amazon S3 buckets operating without any of the application in the cloud as a FaaS framework. Once code is inserted into AWS Lambda software, it is able to handle all the functionality, scaling, patching and network maintenance to execute the code and providing the performance monitoring by publishing in Amazon Cloud Watch real-time measurements. Cost of AWS Lambda is less, which means that the payment is made for

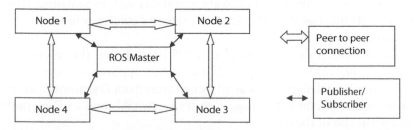

Figure 1.6 Illustrates the connection establishment.

the computation time. There is no need of new languages to be used in the framework so getting started to Lambda is easy. Any libraries of third parties can be included. The AWS Lambda code is the Lambda function. The code is to be uploaded in the code editor or in AWS Management console. We may also choose from the sample function list provided for normal use cases like encoding of images, processing of real-time files, filtering of data etc. When the code is loaded, pick the S3 bucket for AWS Event Source and the Lambda table is ready to start it in a couple of seconds. Some event with Lambda could cause the feature to make the application simple to implement.

An Event source is AWS administration or custom applications. Occasion source mapping is utilized for interfacing or mapping between occasion sources and the capacity of lambda can be either Synchronous Pull Invocation (stream-based) or Asynchronous Push Invocation (non stream-based).

Lambda limits license to change the figure resource, the memory entirety for the component and the most extraordinary runtime. The allotted memory corresponds to the speed limit for the CPU, the total capacity is between 128 and 3,008 MB.

iv. Amazon DynamoDB

The Amazon DynamoDB [20, 21] is the non-social management of the SQL serverless servers. The main focus and document storage provides millisecond output in one digit on any size. DynamoDB stores information in things comprising of a segment key, a sort key and traits. The essential key is made by segment key and sort key and the key worth must be exceptional. Character of everything depends on the essential key. It is a fully managed, multi-region, multimedia, durable database with built in internet security, backup and restoration and in-memory caching. DynamoDB handles 10 trillion requests every day and can process more than 20 million requests every second every day.

Most organizations such as Uber, Airbnb and Redfin in the world are the fastest rising companies and so are businesses such as Samsung, Nissan and Capital One, based on DynamoDB's size and efficiency to sustain their workloads.

Tens of thousands of clients from AWS have chosen the smartphone, cloud, gamer, ad technology, IoT and other applications which have low-latency knowledge access at all dimensions from DynamoDB as their core value and document storage. Creates a new table and let DynamoDB manage the rest of the data.

v. Amazon CloudWatch

Amazon CloudWatch screens tools and software running on AWS regularly with the Amazon Web Services (AWS). CloudWatch can be used to capture and track measurements [22, 23] that are variables for the properties and applications that can be quantified.

The CloudWatch landing page consequently shows measurements about each AWS administration used. This can make custom dashboards to show measurements about custom applications, and show custom assortments of measurements selected.

For e.g., show the use of the CPU and plate peruses and the Amazon EC2 cases and then use [24–26] to determine if additional cases can be submitted to deal with increased pressure. Use this information to avoid unused cases to remove cash. Through CloudWatch, a broad structure for the use, deployment and running health of infrastructure can be obtained.

1.2.6   Interconnection Design

The interconnection moves data between the administrations on different stage. The network use distribute/buy in informing design, simultaneous draw and nonconcurrent push informing designs.

i. ROS and AWS IoT Core

The two ROS [10] and AWS IoT use distribute/buy in informing design causing the two administrations to bury operable. Every distributer characterizes the theme/channel to distribute to and the endorsers buy in to a subject/channel of decision.

ROSBridge is used for shift to JSON array over ROS messages [27]. The transition in payloads significantly improves ROS and MQTT communications. The ROSBridge associate [28] is usable for two-way messaging between ROS and the focuses/channels of MQTT as it places the JSON payload within a MQTT document [29]. Python [30, 38] IoT SDK code. SDK IoT software AWS offers a guaranteed connector between any Python program and AWS IoT Core subject/channel, which can be used for the sale/scatter of educational transport via the MQTT display. Mixing the two distribute/buy in administrations together making a heterogeneous circulated arrange.

ii. AWS IoT Rules

Rules are IoT-based APIs which provide IoT applications which respected AWS organizations [32, 33] with an interoperability. The concepts allow IoT

Center Themes/Channels to work together in a number of AWS advantages, as seen in Figure 1.5.

DynamoDB table messages concerning other topic/channel may not be advanced or collected with the Lambda rule at the same time.

In order to publish messages continuously and do computation among companies directly AWS IoT point/channel using IoT rule republish [34] is used.

iii. DynamoDB and AWS Lambda

DynamoDB underpins simultaneous summons through DynamoDB streams [35–37]. Such streams allow AWS lambda to monitor the process and create a lambda function. It is part of the DynamoDB table. In fact, a synchronized call requires new information to be stored in a DynamoDB table during one operation. The calls are often made into a requested/interaction configuration to facilitate the continuous monitoring of approaching information.

iv. Push and Pull

Any stream- or non-stream-based data source may be an event source. Stream-based models take the stream when another record is remembered, naming a lambda task. Every time users push a message, non-stream models invoke a lambda function. The way they treat adaptability affects the ratio between the two event streams. Stream dependent event origins process-advance shard scenario, which relies upon the number of shard lambda limits. Based on the stream classification, it is the sum of fragments. In the case where a stream is separated into 100 fragments, 100 lambda limits are the worst. Non-stream sources of events request a lambda for any event to boost efficiency to a very great extent [38, 39]. The versatility limit for DynamoDB read/form is calculated by the planner every second and can be modified according to the indications in the layer.

v. AWS Software Development Kit

The Boto3 AWS software development kit (SDK) is used to facilitate process changes. This allows simple assistance and item-setting APIs at a low level. A meeting is held between AWS and any application for pythons.

vi. Analysis of Data

Data analysis is a framework which consolidates various approaches and methodologies, and their depiction can change, especially according to the strategy and applications. The Data Mining method, a technique called Information Discovery in Databases, has been a striking investigation [40, 41]. It makes clear that data extraction can be regarded as an analogous word for KDD and as a fundamental component of the KDD operation.

The method of data investigation is used as a context analysis framework to validate the IoRT level capabilities.

1.2.7   Research Methodology

The procedure is as per the following:

    a.   Outline of the exploration domain to perceive and examine new regions of premium.
    b.   Map main elements, review and relevant information.
    c.   Study the gaps in previous stages and tackle them.

1.2.8   Advancement Process—Systems Thinking

Frameworks believing is a mix of logical aptitudes about frameworks utilized together to make an arrangement of frameworks [5] with a worth more noteworthy than the total of its parts. In addition, it is necessary to comprehend the frameworks and foresee their practices so as to accomplish the reason [42]. The mechanisms for the definition will include components, interconnections and a target as described in the media [43, 44].

- *Intention:* Describe why the structure is?
- *Components:* The features of the framework.
- *Interconnections:* The connection between the components.

Framework believing is utilized as a system to structure the advancement procedure of the stage that fulfills the examination questions.

1.2.8.1   Development Process

The advancement procedure is structured using together investigative study and frameworks view method. It considers six important stages. They are:

    i.   Relating reasons, list of qualities and it capacities.
        (a) Classification of necessary zones of innovation to satisfy the reasons.

(b) Classification of interconnections with the territories of advances.

ii.   Characterize stage estimations dependent on the qualities formed by the framework.

(a) Define the measurements (for example Flexibility) identified with the estimation and the measures (for example Can the administration naturally adjust the remaining task at hand on request?) it decides the inquiry regarding the measurement.

(b) Describes the standards condition that responds the measurement inquiries.

iii. Recognize required administrations for the stage dependent on the qualities of the framework to fulfill the reason.

iv.   Recognize the interconnections between the administrations. How would they connect with one another?

v.   Incorporate the administrations together using the interconnections recognized.

vi.   Survey the administrations utilizing characterized estimations.

1.2.9   Trial Setup-to Confirm the Functionalities

An information examination process is inspected and utilized as a format to plan a stage; the means of the procedure is introduced in Figure 1.7. The robot stage comprises with an Internet of things stage, computing and cloud capacity administrations, also perception and checking administrations [44–47]. Test arrangement covers the stages capacity to picture, procedure and store information from the robots in close to constant, moreover the deferrals between the administrations utilized in the stage is estimated.

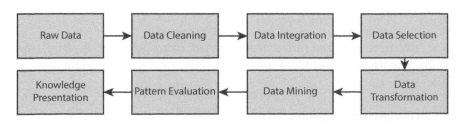

Figure 1.7 Data analysis.

The stage is assessed with the estimations: usefulness, composability, interoperability, versatility and figuring time. Each estimation has relating measurements and standards [48, 49], the rules of every measurement. The measures are replied in the outcomes with a standards condition [50, 51]. The stage is estimated with the accompanying estimations and measurements:

- Usefulness: The administrations capacity to interface in its encompassing, screen administration measurements, store and procedure information.
- Communication: Can the administration connect with its environmental factors?
- Calculation: Can the administration give an execution domain?
- Capacity: Can the administration store information?
- Observing: Can the administration screen own help measurements and additionally other assistance measurements?
- Composability: The administrations capacity to be measured and stateless.
- Measured quality: Can the administration be conveyed freely?
- Stateless: Can the administration treat summons freely?
- Interoperability: The administrations capacity to trade information with different administrations in the stage.

Example: What informing design does the administration give?
Programming interface/Protocol: What correspondence convention or API (Application Programming Interface) does the administration sustain?

- Adaptability: Administrations capacity to scale on request.
- Simultaneousness: Could the administration scale in number of examples?
- Versatility: could the administration consequently adjust outstanding tasks at hand on request?
- Time to register: Network idleness and cloud handling.
- Beginning to complete delays: How long does it take for a message to hit its goal?
- Time Use: How long does it take to use a procedure?
- Payload: What government uses for payload?

1.3   Conclusion

In this proposed work is associated with IoT based independence building design—IoRT and a down to earth approach of an IoRT stage. Web of Robotic Things permits robots or mechanical frameworks to associate, contribute, and enhance the appropriated computation resources, industry movements, and ecological data with each other, with retrieving new information and particular aptitudes unlearned without anyone else, everything is under the advanced structural system. It opens the entryway in the field of associated mechanical autonomy to energizing advances. Enormous developments might be required to exploit the IoRT strategy, for example, route. Approve the attainability of the proposed engineering by indicating hardly any parts, which incorporate current mechanical framework, their border gadget, Internet of Things arranging the units and practical automated levels in the cloud or conceivable outcomes of rise. Key attributes are likewise explained. Research difficulties portrays about the advancement procedure and trial arrangement.

In the stage three principle advancements are explored and applied: apply autonomy, cloud administrations and IoT. Furthermore, an information examination process is researched and utilized as a format to structure the test stage.

All in all, this methodology makes three principle commitments:

i.   A stage joining the automated stage Robot Operating System and Internet of Things stage center which circulates data above the system internet with typical correspondence design.

ii. The automated stage joining Robot Operating System and brought together cloud administrations: DynamoDB and Amazon Web Service Lambda, it stores with procedures sensor information in close to ongoing cloud environment using smaller scale administrations.

iii. A stage that envisions spilling information from the miniaturized scale benefits in close to ongoing.

Therefore Internet of Robotic Things stages to appropriate data, store information, process information and picture information from numerous robots in close to ongoing.

1.4   Future Work

Upgrade a Complete Cycle of Research Using Micro-Administrations
In present execution of exploratory arrangement, examination procedure is to just utilize the format of assess the cloud system administration abilities. There was not sufficient opportunity to actualize an examination procedure, moreover appropriate it more than a few lambda works.

Associate Several Robot Machines
Test the capacities of the stage associating more robots to the dispersed system.

Check the Wider Text Size Range Platform
Burden the disseminated connect with bigger message size, for example sending a video stream and calculating the deferrals.

Actualize Cloud File Storage
Use S3 Amazon pails to use crude documents in the environment of cloud. The Amazon Web Service system gives Application Programming Interface to Dynamo DB, IoT AWS and Lambda in the legitimately interface with the S3 basin.

References

1. Ray, P.P., Internet of robotic things: Concept, technologies, and challenges. *IEEE Access*, 4, 9489–9500, 2016.
2. W. Lin *et al.*, Tracking Causal Order in AWS Lambda Applications, in: *2018 IEEE International Conference on Cloud Engineering (IC2E)*, pp. 50–60, 2018, https://ieeexplore.ieee.org/document/8360312.
3. Håkansson, A. Portal of research methods and methodologies for research projects and degree projects. In *The 2013 World Congress in Computer Science, Computer Engineering, and Applied Computing WORLDCOMP* 2013, pp. 67–73, CSREA Press USA, Las Vegas, Nevada, USA, 22-25 July, 2013.
4. Arnold, R.D. and Wade, J.P., A definition of systems thinking: A systems approach. *In Procedia Computer Science*, vol. 44, pp. 669–678, 2015.
5. Edson, R. Systems Thinking. Applied. A Primer. *Applied Systems Thinking (ASYST) Institute*, vol. 8, Analytic Services Inc., version 1.1, Arlington, VA, USA, 2008.

6. Zhang, Q., Cheng, L., Boutaba, R. Cloud computing: state-of-the-art and research challenges. *J. Internet Serv. Appl.*, 1, 7–18, 2010. https://doi.org/10.1007/s13174-010-0007-6. K. Kamei, S. Nishio, N. Hagita and M. Sato, Cloud networked robotics, in *IEEE Network*, vol. 26, no. 3, pp. 28–34, May-June 2012.

7. Wan, J., Tang, S., Yan, H., Li, D., Wang, S., Vasilakos, A. V., Cloud robotics: Current status and open issues, in *IEEE Access*, vol. 4, pp. 2797–2807, 2016.

8. Waibel, M. *et al.*, RoboEarth, in *IEEE Robotics & Automation Magazine*, vol. 18, no. 2, pp. 69–82, June 2011.

9. Mohanarajah, G., Hunziker, D., D'Andrea, R., Waibel, M., Rapyuta: A cloud robotics platform. *IEEE Trans. Autom. Sci. Eng.*, 12, 2, 481–493, 2015.9.

10. Pereira, A.B.M., Julio, R.E., Bastos, G.S., Rosremote: Using ROS on cloud to access robots remotely, in: *Robot Operating System (ROS)*, pp. 569–605, Springer, 2019.

11. Protskaya, Y. and Veltri, L., Broker Bridging Mechanism for Providing Anonymity in MQTT, *2019 10th International Conference on Networks of the Future (NoF)*, pp. 110–113, 2019.

12. Pereira, A. B. M., and Bastos, G. S., ROSRemote, using ROS on cloud to access robots remotely, *2017 18th International Conference on Advanced Robotics (ICAR)*, pp. 284–289, 2017.

13. Sung Wook Moon, Young Jin Kim, Ho Jun Myeong, Chang Soo Kim, Nam Ju Cha and Dong Hwan Kim, Implementation of smartphone environment remote control and monitoring system for Android operating system-based robot platform, *2011 8th International Conference on Ubiquitous Robots and Ambient Intelligence (URAI)*, pp. 211–214, 2011.

14. Bore, D., Rana, A., Kolhare, N. Shinde, U., Automated Guided Vehicle Using Robot Operating Systems. *2019 3rd International Conference on Trends in Electronics and Informatics (ICOEI)*, pp. 819–822, 2019.

15. Imtiaz Jaya, N. and Hossain, M. F., A Prototype Air Flow Control System for Home Automation Using MQTT Over Websocket in AWS IoT Core. *2018 International Conference on Cyber-Enabled Distributed Computing and Knowledge Discovery (CyberC)*, pp. 111–1116, 2018.

16. Tomar, N. and Gaur, M. S., Information theft through covert channel by exploiting HTTP post method, *2013 Tenth International Conference on Wireless and Optical Communications Networks (WOCN)*, pp. 1–5, 2013.

17. Gandhi, S., Gore, A., Nimbarte, S., Abraham, J., Implementation and Analysis of a Serverless Shared Drive with AWS Lambda, *2018 4th International Conference for Convergence in Technology (I2CT)*, pp. 1–6, 2018.

18. Lin, W. *et al.*, Tracking Causal Order in AWS Lambda Applications, *2018 IEEE International Conference on Cloud Engineering (IC2E)*, pp. 50–60, 2018.

19. Yin Mok, W., A Feasible Schema Design Strategy for Amazon DynamoDB: A Nested Normal Form Approach, *2020 IEEE International Conference on Industrial Engineering and Engineering Management (IEEM)*, pp. 903–907, 2020.

20. Kerr, J. and Nickels, K., Robot operating systems: Bridging the gap between human and robot, *Proceedings of the 2012 44th Southeastern Symposium on System Theory (SSST)*, pp. 99–104, 2012.
21. Mahalleh, V. B. S., Chand, A. N., Rahman, A., Design, Implementation and Evaluation of Ultrasonic Measurement System using ROS and MQTT, *2020 IEEE 8th Conference on Systems, Process and Control (ICSPC)*, pp. 80–85, 2020.
22. Bhatnagar, A., Sharma, V., Raj, G., IoT based Car Pollution Detection Using AWS, *2018 International Conference on Advances in Computing and Communication Engineering (ICACCE)*, pp. 306–311, 2018.
23. Pierleoni, P., Concetti, R., Belli, A., Palma, L., Amazon, Google and Microsoft Solutions for IoT: Architectures and a Performance Comparison, in *IEEE Access*, vol. 8, pp. 5455–5470, 2020.
24. Sun, C., Guo, K., Xu, Z., Ma, J., Hu, D., Design and Development of Modbus/MQTT Gateway for Industrial IoT Cloud Applications Using Raspberry Pi, *2019 Chinese Automation Congress (CAC)*, pp. 2267–2271, 2019.
25. Sadavarte, S. S. and E. Bodanese, Pregnancy Companion Chatbot Using Alexa and Amazon Web Services, *2019 IEEE Pune Section International Conference (PuneCon)*, pp. 1–5, 2019.
26. Arnold, R.D. and Wade, J.P., A definition of systems thinking: A systems approach. *Proc. Comput. Sci.*, 44, 669–678, 2015.
27. Hu, G., Tay, W.P., Wen, Y., Cloud robotics: Architecture challenges and applications. *IEEE Network*, 26, 21–28, May/Jun., 2012.
28. Kehoe, B., Patil, S., Abbeel, P., Goldberg, K., A survey of research on cloud robotics and automation. *IEEE Trans. Autom. Sci. Eng.*, 12, 2, 398–409, Apr. 2015.
29. Campo, A.D., Gambi, E., Montanini, L., Perla, D., Raffaeli, L., Spisante, S., MQTT in AAL systems for home monitoring of people with dementia. *Proc. IEEE 27th Annu. Int. Symp. Pers. Indoor Mobile Radio Commun. (PIMRC)*, pp. 1–6, Sep. 2016.
30. Shamszaman, Z.U. and Ali, M.I., Enabling cognitive contributory societies using SIoT: QoS aware real-time virtual object management. *J. Parallel Distrib. Comput.*, 123, 61–68, 2019.
31. Grieco, L.A. *et al.*, IoT-aided robotics applications: Technological implications target domains and open issues. *Comput. Commun.*, 54, 1, 32–47, 2014.
32. Girau, R., Martis, S., Atzori, L., Lysis: A platform for IoT distributed applications over socially connected objects. *IEEE Internet Things J.*, 4, 1, 40–51, 2017.
33. Komei, and Koji, Z., Rospeex: A cloud robotics platform for human-robot spoken dialogues. *Proc. IEEE/RSJ Int. Conf. Intell. Robots Syst. (IROS)*, pp. 6155–6160, Sep./Oct. 2015.
34. Banafa, A. 6 Three Major Challenges Facing IoT, in *Secure and Smart Internet of Things (IoT): Using Blockchain and AI*, pp. 33–44, River Publishers, 2018.

35. Muhammad, K., Khan, S., Palade, V., Mehmood, I., Albuquerque, V.H.C., Edge intelligence-assisted smoke detection in foggy surveillance environments. *IEEE Trans. Ind. Inf.*, 16, 2, 1067–1075, Feb. 2020.

36. Chen, X., Jiao, L., Li, W., Fu, X., Efficient multi-user computation offloading for mobile-edge cloud computing. *IEEE Trans. Netw.*, 24, 5, 2795–2808, Oct. 2016.

37. Guo, H. and Liu, J., Collaborative computation offloading for multiaccess edge computing over fiber-wireless networks. *IEEE Trans. Veh. Technol.*, 67, 5, 4514–4526, Jan. 2018.

38. Wang, K. *et al.*, Green industrial internet of things architecture: an energy-efficient perspective. *IEEE Commun. Mag.*, 54, 12, 48–54, Dec. 2016.

39. Wu, J. *et al.*, Big data meet green challenges: Big data toward green applications. *IEEE Syst. J.*, 10, 3, 888–900, Sep. 2016.

40. Zheng, M. *et al.*, Energy-efficiency maximization for cooperative spectrum sensing in cognitive sensor networks. *IEEE Trans. Green Commun. Netw.*, 1, 1, 29–39, Mar. 2017.

41. Yin, S. and Qu, Z., Resource allocation in multiuser OFDM systems with wireless information and power transfer. *IEEE Commun. Lett.*, 20, 3, 594–597, Jan. 2016.

42. Chen, Y., Li, Y., Xu, D., Xiao, L., DQN-based power control for IoT transmission against jamming, in: *Proc. of the IEEE 87th Vehicular Technology Conference (VTC Spring)*, pp. 1–5, Porto, Portugal, Jul. 2018.

43. Chen, X., Zhang, H., Wu, C., Mao, S., Ji, Y., Bennis, M., Optimized computation offloading performance in virtual edge computing systems via deep reinforcement learning. *IEEE Internet Things J.*, 6, 3, 4005–4018, Jun. 2019.

44. He, X., Wang, K., Huang, H., Liu, B., QoE-driven big data architecture for smart city. *IEEE Commun. Mag.*, 56, 2, 88–93, Feb. 2018.

45. Sharma, S.K. and Wang, X., Collaborative distributed Q-learning for RACH congestion minimization in cellular IoT networks. *IEEE Commun. Lett.*, 23, 4, 600–603, Apr. 2019.

46. Wang, K., Wang, Y., Sun, Y., Guo, S., Wu, J., Green industrial Internet of Things architecture: An energy-efficient perspective. *IEEE Commun. Mag.*, 54, 12, 48–54, Dec. 2016.

47. Chen, J. *et al.*, Narrowband Internet of Things: implementations and applications. *IEEE Internet Things J.*, 4, 6, 2309–2314, Dec. 2017.

48. Xu, C., Wang, K., Li, P., Guo, S., Luo, J., Ye, B., Guo, M., Making big data open in edges: A resource-efficient blockchain-based approach. *IEEE Trans. Parallel Distrib. Syst.*, 30, 4, 870–882, Apr. 2019.

49. Newman, P., 2017, The Internet of Things 2017 Report: How the IoT is improving lives to transform the world, 2017, http://www.businessinsider.com/the-internet-of-things-2017.

50. Nitti, M., Girau, R., Atzori, L., Trustworthiness management in the social internet of things. *IEEE Trans. Knowl. Data Eng.*, 26, 5, 1253–1266, 2014.

51. Chen, J., Chen, S., Wang, Q., Cao, B., Feng, G., Hu, J., iRAF: A deep rein-forcement learning approach for collaborative mobile edge computing IoT networks. *IEEE Internet Things J.*, 6, 4, 7011–7023, Aug. 2019.

2

Brain–Computer Interface Using Electroencephalographic Signals for the Internet of Robotic Things

R. Raja Sudharsan* and J. Deny

Department of Electronics and Communication Engineering, School of Electronics and Electrical Technology, Kalasalingam Academy of Research and Education, Krishnankoil, India

Abstract

Enlistment of brain (cerebrum) signals can be arranged by a few techniques, for example, invasive and non-invasive. On the off chance that the biosensor is inserted in the cerebrum, at that point, the invasive procedure, has the advantage of high-frequency parts will estimate clearly and exact, yet because of wellbeing dangers and a few moral angles, they are essentially utilized in animal experimentations. If there should arise an occurrence of non-invasive technique, the surface electrodes are made available at the outer portion of the cerebrum, as per 5 to 15 global norms and standards. This application technique is substantially more likely utilized on people (human beings) since it doesn't jeopardize them because of the implantation, however, it has the detriment, that the deliberate signals are noisier. This noisy signal can be removed by using a digital filter, named: Finite Impulse Response (FIR). In the previous years, a few electroencephalography headsets have been created not just for clinical use, which is worked from own batteries to guarantee versatile use. Presently some across the board Electroencephalography headsets are being presented, which are additionally reasonable for accomplishing one of a kind created Brain-Computer Interface. This kind of Headsets can be developed with the architecture of the Internet of Robotic Things (IoRT), where it can analyse the incoming electroencephalographic signals for corresponding actions of human beings. These recordings can be sent to the remote area and stored in the server through Bluetooth or Wi-fi mediums using the Gateway. This

Corresponding author: ajasudharsan@klu.ac.in

R. Anandan, G. Suseendran, S. Balamurugan, Ashish Mishra and D. Balaganesh (eds.) Human Communication Technology: Internet of Robotic Things and Ubiquitous Computing, (27–54)

communication will help the remote person to track the targeted human being. This framework will reduce the latency of the electroencephalography concerning network and speed of data transfer.

Keywords: Electroencephalography (EEG) signals, Internet of Robotic Things (IoRT), headsets, brain–computer interface (BCI), graphical user interface (GUI)

2.1   Introduction

A few papers center around the Internet of Things running from customer situated to modern items. The Internet of Things idea has gotten regular since the start of the 21st century also; it was presented officially in 2005 [1, 2]. The Internet of Things empowers to make data recognized by these articles transmittable, and the items themselves controllable, by utilizing the present system framework [3]. This gives the chance to incorporate the physical world and Information Technology frameworks in a considerably more prominent scope, which prompts the improvement of effectiveness, precision, and financial aspects by insignificant human intercession. Brain–Computer Interface framework-based human–robot test condition is executed utilizing Transmission Control Protocol/Internet Protocol correspondence, where the inactivity of human incitation has been examined.

The Internet of Things innovation gives a few prospects to extending chances of robots, for instance, the use of keen incited gadgets. The IoRT is another idea [4] dependent on the Internet of Things for supporting automated frameworks including mechanical, home robots or other complex programmed frameworks with humanlike aptitudes, where somewhat independent frameworks can speak with one another. These gadgets use specially appointed, neighbourhood, dispersed or fog administered knowledge to upgrade performances and movements in this world considering a few factors, for instance, agreeable, adaptable, security, creation, and coordination angles utilizing data trade, furthermore, information sharing.

At the point when the data checked by the robot isn't sufficient for the ideal activity, the robot can gather extra data from nature as well as can utilize extra cloud administrations to decide the fitting activity. To accomplish this usefulness a few innovations as depicted in Figure 2.1 must be applied dependent on the information on mechanical technology, mechatronics, digital material science, man-made consciousness, bio-designing, data trade system or collaboration.

The Internet of Robotic Things idea managing the expansion of the Internet of Things and mechanical gadgets to give progressed, versatile, progressively keen, shared, and heterogeneous mechanical abilities utilizing

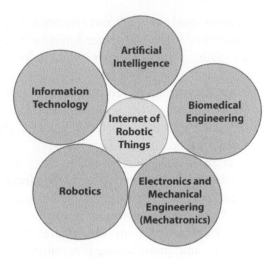

Figure 2.1 Foremost branches of IoRT.

the innovations, among others, Networked Robots, Cloud Mechanical technology, Robot as assistance. To accomplish the referenced points various significant angles must be considered, for example, institutionalization, interoperability, normal engineering/framework configuration including time-fluctuating system inertness, security.

On the Internet of Robotic Things framework, the robot is coordinated into the brilliant condition. Internet of Things innovation, the agreeable robots, and the correspondence of the gear fundamentally add to the computerization and improvement of the frameworks yet in a few things. HMI empowering correspondence between systems, people are stressed, in which field there are numerous investigates in progress, for example, forms dependent on the perception of signals, eye moves or mind movement. There are a few techniques accessible for cerebrum action, however, as far as versatility furthermore, value, the utilization of Electromyography put together gadgets worn concerning the head guarantees the most chances. Electromyography gadget estimating human cerebrum movement was concocted [5], looking for the appropriate response by utilizing this gadget, what sort of associations amid variance mental and biological environments can be appeared. This arrangement was better in the previous eras [6], a few vagaries happening in the movement of various mind sores was watched.

The innovation has been empowered a plan of portable earpieces fit for enlisting Electromyography signals. The mind PC interface is one of the most quickly creating multidisciplinary inquire about fields these days. Brain–Computer Interface framework, which can transmit diverse data (directions) given mind movement by preparing signals showing up from humanoid cerebrum, makes a station amid the cerebrum and outside gadget (portable robot). The main objective of Brain–Computer Interface investigates was to upgrade the existence nature of patients experiencing a diverse neurological issue. In any case, these days [7], investigate fields have just grasped other application fields, for example, the utilization of control highlights. Brain-Computer Interface frameworks dependent on the activity of Electroencephalography type gadgets have a moderately straightforward structure, they are convenient, safe, and their activity is additionally very basic [8].

The article looks at the plan chance of supervisory accomplished by moving of portable robot applying Internet of Things innovation using a cerebrum PC interface, which can use some subjective human abilities and highlights by a Brain–Computer Interface framework.

To structure a BCI framework, an earpiece at less cost Electroencephalography sensor, and manufactured versatile robot is utilized. During testing condition developed by the assistance of these gadgets, the client's mind movement is inspected by an Electroencephalography headset, which transmits information to a PC for procedure and assessment. Brain–Computer Interface successively been running on PC, panels the speed of Wi-Fi portable robot as per the prepared data and empowers remote perception via camera. This research inspects the inactivity of testing condition when the client can straightforwardly observe the versatile robot. This Robot is made realized via a camera placed on the region of vision and it is impacted by evolving considerations.

2.2   Electroencephalography Signal Acquisition Methods

There are two kinds of strategies that are commonly utilized in Electroencephalography obtaining: obtrusive and non-invasive [9, 10]. Figure 2.2 portrays the working procedure of Electroencephalography securing. From the outset, the Electroencephalography signal is gotten by setting the anodes on the mind. After the sign securing the sign gets prepared furthermore, as per the orders set on it, applied in the Internet of Robotic Things area applications.

While securing the Electroencephalography signals from anthropoid, the accompanying encounters are confronted:

- Attainment of correct codes for wanted securing signs
- Evading harm to the humanoid mind
- Averting assaults of infection, though getting signs

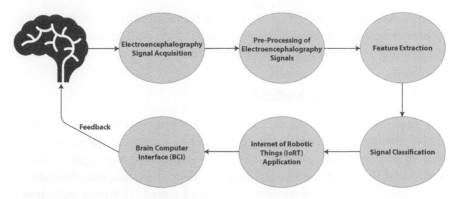

Figure 2.2 Process flow of electromyography signal acquisition.

- Morally demo the information ensuing legitimate human rights
- Prerequisite of broad preparing of subjects earlier enchanting the information.

Advantages and disadvantages of effectively expressed obtaining strategies are depicted in regard of the difficulties are given in the accompanying subsections.

2.2.1   Invasive Method

This strategy is otherwise called profound cerebrum recording [11]. To execute Electroencephalography procurement a gifted individual needs to put cathodes inside the scalp utilizing the medical procedure. As the terminals for the intrusive method are put on the uncovered cerebrum and subsequently, the nature of the sign is far superior to the non-invasive procedure. This kind of intrusive procedure is frequently utilized for serious epileptic patients to distinguish the area of appropriations [12]. Even though this procedure delivers top-notch Electroencephalography signal, here and there scar tissues can develop, which, thusly, make the sign more vulnerable and, in the most noticeably terrible case, the sign may get lost [13]. There are different electrode materials available to measure and record the electroencephalography signal from the brain of the human body. They are listed as follows:

- Needle Electrodes made of AgCl
- Needle Electrodes made of Stainless Steel
- Needle Electrodes made Gold
- Needle Electrodes made of TiO_2.

These electrodes are inserted into the human brain for recording the electroencephalography signal, which causes pain during the test and also the patients feel discomfort during measurements.

2.2.2   Non-Invasive Method

For non-invasive method the terminals are put an external portion of the cerebrum; consequently, nope medical procedure is obligatory. This sort of strategy needs nature of Electroencephalography signals. As the account of the sign is removed a long way from the basis, thus indications get contorted. Also, the quality of acquired signals is minor sufficiency that for obtrusive case [14]. A procurement framework can be isolated dependent on cathodes categories such as surface, needle, or other electrodes [15]. Short out commotion level is low if there should be an occurrence of the water-based framework. The most elevated P300 spelling exactness' are acquired in the hydrogel-based framework. The minimum burden is accessible through needle terminal-based framework. There are different electrode materials available to measure and record the electroencephalography signal from the brain of the human body. They are listed as follows:

- Surface Electrodes made of AgCl
- Surface Electrodes made of Stainless steel
- Surface Electrodes made of Molybdenum
- Dry Electrodes.

These electrodes are placed over the brain of a human being for testing and recording the electroencephalography signal. The main advantage of this type of surface electrodes (Non-Invasive) is it does not cause any pain during tests. Moreover, the surface electrode made of Silver Chloride is widely used because of its temperature co-efficient and efficient Signal to noise ratio compared to other materials of surface electrodes.

2.3   Electroencephalography Signal-Based BCI

Humanoid cerebrum movement actuates negligible power variations, estimated on the epidermis of the head, then this data might enrol Electroencephalography gadgets. This enrolled data signals would interpret using Brain–Computer Interface, that can change the director positions.

2.3.1 Prefrontal Cortex in Controlling Concentration Strength

The anterior projection of the humanoid cerebrum is answerable for a few obligations. Amid supplemental, it controls cognizant changes and reasoning and also social conduct is additionally overseen. The initial segment of the flap is PFC, important for controlling the focal point of concentration, moreover, tensions arrive at flap after the entirety of faculties and the area was significant controller consideration capacities also [16–18]. During the anatomical assessment of the cerebrum, it has been demonstrated, that frontal flap comprises of the groundwork motoric flap, and the Prefrontal Cortex before it, wherein ventral and dorsal locales liable for various functionalities can be watched [19, 20]. The organic complex job of Prefrontal Cortex is exhibited by different trade associations between fore-mind and cerebrum stem [21, 22], besides, it assumes a key job in such intellectual procedures, such as progressing support of consideration, getting the hang of, recollecting, also, self-sufficient activities, so Prefrontal Cortex districts are huge in controlling the quality of focus [23].

The accompanying three capacities can be perused: consideration, passionate response, conduct and dynamic, besides, the area of mind areas liable for these capacities is likewise unmistakable. Among these territories, concerning the cerebrum PC interface, for accomplishing the objectives of the calling, consideration is utmost significant. For assessment of consideration, amid future exhibited estimating territories, the alleged anterior region is utmost appropriate, that is a significant point of view concerning the framework to be set up. It has watched such patients, Prefrontal Cortex was harmed, scarcely, or not ready toward securing novel information, adjust to various undertakings, take care of issues, or on the other hand execute assignments requiring significant level fixation [24–26]. Prefrontal Cortex, close to the controlling of the estimation of consideration, assumes a significant job in the ideal activity of transient remembrance, whereas, the transitory stockpile of biosensor data, and aimed at associating responses on outer upgrades, the immaculate activity of PFC is inescapable [27].

For observing the PFC action of the human cerebrum, a few innovations are applied, essentially in clinical advancements are applied, basically in clinical and research facility condition, for example, CT, EEG MRI, and FMRI [28]. The above recorded diverse imaging gadgets give a significant exact picture of the basic and useful activity of the cerebrum (brain); however, these gadgets are not portable. By the advancement of Electroencephalography gadgets, portable Electroencephalography put together gadgets worn concerning the head have opened up, which relying upon the number of sensors, give a picture about the useful activity of every territory of the mind [29]. The wear planned Electroencephalography based headsets aren't too awkward significantly after a more extended timeframe, so it very well may be applied in a lab domain as well as in ordinary use.

2.3.2 Neurosky Mind-Wave Mobile

The Mind-Wave Mobile Electroencephalography headset (Figure 2.3) is the advancement of Neurosky. A few colleges coordinated in the advancement of Neurosky Think Gear Electroencephalography innovation. In the gadget, a surface Electroencephalography electrode finished of a spotless compound is pragmatic at Frontalpole1 region, and a locus surface electrode, by an indicator interfacing with the ear cartilage. The gadget transmits pre-prepared information through Bluetooth remote association. Electroencephalography signals are tested with 512 Hz recurrence and digitalizes with an 8-piece analogue to digital converter [30]. The gadget, because of Think Gear innovation is appropriate for ascertaining consideration esteem [31] this worth is utilized in the assessments.

2.3.2.1 Electroencephalography Signal Processing Devices

Enrolment of cerebrum signs can be classified by a few strategies, such as intrusive and non-obtrusive. On the off chance that the locator electrode is placed over the outer surface of the head, especially in brain nerve, at that point the importance of discussing intrusive procedure is made, whose

Figure 2.3 Neurosky electroencephalograph headset available in Market.

advantage is that high-recurrence parts can be estimated much more clear and progressively exact, however because of wellbeing dangers and a few moral perspectives, they are principally utilized in creature tests. If there should arise an occurrence of non-intrusive technique, cathodes are put outside the skull, as indicated by the 5–15 global norm as depicted in Figure 2.4.

This application technique is considerably more likely utilized on people, since it doesn't imperil them due to the implantation, yet it has the inconvenience, that the deliberate signs are noisier [32]. During the previous years [33], a few Electroencephalography earpieces are created not for clinical purpose, are worked by batteries to guarantee versatile usage. Presently a few far-reaching electroencephalography headsets are being presented, which are likewise reasonable for accomplishing interesting created Brain–Computer Interface.

Pre-processing of the Electroencephalography signal is a basic and significant advance in any cerebrum PC interface-based applications. It helps to wipe out undesirable curios from the Electroencephalography sign and makes it reasonable for additional handling. The pre-processing method utilized is visually impaired source division (ISD).

The Electroencephalography signal is at first sifted utilizing a step channel focused at 60 Hz, trailed by ISD for Electroencephalography curio expulsion. A limited drive reaction channel has been utilized somewhere in

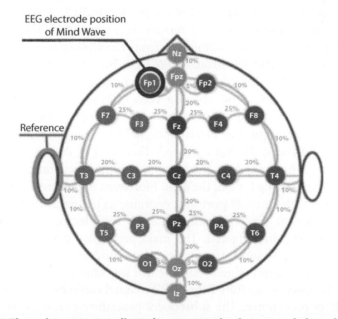

Figure 2.4 Electrode positioning of brain for extracting the electroencephalography signals.

the range of 10–30 Hz to get the necessary Electroencephalography signal for include extraction [34]. Essential separating is to complete expel undesirable curios from Electroencephalography signals. These signs are being given to HP channel with *lower*$_{cutoff}$ recurrence 1.2 Hz and then given to LP Channel with *upper*$_{cutoff}$ recurrence 60 Hz. This signals between the HP and LP channels are known as bandpass (BP) channels, which is separated by the expulsion of electrical cable commotion [35]. The signals sifting is utilized to kill any sign that isn't in the scope of P450 recurrence scope of the Electroencephalography signal. Also, information averaging over numerous preliminaries have been done to update the sign to-commotion proportion. An Electroencephalography signal is separated utilizing a band channel somewhere in the range of 8 and 12 Hz, which relates to the Mu cadence recurrence extend [36]. Another strategy, MWT is proposed for the upgrade of the Electroencephalography signal. It is a propelled strategy than the ISD technique and the other strategy called JRD of Eigen-lattices technique are executed to figure free segments and subsequently expel undesirable antiques from the Electroencephalography signal [37, 38]. An ancient rarity evacuation procedure has suggested that fuses LWT, instead of WT, with an autonomous part examination (APE) strategy for compelling expulsion of antiquities from the Electroencephalography signal. This strategy gives a superior and effective approach to wipe out antiquities than the customary APE technique [39]. The Electroencephalography signals from BP are separated to contract the ideal BP of recurrence, trailed by ISD method to evacuate any undesirable ancient rarities from sign [40]. The DWTs are executed to dispense with commotion from Electroencephalography data signal. A versatile channel through DWT has been executed for antiquity expulsion since the Electroencephalography signs [41, 42]. The sign is initially deteriorated to 8-bit utilizing Wavelet Transform, afterwards it is exposed to the versatile sifting progression. The reproduction of WTs utilized to develop antique-free Electroencephalography data signal. An IWT method, called the WBT, has executed. This WBT is the upgrading technique for this situation while dividing the sign into recurrence sub-bands, it keeps up the fleeting type of the sign. Moreover, the examples of the sub-bands after wavelet bundle portrayal continue as before as that of the first sign. The different pre-processing methods for Electroencephalography signals have been investigated. The main procedure depicted is the utilization of essential separating to expel an undesirable relic from the Electroencephalography signal. An essential step channel can be utilized to expel 60 Hz power gracefully flags. A BP channel could be likewise utilized to get IBP of recurrence. The subsequent procedure examined is versatile sifting. Here, rather than a fixed channel, a channel that adjusts to the range of the recorded Electroencephalography is utilized for compelling ancient rarity evacuation. The last method talked about is ISD [43, 44]. Additionally, other pre-processing methods have been dissected. Methods, for example, Wiener channels or versatile channels, give preferable execution over traditional essential separating of Electroencephalography signals [45]. Another powerful procedure talked about in the part for relic evacuation is the APE, which is executed for the expulsion of electrical cable clamor.

2.3.3 Electromyography Signal Extraction of Features and Its Signal Classifications

In attendance, several element extraction calculations rummage-sale to dissect Electroencephalography data signal. A portion from notable sign handling methods utilized in Electroencephalography signals for the Internet of Robotic Things applications are depicted in this area. There are a few signs include extraction calculations that are utilized at present. There are numerous research partners who once in a while consolidate different element extraction strategies for information examination. However, this procedure regularly prompts include measurement extension and the making of specific highlights that are excess. The decrease of highlight space measurement should be possible through element choice, in this manner expanding better outcomes for the Internet of Robotic Things applications.

All in all, the accompanying three kinds of highlight extraction strategy are utilized, as appeared in Figure 2.5.

- Time-space signal extraction
- Spatial space include extraction
- Extraction of Electromyography signal features change model.

Highlight abstraction of Electroencephalography data signal is a significant advance in Brain–Computer Interface-based applications. It assists with

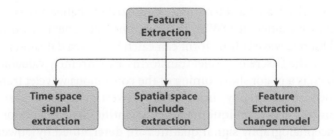

Figure 2.5 Categories of feature extraction techniques.

extricating the most applicable highlights from the Electroencephalography signal, consequently giving an increasingly exact portrayal and thus making it appropriate for additional handling.

An Electroencephalography is a self-assertive and flimsy sign; hence just FFT can't productively separate Electroencephalography signals. A non-deterministic polynomial issue regularly emerges out of ideal include subset determination; henceforth, for ideal element subset looking, the hereditary calculation is regularly utilized [46]. A double exhibit having data signal length equivalent to the number of highpoints of abstractions are utilized by computation by way of people. The worth comes to 'one' for an element whenever chose in the cluster, else it is 'zero'. The calculation work is least of (FPRate * 2(12 * TPRate)), in which TPRate and FPRate are valid positive rate (affectability) then bogus PR separately. These calculations are utilized to regular sifting besides can't be utilized in ancient rarity. Since the Electroencephalography signal ancient rarity has covering spectra. It is adjusted to streamlining calculations. The versatile component is shown by fault motion amid primary sign ($primary_{signal}$) and yield ($yeild_{signal}$) acquired from the channel. The LMS calculation [47] is the most regularly utilized rule for advancement reason.

The DFTs [48] are an advanced sign portrays data sufficiency as opposed to examining time consistently in time area recurrence. Looking at between the sign recurrence and advanced sign examples, it tends to be derived, the previous is valuable. It is a necessity on the way to build up advanced sign dependent on recurrence So that, one can do examination recurrence by this Discrete Fourier Transform calculations of a period area grouping.

Discrete Cosine Transform [49] is extremely helpful for changing the indoctrination cinematic and sound ways on PCs. This calculation computerized data handling then especially in programming change for information pressure [50]. Associated input information and concentrate of Discrete Fourier Transform are utilized in its vitality in initial barely any coefficients of change. Continuous wavelet transform [51] technique is utilized to speak to the interpretation furthermore, scale boundary for the wavelet persistently. Discrete Wavelet Transform technique is utilized to change any WT to DWT test. In utilizing different DWTs, the fundamental benefit is worldly goals over FT. Discrete wavelet transform can catch both area data and recurrence regarding T. The Discrete wavelet transforms are extremely valuable for portrayal, which is a major shortcoming of the continuous wavelet transform.

Electroencephalography information investigation by Fast Fourier Transform [52, 53] technique includes scientific instruments or implies. Electroencephalography signal qualities are determined by power ghastly thickness (PGT) estimation [54]. A case of this technique is Welch's strategy [55]. Wavelet Transform plays out an important in acknowledgement.

The Electroencephalography data signals are period shifting elements, these strategies are appropriate to include abstraction from crude information in period-recurrence space. These techniques are an otherworldly figuring strategy where any broad capacity of wavelet can be showed as an endless arrangement. Since wavelet transform is appropriate for variable measured windows, it gives a progressively customizable way speaking to signal in the time-recurrence area.

To appraise the recurrence of sign and force from relic inclined estimation of Electroencephalography signals, eigenvector procedure has been utilized [56]. The Pisarenko procedure is to clamour sub-space $E_{vectors}$ relating to base E_{values} by discovering a direct blend of the entire commotion $E_{vectors}$ with the assistance of base standard procedure [57].

Utilizing evaluating the constant, the boundary of straight condition viable, we get the estimation of PGT. Coefficient and autoregression boundary is estimated by the aftereffect of misusing one-sided in the Yule–Walker strategy [58]. It approximates the information work utilizing autocorrelation. Utilizing this strategy, we discover the LMS of advancing expectation blunder. Burge's strategy [59] depicts an autoregression unearthly approximation that decreases the blunder of expectation of advancing and in reverse mistakes fulfilling a recursive function. Burge's strategy figures the constant of replication legitimately not evaluating the capacity of $A_{correlation}$. These strategies take a few favourable circumstances. Burge's strategy will quantify the greatest PGT observing precisely like unique information. The entropy [60] brings about preferable execution over inexact entropy proposed [61] which is a strategy to gauge consistency for measuring the multifaceted nature levels inside a period arrangement. Test entropy is here and there valuable for extraction of sign highlights and characterized by the given condition.

$$F_{es} = S_E\ (y,\ Signal_L;\ Signal_{ED};\ Signal_T) \qquad (2.1)$$

Where, $Signal_L$ denotes the length of the signal, $Signal_{ED}$ represents the dimensions and $Signal_T$ is the tolerance level of the signal. Using the Chaos-fractal analysis, the time-series data can be given by,

$$F_{hust} = H_{exponent}\ (u) \qquad (2.2)$$

Equations (2.1) and (2.2) above give the feature extraction and classification of the electromyography signals.

2.4   IoRT-Based Hardware for BCI

A versatile robot is an independent unit gathered from primary parts fit for Wi-Fi remote correspondence, which empowers simple connection with essentially all PC-based control units, and even accomplishment of Internet of Robotic Things usefulness. At the structure of the portable robot, straightforward plan, redesign capacity, and IoT dependent on remote interchanges were the fundamental angles. To accomplish the trials, basic control highlight, the speed control must be guaranteed. On account of the versatile robot, a component dependent on ESP3266 produced by Express if Classifications picked, in which the microcontroller and Wi-Fi correspondence element was accomplished in the incorporated circuit.

A gadget is accessible in few planned components, in which improvement resolves, the ESP12F containing incorporated elevated creation significant yields of the circuit accessible was picked. To a component, the second era NodeMCU engineer was picked, has the voltage of 5 V controller mandatory for the main function flexibly through Universal Serial Bus, and Universal Serial Bus/Universal Asynchronous Receiver Transmitter sequential converter depends on CP2102 is programmed via the port called Universal Serial Bus. An association of additional components to NodeMCU has been upheld by the different Input/Output component.

With the end goal of the versatile robot, fundamentally the straightforward plan, anyway generally appropriate plan giving redesign capacity, empowering body moving component was liked. As to the moving system, the wheels of 2 is place side at the front, 1 of the wheel in the backside is free of configuration was liked and 2 wheels are at the back. The front wheels are known as driven wheels. The versatile BCI-based robot pack comprises of driven wheels, removable coarse, straightforward Poly methyl frame, a 2:50 apparatus current-powered engines, and a different enhancement obligatory for gathering. To drive the immediate current-powered engines, an element depends upon L911S engine regulator unit was picked. Before the robot, a BCI-based, 3 separation locators was connected, to recognize earth and evade impacts.

2.5   Software Setup for IoRT

For ESP3266 small scale controller equipped for Wi-Fi correspondence, a few turns of events situations are accessible, for example, the Arduino improvement condition. The CP2102 is programmed via a driver and coordinated unit empowering Universal Asynchronous Receiver Transmitter association must be introduced, which makes a virtual sequential port on the PC.

The programming of Wi-Fi correspondence association is upheld by the ESP3266. The Brain–Computer Interface framework directs information differing amid 1–99, characterizing the portable robot speed, to the versatile robot's engine component, connecting as a customer to the server through Transmission Control Protocol association. Stream diagram of the program empowering speed control of the portable robot.

In the supposed review period of the turn of events, various parts of the Brain–Computer Interface based testing framework, and its associations have been uncovered. Other than that, the auxiliary plan of the framework, the components partaking in the structure, their correspondence advancements, and they are transmitted media were resolved.

During the product plan, programming structures, information structures and calculation depictions to execute the characterizations. Throughout arranging a legitimate strategy of a framework is made. Figure 2.6 depicts the principle legitimate arrangement of the actualized

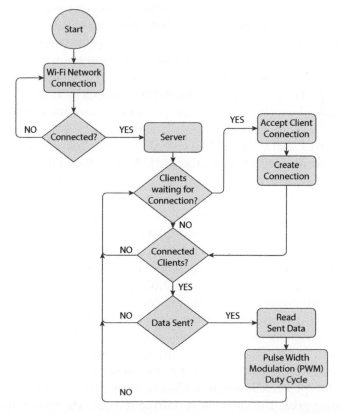

Figure 2.6 The flow of data speed, client connection and data transfer of mobile robot.

framework by a flowchart. On the stream graph, principle steps of the project's activity are very much appeared; information process, information correspondence obligatory for speed control of the robot's engine, and information capacity are executed.

2.6   Results and Discussions

The product of the Brain–Computer Interface-put together framework was acknowledged concerning the premise of the arranging models presented in the previous section. A fashioned Brain–Computer interface is a fitting trial condition for assessment of Brain–Computer interface dormancy. This section deals on the test condition, the assessment, and trial outcomes. The actualized application, for example, the Brain–Computer interface, understands the adjustment of electroencephalography earpiece, the procedure of data directed by the earpiece, their introduction, and regulator of gadgets fit for detached correspondence using Transmission Control Protocol/Internet Protocol convention, as well as the checking of the procedure using a camera. These claims are proficient of the concurrent introduction of a few prepared data, showing both the real estimations of cerebrum wave qualities characterized by the range examination of mind bioelectrical indications and its progressions by T. This framework arrangement along these lines accomplishes the assessment of some psychological variables, similar to consideration level, by utilizing the quality of mind waves characterized by cerebrum action. The gaming control is the widely recognized application of BCI. By actualizing Brain–Computer Interface, console or game comfort can be supplanted by electroencephalography headset. Aside from that, Brain–Computer Interface is additionally executed in applications that are identified with the entity controller. Electroencephalography signal recording used as a controller for chair car via Brain–Computer Interface is the major application discussed in this article and the flow of its control action is illustrated in Figure 2.7. The application runs based on incoming EEG signals from the Human brain, that signal will symbolize the action of control.

The way pf implementation [62] is to control the chair car by alluding to iris movement electroencephalography highlights. Brain–Computer Interface can likewise be utilized for the robot, which regularly expects the client to symbolism development [63–65]. Brain–Computer Interface can be utilized to perceive symbolism objects, taste, picture commonality, and development goal. The classifier is utilized to order the yield into various

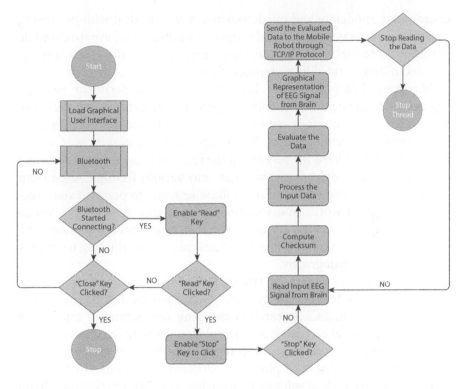

Figure 2.7 The logical flow of brain–computer interface system software.

classes. Other than the referenced applications, Brain–Computer Interface can be additionally used to order consideration stages.

The framework can separate administrator consideration states. In future improvement, this methodology can give consideration state alarm to drivers, what's more, lessen street mishaps. Like consideration state acknowledgement that has been referenced as of now, the sluggishness location framework is additionally a helpful Brain–Computer Interface application that can evade serious mishaps from occurring on the activity line or out and about. Refs. [66, 67] propose an identification strategy for languor through consistent checking. A multivariate typical dispersion is utilized to prototypical the allocation of force range in caution phase.

Besides, a look characterization approach is proposed [68–71]. In their methodology, electroencephalography is recorded when subjects are gazing at a turning vane, both moderate and quick speed. The recorded electroencephalography is utilized to train a classifier, which thusly used to characterize moderate and quick looking. A way to deal with perceiving human reactions is executed and propose a multichannel event-related lie detection potential. The hardware can perceive when the client is lying, which can be separated by a prepared classifier.

Moreover, Brain–Computer Interface is likewise pertinent for feeling acknowledgement and mental assignment characterization [72]. The Brain–Computer Interface can be utilized for video content examination frameworks for seeing feelings, for example, joy and bitterness. A classifier is regularly utilized for perceiving the feelings to arrange the recorded electroencephalography from the client into various feelings. Aside from feeling, Brain–Computer Interface is likewise ready to perceive voice recognition. In their work, an association of highlights, for example, versatility and unpredictability, are utilized and demonstrated the identifying recognizable and unknown speech indications, just by alluding to chronicled electroencephalography.

Brain–Computer Interface straightforwardly makes an association between the outside outer gadgets and the human cerebrum. These days, the new pattern in BCI research is changing the reasoning capacity of people into physical activities, for example, controlling the chair car. This Brain–Computer Interface has been regularly utilized for giving guidance and straightforwardness to physically challenged persons. To help this kind of persons with development troubles, [73, 74] anticipated a hand development direction remaking approach. The examination proposes a technique to rebuild various qualities of hand development direction from Electroencephalography. Patients (Physically challenged persons) are approached to perform think and that signal is taken by means electromyography and been interfaced with a computer to perform the required task by the patients without any trouble and anyone's help. Multi-dimensional relapses are utilized to foresee the boundaries. Notwithstanding recovery reason, [75] utilize a new Electroencephalography examination technique to coordinate an augmented simulation symbol and a product based mechanical autonomy recovery apparatus. This Brain–Computer Interface is fit for recognizing and foreseeing the upper appendage development. Furthermore, [76–78] recommend a technique to walking preparing. Their methodology deciphers cerebral action from electroencephalography to direct lower-appendage stride preparing exoskeleton. Engine symbolism of flexion and augmentation of the two legs are assessed from the Electroencephalography. ISD is utilized as a measure to speak to engine symbolism. With the end goal of recovery, [79, 80] illustrates the computer-generated strolling symbol regulator for drawing in cerebrum variation. In their methodology, delta band electroencephalography is utilized as the fundamental component for the forecast. Their work gives the achievability by shut circle electroencephalography-based Brain–Computer Interface-computer-generated authenticity toward initiating cerebrum variation, empower cerebrum trap and watch the cerebrum action.

Aside from a consistent state of visual evoked potential technique, an abundancy balanced the upgrade is proposed to diminish eye weariness. The proposed technique prevails to diminish eyes' weariness effectively with plentifulness adjusted boost. Sufficiency regulated improvement figured out how to give $L_{recurrence}$ data by a $H_{recurrence}$ the transporter is being capable of diminishing the iris exhaustion of patients (clients) perusing a conveyed data. Ref. [81] acquaint a Brain–Computer Interface-based game with diminishing understudies' tension science. Patients are obligatory to finish three meetings of scientific meets. This chronicled electroencephalography during these three meetings is dissected for their progressions of tension all through the inclined meeting.

The incorporation of this assessing conditions, with other activity of trailing patients, is being inspected for the inactivity of assessing the patients had the option to provide an order contingent upon consideration level. This assignment of trailing the patients was to expand the consideration near the overhead of about 70%, according to the light the action took place is identifies by interpreting the Brain–Computer interface. For example. If the Red light turns the patient is trying to move from one place to the other. Whereas, the green light turns on the patient is eating. This steps and control activities are programmed by via Universal serial bus to the specified chip. The Transmission Control Protocol/Universal Asynchronous Receiver Transmitter is being used for transferring the patient's information of action to the remote centre. The period gives the inertness of correspondence between the Brain–Computer Interface framework and the portable robot. Concurring to these, three assessments have been performed, in the main instance as shown in Figure 2.8. Brain–Computer Interface framework also, the robot was in a similar sub-arrange, and the challenging patients might legitimately realize a robot. This subsequent circumstance, this robot has been organized and realize the actions using the camera placed on it.

These three situations, this robot must propel multiple epochs straight, expanding their consideration level after the Red-light glows. In the test, 12 optional conservatory understudies, at ages differing somewhere in the range of 10 and 16 partook, especially 3 young men and 2 young ladies. The aftereffects of the two tests appear in Tables 2.1, 2.2 and 2.3. The appeared consequences of initial trails of a regular period, to realize these entrances

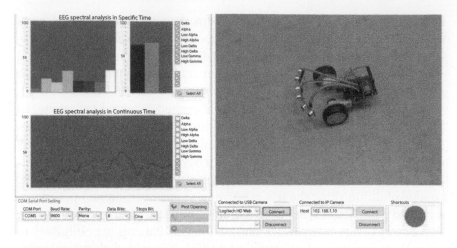

Figure 2.8 GUI of brain–computer interface based software.

Table 2.1 Time-varying latency test concerning speed reference and network latencies.

Test	Speed reference latency	Network latency	Total latency
1	6,012.42 ± 172.32	0.99 ± 0.02	6,013.41 ± 172.34
2	11,582.33 ± 26.1	0.02	11,583.33 ± 26.1
3	10,156.19 ± 21.46	0.97 ± 0.02	10,157.16 ± 21.48
4	7,217.19 ± 19.56	0.91 ± 0.02	7,218.10 ± 19.58
5	7,012.86 ± 13.23	0.98 ± 0.02	7,013.84 ± 13.25

Table 2.2 Time-varying latency test-2 concerning speed reference and network latencies.

Test	Speed reference latency	Network latency	Total latency
1	8,012.42 ± 174.32	1.00 ± 0.02	8,013.42 ± 174.34
2	13,582.33 ± 24.15	0.99 ± 0.02	13,583.32 ± 24.17
3	11,156.19 ± 23.36	0.95 ± 0.02	11,157.14 ± 23.38
4	8,117.19 ± 21.29	0.97 ± 0.02	8,118.18 ± 21.31
5	7,912.86 ± 13.23	0.91 ± 0.02	7,913.77 ± 13.25

Table 2.3 Time-varying latency test-3 concerning speed reference and network latencies.

Test	Speed reference latency	Network latency	Total latency
1	4,061.42 ± 17.32	0.99 ± 0.02	4,062.41 ± 17.34
2	5,282.33 ± 16.96	1.00 ± 0.02	5,283.33 ± 16.98
3	6,106.19 ± 42.46	0.97 ± 0.02	6,107.16 ± 82.94
4	7,217.19 ± 19.56	0.91 ± 0.02	7,218.10 ± 19.58
5	7,997.36 ± 13.23	0.98 ± 0.02	7,998.34 ± 13.25

of signs to dispatch of the robot, around 5 s, more often than not was spent for arriving at a higher consideration level, while robot correspondence required just a few milliseconds, contingent upon organizing idleness. On account of the subsequent test, execution of inaccessible action was like an initial trial, for this situation, normal dormancy was additionally just about 7 s, and obviously, the cognizant impact of consideration level required a few seconds. As an end, notwithstanding, we can pronounce, that cognizant impact of consideration level requires a few periods of seconds. At the time of exhibition of these trials, it was encountered that patient trials are needed to rehearse the utilization of gadgets for 12–15 min beforehand they ready to deliberately impact their consideration echelons in that specific degree can be distinguished by the gadget.

2.7   Conclusion

In the article, the Brain–Computer Interface framework intended for human–PC-based control of Internet of Things-based robot (Internet of Robotic Things) unit has been presented, which bolsters current robots with the chances of innovation based on Internet of Things. On account of the performed Brain–Computer Interface framework, what's more, an Internet of Robotic Things gadget, such challenging condition have been an arrangement, and are reasonable for the acknowledgement of directing both the nearer and farther robots. In this trail condition, execution of humanoid mediation and their inactivity because of Brain–Computer Interface framework have been inspected. As indicated by the encounters of the performed tests, can be expressed, that for the appropriate activity of Brain–Computer Interface framework, trailing patients needed to rehearse the utilization of the gadget in the first place, to arrive at suitable outcomes. Then again, trailing patients is ready to accomplish humanoid intercession just periods of seconds dormancy, even though this inertness didn't rely upon whether the trailing patients controlling robot legitimately before then again by distant action. The Brain–Computer Interface framework gives appropriate premise to test the innovation, also, on pounded of picked-up outcomes, assurance of sequences for additional upgrades. The Internet of Robotic Things and Brain–Computer Interface can be utilized well in instruction likewise to apply in inventive, troublesome, agreeable learning condition and utilizing current Information and Communication Technology innovation

References

1. Schmitt, S.E., Pargeon, K., Frechette, E.S., Hirsch, L.J., Dalmau, J., Friedman, D., Extreme delta brush: A unique EEG pattern in adults with anti-NMDA receptor encephalitis. *Neurology*, 79, 11, 1094–1100, 2012.
2. Sudharsan, R.R., Deny, J., Kumaran, E.M., Geege, A.S., An Analysis of Different Biopotential Electrodes Used for Electromyography. 12, 1, 1–7, 2020.
3. Stanski, D.R., Pharmacodynamic modeling of anesthetic EEG drug effects. *Annu. Rev. Pharmacol. Toxicol.*, 32, 1, 423–447, 1992.
4. Gillin, J.C., Duncan, W., Pettigrew, K.D., Frankel, B.L., Snyder, F., Successful separation of depressed, normal, and insomniac subjects by EEG sleep data. *Arch. Gen. Psychiatry*, 36, 1, 85–90, 1979.
5. Adler, G., Brassen, S., Jajcevic, A., EEG coherence in Alzheimer's dementia. *J. Neural Transm.*, 110, 9, 1051–1058, 2003.
6. Sudharsan, R.R. and Deny, J., Field Programmable Gate Array (FPGA)-Based Fast and Low-Pass Finite Impulse Response (FIR) Filter, in: *Intelligent Computing and Innovation on Data Science*, pp. 199–206, 2020.
7. Alvarez, L.A., Moshé, S.L., Belman, A.L., Maytal, J., Resnick, T.J., Keilson, M., EEG and brain death determination in children. *Neurology*, 38, 2, 227, 1988.
8. Friedberg, J., Shock treatment, brain damage, and memory loss: A neurological perspective. *Am. J. Psychiatry*, 134, 9, 1010–1014, 1977.
9. Waldert, S., Invasive vs. non-invasive neuronal signals for brain–machine interfaces: Will one prevail? *Front. Neurosci.*, 10, 1–4, 2016.
10. Burchiel, K.J., McCartney, S., Lee, A., Raslan, A.M., Accuracy of deep brain stimulation electrode placement using intraoperative computed tomography without microelectrode recording. *J. Neurosurg.*, 119, 2, 301–306, 2013.
11. Deny, J. and Sudharsan, R.R., Block Rearrangements and TSVs for a Standard Cell 3D IC Placement, in: *Intelligent Computing and Innovation on Data Science*, pp. 207–214, 2020.

12. Casdagli, M.C., Iasemidis, L.D., Savit, R.S., Gilmore, R.L., Roper, S.N., Sackellares, J.C., Non-linearity in invasive EEG recordings from patients with temporal lobe epilepsy. *Electroencephalogr. Clin. Neurophysiol.*, 102, 2, 98–105, 1997.

13. Onal, C. *et al.*, Complications of invasive subdural grid monitoring in children with epilepsy. *J. Neurosurg.*, 98, 5, 1017–1026, 2003.

14. Ball, T., Kern, M., Mutschler, I., Aertsen, A., Schulze-Bonhage, A., Signal quality of simultaneously recorded invasive and non-invasive EEG. *Neuroimage*, 46, 3, 708–716, 2009.

15. Pinegger, A., Wriessnegger, S.C., Faller, J., Müller-Putz, G.R., Evaluation of different EEG acquisition systems concerning their suitability for building a brain–computer interface: Case studies. *Front. Neurosci.*, 10, 441, 2016.

16. Alotaiby, T., El-Samie, F.E.A., Alshebeili, S.A., Ahmad, I., A review of channel selection algorithms for EEG signal processing. *EURASIP J. Adv. Signal Process.*, 2015, 1, 66, 2015.

17. Hidalgo-Muñoz, A.R., López, M.M., Santos, I.M., Vázquez-Marrufo, M., Lang, E.W., Tomé, A.M., Affective valence detection from EEG signals using wrapper methods. *Emotion and Attention Recognition Based on Biological Signals and Images*, 12, p. 23, 2017.

18. Dash, M. and Liu, H., Feature selection for classification. *Intell. Data Anal.*, 1, 131–156, 1997.

19. Liu, H. and Yu, L., Toward integrating feature selection algorithms for classification and clustering. *IEEE Trans. Knowl. Data Eng.*, 17, 491–502, 2005.

20. Klimesch, W., EEG alpha and theta oscillations reflect cognitive and memory performance: A review and analysis. *Brain Res. Rev.*, 29, 23, 169–195, 1999.

21. Woehrle, H., Krell, M.M., Straube, S., Kim, S.K., Kirchner, E.A., Kirchner, F., An adaptive spatial filter for user-independent single trial detection of event-related potentials. *IEEE Trans. Biomed. Eng.*, 62, 7, 1696–1705, 2015.

22. Norcia, A.M., Appelbaum, L.G., Ales, J.M., Cottereau, B.R., Rossion, B., The steady-state visual evoked potential in vision research: A review. *J. Vis.*, 15, 1–46, 2015.

23. Palani Thanaraj, K. and Chitra, K., Multichannel feature extraction and classification of epileptic states using higher order statistics and complexity measures. *Int. J. Eng. Technol.*, 6, 1, 102–109, 2014.

24. Picton, T.W., The P300 wave of the human event-related potential. *J. Clin. Neurophysiol.*, 9, 4, 456–479, 1992.

25. Krishna, R.R., Kumar, P.S., Sudharsan, R.R., Optimization of wire-length and block rearrangements for a modern IC placement using evolutionary techniques. *IEEE International Conference on Intelligent Techniques in Control, Optimization and Signal Processing*, pp. 1–4, 2017.

26. Mayaud, L. *et al.*, A comparison of recording modalities of P300 event-related potentials (ERP) for brain-computer interface (BCI) paradigm. *Neurophysiol. Clin.*, 43, 4, 217–227, 2013.

27. Nuwer, M.R., Dawson, E.G., Carlson, L.G., Kanim, L.E.A., Sherman, J.E., Somatosensory evoked potential spinal cord monitoring reduces neurologic deficits after scoliosis surgery: Results of a large multicenter survey. *Electroencephalogr. Clin. Neurophysiol. Evoked Potentials*, 96, 1, 6–11, 1995.

28. Turnip, A. and Hong, K.S., Classifying mental activities from EEG-P300 signals using adaptive neural networks. *Int. J. Innov. Comput. Inf. Control*, 8, 9, 6429–6443, 2012.

29. Sarma, P., Tripathi, P., Sarma, M.P., Sarma, K.K., Pre-processing and feature extraction techniques for EEGBCI applications—A review of recent research, ADBU. *J. Eng. Technol.*, 5, 2348–7305, 2016.

30. Li, K., Sun, G., Zhang, B., Wu, S., Wu, G., Correlation between forehead EEG and sensorimotor area EEG in motor imagery task, in: *Eighth IEEE Int. Symp. Dependable, Auton. Secur. Comput. DASC 2009*, pp. 430–435, 2009.

31. Petrov, Y., Analysis of EEG signals for EEG-based brain-computer interface. *PLoS One*, 7, 10, e44439, 2012.

32. Adelmann, R., Langheinrich, M., Floerkemeier, C., A toolkit for bar code recognition and resolving on camera phones—Jump-starting the Internet of Things. In: Hochberger, C. and R. Liskowsky (Eds.), GI Jahrestagung. (2). *LNI, GI*, 94, 366–373, Informatik 2006, Dresden, Germany, 2006.

33. Arnsten, A.F.T., Berridge, C.W., McCracken, J.T., The neurobiological basis of attention-deficit/hyperactivity disorder. *Prim. Psychiatry*, 16, 47–54, 2009.

34. Baranyi, P. and Csapo, A., Definition and synergies of cognitive info communications. *Acta Polytech. Hung.*, 9, 1, 67–83, 2012.

35. Baranyi, P., Csapo, A., Gyula, S., *Cognitive info communications (CogInfoCom)*, p. 378, Springer, Heidelberg, 2015.

36. Benedek, A. and Molnar, G., Supporting them-learning based knowledge transfer in university education and corporate sector, in: *Proceedings of the 10th international conference on mobile learning 2014*, Madrid, Spain, pp. 339–343, 2014.

37. Brown, V.J. and Bowman, E.M., Rodent models of prefrontal cortical function. *Trends Neurosci.*, 25, 340–343, 2002.

38. Cardinal, R.N., Parkinson, J.A., Hall, J., Everitt, B.J., Emotion and motivation: The role of the amygdala, ventral striatum, and prefrontal cortex. *Neurosci. Biobehav. Rev.*, 26, 321–352, 2002.

39. Cauda, F., Cavanna, A.E., Dágata, F., Sacco, K., Duca, S., Geminiani, G.C., Functional connectivity and coactivation of the nucleus accumbens: A combined functional connectivity and structure-based meta-analysis. *J. Cognit. Neurosci.*, 23, 2864–2877, 2011.

40. Chen, F., Jia, Y., Xi, N., Non-invasive EEG based mental state identification using nonlinear combination, in: *2013 IEEE International Conference on Robotics and Biomimetics (ROBIO)*, 2013, https://doi.org/10.1109/robio.2013.6739789.

41. Christian, F. *et al.*, The Internet of Things, in: *IoT 2008: First International Conference*, Zurich, Switzerland, p. 4952, 378, 2008.

42. Dalley, J.W., Cardinal, R.N., Robbins, T.W., Prefrontal executive and cognitive functions in rodents: neural and neurochemical substrates. *Neurosci. Biobehav. Rev.*, 28, 771–784, 2004.

43. Feenstra, M., Botterblom, M., Uum, J.V., Behavioral arousal and increased dopamine efflux after blockade of NMDA-receptors in the prefrontal cortex are dependent on activation of glutamatergic neurotransmission. *Neuropharmacology*, 42, 752–763, 2002.

44. Fortino, G., Agents meet the IoT: Toward ecosystems of networked smart objects. *IEEE Syst. Man Cybern. Mag.*, 2, 43–47, 2016.

45. Freedman, M. and Oscar-Berman, M., Bilateral frontal lobe disease and selective delayed response deficits in humans. *Behav. Neurosci.*, 100, 337–342, 1986.

46. Friedemann, M. and Christian, F., From the internet of computers to the internet of things, in: *From active data management to event-based systems and more. Papers in Honor of Alejandro Buchmann on the Occasion of His 60th Birthday*, vol. 6462, Sachs, K., Petrov, I., Guerrero, P. (Eds.), pp. 242–259, 2010.

47. Friganovic, K., Medved, M., Cifrek, M., Brain–computer interface based on steady-state visual evoked potentials, in: *2016 39th International Convention on Information and Communication Technology, Electronics and Microelectronics (MIPRO)*, 2016, https://doi.org/10.1109/mipro.

48. Gallo, D.A., Mcdonough, I.M., Scimeca, J., Dissociating source memory decisions in the prefrontal cortex: fMRI of diagnostic and disqualifying monitoring. *J. Cognit. Neurosci.*, 22, 955–969, 2010.

49. Hakiri, A., Berthou, P., Gokhale, A., Abdellatif, S., Publish/subscribe-enabled software defined networking for efficient and scalable IoT communications. *IEEE Commun. Mag.*, 53, 48–54, 2015.

50. Heidbreder, C.A. and Groenewegen, H.J., The medial prefrontal cortex in the rat: Evidence for a dorso-ventral distinction based upon functional and anatomical characteristics. *Neurosci. Biobehav. Rev.*, 27, 555–579, 2003.

51. Horvath, I., Disruptive technologies in higher education, in: *2016 7th IEEE international conference on cognitive info communications*, Wroclaw, Poland, pp. 347–352, 2016.

52. Horvath, I. and Kvasznicza, Z., Innovative engineering training—Today's answer to the challenges of the future, in: *2016 International Education Conference*, Venice, Italy, pp. 647-1–647-7, 2016.

53. Horvath, I., Innovative engineering education in the cooperative R environment, in: *2016 7th IEEE International Conference on Cognitive Info Communications (CogInfoCom)*, Wroclaw, Poland, pp. 359–364, 2016, https://doi.org/10.1109/CogInfoCom.2016.7804576.

54. Horvath, I., Digital life gap between students and lecturers, in: *2016 7th IEEE International Conference on Cognitive Info Communications (CogInfoCom)*, Wroclaw, Poland, pp. 353–358, 2016, https://doi.org/10.1109/CogInfoCom.2016.7804575.

55. Kalaivani, M., Kalaivani, V., Devi, V.A., Analysis of EEG signal for the detection of brain abnormalities. *Int. J. Comput. Appl.*, 1, 2, 1–6, 2014.
56. Cárdenas-Barrera, J.L., Lorenzo-Ginori, J.V., Rodríguez-Valdivia, E., A wavelet-packets based algorithm for EEG signal compression. *Inform. Health Soc. Care*, 29, 1, 15–27, 2004.
57. Kameswara, T., Rajyalakshmi, M., Prasad, T.V., An exploration on brain computer interface and its recent trends. *Int. J. Adv. Res. Artif. Intell.*, 1, 8, 17–22, 2013.
58. Motamedi-Fakhr, S., Moshrefi-Torbati, M., Hill, M., Hill, C.M., White, P.R., Signal processing techniques applied to human sleep EEG signals—A review. *Biomed. Signal Process. Control*, 10, 1, 21–33, 2014.
59. Vidaurre, C., Krämer, N., Blankertz, B., Schlögl, A., Time domain parameters as a feature for EEG-based brain-computer interfaces. *Neural Networks*, 22, 9, 1313–1319, 2009.
60. Chatterjee, S., Pratiher, S., Bose, R., Multifractal detrended fluctuation analysis-based novel feature extraction technique for automated detection of focal and non-focal electroencephalogram signals. *IET Sci. Meas. Technol.*, 11, 8, 1014–1021, 2017.
61. Rejer, I., Genetic algorithms in EEG feature selection for the classification of movements of the left and right hand. *Adv. Intell. Syst. Comput.*, 226, 9–11, 2013.
62. Alın, A., Kurt, S., Mcintosh, A.R., Ozg, M., Partial least squares analysis in electrical brain activity. *J. Data Sci.*, 7, 99–110, 2009.
63. O'Brien, P., A primer on the discrete Fourier transform. *Am. J. EEG Technol.*, 34, 4, 190–223, 2018.
64. Birvinskas, D., Jusas, V., Martišius, I., Damaševičius, R., Data compression of EEG signals for artificial neural network classification. *Inf. Technol. Control*, 42, 3, 238–241, 2013.
65. Chaurasiya, R.K., Londhe, N.D., Ghosh, S., Statistical wavelet features, PCA, and SVM based approach for EEG signals classification. *World Acad. Sci. Eng. Technol. Int. J. Electr. Comput. Energy Electron. Commun. Eng.*, 9, 2, 182–186, 2015.
66. Kim, M. and Chang, S., A consumer transceiver for long-range IoT communications in emergency environments. *IEEE Trans. Consum. Electron.*, 62, 3, 226–234, 2016.
67. Abdellatif, A.A., Khafagy, M.G., Mohamed, A., Chiasserini, C.F., EEG-based transceiver design with data decomposition for healthcare IoT applications. *IEEE Internet Things J.*, 5, 5, 3569–579, 2018.
68. Fisher, R.S. *et al.*, Epileptic Seizures and Epilepsy: Definitions Proposed by the International League Against Epilepsy (ILAE) and the International Bureau for Epilepsy (IBE). *Epilepsia*, 46, 4, 1–3, 2005.
69. Parvez, M.Z., Paul, M., Antolovich, M., Detection of pre-stage of epileptic seizure by exploiting temporal correlation of EMD decomposed EEG signals. *J. Med. Bioeng.*, 4, 2, 110–116, 2015.

70. Abdulhay, E., Alafeef, M., Abdelhay, A., Al-Bashir, A., Classification of normal, ictal and inter-ictal EEG via direct quadrature and random forest tree. *J. Med. Biol. Eng.*, 37, 6, 843–857, 2017.

71. Qaraqe, M., Ismail, M., Serpedin, E., Band-sensitive seizure onset detection via CSP enhanced EEG features. *Epilepsy Behav.*, 50, 77–87, 2015.

72. Mutlu, A.Y., Detection of epileptic dysfunctions in EEG signals using Hilbert vibration decomposition. *Biomed. Signal Process. Control*, 40, 33–40, 2018.

73. Diykh, M., Li, Y., Wen, P., Classify epileptic EEG signals using weighted complex networks based community structure detection. *Expert Syst. Appl.*, 90, 87–100, 2017.

74. Birjandtalab, J., Baran Pouyan, M., Cogan, D., Nourani, M., Harvey, J., Automated seizure detection using limited-channel EEG and non-linear dimension reduction. *Comput. Biol. Med.*, 82, 49–58, 2017.

75. Albert, B. *et al.*, Automatic EEG processing for the early diagnosis of traumatic brain injury. *Proc. Comput. Sci.*, 96, 703–712, 2016.

76. Variane, G.F.T. *et al.*, Early amplitude-integrated electroencephalography for monitoring neonates at high risk for brain injury. *J. Pediatr. (Rio. J)*, 93, 5, 460–466, 2017.

77. Franke, L.M., Walker, W.C., Hoke, K.W., Wares, J.R., Distinction in EEG slow oscillations between chronic mild traumatic brain injury and PTSD. *Int. J. Psychophysiol.*, 106, 21–29, 2016.

78. Weeke, L.C. *et al.*, Role of EEG background activity, seizure burden and MRI in predicting neurodevelopmental outcome in full-term infants with hypoxic-ischaemic encephalopathy in the era of therapeutic hypothermia. *Eur. J. Paediatr. Neurol.*, 20, 6, 855–864, 2016.

79. Nevalainen, P. *et al.*, Evoked potentials recorded during routine EEG predict outcome after perinatal asphyxia. *Clin. Neurophysiol.*, 128, 7, 1337–1343, 2017.

80. Subramanian, R.R. and Seshadri, K., Design and Evaluation of a Hybrid Hierarchical Feature Tree Based Authorship Inference Technique, in: *Advances in Data and Information Sciences. Lecture Notes in Networks and Systems*, Kolhe, M., Trivedi, M., Tiwari, S., Singh, V. (Eds.), p. 39, 2019.

81. Joshva Devadas, T. and Raja Subramanian, R., Paradigms for Intelligent IoT Architecture, in: *Principles of Internet of Things (IoT) Ecosystem: Insight Paradigm. Intelligent Systems Reference Library*, Peng, S.L., Pal, S., Huang, L. (Eds.), p. 174, 2020.

3

Automated Verification and Validation of IoRT Systems

S.V. Gayetri Devi[1]* and C. Nalini[2]

[1]Department of Computer Science and Engineering, Dr. M.G.R. Educational and Research Institute, Chennai, India
[2]Department of Computer Science and Engineering, Bharath Institute of Higher Education and Research, Chennai, India

Abstract

The Internet of Robotic Things (IoRT), an evolving standard draws together autonomous Robotic systems with the Internet of Things (IoT) revelation of linked sensors and smart objects extensively rooted in everyday environments. Some of the concerns in Verification and Validation of IoRT systems involve dynamic environments with multiple sensors and devices in conjunction with robotic things unlike Application testing performed in an established environment, complex real-time Test scenarios, conceiving a Test environment to verify and validate functionality along with scalability, reliability and safety issues.

Ensuring the safety and functional integrity of IORT systems calls for stringent verification and validation. The Formal methods apprehend the intended system behaviour in a formal specification using Mathematical reasoning and facilitate Verification, Synthesis and Validation. Effective validation enfolds automated approach to generating Test cases, Test suite reduction, Test case prioritization and Test execution scheduling in combination with appropriate program verification techniques such as SMT and constraint solvers.

The unified modelling language is used to depict the system requirements and to put forward a base for test case generation. For the test cases to be automatically extracted, the test scenarios are automatically determined using Natural language processing and formal constraints are acquired for the test data to be generated. The formal constraints hence obtain the contexts triggering the execution of test scenarios. This way test cases are generated considering both test scenarios addressed by manually implemented test suites and the vital scenarios identifying critical bugs.

*Corresponding author: gayetri.venkhatraman@gmail.com

R. Anandan, G. Suseendran, S. Balamurugan, Ashish Mishra and D. Balaganesh (eds.) Human Communication Technology: Internet of Robotic Things and Ubiquitous Computing, (55–90)
© 2022 Scrivener Publishing LLC

Constraint programming and global constraints can be utilized to reduce Test suites through constraint optimization models to identify a subset of test cases that encompass all the test requirements and hence optimize the cost of selected test cases as a whole. Constraint model-based test case execution scheduling is performed by assigning Test cases with obvious characteristics to Test agents – Robots with limited time and/or resources capacity. The allocated test cases are the ones that are consistent with the capacity constraints of the Test agents and having optimized time cost functions.

Test cases can be prioritized automatically by observing failing test cases, test results, their actions and effects during run time and thereby adapting the prioritization methods for the test cases continually since the pointers for the failing test cases vary over time according to modifications in the test suite. Evident memory models and reward functions are used for the process.

The magnitudes of IORT systems software failures can be possibly intense. Hence making use of suites formal verification and validation at various levels of abstraction and coverage to help secure certainty of the systems' safety, reliability and functional exactness.

Keywords: Model checking, theorem prover, symbolic checking, abstraction, testing framework, security

3.1   Introduction

Internet of Robotic Things is being extensively applied in many safety-related environments such as aviation, healthcare, etc. Hence, their functional precision is very significant. A fundamental difficulty for the IoRT systems is the capability to demonstrate that the software systems can function securely, efficiently and firmly, with safety as the primary interest. There is a persistent call for a thorough method to establish effectual testing strategies for IoRT solutions along with security testing and qualified Integration testing in addition to the availability of typical platform options for testing. Also, Automation of IoRT Verification and Validation is imperative since the immense number of software variants may not feasible for manual V&V.

Due to the heterogeneity over a large number of devices and service vendors, there is a greater chance of intercepting communications, tamper confidential details or data manipulations. The devices in operation have limited Time and Memory resources to process capacity and storage resulting in complex execution of security procedures. Therefore there is a need to identify potential flaws and vulnerable aspects at the design phase to secure such systems at the very outset. An encouraging technique to locate faults and likely vulnerabilities during design place is Formal

Verification. It confirms the correctness of the design through a distinct set of mathematical as well as logical methods thus conforming to the functional accuracy of implementations, identify confidential data leakage to the adversaries due to physical implementations at the circuit and architectural stages, programming errors, providing security assurances.

System analysis using formal methods assure that a system has coveted properties. The formal methods serve as a multifaceted toolbox for safety and reliability strengthening missions. They are recognized over being robust analysis techniques bringing in mathematical significance into the analysis process. Abstraction leads to over approximations producing counterexamples and false errors. Abstraction refining methods that analyze these erroneous instances strengthen these abstractions and when iterated several times leads to eminent verification of software. Bounded model checking verifies the design conformance to indicated characteristics in a particular modeling language. They represent what can be done wholly in an automated way. Theorem provers also knew as proof assistant incorporate automated verification methods with manual direction to corroborate correctness. They are broadly mightier than model checkers enabling developers with provision to employ built-in schemes or build new ones to prove safety and security constraints. The solid agreements of complete formal verification come at an excessive cost of extremely proficient experts. The tools for automated verification can be classified based on verification of abstract system models, specification of actual software design and those that generate the demonstrably accurate design.

The objective of software validation is to guarantee that the making and quality of the system software are validated following a written process for the proposed use so that it accomplishes as envisioned and satisfies its needs. Acceptable software validation involves a series of characteristics—planning, system software verification and validation, traceability and also configuration management. This relates to both product or device software validation and that which are employed to design, create devices as well as products.

Some of the aspects to be considered during the V&V of IORT systems are:

- Real-time complexities—IORT systems can have several real-time scenarios with enormously intricate use cases
- Extensibility of the system—Developing test environments evaluating functionalities keeping along expandability and trustworthiness is challenging
- Associated third party components and subsystems.
- Complex use cases for test case and test data generation
- Hardware quality constraints and correctness
- Privacy and Security related issues.

3.1.1   Automating V&V—An Important Key to Success

Within time and resource restrained environments, there is one major challenge to increase operational efficacies while developing tests for checking compliances and at the same time offering substantial competences over manual verification and validation. Automated V&V gives important productivity improvements by lessening the necessity for manual resources and reducing the timeline to verify and validate software modules with higher degrees of testing. With automated testing tools, the IORT systems can be verified and validated in considerably lesser time and least number resources.

The general unanimity is that verifying and validating the API that links the related world be automated to the greatest extent possible since when that falls apart, there is no more Internet existing in those things. The IORT systems must tackle the challenges like Security of Data, Security-related threats, Access managing, third party data involvement, Compliance related specifications, Hardware concerns and Integration issues. Performance and Quality are the basis for IORT devices functioning and seamless interconnections. End to end testing of the various functionalities of numerous devices across platforms must be performed across many locations. It begins with integration testing of all the hardware-software alongside usability testing ensuring optimum entire system usage by the end-users. Also, interoperability testing is essential for all the connected applications and devices to provide the necessary functionality for both internally and externally associated devices. And with immense data streaming, testing of security is an obligatory activity.

Automated V&V reduces errors across various phases of the software development cycle:

- Requirements phase: Validation of software requirements with consistency and completeness conformance to the crucial criterion of availability, scalability, maintainability and functionality across the physical layer of Robotic sensors and actuators, Network & Communication layer of Internet routers, Data Acquirement Systems, Edge IT systems and Cloud.
- Design: Identification of software design bugs by conformance of design concerning requirements, and component related interaction anomalies.
- Implementation: Identify programming errors by performing runtime checks, conformance checks with requirements/design, and isolation of Time and memory usages.

Thus, automated V&V of IoRT systems can be applied using the applicable standards like the ones provided below, through which the software teams can find prospective improvement in their efforts:

- Mathematical based methods applying statistical, combinatorial, Domain related concepts etc.
- Fault Attack testing focusing on prevalent error classifications
- Model-based testing performed independently via standards and tools

3.2   Program Analysis of IoRT Applications

Program analysis techniques function on IoRT application source codes to accomplish varied objectives such as comprehending security of applications.

3.2.1   Need for Program Analysis

IoRT devices can access even very private information so IoRT platforms confirm role-based access controls to confidential data and enable only restricted controls over how that data is utilized. The system applications essentially access methods which when misused risks the end-user security and safety. Hence, it is vital to thwart robotic devices being assaulted of their abilities by confirming that the applications handle these devices following functional, security and safety specifications. The authorization model of an IoRT system outlines the access of an application to delicate activities like changes in robotics sensors/actuators states. But these models can be misused when the security access is coarse-grained and when applications try to gain unwanted and threatening accesses of the IoRT devices. To investigate the various attacks and security breaches, Source code instrumentation can first develop application's behavior followed by aggregation of IoRT system information as graph structure for diagnostics.

3.2.2   Aspects to Consider in Program Analysis of IoRT Systems

IORT development platforms are varied and each one employs own programming language. Hence the analysis must apprehend event-driven environment of IoRT applications and accomplish analysis over it. The applications are prone to various vulnerabilities arising out of different physical processes. IoRT apps may interact with each other when they are co-located in an environment. The communication among the system applications takes place when a robotic device operating in an application event handling routine may trigger a different application's routine event handling. Every IoRT program has its particular features challenging the program analysis. These challenges can be managed via static or dynamic analysis.

The static analysis takes advantage of the analysis of entire source code while in the case of dynamic analysis, only a section of the code goes for execution—therefore analysis results are restricted to perceived executions. Besides, static analysis can extend to over approximations by a generalization of all viable program behaviors, chancing false positives. For example, an analysis tool senses a delicate data leak through a part of code in an IoRT application that is not executed at run-time. The dynamic analysis may incorrectly estimate the bugs present in code thus throwing false negatives if any executing path is not analyzed.

Important challenges with IoRT analysis are—deviation of robotic sensor/actuator's intended functionality if the physical processes integrated with digital networks are breached; simulation of widespread and dissimilar IoRT environments demands to acquire the state of multiple IoRT devices, and the interconnection among actions, events and computing intelligence. The additional important issue is the devices' physical processes being difficult to reproduce in a simulation. This requires a discrete-event based simulating engine realized through continuous-time solvers and modeling based on the state machine. There is the main task to automate organized and extendable input creation for IoRT applications controlling various devices via several internal states thereby encouraging the need to intensify the code coverage for automated test case generation. The communication among IoRT devices gives rise to safety, privacy and security related threats despite individual applications being safe at execution. To avoid uninvited and insecure states during the interactions, Program analysis must identify the exchanges among applications, develop guidelines for unwanted states of the device, properties conformance when one application interrelating with another and stalling the states thereby creating violations. Also interaction between IoRT systems and APIs of Trigger action platform services like Zapier, IFTTT, Microsoft flow etc. can also result in security as well as privacy problems. The analysis includes assessing the events and actions and label them with associated confidentiality and integrity-related aspects. Analysis techniques must also address the issues like closures, calls by reflection linked with programming languages adopted by IoRT systems. The context-dependent analysis provides for accurate verification for IoRT applications. Vital sensitivity issues about IoRT systems are concerning execution flow, call site contexts bearing in mind feasible paths for analysis, predicates at conditional-branches, tracking data sources etc.

3.3   Formal Verification of IoRT Systems

Identification of critical flaws to prevent system breakdowns is crucial to IoRT systems whose majority of the activities are associated and interacting with several Robotic sensors, RFID nodes and actuators. To deliver safer systems, Formal verification can be combined with Faults analysis from the system simulations. There are the major verification techniques—model checking, theorem proving and process algebra taken into account to assess the IoRT applications.

3.3.1   Automated Model Checking

The reasoning checks IoRT systems transiting to an incorrect tangible (physical) state is complicated because the degree of devices and applications growing is largely exponential thereby, analysis of all likely exchanges among them may be difficult. Static analysis related tools incline to adopt soundness at the cost of completeness resulting in many false-positives. On the contrary, distinctive dynamic analyses relevant tools validate the properties of a module while executing, however, could again nurture false-negatives. To ensure the correctness of IoRT system, usage of Formal methods has been a desired task. But the complex nature of the methods made them available only to experts like mathematicians. Thereby using them only in critical systems. Evolving Model checking techniques made them open to standard usage. Hence Formal verification has been made easier for a wide range of applications. Model-checking is a method that verifies if a system conforms to a specified specification through a systematic exploration of the states and scenarios of the system modules using a brute-force approach. Faults that stay unidentified using simulation/ emulation and testing can be possibly exposed by model checking. In an optimal instance, the model checker thoroughly scrutinizes all probable states to confirm any safety or vitality relevant specification breach.

In practical situations, the model checker is typically utilized as a falsifier exploring state space (reachable) trying to establish computations violating a particular property. Hence the method is also referred to as bounded model checking with model verifying complexity treated as Propositional-Satisfiability problem.

Model-checking can be accepted as an elementary building block of IoRT systems due to the flexibility in proving the anticipated properties with linear temporal logic, providing concrete counter-examples enabling the capture of the cause of bad states occurring. Also, the checking helps to

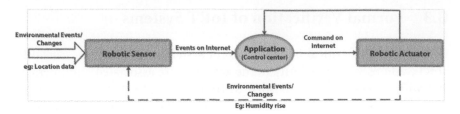

Figure 3.1 Sequence of states in IoRT systems.

identify interactions among several applications with flexible use in concurrent systems. The exploration of sequence of states and scenario of an example IoRT system is illustrated in Figure 3.1.

As the naming suggests, the method verifies the abstract system model described at a higher level without verifying the actual program. The critical aspect of model checking is modeling the system reflecting the actual system. The abstraction must be all-inclusive enough to comprehend all the important characteristics of the system. Else, the model checker might be unworkable if it cannot perform state exploration which can probably result in errors with the safety and reliability of the IoRT systems being compromised.

3.3.2   The Model Checking Process

The three steps of Model checking are—First, construct the system model, usually as a set of Automata. Second, formalization of properties to be verified using expressions in a logic. Third, employing Model checking (tool) for the generation of space of all potential states. And then extensively verify if the properties stay true for every potential dynamic behavior of the IoRT system model. To begin with, a model of the IoRT system is to be created through an applicable Mathematical formal method. We also need to model the system environment. This modeling is accomplished using a specific formal specification language typically a Model description language (MDL) delivered by the Model Checker tool. A high-level language is adopted for practical consideration. Definition of semantical details of the spec languages is done with labeled-transition systems. The semantical information refers to a state-space (all potential behaviors) of the model.

The definitions include aspects of finite state machines definitions with initialization of variables, environmental relevant assumptions, and constraints specifying the preferred system behavior of the system. Complex system properties to be checked for compliance with system model are well-defined through temporal logic related constraints like Linear Time temporal logic—LTL or Branching Time temporal logics namely CTL,

CTL*, etc. Model checkers work based on an exploration of state-space of the IoRT model. The tool proceeds to the next property after the current one is agreed upon. For any violated property, the error trail or counter-example produced by the model checker is analyzed and the system is refined accordingly. This way all the properties are verified. Graph algorithms are employed to verify the required properties, normally on brute-force way—for specific property verification, all the potential behaviors are tested. Through this, the model checkers are completely automatic. The basic method of model checking of IORT system is depicted in Figure 3.2.

Thus the fundamental concept is to model the IoRT system a state transition and define the required properties of the system as formulae in temporal logic. If a property doesn't stay true for a given model of the system, it also provides a counter trace for debugging.

As a side effect, there is a probability of attaining memory faults due to state explosion issue with infinite or very large state-space (exponential growth of the obvious state-space) created by the tool. That is the count of states in the state-space increases very quickly about the model size. Generally, the complications arise when the IoRT system has several components that operate in parallel. The issue can be managed by adopting the following approaches:

- Reducing the count of states for exploration (Abstraction, equivalences based reductions, Compositional techniques).
- Reducing the memory required for storage of travelled states.

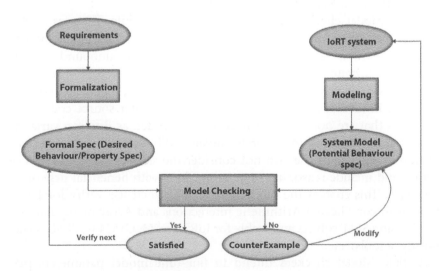

Figure 3.2 Model checking approach.

- Increase obtainable memory
- Balance on completeness requirement and explore essential parts of the state-space.

The symbolic checking is a conservative method of verifying where the transition states are not explicitly generated and Binary decision diagrams are used instead. The space necessities for Boolean functions are comparatively lesser than the explicit way of representation, this way State explosions can be alleviated. In Abstraction method, only important aspects of the IoRT system are represented as states.

Depending on the model spec as well as state-space, the model checkers can be categorized as explicit or implicit. Explicit checkers build a design model representation where the states directly indexed and Graph algorithms for state-space exploration beginning from initial state imparting Partial-Order reduction technique during the exploration. Some tools in this kind for IoRT systems are SPIN (Simple Promela Interpreter), PRISM (Probabilistic Model Checker), etc. Implicit checkers also referred to as Symbolic model checkers utilize logical representations of states (e.g. in the form of Binary decision diagram) to define the areas of model's state space satisfying the evaluated properties. Such compact representations generally allow symbolic model checkers to handle a much larger state space than explicit model checkers. Exploration of state-space is done by symbolical enumeration of states. One important tool to mention in this type for IoRT systems is NuSMV (New Symbolic Model Verifier).

Some model checkers employ Satisfiability Modulo Theories (SMT) solvers that are an extension of SAT (prepositional satisfiability) for verifying constraint satisfaction related issues such as unbounded array structures, infinite-state and recursive function calls. In SAT solvers, the variables should be of type—Boolean. Because of this, it becomes complicated for industrial concerns. For instance, Computer source codes with variables that are non-Boolean need to be encoded as Boolean variables in BIT form resulting in larger formulae. SMT solvers are the alternate option for this since they do not consider the sizes of the data types or arrays and include reasoning of equality along with beneficial first-order concepts. This enables the model checkers to efficiently verify IoRT systems with complicated Arithmetic interactions and Array manipulations. Tools using SMT solvers applicable for IoRT are Z3, CVC4 (CVC-Checker family of tools), etc.

Online Model checkers intend to fine-tune model parameters persistently to reduce modeling errors allowing safety tasks at all times and paves the way to respond before the occurrence of safety violations. An example tool is Java PathExplorer.

3.3.2.1   PRISM

PRISM is a Markov Decision Process (MDP) based model checker tool to formally verify the security and safety aspects of a wide variety of system IORT systems exhibiting probabilistic behavior. The tool provides for probabilistic models such as Discrete-Time Markov Chains (DTMCs), Continuous-Time Markov Chains (CTMCs), Probabilistic Automata (PAs), Probabilistic Timed Automata (PTAs), and Markov Decision Processes (MDPs) along with models extensions. Additionally, the tool comprises of Quantitative abstraction-refinement and statistical model checking relevant engines. The properties to be verified are defined in PRISM language which is state-based working on formalisms for Reactive modules. The PRISM language mainly holds modules as well as variables. The determined model consists of a concurrent arrangement of independent modules that are at the same time interacting. A module has local scalars and commands that are guarded. At any provided instant, the values consigned to these scalars denote the modules states and the commands emulate their behavior. The local state of autonomous modules is incorporated to find the complete state of the entire IoRT model. The software verification with PRISM model checker is shown in Figure 3.3.

For verification and analysis of the IoRT system behavior, the desired functionality is articulated as a property using applicable probabilistic reasoning through property specification language based on temporal logic. Symbolic and explicit state model checking with Symmetric reduction and Quantitative Abstraction refinement are employed further supported with discrete event simulation feature. PRISM tools have optimum strategies generation with a Graphical User Interface that includes a simulator, model editor, graph generation and also a

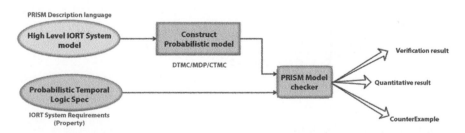

Figure 3.3 PRISM model checking overview.

command-line tool. The tool also contains Benchmark suite for testing of new methods of probabilistic model checkers. Using the PRISM tool, Trustworthiness of IoRT system concerning the system demands is tested. Protocols used in IoRT critical systems can also be modeled and verified.

State-space explosion problems as mentioned earlier can be offset with the help of abstraction and remodeling. For instance, instead of modeling the algorithm entirely for every robotic sensor, detailed modeling can be done for a single robotic sensor and then the remaining of the network of nodes be modeled with a second module in the tool. Thereafter, the size of the module would be retained to the least, still the network node's behavior in reaction to the network can be verified.

3.3.2.2 UPPAAL

UPPAAL is an integrated verification (automatic-model checking) and validation (through Graphical-simulation) toolbox environment for real-time IoRT systems. A description language to model IoRT behavior as Automata-based networks that are finite state machines with the clock as well as data variables extensions is a non-deterministic one with guarded commands. UPPAAL being designed for Real-time IoRT systems verification, clocks are the basic characteristic of modeling and verification. The UPPAAL model is put up as a set of concurrent processes with each process intended graphically as Timed Automation. The graphical representation of UPPAAL timed automation is shown in Figure 3.4.

Timed automation is signified as a graph with locations designated as nodes and arcs in between locations denoted by edges. Guards (indicating

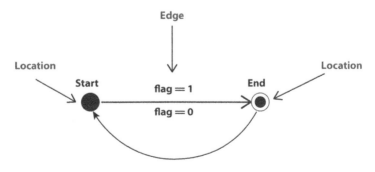

Figure 3.4 UPPAAL basic structure.

when transitions are enabled or fired), synchronizations (coordinating actions of two or more processes), update (expression evaluated when an edge is fired after which the system state is changed) or selections are annotated along the edges. As multiple instances of the same automation are frequently required, templates are employed. A simulator to validate the design stage of IoRT is provided to ensure that the model behaves as the IoRT system that we wished to model and detecting any design flaw, the next step is to assure that the model verifies the properties of the system. Hence formalize the properties and then have them translated into UPPAAL query language. Complex queries are verified by checking multiple different queries. State-space exploration is used for the analysis of properties like reachability, liveness, safety and deadlock related via a time Automata-based Model checker. Automatic generation of diagnostics traces to verify the property satisfiability is viable. The simulator provides for conception and examination of these traces.

3.3.2.3   SPIN Model Checker

Model-checking, as stated earlier, is a computation technique, provided with a Finite-state system model and logical properties, thoroughly verifies if those properties are true for that given model. Thus model checkers can envisage about the validity of the system and expect design-related deficiencies before it is implemented and not holding its role of the final system implementation phase. Eventually, model checkers have the viability to lower rework and failures risks in mission-crucial applications. SPIN (Simple Promela Interpreter) Model checker is an open-source formal verification tool oriented towards asynchronous distributed IoRT systems capable of verifying functional properties. At the same time, the tool does not model Real-time systems yet models timeouts. Developed in ANSI C language, the tool is portable across several platforms. SPIN can be utilized in 2 fundamental modes—As a simulation tool to obtain a swift impression about System behavior captured from the model, and as—Verifier to step through execution traces using simulation when a counterexample is produced. The model checker proves the exactness of interactions among processes. The tool encompasses an innate C language similar Promela scheme to state the system's finite-state abstraction clearly and notations to express the requirements pertinent to general correctness in the form of Linear Temporal Logic. Pamela stands for Process-Meta language and being input to the Tool. It is a non-deterministic language with guarded commands describing the IORT distributed system's behavior.

The formal verification process of SPIN model checker is depicted in Figure 3.5. The Promela model comprises of Data objects, Message channels and Process corresponding to a finite state machine where every object is bounded. More than one process is acceptable inside the model with concurrency among them. The data objects can be local/ global and message channels allow Synchronous as well as synchronous communications. During verification runs. Promela checks for simple and trace assertions, labels namely—Progress-state, End-state, Accept-state and *Never* claims. Also, the model verifies safety and liveness properties. The tool has no real-time aspects and can help get out of deadlocks. The timeout models an exceptional condition that enables the process to abort waiting for a constraint that may never hold. State explosion is a side-effect of the SPIN tool.

SPIN devises Optimization as well as reduction techniques like Partial Order reduction, Hash compaction, Bitstate hashing/supertrace, minimal-ized automation, state-vector compressions, dataflow analysis, slicing techniques to make verification runs more operative.

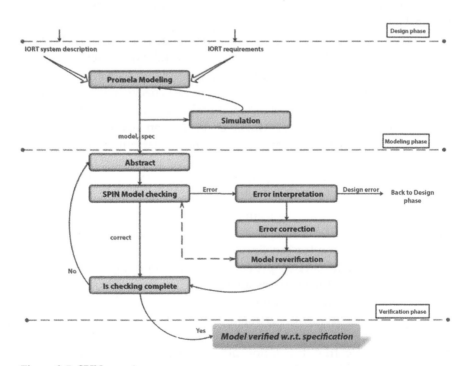

Figure 3.5 SPIN overview.

3.3.3 Automated Theorem Prover

Automated theorem proving verifies mathematical or logical statements that can specify the IoRT system properties through the use of computers. Methods for theorem proving in First-Order logic are complete such that the proof of a formula can be found if and only if it is valid. Theorems form the input to automated theorem provers stated informal logic and could be propositional, first-order, non-classical logic and higher-order logic. The logical language permits an accurate formal statement of the required information that can then be handled by an Automatic Theorem Prover. This aspect is the primary strong point of ATP—there is no uncertainty in the problem statement with the problem being self-reliant and unknown assumptions are not allowed. The output of an automated theorem prover could be a yes or no, otherwise, it can comprise comprehensive proofs with/without counterexamples. The basic automated theorem proving procedure for any real world problem is illustrated in Figure 3.6.

One main necessity is soundness and complete in the sense no proofs are lost and each proof identified by the prover system is proof. Most practical ATP implementations are incomplete because of restricted run-time of the system. Most provers can assure soundness and work with intensive searching. Proof checkers can automatically check the exactness of proof structure by inputting the created proof and formula and verifying that the inference rules are applied correctly and all proof

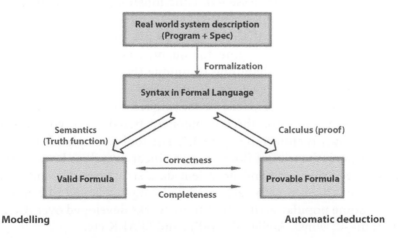

Figure 3.6 Automated theorem proving and logic.

terms are instances of formula terms. But even if the automated prover may operate correctly, faults may occur during formalization, first-order transformation, resultant formula or axioms pre-processing. Hence the precision of the entire system must be judiciously examined. In some applications, AI methods can be combined with automated prover for solution locating by the former and ensuring accuracy by the latter. When the prover is connected to an IoRT application system, it must adhere to interface protocols conformance—how data/control details passed on to the prover, transfer of results, start and stop of prover and finally transfer of arguments. The extent of automation depends on the applied formalism for theorem description and IoRT modeling. Higher-order logic, first-order logic, temporal logic and Propositional logic rank in the increasing level of Automation. The lesser expressive a formalism is, the more automated it can be. Thus, tools for higher-order logic normally operate iteratively with the user being accountable for supplying proofs that are simpler facilitating the verification.

3.3.3.1   ALT-ERGO

Alt-Ergo based on SMT is an automatic theorem solver (open source) of mathematical formulae intended on the context of deductive verification. Alt-Ergo has a built-in input language for first-order logic and capable of reasoning of user-defined data-structures. The language adopts Prenex polymorphism rendering it expressive enough and with fully static type-safety such that the number of quantified axioms and problems complexity are lessened. Functions/data types can be defined generically handling values identical without reliant on their types. The 3 main components of the tool are a Depth First Search-based SAT solver, an instantiation engine for quantifiers based on E-Matching (a heuristic Quantifier-handling technique that works by finding sub-expressions of quantified-formula matched during proof searching) and an arrangement of decision techniques for built-in theories. A higher level view of the three component based Alt-Ergo automated theorem solver is shown in Figure 3.7. The tool also upholds reasoning of quantifiers, theories of floating, non-linear as well as linear rational and integer arithmetic and prevalent data structures. OCaml is used to develop Alt-Ergo with each module being developed in a modular model. Some popular verification frameworks developed over Alt-Ergo are Frama-C, why3, Atelier-B, Rodin, and SPARK etc.

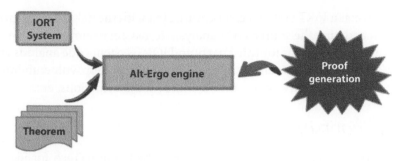

Figure 3.7 Higher level view of alt-ergo.

3.3.4   Static Analysis

Tools for Static analysis perform three kinds of checking—Semantics, syntax and style. Semantic checking is used for code analysis to identify invalid usage of the programming language. Syntax checking averts invalid constructs concerning the grammar. Style checking imposes a certain Coding standards-based Program code writing style. This is beneficial to have a uniform repository of the codebase. Static analysis is an overall approach covering numerous techniques. The techniques incline to be restricted to analysis at the unit level.

Static Analysis tests and evaluates IoRT applications by examining code, bytecode like compiled java program, binary executable codes without execution of the application through reasoning about possible system behaviors. It is reasonably proficient at evaluating a codebase as against dynamic analysis tools. The tools can analyze paths in the code which are not tested by other procedures and can go ahead with tracing data and execution related paths in code. It can be included during the initial developmental phase to analyze present, application source code that is supported any longer as well as third-party binaries and source before being incorporated into the IoRT product. As different sources are included we can go about with incremental analysis along with configuration management for security and quality of software.

Static analysis tools impose coding standards, detect code anomalies, analyze dependencies and structure, compute metrics like nesting levels, cyclomatic code complexity, detection and analysis of tainted data (to catch how possibly unsafe inputs can run through a program to touch-sensitive fragments of code), Uninterrupted assurance of security and quality of the source. Risks in IoRT systems can be mitigated with the help of static analysis by mandating the source code analysis across developmental projects, utilizing Binary analysis for third party and IORT system code analysis and finally incorporate software hardening (reducing system vulnerabilities) advancements like software monitors, Binary transformations, etc.

3.3.4.1   CODESONAR

CodeSonar is a static analysis tool developed by GrammaTech for identifying and fixing bugs and security vulnerabilities in the source as well as binary codes that might otherwise cause failures of IORT system failures, unreliable software, breaching of the system and unsafe contexts. The tool provides crucial support during the coding and integration stages of software development. The tool can statically analyze on both binary libraries and executables capable of examining both stripped and unstripped executables. Figure 3.8 illustrates the basic overview of CodeSonar static analysis tool. Built-in checking comprises of buffer-overruns, variables not initialized, null-pointer dereferencing, divide by zero errors, etc. The tool complies with standards such as MISRA C: 2012, DO-178B/C, US-CERT's

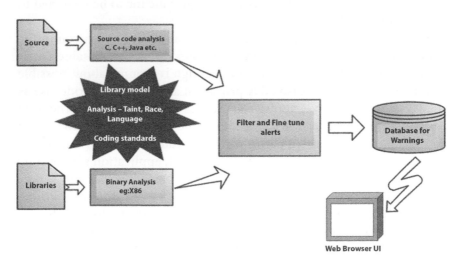

Figure 3.8 CodeSonar overview.

Build Security In etc. Languages supported by CodeSonar are C, C++, C#, Java, Python and Binary code analysis provides for ARM and Intel ×64/×86.

3.4   Validation of IoRT Systems

The main requirement of IoRT systems is to provide stable solutions with higher quality. Devices of IoRT systems constantly produce data challenging the internal testing groups with testing complex solutions. Independent Testing of IoRT warrants quality of the system developed using a multi-disciplinary methodology, test strategies planned well and utilization of suitable automation, simulators service virtualization tools for ubiquitous environment and tools for quality measurement. Some of the fundamental concerns for validating IORT systems are listed in Figure 3.9.

IoRT systems are intricate in terms of several perspectives like diverse components associated such as devices, application and server related server software, client and network platforms, the immense level and production capability with which expected to perform on networks and the end user and other environment related constraints for operation. The testing framework for an IORT system is portrayed in Figure 3.10.

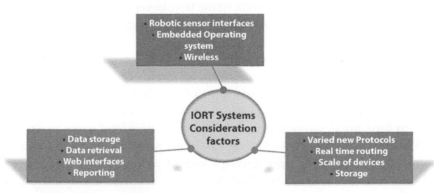

Figure 3.9 IoRT Validation key concerns.

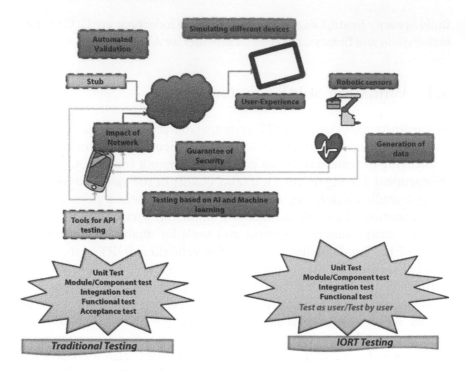

Figure 3.10 Approach to IoRT testing framework.

A higher level of tasks—The multitude of connected devices associated with the cloud or on-prem servers make testing very complicated accompanied by multiple vendor settings and difficult simulations of real-time environments.

The interdependence of Hardware and Software—A unified approach to test IoRT systems is required to operate on interlinked dynamic software structure. We need to test real-world situations that take into account the communication between hardware and software components along with regular functional, safety and security testing of unit-level components.

Platform heterogeneity—Several variations of firmware, hardware and software platforms, different network-related protocols and methods to connect devices to server WebSockets, HTTP etc. make it impractical to test all possible combination. Hence it gets necessary to select appropriate scenarios of test based on end-user conditions, domain information, and a platform-independent and automation of test suites.

Rate of real-time information—Several associated devices lead to substantial load over the network. Undependable internet provisions and hardware for networks degrade the performance of the devices and eventually the quality of the IoRT solutions.

User-experiences-continuous and dependable user-experience across mobile and desktop environments is necessary for IoRT systems. The varied environments of the users must be considered for testing.

Privacy and security aspects—Devices and applications connected over the network might be susceptible to hacking. Recommended security criteria must be complied with by the applications and various Robotic devices. Persistent upgrades of security patches and subsequent testing are vital.

The different types of automated testing frameworks that can be availed for use are shown in Figure 3.11.

1. Linear also referred to as record and playback, used for testing smaller IoRT applications. This type does not involve expertise in automating tests since there is no necessity for custom coding but since the data is hardcoded inside the script, test cases cannot be executed with multiple sets of data.
2. The modular driven type, as shown in Figure 3.12, has the application segmented into small modules based on the specification with the creation of independent test scripts that are easier to maintain and extendible. But it takes considerable time for analysis of reusable flows.

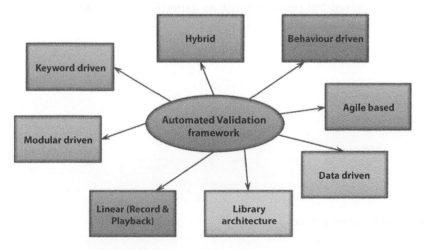

Figure 3.11 Automated test frameworks types.

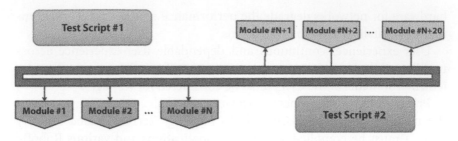

Figure 3.12 Modular driven framework.

3. Library Architecture (refer Figure 3.13) built over module-based framework where the application is segmented into functions that can be utilized by other applications also thereby creating a common library and can be invoked by the test scripts as desired. The type is little complex and holds the merits and demerits similar to the modular framework.

4. Data-driven approach (as shown in Figure 3.14) segregates test script functionality from test data by storage of data in external databases with the data stored as key-value combination pairs enabling the access of data by the use of key and data being populated inside the test scripts. The merit of the approach is a multitude of scenarios tested with lesser code involved but requires quite an expertise to make use of the framework design effectively.

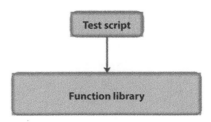

Figure 3.13 Library architecture.

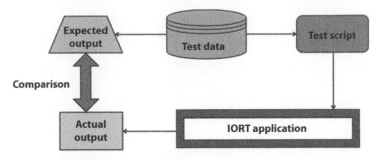

Figure 3.14 Data driven framework.

5. Keyword-driven (illustrated in Figure 3.15) extends data-driven type by retaining groups of code called keywords related to testing scripts in external data files along with the separation of test data and script. The keywords and data are stored as a table and hence the approach is also called as table-driven. The keywords serve as guidelines about the actions done on the application. Both keywords and data are independent of the automation tool employed.

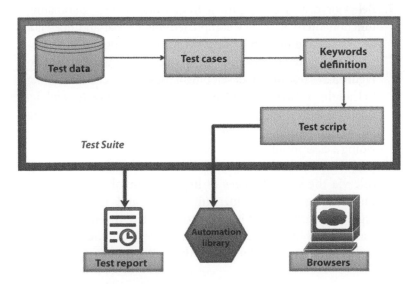

Figure 3.15 Keyboard driven framework.

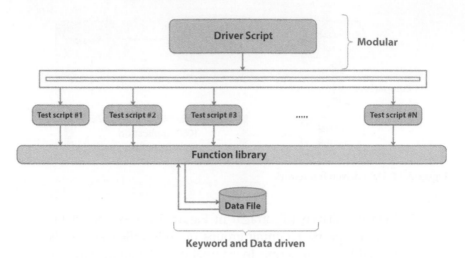

Figure 3.16 Hybrid automation framework.

6. A hybrid approach is an arrangement of data-driven, keyword and modular driven testing and carries the benefits of all the three approaches. The hybrid arrangement is indicated in Figure 3.16.

7. Behavior driven development framework enables automating functional tests in a very comprehensible format and does not necessitate the user to be familiar with the programming language. A basic approach to BDD automation is illustrated in Figure 3.17. Test-driven development uses automated unit testing to lead the software design and dependencies being decoupling. Behavior driven approach extends test-driven type by focusing on the system behavior rather than implementation thereby providing a clear insight into the system purpose.

8. Agile automation framework makes testing have a critical role via the several stages of iterations involving continual unit testing, integration, unit testing and uninterrupted regression testing that is tough to complete thorough testing frameworks. Moreover, attaining highest functionality and code coverage is challenging with testing frameworks.

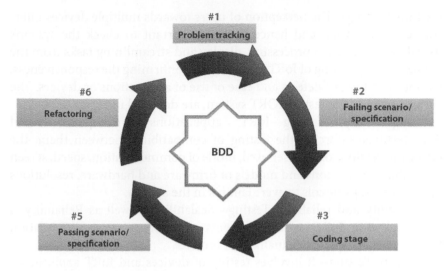

Figure 3.17 BDD automation framework.

3.4.1 IoRT Testing Methods

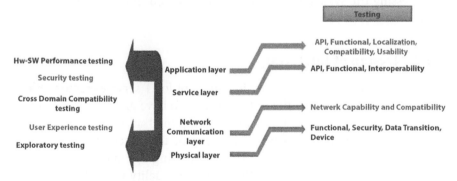

Figure 3.18 IoRT testing.

Usability testing—The perception of users towards multiple devices interconnected is varied and hence it gets important to check the system's usability such as Data processing, display and streamlining tasks from the devices during testing of IoRT systems thus confirming the responsiveness, smooth handling of defects and ease of use of applications or devices. The various methods of testing IORT system, are depicted in Figure 3.18.

Compatibility Testing—IoRT applications encompass several Architectures enforcing the testing of compatibility between them, the types and versions of browser used, mode of communication, speed, screen sizes, different versions and models of firmware and hardware, resolutions of the display, protocols to avert failures in the system.

Scalability and reliability Testing—Scalability as well as Reliability is crucial to set up IoRT test arrangements using robotic sensors' simulation with the help of quality virtualization toolsets.

Security Testing—It involves testing of devices and IoRT applications for various simulated threats against unauthorized access provided to data and devices including OWASP major ten threats.

Performance Testing—Factors like latency and bandwidth of Network, loss of data packet, the high volume of concurrent users, and responsiveness to the actions of end-user, proper handling of spikes on network traffic etc. must be tested. Various Performance measurement tools can be used for assessing the system performance on the cloud under full and normal load conditions.

3.4.2 Design of IoRT Test

The unreliability and dynamic environment of IoRT services require effective resource planning for the testing phase. To have greater test coverage, the test design and execution must be simplified and automated. Wide range of input/output increases the count of test cases making it difficult to develop via manual designing. Generating optimal test cases with higher functionality coverage with maximum quality possible and minimal efforts. Artificial Intelligence and Machine learning can help to create optimum test cases by assessing risks, analysis of previous performances related information, faults and test coverage gap analysis.

3.5 Automated Validation

Constraints of cost and time constraints make it challenging to exhaustively test an IoRT application before the release. When defects go unnoticed, the consequences can be catastrophic. Automating the validation process enables an increased level of testing in a short period thereby higher coverage and helpful for those test cases that are run recurrently during compatibility and regression testing. Automated validation is the usage of frameworks as well as tools to exercise the Test cases execution and then corroborate the outcome with expected outcomes. It can span across mobile and web services thus enabling testing across several browsers on cloud and many mobile devices through any framework. The benefits of efficient automation of IoRT validation are higher because along with testing of software, a complete coexistence of devices, interconnections and real-time situations are also scrutinized and becomes a necessity for the testers to confirm if the IoRT system is reliable and scalable under extreme conditions.

A broad test plan approach involves several forms of testing, setup of test labs, simulators and tools for deployment. It is essential to assess the techniques of simulating and visualizing data. Stubs can be used at the earlier testing stages and recorders at later testing. Along with reasonable test plans & simulation of data, metrics oriented, exhaustive testing accomplishes a stable IoRT system. Testing forms namely Functional, Connectivity, performance, security, security, compatibility, integration, acceptance and testing of devices must be extensively adopted to identify potential faults in the IoRT systems.

Priority is given to automated tests with the usage of stubs or mocks enable automation during the early stages of the life cycle and upsurge the penetration of code. The demarcation of testing performed both manually and in an automated mode, is shown in Figure 3.19. Towards the end, a strong focus is on testing to make sure that IoRT system works fine as a whole.

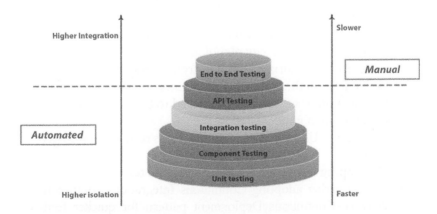

Figure 3.19 Priority of testing mode.

3.5.1   Use of Service Visualization

In wireless and wired component-based—heterogeneous IoRT applications such as service-oriented architectures in smart IoRT and health monitoring systems, cloud-based systems using multiple protocols, Service Virtualization emulates the behavior of the components (virtualized) and aids the development and Quality Assurance teams to reach unavailable components that are dependent and required for testing the application. The activity is thus used to virtualize IoRT systems and services with time, access and availability constraints during unavailability of components and services, especially when under the control of third parties, or available in very less capacity or inconvenient timings for testing with difficulties in configuring tests environments to lessen the dependencies, start development and testing ahead of time, improved test coverage and early detection of defects, thereby lowering the dependency on other groups for testing with different data.

3.5.2   Steps for Automated Validation of IoRT Systems

Implementing automated validation of IoRT systems works simultaneously with the lifecycle process of software development. The lifecycle of automated validation consists of a multi-phase method supporting actions for using the automated testing tool, go about developing and executing test cases, evolving test design, then build and address test environment and data.

The test design represents testing efforts and provides a framework for the magnitude of the test module. The various steps for automated IORT system validation is shown in Figure 3.20.

1. Based on the type of IoRT system, assess the need to automate the testing
2. Set Automation objectives and priorities of testing activities
3. Automated Test strategy planning
4. Choice of appropriate tool and framework for automation depending on the system requirements
5. Confirm on what test cases that need to be automated
6. Generation of good Test data
7. Creation of User Interface modifications resilient automated tests
8. Developing test scripts and executing the tests
9. Testing earlier adopting Continuous Integration–Continuous delivery–Continuous Deployment pattern for quicker feedbacks via CI toolsets, better analysis of entire new builds process,

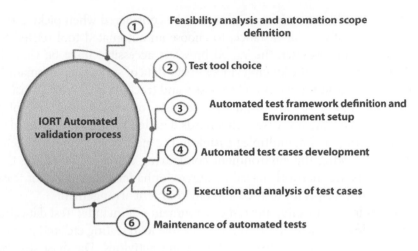

Figure 3.20 Automated validation process.

test outcomes and any new build related problem to identify the cause of the problem thus enabling earlier detection of faults.

10. Maintenance of the test scripts.

Assess the extent of Automation of validation—The first phase of automation to identify the automation feasibility by performing feasibility check on the test case sets developed manually paving the way for Test design. The aspects to analyze are the application modules that can be automated and otherwise, tests that can be automated and the relevant procedure, factors such as testing team's size, cost of automation and expertise level, feasibility for test case automation and application under test automation percentage of User interface components that can be automated by the tool during validation.

Test planning, design and strategy—Comprises of automation framework selection while laying down test strategy while test planning involves deciding on the standards and guidelines for creating test procedures, the hardware-software and networks for supporting test environment, an initial test agenda; requirements for test data, bug tracking method and allied tracking tool and test configuring mechanism. The architecture for tests is then adapted. The strategy for managing tests must have an insight into identifying the test cases that need to be automated, the framework to be adopted, building the automation test suite, assessing the threats and dependencies between the application and the selected tool and capture those details in the test plan and get the plan approved from the stakeholders.

Choosing appropriate Automation Tool—The resources, technics employed for the project, tool acquaintance, work insight, resilience and provisions to address various queries must be considered when picking the tool for automation. For instance, to choose an automated tool related to compatibility for browser, the varied browsers accessible must be viewed. Ability to apprehend the logging videos, meta-data of scripts for automation scripts across various devices and browsers and tracking of bugs is a must.

Creating the Test Environment—Consists of establishing (remote) machines to run the test cases. This needs detailed planning to maximize the test coverage across multiple possible test scenarios and requires scheduling and tracking the environment configuring activities, installing the relevant software, network-based resources, enhancing databases of tests and preparing scripts for testbed and environment arrangement.

Pointers for establishing the test environment—It includes Test data and Front end development environment to enable load testing etc. and preparation of system-related checklist for testing activities, Database server, testing across multiple client OS and several versions of browsers, licenses for tools.

Developing Test scripts for Automation and subsequent Execution— After the test environment is established, the test scripts must be executed with unit testing scripts input to the automation tool. Simplified, reusable and well-structured scripts reviewed by code reviews and capable of being run on multiple environments and platforms are developed based on actual specification.

Testing with CI-CD pattern—A crucial outline of CD embraces continuous integration and automation of validation. It involves code modifications passing a group of tests namely unit, regression, exploratory and usability tests. Each code modification is a release entrant. When regression issues are not identified, the release of the product can be done. For flaws detected at a later stage, tests are added and updated as required. If bugs are exposed to exploratory testing, automated testing should be amended. When bugs are revealed in acceptance testing, unit tests should be enhanced.

Analysis and generation of Test result report—After completion of the different tests, Test outcomes are then evaluated and the test results are documented. This helps in analyzing specific functionalities or components with relative vulnerabilities thereby signifying if further testing efforts and methods are necessary or not.

3.5.3   Choice of Appropriate Tool for Automated Validation

To begin with, the necessity for automated validation must be confirmed taking into account the forthcoming requirements. The next stage is to arrange for selecting the apt tool since certain tools are particular to a specific application kind and some tools fit for all kinds of application. Then begins the analysis of different testing tools via trial versions provided. Preparing sample test cases ahead helps in comprehending how a specific tool runs them. Some key aspects to consider during sample execution are integrating with test management and defect trailing related tools, provision for varied browsers, platforms, strong reporting capability, distributed operations across multiple platforms and machines. Once documentation of requirements and tools experimentation is completed, comparison of the tools experimented is performed to estimate how easy the tool is to learn and use based on automated test framework, the speed with which the test cases are run, the degree of sustenance for the tool of test management and varied platforms. Some of the testings that can be automated are concerning—web and mobile applications, cross-browser compatibilities, web services, database, performance, integration, data-driven and unit testing. Automated testing may not be suitable for UX and UI testing.

3.5.4   IoRT Systems Open Source Automated Validation Tools

In the ecosystem of IoRT applications, the innumerable with several abilities produce huge data which can be exposed to leakages, unapproved retrieval or data loss and can be addressed with appropriate efficient testing. Open Source test automation enables testing with lessened costs, scalability, reliability flexibility etc. It allows concurrent test running across several devices with reusable test cases.

Lowered cost—The main benefit with open source test tools is the lowered cost and comprises fewer hardware necessities.

Highly adaptable—The tools offer models, customized directions, additions, performance modifications, and plugins to tailor the tool.

Community Backing—The open-source toolset largely assist in efficient issue solving.

Faster Testing—Allows smaller test sequences, rapid setup, updates without disturbing throughput along with faster updates in code, lowering replication and refining the ease of maintenance.

Quicker resolution of flaws—With repeated automated execution of tests debugging is simplified enabling faster fixing of bugs.

Quicker Delivery and greater Quality—The tools offer wider coverage of tests and lesser faults in development with lowered associated risks and quicker release sequences.

Support for varied Language—The frameworks have support for numerous languages, platforms and browsers making testing easy for the users.

3.5.5   Some Significant Open Source Test Automation Frameworks

Selenium—a foremost open-source framework for automated testing of web applications. It can automate functional testing responsibilities and delivers various levels of provision for automating tests. Tools namely—Selenium Remote Control, WebDriver, Selenium IDE and Grid. The framework is well-suited with an extensive assortment of browsers and very flexible to develop text and gives strong support for different programming languages like Java, Ruby, C# and python.

Robotium—Framework for android testing for test cases automation for hybrid and native system applications. Enables strong automated development of android GUI test cases. Also provides for system, acceptance and functional test scenarios.

Appium—Open source framework for UI testing for distributed mobiles. Enables hybrid, web application and hybrid testing can accommodate tests on several devices simulators and emulators with cross-platform testing support where one API suits test scripts of both IOS and platforms and provision for languages such as Ruby, PHP, Python, Java, C#, JavaScript with node.js, Objective-C etc.

Espresso—An open-source user interface testing framework for android applications created by Google. The framework coordinates automatically the testing actions with the UI of the application. Also, the activity is well begun before the execution of tests with the tests awaiting the completion of background activities. It is envisioned for testing of single system application but can also span over multiple applications.

XCUITest—A test framework to execute UI tests for iOS devices by Apple and is constructed over the XCTest framework. It is incorporated within iOS Xcode development-related tools. Objective-C/Swift is used to develop tests and being built as a .ipa file. This file is loaded and goes about for execution over the device alongside application under test.

3.5.6   Finally IoRT Security Testing

The increasing challenges of IoRT systems mandate considering security as a crucial factor for business and by progressively refining security the cyber vulnerabilities can be averted. End to end validation of IoRT systems assures greater uniformity, reliability and extensibility, and delivers rich user experience. Security must be handled from the early design phase to functioning level. Secured booting through digital signature and software authorization, Secured control of access via minimal privilege principle restricting any compromised information within the credentials authorized area, authentication of devices, the capability to inspect firewalls for controlling traffic and filtering specific information, security patches and updates safeguarding bandwidth of network and devices connectivity with security well-preserved both at network and devices levels.

3.5.7 Prevalent Approaches for Security Validation

Static Application Security Testing (SAST)—Also referred to as a form of White Box Testing, the testing performs analysis of program code for security weaknesses without any compilation of code. With penetration to design information, requirements, data tables, schemas, architecture-related drawings, firmware and program code. The testers try system attacks to identify flaws.

Dynamic Application Security Testing—Tests the IORT applications in execution state to uncover vulnerabilities. The testers pose real-world aggressor. The testing aims at recuperating firmware or foraging the device. The operation of the system especially about making it possible to detect crucial complete problems.

Threat modeling—possible vulnerabilities are detected, evaluated, and ranked. An exhaustive IoRT system model is developed to find the critical problems with the model being developed and fine-tuned throughout the lifecycle of the system product reflecting the system's actual present state.

IoRT penetration testing—The DAST toolset can be used for application-related attacks to be simulated. It is performed by the testers and can encompass the hardware, software and firmware of the entire IoRT system.

Communications protocol testing—validate communications and the information transmission in the IoRT device inclusive of encryption methods used.

3.5.8 IoRT Security Tools

Tools for IoRT security assess the security of the application system operated by security testers and pen-testers. The chief strategies adopted for assessing the security of IORT systems is depicted in Figure 3.21.

Exploit—a framework for security testing and manipulation of IoRT ecosystem. It is a framework for exploitation and security testing. Tests are structured as plugins extended by custom made plugins. The usual communication practices and message buses are reinforced. Examples are BLE, CoAP, CANBus and MQTT etc.

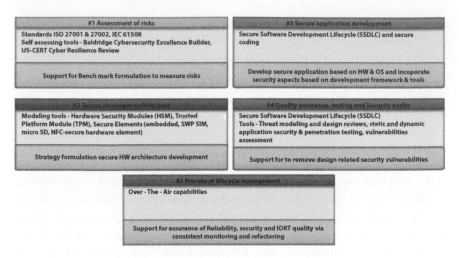

Figure 3.21 Key strategies for IoRT security.

RouterSploit—Framework to manipulate embedded devices and employed during penetration testing for security validation. It is a framework for testing and exploitation tool for embedded system devices. The in-built modules perform scanning and exploitation of robotic devices and perform a range of deployments for attempts on system exploitation.

References

1. Vermesan, O., Bröring, A., Tragos, E., Serrano, M., Bacciu, D., Chessa, S., ... Bahr, R., Internet of robotic things: Converging sensing/actuating, hypoconnectivity, artificial intelligence and IoT Platforms, *in: Cognitive Hyperconnected Digital Transformation: Internet of Things Intelligence Evolution*, pp. 97–155, 2017.
2. Batth, R.S., Nayyar, A., Nagpal, A., Internet of Robotic Things: Driving Intelligent Robotics of Future - Concept, Architecture, Applications and Technologies, in: *4th International Conference on Computing Sciences (ICCS)*, Jalandhar, pp. 151–160, 2018.
3. Ingrand, F., Recent Trends in Formal Validation and Verification of Autonomous Robots Software. *2019 Third IEEE International Conference on Robotic Computing (IRC)*, Naples, Italy, pp. 321–328, 2019.
4. ter Beek, M., Maurice, Gnesi, S., Knapp, A., Formal methods and automated verification of critical systems. *Int. J. Software Tools Technol. Trans.*, 20, 355–358, 2018.

5. Huang, W.-l. and Peleska, J., Model-based testing strategies and their (in) dependence on syntactic model representations. *Int. J. Software Tools Technol. Trans.*, 20, 441–465, 2018.
6. Flanagan, C. and König, B., Developments in automated verification techniques. *Int. J. Software Tools Technol. Trans.*, 16, 123–125, 2014.
7. Souri, A. and Norouzi, M., A State-of-the-Art Survey on Formal Verification of the Internet of Things Applications. *J. Serv. Sci. Res.*, 11, 47–67, 2019.
8. Souri, A., Rahmani, A., Navimipour, N., Rezaei, R., A symbolic model checking approach in formal verification of distributed systems. *Hum.-Cent. Comput. Info. Sci.*, 9, 1–27, 2019.
9. Liang, C.-J., Bu, L., Li, Z., Zhang, J., Han, S., Karlsson, B.F., Zhang, D., Zhao, F., Systematically debugging IoT control system correctness for building automation. In *Proceedings of the 3rd ACM International Conference on Systems for Energy-Efficient Built Environments (BuildSys '16)*. Association for Computing Machinery, New York, NY, USA, pp. 133–142, 2016.
10. Saha, O. and Dasgupta, R., A Comprehensive Survey of Recent Trends in Cloud Robotics Architectures and Applications. *Robotics*, 7, 47, 2018.

4

Light Fidelity (Li-Fi) Technology: The Future Man–Machine–Machine Interaction Medium

J.M. Gnanasekar[1*] and T. Veeramakali[2†]

[1]Department of Computer Science and Engineering, Sri Venkateswara College of Engineering, Kancheepuram, India
[2]Department of Computer Science and Engineering, School of Computing, Vel Tech Rangarajan Dr. Sagunthala R&D Institute of Science and Technology, Chennai, India

Abstract

In the world of communication, the wireless data communication moves to the driver seat. Light Fidelity (Li-Fi) technology becoming as one of the choice in the short distance wireless data communication system. Huge amount of data transmission is taking place through the electromagnetic spectrum. Cisco Visual Networking Index (VNI) reports a sharp traffic of the data has an increase of 69% during 2014 compared to the previous year 2013. More than 80% of mobile data traffic occurs in close door environment and the radio frequency spectrum is the medium for data transmission. Presently, Wi-Fi technology is used extensively for the wireless data communication. The performance of Wi-Fi system is affected by spectrum related issues such as capacity, efficiency, availability and security. The electromagnetic spectrum issue is important problem in the Wi-Fi technology.

The third and fourth Generation technologies consume large section of the electromagnetic spectrum. The volume of the uses affects the performance and efficiency of the Wi-Fi technology. Electromagnetic spectrum consists of harmful waves such as γ-Rays, x-Rays, UV-Rays, ir-Rays, etc. In this scenario, Li-Fi technology is looking as alternative for short range wireless communication solution by the Industries and Research Organizations where Light is used as medium of communication. Li-Fi technology is capable of covering indoor area. The static wireless devices installed

Corresponding author: jmg_sekar@yahoo.com
†*Corresponding author*: umaprabhu81@gmail.com

R. Anandan, G. Suseendran, S. Balamurugan, Ashish Mishra and D. Balaganesh (eds.) Human Communication Technology: Internet of Robotic Things and Ubiquitous Computing, (91–112)
© 2022 Scrivener Publishing LLC

inside the covered region can get benefit out of Li-Fi technology. The research on Li-Fi technology helps to overcome the range limitations and spectrum issues in conventional wireless mode communication systems. In future two nearby devices can be communicated through Li-Fi Technology. Few expecting future applications of Li-Fi are Li-Fi Printer, Internet access in indoor environment without radio frequency, short distance mobile to mobile data transfer, Vehicle to Vehicle communication, under water communication, navigation for blind people and etc.

Keywords: Li-Fi, human machine interaction (HMI), LED, machine to machine interaction (MMI), V2V communication, visible light communication, Wi-Fi, radio frequency

4.1   Introduction

Light Fidelity (Li-Fi) uses LEDs (Light Emitting Diodes) to transmit the data without wire. The Visible Light Communication makes the use of intensity modulation, for wireless data transmission. Photo diode acts as the receiver, to detect the signal. It forms the point to point communication and multiuser bi-directional communication. That is, single point-to-multipoint and multi-point-to-single point Communication. Also, Li-Fi enables to access multiple access points to form smooth communication in the wireless network. This enables the portability of the wireless connection during the movement of users within the short range. To enable this, need more light sources to form a wireless network. The speed of light is so high, so the speed of data delivery is also high compared to existing system. This system can also be implemented for fast accessing data between the electronic systems and laptops when they will be transmitting the beam of light inside the small place.

Li-Fi is the most prominent technology for the information communication. It will act as a substitute for Wi-Fi and even act as Optical Wi-Fi. Li-Fi uses the light for data transmission which actually falls in the electromagnetic range between 400 and 800 THz. This light is acting as Information carrier and brightening material.

It uses the light beats for the data transmission. The basic parts of a Li-Fi framework may essentially contain the components:

  i) A light transmission source with high luminance
  ii) A silicon photograph diode with capacity to react with light
       as the accepting component.

The LEDs are having basically two stages as ON and OFF which can be mapped to 1 and 0 respectively. Using this phenomenon, we can easily generate any string as a collection of 0s and 1s. The Information can be converted into a stream of 1s and 0s using optical encoding technique by fluctuates the glinting pace of the LED.

Thus, the LEDs output light is loaded with the sender information. Actually the light is flicking in nature, because of the data loaded on it. This cannot be visualized by the naked eye since the light is made to flash at much higher frequency.

Correspondence rate more than 100 Mbps can be used with the help of fast LEDs with the support of diversified multiplexing approaches. The VLC information rate can be furthermore lengthened to a greater value up to 10 Gbps through which, the information communication applying a different collection of LED units. In this system individually every LED transmits a different information stream.

Once LED light is switched on, huge number of photons (light) starts transmitting from the bulb. These LEDs are made up of semiconductor materials and emits high luminous light. This light will permit us to change the speed. Using this property, the data can be loaded into the light.

The working principle of Li-Fi framework is explained (Figure 4.1) as follows. This system has the transmitter which contains the data to be transmitted, a timer circuit and a LED as light source. The input data can be any sort of information like content, voice, and so on. The timer circuit of the transmitter controls the essential time spans of the LED glow, based

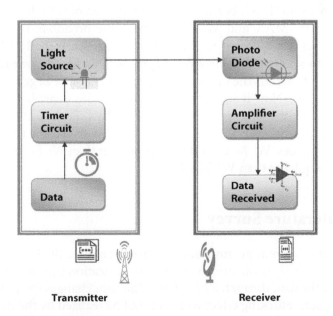

Figure 4.1 Working principle of Li-Fi.

on the input data. This modulated signal is transmitted and the receiver will collect it.

The receiver contains the photodiode and amplifier circuit. The main function of the photodiode is to collect the light with the data. Based on the intensity of the light received, an electrical signal was generated. The light to electrical signal conversion is done by the photodiode. The amplifier circuit gets the electrical signals from the photodiode and boosted the signal.

The variation in the light intensity is invisible for the naked eye. However, this system is as consistent as the other radio frameworks. It allows the clients to link itself with the Li-Fi authorized light. This method supports transmission of high speed data using LED light.

4.1.1   Need for Li-Fi

The main idea behind the Li-Fi is the light can act as the data carrier. The bulbs made up of Light Emitting Diode (LED) can be the source of light. The data transfer rate is depending on the intensity of the light. Light power is fast, so the naked eye can't detect any variation in the light. The speed of data around is 130 Mbps, which is double the speed of Wi-Fi in the wireless communication. Li-Fi is the quick and modest remote correspondence framework. It is an optical equivalent of Wi-Fi. Light is effectively accessible and spreads about all over, so the communication can be achieved using the light without any issues. This is because of less obstruction of light than RF waves.

Both the Wi-MAX and Wi-Fi fall under the broadband technology. However, they are different in the way of execution. Initially Wi-Fi was developed to support the portable gadgets such as Laptop, workstations, etc. Later on it extends the supports the applications such as game stations, VoIP telephones. Now it supports in establishing the smart home by connecting the house hold basic devices such as TVs, Fridge, DVD players, surveillance camera, etc. Wi-MAX is developed to overcome the last mile connectivity issues. Wi-MAX is 100 times quicker than Wi-Fi and the Li-Fi is 100 times quicker than Wi-MAX.

4.2   Literature Survey

A Li-Fi is another remote innovation to give the availability inside network environment. It gives the information communication through lightening by sending the data through a LED light. The light changes the power level and introduces a flicking effect which cannot be realized by the naked eye. The infrared based remote control is also working in the similar principles.

Li-Fi can produce information at a rate faster than 10 megabits per second. It can be faster than the conventional broadband data transfer. The LED is utilized in various zones of regular daily existence. It can utilize the lighting capacity to convey the information from one source to the subsequent source. The huge use of Li-Fi may clear up some restrictions in information communication in the Wi-Fi techniques. The innovators have made an attempt to observe the future of this new invention which is using the light as the transporter in information communication and system management.

4.2.1   An Overview on Man-to-Machine Interaction System

Knowledge based systems required to completely comprehend human aims and activities so as to help or team up with people, to finish entangled assignments, which is normally actualized by utilizing human–machine association methods [1]. This author proposes another robotic education structure to perform numerical errands through exploring man–machine collaborations with man inclinations. This method builds up a human inclination input framework to empower the robot to learn human inclinations.

Viable communications among people and machines are fundamental for superior of intelligent machines. By powerful data trade and translation, intelligent machines can comprehend the human goals, and therefore, human–machine collaborations are viewed as a significant exploration point to help people in finishing tasks. Various HMI techniques have been created to advance the capabilities of intelligent machine.

These HMI-based methodologies just permitted robots to legitimately utilize guidelines specified by a person to compose characters or literals, instead of deciphering person inclinations by means of HMI. Subsequently, the robots can utilize just one fixed composing style, which probably won't follow a human client's inclinations. Besides, to build the assorted variety of composing results, human designers must play out countless showings for preparing. In this manner, it may be tough to make novel composing styles for inscription robots utilizing this sort of HMI technique

The versatile industrial human–machine association assumes a significant job in the modern IoT, since the architects can utilize a cell phone to communicate with machines that extraordinarily improves the proficiency and security [2]. The author talked about the personally nearness estimation of the interpersonal organizations. Consolidating information leveling with the predefined closeness limit, this effort enhances the assessment exactness to 1–1.5 m which satisfies the interest of estimating in person distance.

The author also discusses about the huge amount of machine nodes in the industrial IoT scenario. It becomes an important issue for the designers. They need to interface with them in the industrial arena. We are focusing on the association of components, whereas the designer needs to differentiate the objective machine and the association of huge number of hubs. We right off the bat concentrate how the size of the association list influences the multifaceted nature of manual association. At that point the exhibition of closeness estimation is concentrated to demonstrate that the current works isn't adequate to take care of the issue.

Xu [2] talked about the difficulties of the view association in the portable industrial HMI. A test bed is actualized to contemplate the issue, and afterward the Light on plot is proposed to utilize vicinity estimation and obvious image task to streamline view associations. The image task calculation is intended to decrease the intricacy of image determination, and its presentation is examined hypothetically. The exhibition of Light on is assessed in the test bed, and the test results demonstrate that Light on is a promising answer for rearrange view associations with low unpredictability.

4.2.2   Review on Machine to Machine (M2M) Interaction

M2M communication is an advanced data transmission technology which allows two devices to exchange the information between them. The M2M communication that occurs between the machines which are autonomous, there is no need for human intervention for this data exchange [15]. M2M system is time and cost efficient system. Its functionality is based on the Supervisory Control And Data Acquisition (SCADA) structures. The sensory devices and different components are linked via wire or radio frequency. The computers are available in M2M systems for monitoring and controlling the process in automatic manner.

A main reason for the development of M2M communication nowadays is the persistent ease of understanding of price benefit and everywhere connection availability. 3G and Long Term Evolution (LTE) mobile networks are offering high speeds at highly competitive prices. In home and industries, the IP enabled equipment like sensors, actuators and monitors has facilitated interconnected and inter-operable services. The first and most important issue in this M2M communication is that the overload and congestions in the networks. So different kinds of traffic issues are rising up. Few of the significant issues in M2M communication comprises of energy efficiency [16], reliability, security, ultra-scalable connectivity.

4.2.2.1   System Model

Figure 4.2 shows the M2M communication system. This diagram explains about the interaction between the device and the network components. These two entities are interconnected using Internet.

M2M Device Entity
A big quantity of devices such as sensor devices, actuators and smart meters are connected together through the network and a gateway is used to connect with network entity. The decision making intelligence of the system is based on the monitored information. It has been passed to the gateway. The M2M network is comprised of devices like sensors, actuators, and smart meters. The gateway will act as data aggregation points.

The M2M network will the data and make an appropriate decision to transmit the collected data to the gateway. The gateway component act smartly and manages intelligently on the received packcts. With the help of the network entity, the gateway component transmits the data packet to the back-end application entity server using the available efficient paths. In the multiple gateways scenario, the gateways can communicate themselves to select the optimal destination path. The components involved in the M2M Entity are not fixed but purely depends on the type of the underlying application.

Network Entity
The network entity is the bridge between the Device Entity and Application Entity. Generally, the Application Entity and M2M device entity are in

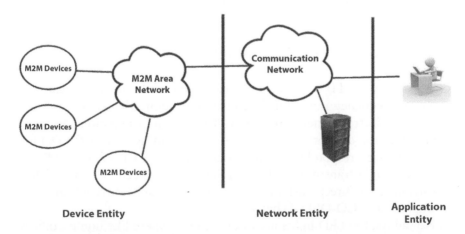

Figure 4.2 M2M communication system.

different locations. The network entity binds them using the long-range wired/wireless network protocols. The network entity uses telephone networks, and/or 3G/4G cellular networks. This network setup is cost effective and ensures the reliable communication across the M2M devices and Application entity.

Application Entity

The collection of servers at the back end (BES) and M2M application clients form the Application Entity. The servers at the back end are the key module in the Application entity. It stores all the data generated from M2M device entity. The Application Entity the feeds the data to real-time remote monitoring management (RMM) client applications such as healthcare, traffic observing, etc. The BES are an application dependent one. The M2M health-monitoring servers are doing the BES role in Healthcare systems, whereas the control centres will perform this task in Smart Grid systems.

Considering M2M entity in Figure 4.2, there are two different communication scenarios possible. The Client/Server architecture is the first scenario. Here the deployed M2M devices are the clients and the Application Entity is the server. This architecture is most common one. The home automation, environmental monitoring is few applications which follow the Client/Server architecture.

The M2M entity uses the standard peer-to-peer (P2P) as the communication model in certain applications. In these P2P systems the components of M2M entity will interconnect openly between themselves. These types of applications become the source of the additional scenario. The P2P systems use Mobile networks and/or adhoc network connections.

4.3   Light Fidelity Technology

Light-Fidelity (Li-Fi) is basically an extension of the operative electromagnetic frequency range for data communication. This system utilizes the higher electromagnetic frequency. It falls under the nanometer wave communication category. Li-Fi utilizes Light Emitting Diodes (LEDs) for rapid remote correspondence, and velocities of over 3 Gb/s from a solitary small scale light transmitting diode (LED) [3] have been exhibited utilizing streamlined Direct Current Optical Symmetrical Recurrence Division Multiplexing (DCO-OFDM) balance.

Nowadays, the LED lights are available everywhere like homes, offices and Streets as Streetlights which can be used as the source of light for data

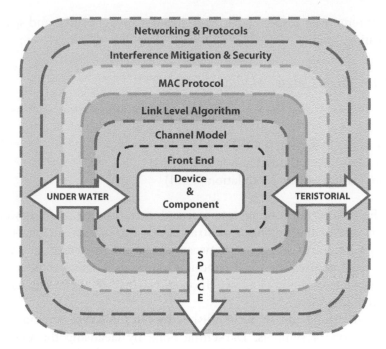

Figure 4.3 Basic building blocks of Li-Fi & its applications.

transmission. The Li-Fi system can make use this existing setup. There is an additional benefit for Li-Fi cell organization, where it can expand on the existing lighting infrastructure. In addition, the cell dimensions can be modified with milli-meter-wave correspondence driving with idea using Li-Fi attocells. The Li-Fi attocell is an additional arrangement layer in the current remote structures. They also have provided smooth data transmission with zero impedance the light on both the directions. For example, femtocell systems. A Li-Fi attocell organize utilizes the lighting framework to give completely arranged (multiuser access and handover) remote availability.

The main components of Li-Fi and its application zones are depicted in Figure 4.3.

4.3.1   Modulation Techniques Supporting Li-Fi

The Li-Fi Communication system works based on the electromagnetic radiation for the data transmission. Hence, all the basic regulations of RF Communication systems are also applicable for Li-Fi also with some fundamental adjustments. Additionally, because of the utilization of noticeable light for remote correspondence, Li-Fi likewise gives peculiar and specific modulation types.

4.3.1.1   Single Carrier Modulation (SCM)

Li-Fi technology uses the Single Carrier Modulation schemes such as

- On Off Keying (OOK)
- Pulse Amplitude Modulation (PAM)
- Pulse Position Modulation (PPM)

uses the concentrated in remote infrared correspondence frameworks. OOK is one of the notable and straightforward adjustment plans, and it gives a decent exchange off between framework execution and usage multifaceted nature. The OOK conducts information using consecutively changing state of the LED as switch on and switch off, it can intrinsically give darkening help.

OOK dimming can be accomplished by On Off Level refinement (b) compensation of symbols. Darkening done by cleansing the ON/OFF degrees at different level of the LED start keep up similar information rate, in any case, the dependable correspondence range would be dimming at low darkening levels. Then again, darkening by sign reimbursement can accomplished using embedding extra ON/OFF signal, which will have controlled by the ideal darkening level. The greatest information amount is accomplished by a half darkening level expecting equivalent value of 1 and 0 s by and large, expanding or diminishing the luminance of the LED would cause the information rate to diminish.

Optical Spatial Modulation is one of the important SCM methodology used for data communication in Li-Fi technology. It has the both force and data transfer capacity effective for indoor optical wireless communication. The Quadrature Amplitude Modulation (QAM) for unique carrier structures, carrier free amplitude and phase modulation utilizes bi-symmetrical signs, instead of the genuine and fanciful pieces of the QAM flagging arrangement, for range effective signal transmission in Li-Fi systems.

4.3.1.2   Multi Carrier Modulation

As the necessary information rate increments in Li-Fi systems, SCM schemes like OOK, PPM and PAM begin to experience the unexpected effects of undesirable impacts, for example, non-straight sign bending on LED face and image obstruction carried about through the reappearance choosiness in diffusing visual wireless channels. Hence, for rapid optical remote correspondence, activities are fascinated to Multi Carrier Modulation (MCM). When compared with different modulation schemes it gives an illusion that more data communication takes place, however it is less in real.

OFDM is broadly recognized substitution of MCM in Li-Fi systems. Where concurrent information streams are transmitted over an assortment of symmetrical subcarriers and complex leveling can be precluded. On the off chance that the quantity of symmetrical subcarriers is picked so the transmission capacity of the regulated sign is littler than the intelligibility data transfer capacity of the optical network, each sub part of the channel can be treated as a smooth fading channel.

Methods previously created aimed at smooth diminishing channels can in this way be applied. The utilization of OFDM takes into consideration more versatile piece and control stacking procedures separate subcarrier with the goal which improved framework execution is accomplished. An OFDM modulator is used to increase the Discrete Fourier Transform area, that is, effectively acknowledged utilizing Inverse Fast Fourier Transform (IFFT), trailed by a conversion unit which consume digital signal as input and delivers the analog signal in the output. Accordingly, the OFDM produced output is circuitous and dual polar ordinarily. So as to fit the IM/DD prerequisite forced by industrially accessible LEDs, vital changes to the customary OFDM procedures are required for Li-Fi.

4.3.1.3   Li-Fi Specific Modulation

Li-Fi transmitters are commonly structured for wireless communication as well as for lighting, that is acknowledged either by utilizing the color of the LEDs with appropriate chemical covering or by shading blending using hued LEDs. Luminaries furnished using multi shaded LEDs give additional prospects to modulation and location of Li-Fi frameworks. Color Shift Keying (CSK) is an IM conspire laid out in IEEE 802.15.7, tells about the sign encoded into shading forces emitted by Red, Green and Blue (RGB) LEDs. In CSK, the data are plotted on to the immediate chromaticity in matching shade in diode output light while maintaining the steady normal saw shading. The upsides of CSK on normal IM plans are two stages. Initially, a stable radiant flux ensured, nearby there is no glint impact covering completely the entire frequency spectrum. Also, consistent radiant flux infers an about steady LED operating current, that decreases conceivable incoming current in the light signal balance, and consequently increases LED dependability. In view of CSK, tweak was produced, which can accomplish advanced vitality proficiency. This will give additional control of the shading superiority, notwithstanding, by the detriment of need an extra and freely organized green LED. From the viewpoint of augmenting the correspondence limit, Color Intensity Modulation (CIM) is suggested in the symmetrical and non-symmetrical form of the optical networks.

4.3.2 Components of Li-Fi

The key parts are an Arduino Uno board, frequency explicit LED and photodiode [4] as in Figure 4.4.

Other than the segment dependable of creating and catching the light signals, additional equipment is expected to network and decipher signs. For example, a reasonable band allow pass channel is used to shift through approaching signs with non-ideal frequencies. The optical network channel is a preferable method to analyze through brightness of dissimilar frequencies. The focal point of the light approaching the center is suitable for the light with less power. The computerized information communication, a digital signal processor is applied to process the signal at both the ends [5].

4.3.2.1   Light Emitting Diode (LED)

Light emitting diodes are the semiconductor devices that generate light energy. When the electron arrives into the semiconductor, it will recombine

Figure 4.4 Arduino Uno development board.

with holes available in the media and energy is released as photons. Certain basics need to be considered on selecting the LED. These factors are interdependent and contribute each other. The ascent time is the important which decides the LED selection. A short ascent time is the result of a low force makes it conceivable whereas the growing the power results in higher ascent time. The higher force on the LED creates more light and also more heat. The Arduino has a greatest operating voltage at 5 V, most extreme current yield of 1 A and produce a square wave with the most extreme recurrence of 50 kHz. The OSRAM LED satisfies the above requirements and hence it was selected.

4.3.2.2 Photodiode

The photodiode is a semiconductor device which converts the light into electrical signal. The majority of the photodiodes designed to suit the fiber optics based applications. The photodiodes are widely used in the fiber optic communication system to convert the light into current mostly in the receiver section. Technically the radiant delicate territory of the photodiode is small and the ascent time is lesser.

In a large area, the reaction time of the system is extra sluggish. Without fiber optics a bigger radiant delicate territory takes into consideration all the additional light to be caught by the recipient. In this way, the decision of photodiode is restricted. The reaction time of LED is the important factor which decides the range of operation. It has suitable frequency top disturbance at 565 nm. The spectral bandwidth ranging between 420 and 675 nm provides a perfect range for the Li-Fi applications. It has the fastest light intensity so far and the radiation area is 7.5 mm, which was larger than most photodiodes found. It has a rise and fall of 3 μs each, which gives a trading frequency of 166 kHz [4].

4.3.2.3 Transmitter Block

The main function of transmitter is to change the computerized information i.e. Data, into the light. A LED will do this job perfectly due to its moderately conventional connection between the current and light energy. The light power of the LED represents the Data i.e., the amount of the light decides the image transmitted. The Arduino ports are not fast enough for conveying the seamless quantity of current to make the light force. To get around this issue a transistor is utilized as a switch, which made it imaginable to switch a more current quicker. In Figure 4.5, schematic is appeared to give a review of the transmitter.

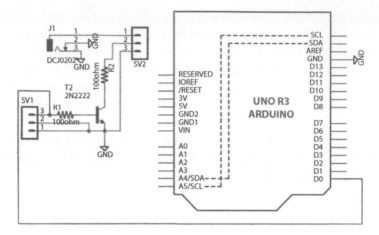

Figure 4.5 Li-Fi transmitter circuit.

4.3.2.4   Receiver Block

The receiver performs the opposite functionality of the transmitter. It converts the upcoming light into current using a photo diode. The Arduino can't get a voltage over 5 V for digital signal. Along these lines, the electrical circuit between the photo diode and the Arduino needs to process the electrical signal, so it perform well and translated accurately [7] into the original data.

The gatherer's contraptions need to change over the current to voltage in order to improve and take a gander at it. The separation between the transmitter and the recipient cannot be a fixed one. Anyway to protect a vital good way from incredibly little or very high sign, an Automatic Gain

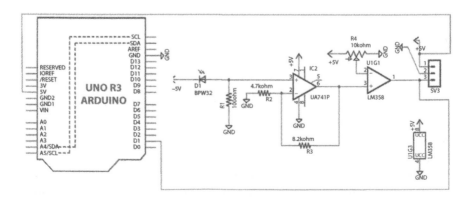

Figure 4.6 Li-Fi receiver circuit.

Controller (AGC) can be planned, rather than a variable resistor. This AGC unit improves or diminishes the information voltage to a picked yield voltage. An Op-Amp comparator is employed to ensure the signal is properly digitalized and also steady before the Arduino unit. The schematics appears in Figure 4.6.

4.4   Li-Fi Applications in Real Word Scenario

4.4.1   Indoor Navigation System for Blind People

The Li-Fi innovation can move the information through LEDs. It is a rapid and ease remote correspondence framework, contrasted with Wi-Fi. It can give high security, huge data transmission, and ease. Li-Fi utilizes normal family unit LED (Light Emitting Diodes) lights to empower information move, bragging speeds up to 224 G for each second. Light Fidelity (Li-Fi) is a bidirectional, fast and supports remote communication innovation similar to the Wi-Fi system. The term Li-FI was coined by Prof. Harald Haas. Fundamentally Li-Fi is a medium of Communication. It is a subset of optical remote exchanges and also a complement to RF communication (Wi-Fi or Cellular system), or even a substitution transmission media for information broadcasting. Li-Fi can be viewed as better than Wi-Fi on the grounds that there are a few restrictions in Wi-Fi. Wi-Fi utilizes 2.4–5 GHz radio frequencies to convey remote web access and its data transmission is constrained to 50–100 Mbps. This innovation has been proposed as an answer for the RF transfer speed constraints. Indoor course is useful to everyone and it is especially basic for the apparently debilitated. Li-Fi uses a free, unlicensed reach and isn't impacted by RF clatter. Likewise, most indoor territories would have a sufficient proportion of light sources and give additional security since Li-Fi can't invade through dividers [14].

High brilliance LED goes about as a correspondence source. The transmitter unit is fitted to the divider/roof. In the transmitter the adjusted data is transmitted through LED. Silicon photograph diode which fills in as an accepting component. The beneficiary unit demodulates the encoded paired information and gives the reaction as voice to the individual. The collector unit comprises a photograph transistor which gets the data from the LED associated with the transmitter. The data comprise of area, and at whatever point recipient module comes in the scope of that transmitter zone than relating area message is send to beneficiary is put away in the IC APR33A3 and handled further to start voice to manage the individual and vibrator engine to explore the individual which can help outwardly

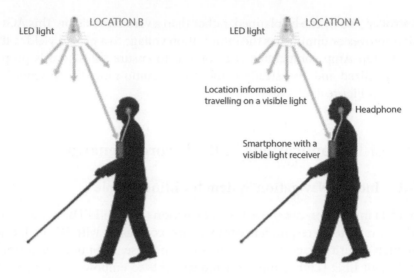

Figure 4.7 Li-Fi navigation system for blind people.

disabled individuals at indoor spots [6]. Figure 4.7 shows that the working procedure of the Li-Fi navigation system to the visually challenged people.

4.4.2   Vehicle to Vehicle Communication

Figure 4.8 shows that, the vehicle to vehicle correspondence is the best course of action we have used in order to reduce accidents that goes ahead step by step news. In Li-Fi advancement for vehicle-to-Vehicle data transmission use LED light. In this innovation, the end vanishing of conventions are utilized so in Li-Fi innovation intricacy isn't excessively. The point of structuring this framework is profoundly solid which will give any ideal information transmission among transmitter and collector mounted on the vehicle. The Li-Fi innovation utilizes the light to transmit the information so that the space prerequisite is less. The System is controlled with Micro-controller that has been executed utilizing an Arduino and along these lines decreasing the time squandered by the framework. In this

Figure 4.8 Vehicle to vehicle communication using Li-Fi.

introduced model, Li-Fi brings the information move rate undeniably of worth. It additionally comprises of a LED and which is acceptable yet in this the speed of transmitting rate becomes higher which is its legitimacy.

This Li-Fi in 2011 was created and presented in the thought of Wi-Fi so the name is Li-Fi just in this framework utilized noticeable light rather than radio recurrence [8]. So as to analyze the speed both the tech also, to defeat with the jam of system let us look at that as a Li-Fi/Wi-Fi cross breed down-interface framework model is thought of. This mixture organize covers a specific indoor region by NC Li-Fi applications and a solitary Wi-Fi AP. In the circumstance, customers are reliably appropriated and move aimlessly. The aggregate of the passageways is related with a control unit through goof free between affiliation joins. Each Li-Fi is a colossal light producing diode (LED) light which contains many low power LEDs, and each customer has a Photo Diode (PD). It is acknowledged that the sum of the PDs is arranged inverse to the oar. The point got by the structure is light is comparable when stood out from edge of event.

The Field of View (FoV) of the LEDS can be organized with the goal that the transmission can be contained inside a particular space. The dividers likewise here and there hinder the light and make its power to be exceptionally low and obstruction between rooms. The gct segment comprises of a photodiode, for example silicon photograph identifier or an Infrared germanium tube shaped locator. The photograph identifier goes about as the demodulator and when the approaching gotten signal dependent on the grouping of 1s and 0s. The demodulated signal is then sent to a channel to expel undesirable clamor. This isolated sign is presently increased using signal strengthening part. The isolated and strengthened sign is by then given to a yield device, for instance, a LCD show or a speaker. The information signal is in this manner distantly communicated and gotten.

4.4.3 Li-Fi in Hospital

As Li-Fi doesn't meddle with radio recurrence gadgets, Li-Fi can be securely utilized in numerous emergency clinic applications. For example, in foyers, sitting territories, getting rooms and working theaters, Li-Fi development will allow a light correspondence orchestrate, which will remove electromagnetic impedance issues from phones and the use of Wi-Fi in crisis centers. Li-Fi can similarly be used for continuous checking and report of patient turn of events and basic signs without the need of wires.

In clinic drug stores and explicitly kept in sterilized assembling locations. The Li-Fi can be applied by drug specialists for receiving and scrutinizing electronically suitable remedies directly in the unit. Li-Fi can be utilized for the following up of the current suggested sterile medications like cytotoxic medications, Parenteral medications and brought together intravenous added substance administrations in the unit. Also, one can able to follow the attendants and other medicinal services experts from the ward and can check the status without the need of calling or going rightfully in the sterile wards [9]. The Li-Fi system ensures the sharing of the patient records fast and remarkably secure way. In the case of drug store units, Li-Fi can be utilized by the patients to check the available results on their cell phones or drug store unit interface and even book the doctor appointment. Li-Fi can used to display the authorized information on the standard devices inside a hospital for the purpose like querying about patients, drug status in pharmacy and or doctor appointment. In the Li-Fi connected campus the information can be collected using any Li-Fi empowered gadget.

Li-Fi can empower patients on their beds associating with web news, messages, computer games and internet based life stages through their cell phones. This will assist them with breathing easy during the inconvenient period. For clinical laborers, Li-Fi will empower the following and movement of the places of key clinical gadgets particularly those routinely shared by various offices. Check the beneath outline for a synopsis of the advantages of Li-Fi in emergency clinics. Figure 4.9 shows that the visualization for the ICU care by which patient can be protected from Radio waves.

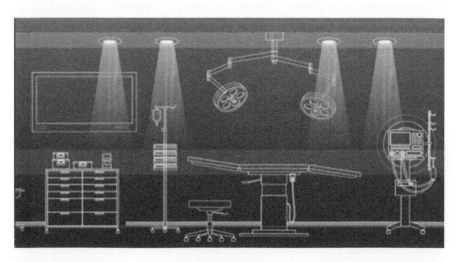

Figure 4.9 Li-Fi at ICU room.

4.4.4   Li-Fi Applications for Pharmacies and the Pharmaceutical Industry

In crisis center medication stores and explicitly in the clean gathering areas, Li-Fi could be used by drug experts for tolerating and screening electronically asserted cures legitimately in the unit. Li-Fi can be used for constant after of embraced clean prescriptions like cytotoxic meds, Parenteral meds and united intravenous added substance organizations (CIVAS) in the ward. The patients and the restorative assistance people from the ward can get the refreshed data without the need of calling or going straightforwardly to the sterile units.

Automation, including electronic assessment and packaging, is transforming into a verifiably critical bit of drug gathering. The various focal points of computerization join capability, saving pros from dangerous conditions or dull tasks, decreasing getting ready overhead, murdering human goof, extending repeatability and reproducibility, and in tidy up rooms, removing the potential for human contamination.

In 2001, the Audit Commission's "Spoonful of sugar" report pushed the use of robotization to change drug store organizations and, starting now and into the foreseeable future, various UK clinical facilities presented dispensary robots. Medication store robots have been appeared to diminish the event of regulating botches, improve the speed and capability of the allotting strategy, and advance the usage of room in the medication store.

In the UK, the utilization of robots in the network drug stores is as yet constrained. In any case, robots can possibly deal with high volumes of apportioning in network drug stores or administering "centers", and to discharge drug specialists to create and convey tolerant focused administrations. Li-Fi can guide the robots in drug stores to speak with staff and other IT frameworks, conveyance of medications, stock piling racks and many more such applications.

These days an upward steep bend is seen in the beneficial machines become self-flexibility and programmed dynamic are permitted. It is affecting the utilization of the robots in all the divisions of medication store additionally going to augment. Apart from that, the modernized methadone allotting machines (e.g., Methameasure, Methadose) offer accuracy and capability in the determined methadone controlling cycle, and their use will presumably augment, also, especially in drug stores with a high volume of methadone distributing. Li-Fi will be on the one of the far off correspondence progresses that will engage robots to play out their endeavors suitably and talk with various structures and robots.

The Internet of Things (IoT) is at present influencing various endeavors, including the drug business. Drug creation structures must be a lot of answered to develop and keep up unsurprising regulatory consistence. Li-Fi development can enable the pharma IoT related devices to continually send data at a high transmission rate to a worker to satisfy out the quality guidelines, which will reasonably decrease the proportion of manual work area work and conceivable edge for botches.

4.4.5 Li-Fi in Workplace

Travelling is one of the big industries. It takes care of the passengers and their needs. The travel planners are going about as an interface between the clients and the specialist organizations. An overview gives a report as, about the 67% of explorers would be bound to rebook with a transporter if inflight web accessibility were available. It shows that the web access plays a significant part on making the inflight appointments. About 66% of the shoppers acknowledge inflight accessibility is significant. 65% of explorers that have drawn closer inflight web network in the latest year used it. The 54% of travelers concurred that if simply bad quality Wi-Fi was on offer, they would slant toward not to have it using any and all means.

Li-Fi will allow the travelers to improve level of information correspondence than the one at present gave by Wi-Fi framework. Traveler will get to faster web access, download and stream content at the solace of their area.

Li-Fi has an unmistakable bit of leeway for three reasons. At first, it explains a 'blockage' issue. In the data driven world that we live in, we are having an issue of short on radio reach. This is an issue in crowed areas, for example, air terminals and plane. It deduces that the present accessible exchange rate doesn't reinforce the numerous characters wishing to utilize the data centered applications and the web in a comparative spot simultaneously. Li-Fi brightens this issue by using on different occasions the exchange speed thought about and the entire radio return territory [11]. This is accomplished without extra, unregulated information correspondence in the distinguishable light reach.

Second, it prepares for territory to be developed, which suggests that travelers can settle on decisions, use the web and access in-flight theater arrangements even more with no trouble. Third, in a universe of quick being coordinated by an enormous data, shielding the information is essential assignment. In the shut locale, disregarding the way that Li-Fi signs can spill through windows, the development offers more conspicuous security to travelers than the Wi-Fi frameworks. Their amassing anterooms every now and again have loads of LED lighting and relatively few windows, which will improve the data security in their workplaces. Verizon, Nokia and Aegex Technologies hold a fiasco testing flexibility testing of the light-based Li-Fi courses of action from unadulterated Li-Fi, to show Li-Fi application in rescue exchanges and emergency response in the event of a catastrophe event.

The show, called Operation Convergent Response (OCR), was held at the Guardian Centers planning office in the United States [13]. Unadulterated Li-Fi indicated the use of Li-Fi development in a metro fiasco circumstance. Li-Fi development was used to keep up, consistent, bi-directional correspondences that could enable exchanges with a war room allowing the emergency organizations to take care of ensured, strong organization during a response.

4.5   Conclusion

Various industries, research affiliations and associations are focusing in Li-Fi Technology. In this advancement light is used as correspondence media. Li-Fi development is having the constraint of low consideration locale. Thusly, non portable far off devices are giving indications of progress utilization of Li-Fi advancement in an indoor area. Various researchers finished the tests towards the Li-Fi development would be crushed the limitations and disservices of the Radio Frequency based distant correspondence. In future two near to contraptions can be passed on through Li-Fi Technology. Barely any applications, for example, indoor route for dazzle individuals, vehicle to vehicle correspondence, Li-Fi in Pharmacies and the Pharmaceutical Industry, Hospital and Workplace have been talked about in this article.

References

1. Gao, X., Zhou, C., Chao, F., Yang, L., Lin, C.-M., Shang, C., A Robotic Writing Framework–Learning Human Aesthetic Preferences via Human–Machine Interactions. *IEEE Access*, 7, 144043–144053, Sep-2019.
2. Xu, Z., Liu, A., Yue, X., Zhang, Y., Wang, R., Huang, J., Fang, S.-H., Combining Proximity Estimation With Visible Symbol Assignment to Simplify Line-of-Sight Connections in Mobile Industrial Human-Machine Interaction. *IEEE Access*, 7, 133559–133571, Sep-2019.
3. Haas, H., Yin, L., Wang, Y., Chen, C., What is Li-Fi? *J. Lightwave Technol.*, 34, 6, 1533–1544, Mar-2019.

4. Chao, F., Huang, Y., Lin, C.-M., Yang, L., Hu, H., Zhou, C., Use of automatic Chinese character decomposition and human gestures for Chinese calligraphy robots. *IEEE Trans. Hum.–Mach. Syst.*, 49, 1, 47–58, Feb. 2019.

5. Wang, Y. and Haas, H., Dynamic load balancing with handover in hybrid Li-Fi and Wi-Fi networks. *J. Lightwave Technol.*, 33, 22, 4671–4682, Nov. 2015.

6. Chen, C., Basnayaka, D. A., Purwita, A. A., Wu, X., Haas, H., Wireless Infrared-Based LiFi Uplink Transmission With Link Blockage and Random Device Orientation. *IEEE Trans. Commun.*, 69, 2, 1175–1188, 2021.

7. Islim, M.S., Videv, S., Safari, M., Xie, E., McKendry, J.J.D., Gu, E., Dawson, M.D., Haas, H., The impact of solar irradiance on visible light communications. *J. Lightwave Technol.*, 36, 12, 2376–2386, 2018.

8. Papanikolaou, V.K., Bamidis, P.P., Diamantoulakis, P.D., Karagiannidis, G.K., Li-Fi and Wi-Fi with common backhaul: Coordination and resource allocation. *IEEE Wireless Communications and Networking Conference (WCNC)*, pp. 1–6, 2018.

9. Yin, L. and Haas, H., Physical-layer security in multiuser visible light communication networks. *IEEE J. Sel. Areas Commun.*, 36, 1, 162–174, 2018.

10. Ayyash, M. *et al.*, Coexistence of Wi-Fi and Li-Fi toward 5G: Concepts opportunities and challenges. *IEEE Commun. Mag.*, 54, 2, 64–71, 2016.

11. Goswami, P. and Shukla, M.K., Design of a Li-Fi Transceiver. *Wirel. Eng. Technol.*, 8, 71–86, 2017.

12. Badamasi, Y.A., The Working Principle of an Arduino. *11th International Conference on Electronics Computer and Computation (ICECCO)*, 2014.

13. Rosli, M.A. and Ali, A., Development of RD ENERGY harvesting technique for Li-Fi application. *Intelligent and Advanced Systems (ICIAS)*, 15–17 Aug 2016, 2016.

14. Jaswal, A., Mahal, V., Ahuja, B., Khatri, A., Navigation System for Visually Impaired Using Li-Fi Technology. *Soft Computing: Theories and Applications. Advances in Intelligent Systems and Computing*, vol. 1053, pp. 695–702, Feb. 2020.

15. Pavan Kumar, V., Rajesh, V., Prakash, A., Machine-to-Machine Communication: A Survey. *J. Netw. Comput. Appl.*, 66, 83–105, 2016.

5

Healthcare Management-Predictive Analysis (IoRT)

L. Mary Gladence*, V. Maria Anu and Y. Bevish Jinila

Sathyabama Institute of Science and Technology, Chennai, India

Abstract

Big Data Analytics is that the strategy for analyzing enormous and changed information sets—i.e., huge learning—to reveal unseen patterns, trends in marketing, unknown correlations, customer inclinations and distinctive supportive data that may encourage associations make more-educated business determinations. There are various techniques to manage these data, among that Sequential Pattern Mining plays a vital role. From the inferences of several Sequential Pattern Mining techniques, Mine Fuzz Change Model is found to be interesting. It performs Sequential Pattern Mining Process by using Similarity Computation Index (SCI). In addition to this, it performs pattern classification process and significant changed pattern set by undertaking the patterns SCI and support values. But this model has the pitfall in the computation of SCI and significant pattern set since it uses the raw data. To avoid this, optimized Fuzzy Time Interval (FTI) is used. It comprised of (i) Fuzzy time interval sequential pattern mining using GA algorithm, (ii) Patterns matching using SCI, (iii) Patterns classification based on SCI value and (iv) Significant pattern evaluation process. Second part of this work is prediction. Here, how the patients have been assessed using belief network has been automated through Internet of Robotic Things (IoRT).

Keywords: Pattern mining, classification, voice commands, similarity, belief network, Internet of Robotic Things

*Corresponding author: lgladence@gmail.com

R. Anandan, G. Suseendran, S. Balamurugan, Ashish Mishra and D. Balaganesh (eds.) Human Communication Technology: Internet of Robotic Things and Ubiquitous Computing, (113–136)
© 2022 Scrivener Publishing LLC

5.1   Introduction

Data Mining or Information Mining is the procedure of burrowing through and breaking down tremendous arrangements of information and afterward extracting the importance of the information such as knowledge rules, constraints, prediction of future use given by Han, Pei and Kamber [1]. The extent of data mining is automated prediction of patterns and its behavior, discovery of previously unknown patterns. Bhatnagar *et al.* [2] proposed a data mining approach for handling the enhanced patterns and new links concerns processing decision making efficiently. Prerequisite skill for extracting the frequency patterns that establishes effective relationships executes categorization and forecasting them. Data mining techniques efficiently execute the pattern extraction from database with incredible alleviation and enthusiastic patterns for database and knowledge acquirement with smart systems. There are various techniques to manage these data. Among that sequential pattern mining plays a vital role. Sequential Pattern Mining (SPAM) is one which can compute set of frequent sequential pattern by satisfying minimum support threshold value with time interval. Idhammad *et al.* [2] state that a cardinal problem with data mining extracts the sequential patterns within data sequence set. Efficient changes occur in the behavior of launching identical changes in the details of data records. The large amount of data can have decision making relationships focus the mining on sequential patterns within the data sequence. Comparative model connecting guessable and performance predictions extract patterns for knowledge acquisition over the building of expert systems. Decision making methods in data mining with extraction of pattern alleviations acquire comprehension with smart systems.

According to Chen *et al.* [3], time interval sequential pattern mining finds sets of patterns which cannot be influenced by others/events in a sequence with time interval. By analyzing this concept, we can make prediction on future use. For example, a doctor can find the development procedure of sicknesses as far as patient therapeutic record to avoid and cure ailment sooner. Even though Time Interval Sequential Pattern Mining presents additional information than without time interval, it may cause a sharp boundary problem whenever time interval is close to boundary region. To avoid this drawback which is exists in Time interval sequential Pattern Mining Fuzzy Time Interval Sequential Pattern Mining is introduced by Chang [4].

Fuzzy Time Interval Sequential Pattern Mining (FTI-SPAM) performs the sequential Pattern Mining using Similarity Computation Index (SCI) given by Huang [5]. Unwanted data as well as unmatched data are pruned while performing Similarity Computation Index Pattern Matching Process. After that they perform Pattern Classification and Significant Changed Pattern set by using SCI. This Mine fuzz change Model successfully finds the significant Patterns set and avoids the drawback which is presented in existing work.

5.1.1   Naive Bayes Classifier Prediction for SPAM

The frequent subsequences of given data for sequential pattern mining finds intersession pattern present in set of items in a time ordered set of sessions. Naive Bayes classifier develops Automatic classifier used for recognizing patterns especially for medical diagnosis. The iteration and splitting of Naive Bayes algorithm based on various criteria produces decision tree. Discovering sequential patterns from a large database of sequence is an important problem in the field of knowledge discovery and data mining described by Lin *et al.* [6].

5.1.2   Internet of Robotic Things (IoRT)

The Internet-of-Robotic-Things (IoRT) is a developing model that unites self-governing automated frameworks with the Internet of Things (IoT) vision of associated sensors and savvy questions widely installed in our ordinary condition. This merger can empower inventive applications in pretty much every division where participation among robots and IoT innovation can be envisioned: From helped living, to accuracy cultivating, to bundling and dispatching products in assembling and strategic applications, to cleaning and support of common foundation, to squander assortment and reusing, to mapping, assessment, fix and destroying in seaward by Sharif *et al.* [7].

Early indications of the IoT-Robotics assembly can be found in ideal models like system robot frameworks, robot ecologies, or in approaches, for example, cloud apply autonomy. In any case, every one of these endeavors have delivered techniques, devices and stages that remain to a great extent particular from those being produced inside IoT activities. All things considered, progress in our capacity to create incorporated frameworks is as yet divided with covers restricted to barely any application areas. So as to open the capability of IoRT arrangements, various major innovative and logical difficulties must be handled to address the multifaceted nature, profound clashes and furthermore the security, wellbeing and protection concerns achieved by different heterogeneous things detecting, taking self-ruling choices, and moving and acting inside a similar powerful condition.

5.2   Related Work

Chena *et al.* [3] have addressed the issues regarding discovery of sequential patterns occur from vast collection of sequence, knowledge extraction, knowledge dredging and data extraction, etc. The problem regarding sequential pattern mining must get complete solution for frequent satisfaction of sequential pattern with assured support of minimizing the sequence of database. Mining applications based on medical records, telecommunications, web applications and analysis need more sequential patterns as host of applications. Thus, it motivates us to research over repeating patterns with frequent sequences using fuzzy rules of different time interval applications. Most of the patterns are not required for mining data tasks, since it has useless pattern redundancy which is not required for new type of patterns.

The sequential pattern mining faithfully discharges the assignment of locating the sequential patterns which habitually happen in time sequence or specific order [12]. Thus, it is very easy to predict the upcoming scenarios, by means of a deft appraisal of the variation in the state of the sequences.

Consequently, the physicians are capable of identifying the fruition course of ailments with regard to the medical history of the subjects with the intention of averting and healing the diseases with no loss of time. The major motive of the Sequential Pattern Mining technique is devoted to the determination of the frequent sequences in the specified database by Anu *et al.* [19]. It has, over the years, emerged as a significant data mining issue with extensive applications, like the web log mining, DNA mining, and so on. It represents a daunting challenge in as much it is essential to scrutinize the combinatorial explosive number of potential subsequent patterns.

Gowri *et al.* [20] have designed a robotic arm using Internet of Things and Arduino. Author has used servomotor 6 to understand the concepts behind their invention. Vimali *et al.* [14] have discussed about temporal data mining i.e. time related data mining using greedy algorithm which can be used in time related application such as weather, trend in marketing etc.

One of the striking features of the Sequential pattern Mining is its innate skills in the effective identification of the frequent sub-sequences in a dataset. Further, the sequential pattern mining is extensively applied in many an application. It has a vital part to play in the DNA Sequence patterns which are highly fruitful in the domain of the Medical applications by Gladence and Ravi [13]. It has also metamorphosed as an indispensable data mining function with several applications, encompassing market and customer appraisal, web log evaluation, pattern identification in the protein sequences, and extracting the XML query access patterns for the purpose of caching said by Chen *et al.* [9].

Islam *et al.* [10] have discussed many things related to IoT heath care management which can be concentrated on privacy, security, threat model etc. In addition, this research made a way for new challenges to the people who are interested in automation by Gladence *et al.* [17]. Proposed a recommender system which can help elderly people and disable people for their day to day activities through their voice commands. Authors have used natural language processing concepts to know the semantics of user needs.

Simoens *et al.* [15] addressed the Internet of Robotic Things is a rising vision that unites articles and sensors which are in escapable by means of automated frameworks. This overview analyzes how the combination of robotic and Internet of Things advances will progress the capacities of both the present internet related works and the current robotic frameworks. In this way it empowers the production of new, conceivably troublesome administrations. Srinivasulu *et al.* [8] have done a work based on sentiment analysis to identify the disease. This work describes the classification in the form of three different categories such as positive, negative, neutral. Using the above said work user can easily track their situation and act accordingly.

Patel *et al.* [16] discussed that with the invention of the Internet of Things (IoT), robots are incorporated as a 'thing' and build up associations with different things over the Internet. This part plainly demonstrates the drawn-out advantages of person in social insurance division, health related crises, e-wellbeing, and so forth utilizing mechanical autonomy and IoT.

Rezig *et al.* [18] stated that an information mining approach is coordinated in this work for predictive consecutive support alongside data on sparse parts dependent on the historical backdrop of the support information. Proposed technique predicts the event of the support movement with data on the expended sparse parts.

5.3   Fuzzy Time Interval Sequential Pattern (FTISPAM)

Sequential Pattern Mining (SPAM) involves the discovery of frequent sequential patterns of database in data mining. The process of sequential pattern mining involves many algorithms and techniques perform efficient mine fuzz change model using similarity computation index (SCI). Pattern classification process involves in pattern mining uses Fuzzy Time Interval (FTI) to overcome the problem of raw data computation collected from number of time interval that creates time complexity in pattern mining process [11].

The problem regarding sequential pattern mining must get complete solution for frequent satisfaction of sequential pattern with assured support of minimizing the sequence of database. Mining applications based on medical records, telecommunications, web applications and analysis need more sequential patterns as host of applications. Thus, it motivates us to research over repeating patterns with frequent sequences using fuzzy rules of different time interval applications. Most of the patterns are not required for mining data tasks, since it has useless pattern redundancy which is not required for new type of patterns.

Sequential Pattern Mining is intimately linked to theory of the Data Mining. The location of the sequential patterns, which is an improvement over the frequent item-set finding of association rule mining, has emerged as a daunting challenge thanks its incredible intricacy. The literature is flooded with several diverse algorithms and methods which are employed in the task of the sequential pattern mining. One of the out-of-the-ordinary modern sophisticated methods is the Mine Fuzz Change model, which is envisioned for the Sequential Pattern Mining process by employing the Similarity Computation Index (SCI) which effectively carries out the pattern classification process. But the captioned model is plagued by certain deficiencies in the SCI evaluation.

Since, the SCI value is estimated by means of the raw data which is gathered from diverse time intervals, it leads to the time intricacy in the pattern mining task. Further, there is a dearth of works related to the mining of the change in the patient behavior in the fuzzy time-interval sequential patterns employing the Hybrid Genetic technique. When the entire deficiencies illustrated in the literary works are efficiently overwhelmed, the mining accuracy is augmented together with the superlative efficiency. However, the absence of effective solutions for the deficiencies has inspired us to carry out the investigation work in the area concerned.

5.3.1   FTI SPAM Using GA Algorithm

The pattern mining from databases D^t and D^{t+1} mines the length of frequent pattern from different databases that has support values. The set of tuples contained in the support value defined as (id, s). The support value in number of tuples for the sequence of database D containing the sequence s is known as support of s that can be denoted as $su(s)$. The mined patterns with great support value given in the user define value termed to be α known as frequent one length patterns. After one length pattern, other length patterns mined using the renowned optimization algorithm known as GA. The objective of using Genetic Algorithm for pattern mining process is as databases collected from various time intervals having a greater number of raw data. The increase in raw data creates the time complexity towards pattern mining. To overcome this, optimization algorithm in pattern mining is used to reduce the time complexity. In addition to this, most useful data from its database is found. The genetic algorithm-based pattern mining process is described in following terms such as the following.

5.3.1.1 Chromosome Generation

Chromosomes are generated arbitrarily based on initial population. The represented chromosomes are frequent among the one length patterns where each position of the chromosomes denotes the gene. The chromosomes generated are as follows.

$$C^j = \{i_1, l_i, i_x\}; 0 \leq j \leq n_c - 1 \tag{5.1}$$

Here the gene value i_x represents one length pattern of frequent items value and l_i represents the linguistic terms. This one length frequent pattern is involved in the process of chromosome generation. The one length frequent patterns phrased as $\{c, d, e\}$ means the generated chromosomes for this one length patterns that are listed as in Table 5.1 along with va. This kind of fitness function calculation is for the jth chromosome as defined.

Table 5.1 Generated chromosomes.

Sample chromosomes		
c short d	c short e	d short e
c long d	c long e	d long e
c middle d	c middle e	d middle e

5.3.1.2   Fitness Function

In the stage of generated chromosomes, the evaluation of fitness function is applied for choosing the best chromosomes. The fitness function is intended for every chromosome generated. It is considered as one of the best chromosomes that defines the fitness functions and it is termed to be as

$$f^{ij} = su(c^j) \tag{5.2}$$

The best selected $n_c/2$ chromosomes can satisfy the conditions given in Equation (5.2) subsequently by the selected best chromosomes which are subjected to the crossover and mutation operations.

$$Su(c^j) > \alpha \tag{5.3}$$

Selected chromosomes are checked with Equation (5.3) and chromosome which are satisfying $Su(c^j) > \alpha$, are taken in for the next step i.e. crossover.

5.3.1.3   Crossover

Here, we perform crossover with a crossover rate of c_r. We generate random value r which is generated within the interval of [0, 1]. The generated random value is less than the crossover rate c_r means change the chromosomes gene values otherwise do not change the gene values. Finally, $n_c/2$ children chromosomes are obtained. The process of crossover operation is given in Figure 5.1.

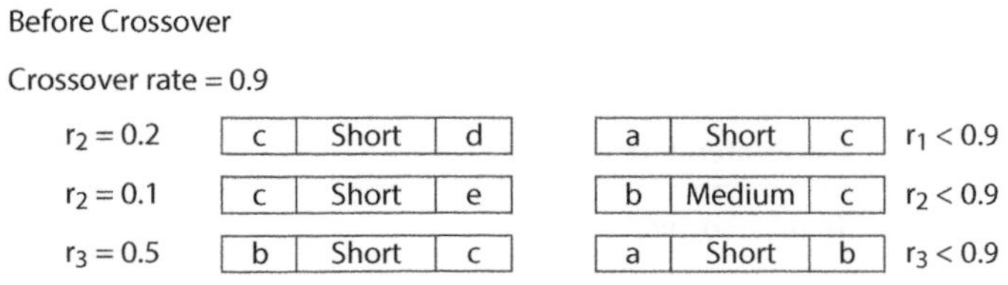

Figure 5.1 Cross-over representation.

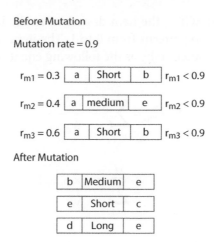

Figure 5.2 Representation of mutation process.

5.3.1.4 Mutation

The children chromosomes obtained are mutated at the mutation rate of m_r to obtain the $n_c/2$ values as new chromosomes. For every child chromosome, the randomly generated value r_m will be within the time interval of [0, 1]. The r_m value of chromosomes compared with the mutation rate m_r. The r_m values are lesser than the mutation rate which means the chromosome gene values which are mutated and otherwise the gene values cannot be changed. To obtain the consequent $n_c/2$ new children chromosomes and $n_c/2$ will be the best parent chromosomes. The process of mutation operation is shown in Figure 5.2.

5.3.1.5 Termination

The above process is repeated until it reaches the maximum number of iterations I. Once it reaches I, the best c^j chromosomes are stored in p^t. By using the abovementioned process, the fuzzy time interval sequential pattern sets P^t and P^{t+1} are extracted from the data base D^t and D^{t+1}.

5.3.2 Patterns Matching Using SCI

The similarity between two different patterns understands the computation of SCI described as

$$SCI_{mn} = \eta \times SCI_{mn}^o + (1-\eta) \times SCI_{mn}^e \tag{5.4}$$

In Equation (5.4) SCI°$_{mn}$ the item described as the linguistic term has similarity between two patterns from 0 to 1. The item SCI^o_{mn} and the linguistic term are computed to be as the following equations.

$$SCI^o_{mn} = \sum_{p=1}^{il} \frac{(w_o \times S^o_{mnp})}{w_o} \tag{5.5}$$

$$SCI^e_{mn} = \sum_{p=1}^{ltl} \frac{(w_e \times S^e_{mnp})}{w_e} \tag{5.6}$$

Equations (5.5) and (5.6) computed based on the positions of patterns p is the odd or even. i^l is the maximal item length of patterns where the weight in odd position has different patterns. From Equation (5.6) we infer l^l_t has the maximal linguistic term regarding the length of the patterns where w_e are the weight in even position. The items that have linguistics were similar to the patterns regarding odd and even position. The similarity item along with linguistic term has similarity computations using item similarity and linguistic similarity computation algorithms as explained in the equations.

5.3.3   Pattern Classification Based on SCI Value

SCI computation process after change in the pattern classification will be termed as

1. Emerging Patterns: if the value of SCI$_{mn}$ = 1.0 or SCI°$_{mn}$ = 1.0. If the support of two different pattern user could able to get the same value for item and linguistic term, that particular pattern is called as emerging pattern.
2. Unexpected Changes: If the value of $MiSCI_n$ >pt. The above said criteria is met with respect to p_m those patterns are called as unexpected pattern or unexpected change.
3. Added/Perished Patterns: If the value of $MaSCI_n$ <pt meant by the FTI sequential pattern defined to be the added patterns relevant to all discovered patterns in D^t.

Hence if the value of $MaSCI_n$ ≤pt meant by the FTI sequential pattern defined to be the perished patterns relevant to all discovered patterns in D^{t+1}.

5.3.4   Significant Pattern Evaluation

The change of patterns classification after the significant patterns are calculated based on user specified value of α. Most specifically the similarity values of patterns can be computed using their support and $MaSCI_n^{t+1}$, $MiSCI_n^{t+1}$ values. The patterns emerged by the significant computations as below.

$$E_{mn} = \frac{(su(p_n^{t+1}) - su(p_m^t))}{su(p_m^t)} \tag{5.7}$$

In Equation (5.7) the values denoted supports pattern through p_n^{t+1} in D^{t+1} and p_m^t in D^t. Equation (5.8) signifies the unexpected change according to the computations involved.

$$U_{mn} = SCI_{mn} \times \frac{su(p_n^{t+1})}{su(p_m^t)} \tag{5.8}$$

The perished and added patterns of significance calculated by multiplying the $MaSCI_n^{t+1}$, $MiSCI_n^{t+1}$ by supporting their values. The perished and added patterns significance computed will be termed as follows.

$$P_{mn} = MiSCI_n^{t+1} \times su(p_n^{t+1}) \tag{5.9}$$

$$A_{mn} = MiSCI_m^t \times su(p_m^t) \tag{5.10}$$

Based on the description of the above process the significant change of patterns mined from the databases. The mined pattern supports the managers for easy understanding of the client behaviors. Data mining techniques are capably being used in healthcare fields, such as diagnosing of disease. Heart disease is causing death all over the world. Different Data Mining tools are obtainable while using any one of the tools has showed suitable intensity of exactness. Our research establishes the loopholes in the Disease prediction about coronary disease investigations additionally the curable medicine. More-over constructed a model capable of determining the application of information mining systems with coronary illness detection. Disease related medicine information might provide satisfactory and trustworthy execution accomplishes the identification of coronary disease.

The forecasting of sequential pattern mining finds the occurrence of subsequences from the given data for providing the intersession pattern with set of items following another item by time ordering the set of sessions. Especially heart disease was predicted using Naïve Bayes Classifier by finding the severe congestive heart failures using short term HRV measures. High risk patients were considered by the suffering from severe CHF whereas the risk will be less in low risk patients having mild CHF.

5.4　Detection of Congestive Heart Failure Using Automatic Classifier

Congestive Heart Failure (CHF) is the one in which human life leads to a critical state because of malfunction of the heart to pump enough blood to the body which is required for the human to live a normal life without disturbance. New York Heart Association classification has taken the NYHA scale as one of the risk factors for people's death if it increases the threshold level.

Difference between two consecutive heart beat which has been extricate from electro cardio graphic signal which is recorded by non-invasive strategy is called heart rate variability. Most of the time HRV is identified as a part of the impact of the Automatic Nervous System (ANS) in the heart. HRV is one which can find out whether the patient is experiencing congestive heart disease or not. Many literatures proved that HRV is the successful method of hazard estimation which prompts the sickness of heart perfectly. Additionally, it arranges a classifier in view of long haul HRV procedure to individual malfunctioning of CHF. The systematic procedure or method which is used to develop the classifier is Bayesian classifier. Invented method separates higher risk patients from lower risk patients by examining long term heart rate variability measures. Here based on the measures of New York Heart Association order patients are categorized as low/high risk patients.

Once data classification is done using sequential pattern mining, classified data are taken into consideration for predicting disease through Internet of Robotic Things devices. Diagrammatic representation of work flow is given in Figure 5.3. All communication which is going to happen to predict or manage health records is done via robot. This system must have wifi connection to perform automation via robot. Through wifi robot will get patients' details and these details are fed to the belief network. Belief network is a statistical classifier which will have prior knowledge about the dataset and it will produce the result in the form of probabilistic manner.

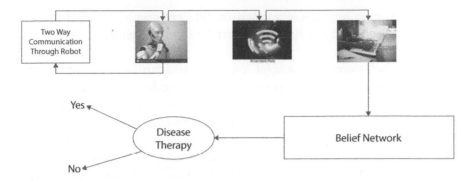

Figure 5.3 Robot interaction for disease prediction—belief network.

Through the belief network robot will come to know whether the patient have to undergo disease therapy or not. Major advantage of using robot is its interaction ability. Interaction ability is concerned about interaction between human and robot either socially, physically or cognitively. This work can be extended to home cleaning, home automation, choice of foods based on human's interest etc. The above said task can be done based on change in environment, natural language processing.

5.4.1   Analyzing the Dataset

Experimental Datasets enclose huge quantity of data records about the patients and also their health examination report. Data set which is taken as the input comprises of variety of diseases that concern about people's health records. Health issue is measured by the origin of symptoms which have details about patient's health considering certain places. Documentation sets with health attribute are combined together and with the assistance of it the models significant to the heart attack forecast are extracted.

The attribute class is acknowledged as the predictable feature with value "1" for patients with disease and patients with no sickness with the value of "0". In this module we analyse the records which are registered in the database. Initially major required attributes were taken to find out the disease. Patient's ID is taken as the key attribute to discriminate between one patient and another patient. The minority of them play a major role in foreseeing the heart sickness and those are described below.

a.   Angina: It is often referred to as "angina pectoris" is an intellect of twinge occurring in the chest. It happens when the heart muscle does not receive enough oxygen-rich blood.

Angina happens in models in different manner. They are categorized as Chronic Angina, Unstable Angina and variant angina.

b. Cholesterol: Cholesterol assists in structuring our body's new cells, protecting nerves and even producing hormones. In general, high cholesterol leads to a heart attack. High cholesterol builds up in the artery walls and leads to a procedure called atherosclerosis. Atherosclerosis is one heart disease presentation. Additional cholesterol can be known as Low Density Lipoprotein (LDL or "Poor" and high-density lipoprotein (HDL or "good" Cholesterol). These describe the structure in which cholesterol actions in the blood. Intensity of cholesterol is measured to be high if acquired 240 and beyond, borderline high if accurate between 200 and 239 and enviable if less than 200.

c. Blood Pressure: It is the determination of the obliged at which the blood flows next to your blood vessel walls. In two patterns known as systolic and diastolic the velocity of blood pressure can be considered. This measures pressure force as the heart contracts and the blood is squeezed out, known as systolic. This is the diastolic number that determines when a heart relaxes between beats.

d. Electrocardiogram: In control of recognizing a patient's heart hindrance, doctors make the use of an examination known as electrocardiogram (ECG). This is used for characteristics and pursues a heart's electric stroke when it undergoes depolarization (over joy) and polarization (resurgence) to instigate each and every heartbeat. ECG maps electrical activity of the heart into line tracings on a paper. Signals are displayed at the dots and dips in the graph. Doctor uses the points and dips to resolve your heart's electrical movement. The grouping of spikes and dips into various sections will determine the heart functions specified. The results of the ECG are determined to be normal when the heart beats at the regular rhythm and it mostly lies between 60 and 100 beats per minute.

5.4.2   Data Collection

Here, input data is patient data which consists of attributes like gender, age, blood pressure, cholesterol, LDL, exang, thalach etc. These data are fed to

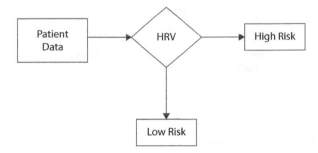

Figure 5.4 Data collection.

high rate variability measure which separates patients in to two categories such as high-risk patients and low risk patients which is shown in Figure 5.4. Based on this patient treated well to diagonize and cure their disease and live happily.

5.4.2.1 Long-Term HRV Measures

Difference between sequences of heartbeats which is taken from electro cardio graphic signal recorded by non-invasive strategy is called heart rate variability. Most of the time HRV is identified as a part of the impact of the Automatic Nervous System (ANS) in heart. HRV is one which can find out whether the patient is experiencing congestive heart disease or not shown in Figure 5.5. Many literatures proved that HRV is the successful method of hazard estimation which prompts the sickness of heart perfectly. Additionally, it arranged a classifier in view of long haul HRV procedure to individual malfunctioning of CHF. The systematic procedure or method which is used to develop the classifier is Bayesian classifier. The novelty presented in this work using classifier differentiates higher risk patients from lower risk patients by examining heart beat measures under long period of time. Here based on the measures of New York Heart Association order patients are categorized as low/high risk patients.

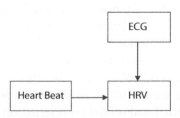

Figure 5.5 HRV measures prediction.

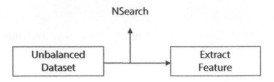

Figure 5.6 Attribute selection.

5.4.2.2   Attribute Selection

Regardless of the possibility that Bayesian belief network calculations execute a stepwise element determination, it might happen that one element is prohibited in light of the fact that different factors veiled its impact. It is a challenging work when there is a situation to use unbalanced or tiny data set.

To make the tree to produce best subset of variables, adopted a technique called exhaustive search method to produce all mixture of k from N elements (k ranges from 1 to N). For example, quantity of element N is 13, using exhaustive search method produced N13 = 8,092 subset of elements and preparing and testing them in a required number of classifiers as discussed earlier. Here among calculated classifiers through exhaustive search method one with minimal calculation of misclassification which is appraised by ten-fold cross validation is chosen. Since probability of cross validation technique could give accurate result for unbalanced and tiny data, above said method is chosen shown in Figure 5.6. Here feature selection method enhances classification since it takes all possible considerations.

5.4.3   Automatic Classifier—Belief Network

Bayes network or Bayesian belief network or dependencies among attributes is one of the statistical classifiers which can play a major role in prediction. In this marvelous invention, prediction is in the form of probabilities. For this reason, it is also called as probabilistic graphical model or probabilistic acyclic graphical model. For example, this model could represent the work in the form of relationship between symptom and disease if you consider disease as the example. In a nutshell, Bayesian belief network can take input as the symptom of any disease and compute the probabilities of existence or not-existence of any disease. This network can allow conditional independence among other attributes. In general, we can specify a Belief network as a graphical model representation of relationship which can show dependencies among variables, joint probability distribution.

Thus, the independence expressed in the above network is that G is independent of B given C. In case of Bayesian belief probabilities ranges from 0 to 1. Suppose one probability is given another possible probability is identified easily from the range. This network has been widely applied in many of the pattern recognition application, especially in medical diagnosis due its attractiveness towards statistical classifier which can perform probabilistic prediction. Only flaw in this network is one who is performing research in this, need to have prior knowledge about probability. Here Bayesian belief network is adopted due to feature selection method which can handle very little and unbalanced data set. Belief network need to have conditional probability table for each and every variable which is taken in to consideration, from this conditional probability table probabilities of variables which are not given directly are calculated.

Bayesian or belief network defined by two wonderful components such as conditional probability table and directed acyclic graph. Figure 5.7 represents the directed acyclic graph for the example taken to appraise the work. Each variable or attribute taken in this said example is in the form of discrete or continuous value. Since it accepts class conditional dependence among the attributes this technique can be taken to classify disease. Each node in the directed acyclic graph is the random variable. Whenever you are looking for Bayesian belief network whether the graph is represented in the form of directed acyclic graph or not. Figure 5.7 arc is drawn from node A to node D, then A is considered as immediate predecessor of D or parent of node D and node D is the descendent of node A.

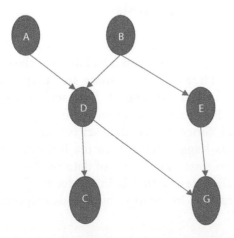

Figure 5.7 Graphical representation of Bayesian belief network model.

For every vector a beliefs network has one conditional likelihood table (CPT). The CPT for a Y vector defines the P(Y) conditional distribution, where parents(Y) are parents of y. The conditional probability for every known value of variable is given for every possible combination of its parents' values.

Notations used from Figure 5.7 are D → Diabetes A → Hereditary, B → blood pressure

P(Diabetics = yes|Heriditary = yes, Blood pressure = yes) = 0.8

P(Diabetics = no|Heriditory = no, Blood pressure = no) = 0.9.

Let M = (x1, ...,xn) be a data tuple described by the Y1, ..., Yn, respectively. Note that in the network graph, provided its kin, each element is conditionally independent of its no descendants. This allows the network to fully represent the existing joint probability distribution using the following equation:

$$P(X_1,...,X_N) = \prod_{i=1}^{N} P(X_i \mid Parents(X_i)) \qquad (5.11)$$

Equation (5.11) is used to find the joint probability from the conditional probability table.

5.5   Experimental Analysis

Proposed classifier has highest attractiveness towards different strategies such as classification and regression tree, Bayesian classification, decision tree induction etc., Here as a preliminary step preprocessing is done to replace the empty field in the data set. Data set has been extracted from Kaggle repository. Preprocessing is done using replace missing value filter from weka tool. Since disease data set is taken from freely available data source such as Kaggle, result is in the form of two classes such as Yes and No. Due to class description of data set 2 × 2 confusion matrix is used. Assume class description is in the form of C and D. Output of the network is displayed in the form of class description which are listed below.

Class C = Yes (Disease Present)

Class D = Yes (No disease).

The Internet of Robotic Things (IoRT) is a developing model that unites self-governing automated frameworks with the Internet of Things (IoT) vision of associated sensors and savvy questions widely installed in our ordinary condition. This merger can empower inventive applications in pretty much every division where participation among robots and IoT innovation can be envisioned. Early indications of the IoT-Robotics assembly can be found in ideal models like system robot frameworks, robot ecologies, or in approaches, for example, cloud apply autonomy. In any case, every one of these endeavors have delivered techniques, devices and stages that remain to a great extent particular from those being produced inside IoT activities.

Whenever you are using a classification analysis, users always need to look for a class label which is the subset of supervised learning. In supervised learning user will provided with input variable and a output variable, then user will use an classification or regression algorithm to learn the mapping function from input to the output(output = function(input)). Classification techniques or algorithms are used to separate the data from one with another. Whereas regression techniques or algorithms try to fit the data in many forms such as linear non-linear etc.

In this automatic classifier, heart disease data set is taken to validate the work using Bayesian belief network. Since this statistical classifier uses probabilistic prediction model one that is involving in this work must have prior knowledge about it. This is also one kind of boosting the performance of the network. Sample model tree for the data which is used in automatic classifier is shown in Figure 5.8. In the tree each node is the graphical representation of if followed by then rules i.e. in the form of decision rule which is the output format of decision tree. For example, if age >55 and the values for attributes which is taken to identify the disease go beyond threshold value probability of having disease is more. If the attribute value is less than threshold value probability of having disease is less. In this manner people can identify whether they are having heart disease or not. This method is compared with the classification methods which are used earlier to find out heart disease and results have clearly stated that proposed work is much superior. This work is evaluated using the performance measures such as predictive accuracy, sensitivity, true positive, false positive, true negative, false negative, recall, etc., and the results are shown in Figure 5.9.

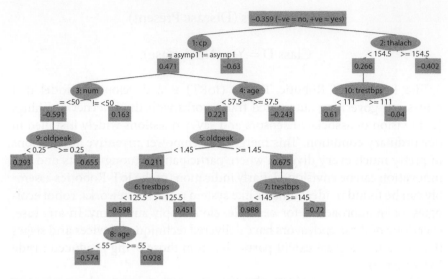

Figure 5.8 Final model tree for the combination of attributes.

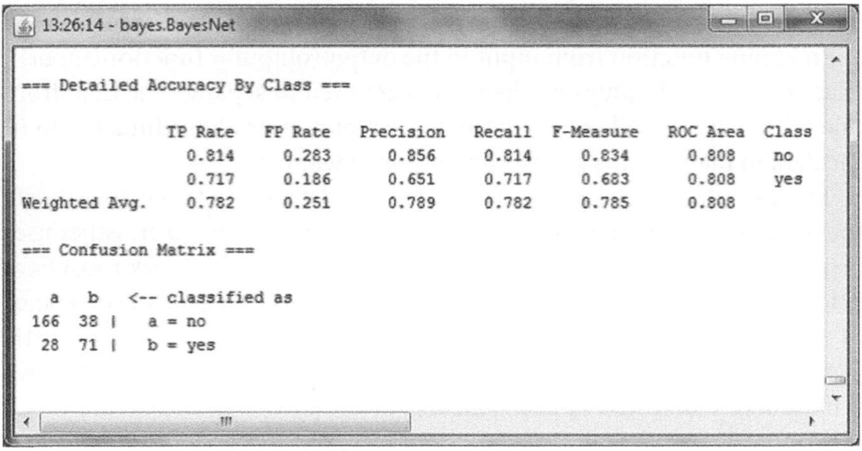

```
13:26:14 - bayes.BayesNet                                        ▭ ▢ ✕

=== Detailed Accuracy By Class ===

                TP Rate   FP Rate   Precision   Recall   F-Measure   ROC Area   Class
                0.814     0.283     0.856       0.814    0.834       0.808      no
                0.717     0.186     0.651       0.717    0.683       0.808      yes
Weighted Avg.   0.782     0.251     0.789       0.782    0.785       0.808

=== Confusion Matrix ===

   a    b    <-- classified as
 166   38 |   a = no
  28   71 |   b = yes
```

Figure 5.9 Final output of in terms of performance measures with classified result.

5.6   Conclusion

This work has been developed to classify pattern at first in the form of emerging pattern, perished pattern and unexpected pattern for the disease data set. These patterns are generated by checking their similarity using similarity computation index. After classifying the patterns based on similarity computation index, it has been evaluated based on significant pattern evaluation. Since, it uses fuzzy time interval sequential pattern mining algorithm that classifies the dataset given along with reduced computation of time complexity. It efficiently describes the pattern classification and sequential pattern changes illustrating the change of patterns for the input which is taken to appraise the work.

Bayes network or Bayesian belief network or dependencies among attributes is one of the statistical classifiers which can play a major role in prediction. In this marvellous invention, prediction is in the form of probabilities. For this reason, it is also called as probabilistic graphical model or probabilistic acyclic graphical model. For example, this model could represent the work in the form of relationship between symptom and disease if you consider disease as the example. In a nutshell, Bayesian belief network can take input as the symptom of any disease and compute the probabilities of existence or not-existence of any disease. This network can allow conditional independence among other attributes. In general, we can specify a Belief network as a graphical model representation of relationship which can show dependencies among variables, joint probability distribution. The HRV classifier for regular classifier, based on various experimental & influential parameters have been proposed to sustain CHF evaluation. Considering only the small intensity types and to load their space between low level and high-level causes CHF it makes results probably and classifies the personal CHF. All communications which are going to happen to predict or manage health records is done via robot. This system must have wifi connection to perform automation via robot. Through wifi robot will get patients details and these details are fed to the belief network. Belief network is a statistical classifier which will have prior knowledge about the dataset and it will produce the result in the form of probabilistic manner. Through the belief network robot will come to know whether the patient have to undergo disease therapy or not. Major advantage of using robot is its interaction ability. Interaction ability is concerned about interaction between human and robot either socially, physically or cognitively. Thus, this work deals with classification which can deal with sequence of patterns and classify them in to emerging pattern, unexpected change, perished pattern. Classified data is automated based on Internet of Robotic Things using Bayesian belief network. Based on the above discussion patients were given with the instruction via robot whether a patient has to undergo disease therapy or not. This work can be extended to home cleaning, home automation, choice of foods based on human's interest etc.

References

1. Han, J., Kamber, M., Pei, J., Data mining concepts and techniques third edition. The *Morgan Kaufmann Series in Data Management Systems*, 5.4, pp. 83–124, 2011.
2. Idhammad, M., Afdel, K., Belouch, M., Distributed intrusion detection system for cloud environments based on data mining techniques. *Proc. Comput. Sci.*, 127, 35–41, 2018.
3. Chen, Y.L., Chen, J.M., Tung, C.W., A data mining approach for retail knowledge discovery with consideration of the effect of shelf-space adjacency on sales. *Decis. Support Syst.*, 42, 3, 1503–1520, 2006.
4. Chang, J.H., Mining weighted sequential patterns in a sequence database with a time-interval weight. *Knowl.-Based Syst.*, 24, 1, 1–9, 2011.
5. Huang, T.C.K., Mining the change of customer behavior in fuzzy time-interval sequential patterns. *Appl. Soft Comput.*, 12, 3, 1068–1086, 2012.
6. Lin, N.J., Bailey, L.O., Becker, M.L., Washburn, N.R., Henderson, L.A., Macrophage response to methacrylate conversion using a gradient approach. *Acta Biomater.*, 3, 2, 163–173, 2007.
7. Sharif, M.S. and Alsibai, M.H., Medical data analysis based on Nao robot: An automated approach towards robotic real-time interaction with human body, in: *2017 7th IEEE International Conference on Control System, Computing and Engineering (ICCSCE)*, 2017, November, IEEE, pp. 91–96.
8. Srinivasulu, S., Mahesh, C., Manikanta, I., Emotional antinomy classification of sentiments for healthcare systems. *Int. J. Pharm. Technol.*, 8, 2, 11943–11950, 2016.
9. Chen, Y.L., Chen, J.M., Tung, C.W., A data mining approach for retail knowledge discovery with consideration of the effect of shelf-space adjacency on sales. *Decis. Support Syst.*, 42, 3, 1503–1520, 2006.
10. Islam, S.R., Kwak, D., Kabir, M.H., Hossain, M., Kwak, K.S., The internet of things for healthcare: A comprehensive survey. *IEEE Access*, 3, 678–708, 2015.
11. Mary Gladence, L. and Ravi, T., Mining the change of customer behavior in fuzzy time-interval sequential patterns with aid of Similarity Computation Index (SCI) and Genetic Algorithm (GA). *Int. Rev. Comput. Software (IRECOS)*, 8, 11, 2552–2561, 2013.
12. Soliman, A.F., Ebrahim, G.A., Mohammed, H.K., Collective sequential pattern mining in distributed evolving data streams, in: *Proceedings of the International Conference on Innovation and Information Management*, Singapore, 36, 2, pp. 141–148, 2012.
13. Gladence, L.M. and Ravi, T., Heart Disease Prediction and Treatment Suggestion. *Res. J. Pharm. Biol. Chem. Sci.*, 7, 2, 1274–1279, 2016.
14. Vimali, J.S., Gupta, S., Srivastava, P., A novel approach for mining temporal pattern database using greedy algorithm, in: *2017 International Conference*

on *Innovations in Information, Embedded and Communication Systems (ICIIECS)*, IEEE, 2017.

15. Simoens, P., Dragone, M., Saffiotti, A., The Internet of Robotic Things: A review of concept, added value and applications. *Int. J. Adv. Rob. Syst.*, 15, 1, 1–11, 1729881418759424, 2018.

16. Patel, A.R., Patel, R.S., Singh, N.M., Kazi, F.S., Vitality of Robotics in Healthcare Industry: An Internet of Things (IoT) Perspective, in: *Internet of Things and Big Data Technologies for Next Generation Healthcare*, pp. 91–109, Springer, Cham, 2017.

17. Gladence, L.M., Anu, V.M., Rathna, R. *et al.*, Recommender system for home automation using IoT and artificial intelligence. *J. Ambient Intell. Hum. Comput.*, https://doi.org/10.1007/s12652-020-01968-2, 2020.

18. Rezig, S., Achour, Z., Rezg, N., Using data mining methods for predicting sequential maintenance activities. *Appl. Sci.*, 8, 11, 2184, 2018.

19. Anu, M., Anandha, V., Mala, G.S., RFID data encoding scheme in supply chain management with aid of orthogonal transformation and Genetic Algorithm. *Int. Rev. Comput. Software (IRECOS)*, 8, 11, 2562–2569, 2013.

20. Gowri, S., Srinivasulu, S., Blessy, U.J., Vinitha, K.M.C., Implementation of IoT in Multiple Functions Robotic Arm: A Survey, in: *International Conference on Computer Networks, Big Data and IoT*, 2019, December, Springer, Cham, pp. 948–952.

17. Macgregor, R., DeLangre, M., Gallotti, A., The Internet of Robotic Things: A review of concept, added value and applications. Int. J. Adv. Robot. Syst. 15, 1, 1–41, 1729881418759424, 2018.

18. Patel, A.R., Patel, R.S., Singh, N.M., Kazi, F.S., Vitality of Robotics in Healthcare Industry: an Internet of Things (IoT) Perspective, in Internet of Things and Big Data Technologies for Next Generation Healthcare, pp. 91–109, Springer, Cham, 2017.

19. Dharmaraju, A.M., Ang, V.M., Belman, R. et al., Reconfigurable System to Ignite appropriate living IoT, and artificial intelligence. J. Ambient Intell. Hum. Comput. https://doi.org/10.1007/s12652-020-01605-y, 2020.

20. Peng, S., Schaar, P., Keng, N., Using data mining methods for preventing failure of innocuous actions. Ample Soc. de. Hci. 764, 2018.

21. Kim, M., Sundada, K., Vlok, S-S., FETU data processing scheme in sensor data integration with an millisecond measurement and Gendse Algorithm. Inst. Comput. Science IFECSINTE 11, 232, 240, 2013.

22. Garcia, S., Sudhvapho, J., Prem, Li-Pulpofon, K.M., Implementation of IoT Method, Teaching, Research, Trial. A Survey, in Internet and Code-Scene, Machine, Networks. of cyptome of procedures. Springer, Cham, pp. 238–252.

6

Multimodal Context-Sensitive Human Communication Interaction System Using Artificial Intelligence-Based Human-Centered Computing

S. Murugan[1], R. Manikandan[2*] and Ambeshwar Kumar[2]

[1]Department of Computer Science, Sri Aravindar Engineering College, Viluppuram, India
[2]School of Computing, SASTRA Deemed University, Thanjavur, India

Abstract

Human-Centred Computing (HCC) is emerging technology which aimed to overcome limitation associated with existing technology related to design and implementation of the computation process for monitoring human activity. HCC provides integration of human science and computer science for computing system design based on the visualization of humans from beginning to end. Human-Centered computing (HCC) incorporates a set of methodology that can be applied to any field which uses computers, any applications where humans communicate directly with devices or system which uses computer technology. The interfaces are provided for transcending with the use of traditional keyboards and mouses and capable of understanding human behaviour and emulating human communicative interaction characteristics with an expression of behavioural cues related to affective and social signals. Most techniques related to human sensing, human behaviour and context sensing analysis are performed effectively in a constrained environment. The factors such as fast movement, illumination changes and also other factors affect the performance. Also, many traditional methods cannot perform effectively for offering interactivity support with the system. To overcome this limitation, in this workshop designed a Multimodal Human Communication Interaction system for an effective communication process. The design modulates all modes of communication

Corresponding author: srmanimt75@gmail.com

R. Anandan, G. Suseendran, S. Balamurugan, Ashish Mishra and D. Balaganesh (eds.) Human Communication Technology: Internet of Robotic Things and Ubiquitous Computing, (137–162) © 2022 Scrivener Publishing LLC

received from humans, such as gestures, posture, voice tone, facial expression, respiration, the temperature of the skin, clamminess, word selection and so on. In Multimodal Human Communication Interaction System, the best emotional inference is achieved through a combination of low-level features and high-level reasoning and natural processing for achieving high emotional inference. Also, it is stated to facilitate multimodal context-sensitive based human-computer interaction is observed as a widespread research topic in the field of the research community. The proposed method CNN_LSTM is categorized into different modality data which achieves better results of accuracy of 82.4%, specificity achieves 56% and sensibility achieves 52%.

Keywords: Human-centered computing, communication, interaction, multimodal context, sensitive, artificial intelligence

6.1   Introduction

In the past era, computing technology is considered a promising evolution; it involved in characterization and monitored human activities. For computation process information is collected from different sources, data are in various media forms. Usually, that information is collected from the sensor and other devices. Due to the drastic development of technology amount of data collection increases drastically; on the other hand, demand for a new paradigm for organizing, search and integrate data related to human activities also increased.

Humans express the higher quality of emotional channels in social communication with modulating their speech utterances, body gestures and facial expression. That relies on emotional cues for resolving semantics in the received information. Interestingly, emotional information also shared by a human while interacting with machines. In human–machine interaction, people express their effects and respond emotionally. However, the machine is considered the simplest model of intelligently designed by humans; conventionally, machines can be oblivious to the emotional intelligence system. This fact is changed from the evolution of affective computing technology.

The emerging field recently is Human-Centered Computing (HCC), which aims to interlink the gaps among different techniques that involve computing system design and implementation based on people's activity support. The main aim of HCC is integrating tightly computer science and human science to design the system based on human can focusing from beginning to the end. Computer science involves signal processing, ubiquitous computing, human–computer interaction and machine learning. Human science may involve cognitive and social. The integration of HCC is focused on considering the social, personal, and contexts of culturally based on the system that can deploy [1].

Human Centered Computing (HCC) focused on design, implementation and evaluation of interactive information gathered from the technological system in terms of usable and accessible information gathering. The aim of Human-Centered Computing is evaluation of human interaction performed with information technologies that utilize that information about improving the quality of individual lives. Figure 6.1 illustrates Human-Centric computing technology. The main objective of this Human-Centric approach is to examine human–computer interaction (HCI) for the recorded data onto individual interaction obtained between user and machine by use of automatic logging function, or basic information are recorded based on the audio and video with the use of manual annotation. For several purposes, collected data can be analyzed both qualitatively and quantitatively [2].

Multimodal Human–computer interaction (MMHCI) comprises more than a few research domains like artificial intelligence, computer vision, psychology and many other applications. As in human lives, computers are integrated into everyday activities, which include ubiquitous and pervasive computing processes; it is critical for effective human–computer interaction. In several applications, users can able to communicate with computers using face-to-face communication with human–human interaction. Human communication with speech and use body language for expressing their attitude, mood, emotion, also attended. Also, in human–human communication, interpretation of audio-visual signals is an important task for understanding the message. Several researchers stated this, to resolve this

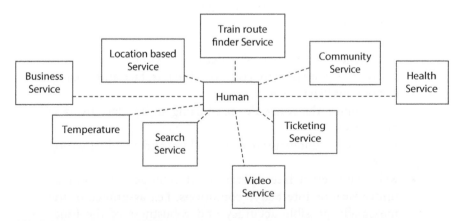

Figure 6.1 Human-centric computing.

constraint, unimodal techniques are developed. The unimodal techniques perform computer vision, audio processing, speech processing, etc. In the case of hardware technology, minimal cost sensors and cameras are utilized, which exhibits significant growth in MMHCI domain. In traditional HCI applications, a single user is included within computers and performs interaction through a mouse or keyboard. The new applications explicit commands are provided for multiple user applications such as intelligent homes, remote collaboration, arts, etc., interactions are not often engaging multiple users, also explicit commands.

With the development of multimedia workstations and high-speed data-links, information delivery and transmission demand also increased. The limitation is observed in the analysis and interpretation of the human communicative signal analysis. Human interaction is categorized through the multiplication of signal, which generates complementary information and redundant, which facilitates human communication more flexible, nature and robust.

Computer interfaces with similar human behavior flexibility, robustness and natural characteristics, multimodal human–machine interfaces system incorporate face recognition, gesture, lip and hand models. Further, it includes character recognition, eye-tracking and other human feature for the understanding goal of human users. Those multimodal features are effective against human-to-human communication, specifically for speech translation and video conferencing. Further, it can be effective against database access, scheduling on the appointment, production of a document, CAD design, machinery operation and other applications of human–computer interaction [3].

State-of-the-art user interfaces that ensure human–computer interaction should meet the principal requirements of end-users and should rely on several basic principles [4]:

- Naturalness (intuitiveness): interaction without the need to instruct the user how to work with the interface and to carry various auxiliary devices;
- Ergonomics: the convenience of using an interface by various users;
- Friendliness: unobtrusive user tracking and avoiding wrong user actions;
- Reliability: error-free operation of interface components under various interactive conditions, i.e., assurance of the maximally possible accuracy and robustness of the functioning of interface recognition components;

- efficacy: a minimal number of operations on the part of the user and minimal time for performing the required task;
- universality: applicability to various user categories, including, e.g., the physically disabled, older people, or expert operators who act under extreme conditions, such as weightlessness, underwater situations, etc., without the need for adaptation;
- multimodality: simultaneously provides a vast range of communication features such as texture, speech, gesture and so on, through which users can able to select from intelligent and convenient tools.

6.2   Literature Survey

From the point of human perspective, the challenges observed are new users, diverse device location and multiple interactions of devices. The device interaction such as shaking, positioning, touching, voice diction are performed at large scale and diverse factors in the device are arisen due to the introduction of albeit flexibility leads to incidental complexity. The present is related to the field of description based language interface.

Through analysis of the context in scientific terms, this research introduced HCIDL modeled for analysis of various stages in language integrated with model-driven engineering technique. Among the several characteristics incorporated in the human–computer interface, the proposition involved in designing of multi-target, the interface of plastic interaction, multimodal with the inclusion of language description through the user interface. Through the integration of multimodality and plasticity, HCIDL improves user interface usability using adaptive behavior with the provision of end-user interaction establishment between terminals of input or output, an optimum layout. Elsevier B.V is hosting and also production. This article is open access under the license of CC BY-NC-ND [5].

In the multimodal human–computer dialogue, non-verbal channels, such as facial expression, posture, gesture, etc., combined with spoken information, are also important in the procedure of dialogue. Nowadays, despite the high performance of users' single-channel behavior computing, it is still a great challenge to understand users' intentions accurately from their multimodal behaviors. One reason for this challenge is that we still need to improve multimodal information fusion in theories, methodologies, and practical systems. This paper presents a review of data fusion methods in the multimodal human–computer dialog. We first introduce the cognitive assumption of single-channel processing and then discuss its implementation methods in the human–computer dialog. In the task of multimodal information fusion, several computing models are presented after we introduce the principle description of multiple data fusion. Finally, some practical examples of multimodal information fusion methods are introduced and the possible and important breakthroughs of the data fusion methods in future multimodal human–computer interaction applications are discussed [6].

In collaboration with a human–robot system with a dynamic environment, the efficiency of human workers is improved using the provision of work instruction with context-dependent factors delivered through communication modalities to match actual context. The term workers represented, it needs to support controlling robot or further components of robot included in a production system with the inclusion of the most effective modality factor; this improves the performance rather than conventional interfaces as a push button that is installed in fixed locations. Here, we introduced the context-dependent multimodal communication workflow with a working atmosphere that collaboration and performed implementation using the Human–Machine Interface Controller system [7].

In the manufacturing sector integrated with human–robot, dynamic changes are performed through industrial robots through pre-programmed tasks and within the same workstation, human operators collaborate. In the case of traditional industrial robots, control codes are pre-programmed for robot control; this leads to the development of human–robot collaboration. Upon the reception of the request, this research explored a robot control interface using deep-learning-based multimodal with collaboration with human–robot.

In the multimodal interface system, three methods are integrated, like body posture recognition, hand motion recognition also voice recognition. For classification and recognition, deep learning is adopted. Human–robot collaboration is adopted through the inclusion of a specific dataset. Results illustrated that in the robot collaboration environment, a deep learning approach based on human–robot offers significant performance [8].

Activity recognition technology is a useful technology for elderly person life-logging. Mostly older people preferred to stay in their own house and locality. If they can do, they can receive several benefits from both economic and social backgrounds. However, at older age living alone leads to several risk factors. Those risks are overcome with the development of a wearable sensor; this sensor is actively involved in medical applications. The wearable sensor is actively involved in older people's wellness monitoring with interfering in their daily activity. The research conducted by Ref. [9] reviewed treads and technology involved in wearable sensor devices with multimodal recognition combination with continuous or discontinuous human activity monitoring. Through biological signals analysis like Electrooculogram (EOG), Electrocardiogram (ECG), Electroencephalogram (EEG), Electromyogram (EMG), health conditions are monitored. This enables appropriate assistance within a specified period; this leads to a crucial development in the diagnosis of diseases and treatment. The architecture shared control with the inclusion of multimodal interfaces for different applications. In a complex environment with the utilization of commands for controlling achieved efficient results for controlling.

Deep learning belongs to a class of machine learning technology with the capability of improving algorithm performance for the given datasets with learning. The structure of deep learning included several layers, such as the input layer; deep features from the input are extracted using several hidden layers; also output layer is utilized for interference. With various network layers, the output obtained from the previous layer is providing input to the current layer. Then the data represented in the learner of each layer and construct a concept of the abstracted layer in a hierarchy manner with simple and complex characteristics. In the later 1940s, three deep learning technology based on historical waves are evolved [10]. The deep learning technology is usually based on the consideration of perception, which is a single machine neuron. This can be inspired by a biological mechanism. The historical wave is second, which includes the application of a back-propagation algorithm with minimal cost function in the neural network training process. Algorithm of Back propagation provided the multi-layer neural network architecture.

Currently, the development of neural networks resolve issues such as computational capacity, reduced cost for training; this leads to the development of third historical wave. Third generated wave leads to a breakthrough for triggering a deep brief network; this is proposed by Hinton with the implementation of a pre-training strategy adopted in a greedy layer of the network. The viability of the neural network is applied to another neural network as well. Deep learning-based technology can be applied in a vast range of applications like natural language processing, computer vision, speech recognition and so on.

Several arguments are evolved about AI act as human replacing technology or human assisting technology. However, education does not focus on where the question arises but focuses on its application. Through analysis, it is observed that it has been utilized in a vast range of professional backgrounds AI exact role in education is not easier for its prediction. Ref. [11] argued about AI potential role in education is examined. The argument is based on the evaluation of opportunities provided for human intelligence augmentation, AI role in the decision-making process instead of automation replacing. To offer empirical evidence, this research presented a case study related to debate tutoring. To increase the transparency of tutors' reflection prediction and classification model is utilized for advanced reflection and feedback. Comparatively examined, the unimodal accuracy also classification of a multimodal model for the decision-making process of human expert tutors, to achieve decision-based on social and emotional factors of tutors in training. Results demonstrated that multimodal data provides an accurate classification model.

A novel deep neural network was proposed for effective management of multimodal data [12]. The performance of the proposed model is seamless multimodal input fusion also offers dimensionality reduction of spaces in input features. The proposed model employs a modified stacked autoencoder integrated by multilayer perceptron with the inclusion of the regression model. In the proposed architecture, two variants are incorporated for the application of multimodal benchmark data (RECOLA) for examining the performance of multimodality against a single modality. Experimental results illustrated that through effective multimodal data performance is conducted based on a sequential or concatenated manner. Results provide a promising performance; the proposed approach express minimal computational cost rather than the existing approach. Thus, it can be concluded that proposed architecture exhibits significant performance rather than other techniques.

Ref. [13] presented a novel deep neural network (DNN) for emotional recognition through the multimodal fusion of different modalities such as audio, video and text. The proposed DNN architecture exhibits independent and shared layer performance with the aim of effective representation of each modality through the representation of combination function prediction results that are effective. Experimental analysis of AVEC sentimental analysis is performed on a Wild dataset for evaluation of proposed DNN for achieving higher Concordance Correlation Coefficient (CCC). On the other state-or-art system to perform an early fusion of feature-level modalities as concatenation and late fusion score-level as a weighted average. The proposed DNN provides CCC score of 0.606, 0.534 and 0.170 for the development of partition dataset with the prediction of arousal, valence and liking factors, respectively.

6.3   Proposed Model

Artificial Intelligence (AI) has been widely implemented in a vast range of applications due to its significant functionality. AI has been integrated with several applications such as medical monitoring, multimodal sensory and healthcare measurement it is shown in Figure 6.2. However, AI subjected to several challenges and limitations such as consolidation, ubiquitous information, interpretability, data pre-processing and many others. Hence, resolving these issues related to AI frontier for healthcare applications.

Repetitive Strain Injury (RSI) is a common injury that occurred in humans due to the increased utilization of the computer. The risk of RSI can be minimized by taking pauses and regular exercises. This research focused on monitoring the health of a person working in the computer, in a user-preferred manner person is advised to take a break for a specified period, motoring to exercise execution. Inclusion of vocal and facial signs of pain related to the planning of new break, reports related to the correctness of performed exercise, and provision of feedback related to the impact of exercise on human.

6.3.1   Multimodal Data

From the image, it can be able to observe objects, sounds, texture features, the smell of odours and flavours taste. Modality is defined as something happen or experienced by a person is considered as research problem; this can be characterized by multimodal features when included in several modalities of research. In the case of AI, it offers the progress of things that happen to us; it can be capable of interpretation of such signal multimodal

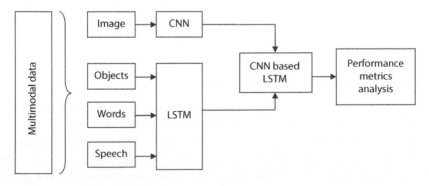

Figure 6.2 Proposed methodology.

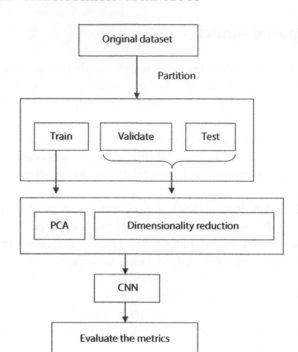

Figure 6.3 Data partition in the network.

together. For example, images are related to tags and explanation of text; here text to include images which provide a clear expression of the main article idea. Different modalities are characterized as consideration of different statistical factors.

Available data can be categorized into three different sets: training, testing and validation (shown in Figure 6.3), also it contains other variants like cross-validation. The network is trained using the training set, in which loss is calculated through forwarding propagation and learner parameters are updated using backpropagation. A validation set is adopted for the evaluation of the training model to process.

6.3.2   Dimensionality Reduction

The process of minimizing the dimension of the feature set is known to be Dimensionality reduction. Dataset of hundred features of the feature set and their array point could create a huge boundary in the space of three dimensions. This reduction of dimension may lead to occupying several columns down to say, twenty else in boundary conversion to a sphere with the space of two dimensions. For training the many numbers of features by using a machine learning model and might get maximized independently on data. It has been trained already along with that this could be overfitted in return, the outputs are also poor for original data and beating the purpose.

Overfitting can be avoided through the main motivation in executing the minimization of dimensionality. When there are minimum features, this proposed model would have only a few assumptions that are made by this model, which is being easier. However, when this is not and dimensionality reduction might have lots of advantages to provide, which are as follows:

1. Minimum data could improve the accuracy of the model.
2. Reduced dimension gives reduced computing; with minimum data, algorithm trains them fastly.
3. Lower data requires a lower storage space.
4. Decreased dimensions access the algorithm utilization that is not fit for the maximized number in dimensions.
5. The repetition of features and noise has been decreased.

6.3.3   Principal Component Analysis

An unsupervised algorithm that generates the linear correlations between initial features is done through Principal component analysis (PCA). Generally, the novel features remain orthogonal that could be uncorrelated. Additionally, their order is ranked by their "explained variance." Nearly all variance in the dataset has been determined by the first principal component (PC1), and then PC2 determines the second most variance, and so on. Karl Pearson was the creator of this method. This method executed on very stages in which the data with maximum dimension space has been mapped with data onto their minimum dimension space; the data variance in minimum dimension space has to be increased. This includes some stages that are as follows:

- The data matrix with covariance has to be constructed.
- Eigenvectors for this matrix has to be calculated.

A higher value of eigenvalues has been generated again with a higher variance fraction of the initial data in correspondence with Eigenvectors.

Therefore only the minimum number of Eigenvectors has remained; also, there occurs some loss in data of this process. Most essentially, the variances remain through retained eigenvectors. Advantages of Dimensionality Reduction

- Data compression is done. Therefore, the storage space is minimized.
- Computation time is reduced.
- Redundant features have been rejected if any.

6.3.4   Reduce the Number of Dimensions

- There are many advantages of Dimensionality reduction from a machine learning point of view.
- This model has some independence, where overfitting is minimized. So this will simply create new data.
- When feature selection is used, the reduction will support essential variables. And its interpretability has been enhanced by this model.
- Many techniques in feature extraction remain unsupervised. Autoencoder or fitted PCA can train the unlabeled data. When many data are unlabeled, this model is used for labeling them without time-consuming and at a lower cost.

6.3.5   CNN

Every desire in a community of deep learning in the present trend is Convolutional neural network (CNN). For most of the varied applications and domains, the CNN model is used, where particularly in the field of image and video processing research. The spatial feature of the image has been captured by CNN. The pixel arrangement has been indicated by spatial features, also the connection between the images. By this method, the object could be detected with higher accuracy, where they can locate the object also their correlation between the objects of an image. Generally, CNN consists of two types of subnetworks (or subnets) such as the decision subnet than the feature extraction subnet.

Various areas in which CNN is used are image and pattern recognition, speech recognition, video analysis, then natural language processing. It has many reasons for CNN to become important. The basic pattern recognition model designs the most important feature extractors [14]. This technique uses the quantity of convolution layer in feature extraction also the fully connected layer where classification is used in strong-minded processes of data training. The network structures that have been enhanced by CNN's might save memory usage and necessity in computation complexity. Also, there must be optimized performance in application, in which their input has a local connection (e.g., speech and image).

In training, the huge necessitate for computation and calculation of CNNs has been carried out using DSP (Digital signal processing), GPU (graphic processing units). Further, the architectures of silicon with efficient throughput, then the characteristic patterns of CNN have been executed; this required low energy for computation. The fact is that processors in advancement, namely the Tensilica Vision P5 DSP are used for Imaging. Then Computer Vision from Cadence possesses nearly standard computation set along with memory resources needed in operating CNNs with maximum optimization.

CNN layers consist of input images. The appropriate features have been extracted by this layer from the trained image. There are 3 Operations. The first step is convolution operation, where the kernel filter 5×5 size has been applied for both the first and second layers. Finally, three layers consist of the filter with size 3×3 for the input. After this process, the nonlinear ReLU function is applied. At the last image, the region has been summarized by the pooling layer, where their outputs have been downsized to the version of the input. When image height is downsized to two for every layer, feature maps have to be added; then, the feature map output has been sized to 32×256.

6.3.6   CNN Layers

In CNN the various layers and many stacking have been done where the complicated architectures have been built for classification problems. Four layers are common mostly: convolution layers, pooling/subsampling layers, nonlinear layers, also fully connected layers.

6.3.6.1   *Convolution Layers*

A neural network of convolution layers varies not by every pixel that is connected with the subsequent layer by their weight and bias. However, the whole image has been divided into small regions with weights along with bias that is applied over it. Where a weight along with bias has been referred with filters else, kernels are the one while convoluting each small area of the input image of yielding the feature maps. They are simple, like features of the filters that have to search for an input image of the convolution layer. This convolution operation is a minimum when a similar filter is transmitted for the whole input image of a single feature that is required for several parameters. The number of filters used, local region size, stride, also padding is convolution layer hyperparameters. Based on input image genre and size, better outputs can be obtained by tuning hyperparameters.

Various features of input have been extracted using this convolution process. Initially, the convolution layer extracts various features that comprise edges, lines, and then corners. Higher-level layers remove higher-level features. 3D convolution process usage in CNN is an example of this method. Size of the input is N × N × D where this has been convoluted by H kernels, individually their every size is k × k × D. Input that has one kernel of Convolution will generate one feature output, then H features have been generated independently with H kernels. From the top-left corner of the input, at a time, only one element is encouraged since the left to right of each. Once upon a time it reached, the top-right corner then the kernel is directed towards downwards for each element also for one element at a time over the kernel can be encouraged since left to right.

The above process has been iterated until kernel attains the bottom-right corner. Consider, in the case when N = 32 and k = 5, 28 distinctive spots are starting left to right and 28 distinctive spots from top to bottom that the kernel can take. In correspondence with this spot, the result of every feature contains 28 × 28 (i.e., (N − k + 1) × (N − k + 1)) components. Where every spot of the kernel in a sliding window process, k × k × D input components and k × k × D, components of the kernel have been multiplied by each component is stored one by one. However, to generate the one component for one feature output, k × k × D multiply-accumulate operations are mandatory.

6.3.6.2   Padding Layer

The process of each layer is generally added from zeros to the input images of avoiding the problem that is mentioned above. Here the sliding window has been considered as the kernel. So the solution we go for is padding zeros on the input array. Rarely, the input image does not have a perfect fit for the filter.

6.3.6.3   Pooling/Subsampling Layers

This layer minimizes the resolution of the extracted features. Here the feature can become strong against noise and distortion. Pooling can be done in two methods: max pooling and average pooling. In the case of both methods, the input has been divided into non-overlapping two-dimensional spaces.

6.3.6.4   Nonlinear Layers

Generally, CNNs and neural networks have been relied on nonlinear triggers specifically, where the signal with unique identification of similar features is available on hidden layers. The various particular operations done by CNNs are rectified linear units (ReLUs) and continuous trigger (nonlinear) functions in executing nonlinear triggering effectively.

6.3.7   ReLU

The function y = max(x,0) has been executed by ReLU, where the size of input and output in this layer are similar. The nonlinear property has been enhanced by the decision operation, also the entire network, which does not affect the field of reception in the convolution layer. Comparatively, CNN uses other nonlinear functions (e.g., sigmoid, hyperbolic tangent, and absolute of hyperbolic tangent), the advantage of a ReLU advantage is that the training of the network is done very earlier than the usual.

This problem can be solved using rectified linear units (ReLU), where they do endure from this tail saturation as much. Consider that the input is smaller than zero, and then the output will be zero for that function. Else, this function will become repetitive of the identity function. Where this is very fast in computing the ReLU function

$$f(x) = \begin{cases} 0, & x < 0 \\ x, & x \geq 0 \end{cases}$$

Further, ReLU is

$$f(x) = \max(0, x)$$

Consider x <0 and 1, if x ≥0, then the derivative is 0; consequently, the error signal does not get weak as it propagates back to the network. However, there is a problem in the negative region (x <0) since the derivative is zero. So the error signal is nullified, while it is good to add a leaky factor of the ReLU unit, also there will be a negative region in the negative slope. And this parameter is fixed or random; here, the parameter is fixed after training the data. They also have max out; however, their weight will be twice as an ordinary ReLU unit.

6.3.7.1　Fully Connected Layers

Generally, this layer is always used as the final CNN layer. This layer is constructed accurately and their way to imply name is: completely related to the output of the preceding layer. The mathematical sum of these layers is calculated by the weight from the feature of the preceding layer. It denotes the accurate combination of variables to estimate the particular result target. The layer characteristic of all the features of the preceding layer has been utilized in evaluation of every component in every output of the feature.

6.3.7.2　Activation Layer

From the input to output, the mappings of complex functions have been implemented where the nonlinearity is produced within the network in this activation layer function. In general, the activation operations used are Rectified Linear Unit (ReLU) [13], softmax, sigmoid and tanh. In this network, ReLU as in $f(x) = max(0,x)$ for all the layers, the activation function has been used in all the layers but not for the final layer of the network. Here the final layer use softmax activation functions as in $\sigma(x) = (1 + e^{-x})^{-1}$. The probability of every target class has been calculated using softmax function; those classes having higher probability has been chosen for the predicted class.

6.3.8　LSTM

LSTM possesses specific CNN architecture, which is being static and powerful for modeling of general-purpose sequence in which distance ranges depend on many previous types of research [15]. LSTM invention is a major for its memory cell that is important plays accumulation in the state of information. The accessed cell is written then cleared through many control gates of self-parameterized. When new input arrives, the data has been stored to the cell while the input gate is activated. And previous cell status $ct - 1$ could be "forgotten" in this process when the other gate ft is switched on. If ct (latest cell output) has been propagated at the final stage ht has been additionally controlled through the output gate ot. The benefit of using cell memory also flows of control information to gates has become gradient and will be trapped within the cell (also known as constant error carousels). It has been conserved from quick vanishing that has a crucial problem with CNN model [16]. The key equations are shown in the equations below, where 'o' denotes the Hadamard product:

$$i_t = \sigma(W_{xi}x_t + W_{hi}h_{t-1} + W_{ci} \, o \, c_{t-1} + b_i)$$

$$f_t = \sigma(W_{xf}x_t + W_{hf}h_{t-1} + W_{cf} \, o \, c_{t-1} + b_f)$$

$$c_t = f_t c_{t-1} + i_t \tanh(W_{xc}x_t + W_{hc}h_{t-1} + b_c)$$

$$O_t = \sigma(W_{xo}x_t + W_{ho}h_{t-1} + W_{co} \, o \, c_t + b_o)$$

$$h_t = O_t \, o \, \tanh(C_t)$$

The weight matrix is denoted as W; the bias vector is represented by b; outputs for the inputs, forget and output gates. It was given by i f, and o correspondingly, cell activations and cell output vector have been denoted by C and h, and sigmoid and tanh are nonlinear activation function. For solving many problems with real-life based on modeling on sequence problems, these models have been applied [17].

The process of forwarding propagation along with the user profiles exploration, formulas mentioned above have pertained, which could be an input for Softmax function [18]. The shilling attacks could be detected through probability when the calculation of processing output from Softmax function. Specifically, error backpropagation has been modified in the training stage of deep neural networks of the proposed algorithm for offsetting updating and iteration of weights until the maximum number of epochs is achieved [19].

6.3.9   Weighted Combination of Networks

The contribution to every ensemble constituent of weight prediction is proportional to the trust and experiments analysis of the element by the dataset holdout is known to be weighted average ensembles. A weighted correlation between subnet has been taken where every input modality can possess learned contribution (Theta) towards the prediction of output. A search process is an Optimization, however rather than sampling space is feasible solutions indiscriminately or comprehensively, the process of searching to utilize any information present that generates in the consecutive stage of the search, namely in the direction of weight set where the error is minimum.

Our optimization problem becomes

$$N_\theta = \sum_{m=1}^{M} \theta_m \left\langle f_{w_1^m, w_2^m, \dots w_{L-1}^m}^m (x_i), W_L^m \right\rangle + b$$

Loss Function after Theta weight is given to each sub-network.

The combining of weights among subnet namely CNN and LSTM along with their predicted output on the basis of subnet weights has been shown by Figure 6.4. Given input has image, speech, text can be combined and predicted with output are referred to as weights.

It is preventing reliance on data restoration and the process of feature extraction that is entirely relied on the advantages of biased perception and human experts. The potential of feature extraction in CNN becomes self-learning and adaptable through their characteristics [20]. For the function of scanning, the entire profile for the user has been attainable for repetitive or counterfeit features of the entire object set that are measured for users by comprising various convolution kernels. Particularly 3-D feature tensor output has been estimated at the convolution network final layer has been expanded on one dimension feature vector in the hybridization feature stage. In specific, the three-dimensional feature tensor output derived from the CNNs' last layer is elaborated into a single one-dimensional feature vector in the stage of feature hybridization. The feature vector for single one-dimensional has been extracted by proposed CNN-LSTM through the inclusion of convolution kernels, which includes inessential information, likelihood information and some blank information, etc.

Moreover, the feature vector has been transmitted into the space of 2-D that has been taken as LSTM input. Separate rows that are correlated by a matrix of the feature have been taken as primary hybridization units. The feature data row is read at every step and the feature matrix is divided as diverged steps of time for identification by using proposed CNN-LSTM.

Therefore individual data has been converted into data sequence by the aforementioned strategy of implementation. For extracting the vital

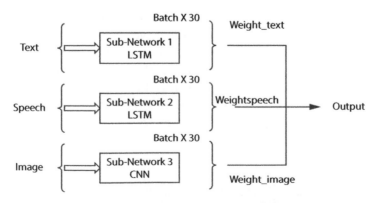

Figure 6.4 The output is predicted after attaching weights to the subnetworks.

dependencies, the LSTM network plays a major role that relied upon the separate feature matrix row. This proposed network also acts as an anchor in filtering and integrating the features that are extracted from the CNN network.

6.4   Experimental Results

The performance analysis shows the CNN based LSTM, which can be calculated by using the metrics.

Figure 6.5 shows the multimodal data performance of the proposed research methodology. Here, consider three types of data called audio, video, and image. The x-axis and y-axis show the data and the values obtained respectively.

When CNN is trained, various metrics such as the accuracy, specificity, sensibility, the negative predictive value (NPV) and then the positive predictive value (PPV), are used for evaluating each dataset, which is test, training, and validation.

6.4.1   Accuracy

Accuracy can evaluate whether a model is being trained correctly and how it may perform generally.

$$\text{Accuracy}(\%) = \frac{TP + TN}{TP + TN + FP + FN}$$

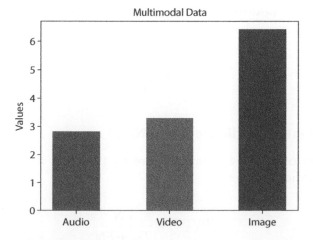

Figure 6.5 Multimodal data performance.

Where TP is true positives, TN is true negatives, then FP and FN is false positives than false negatives, respectively.

6.4.2   Sensibility

It is a measure by the proportion of actual positive cases, which is predicted as positive (or true positive). Sensibility is also called a Recall, which implies that there will be another proportion of actual positive cases, which would get predicted negative as incorrectly (and also called a false negative).

$$\text{Sensibility}(\%) = \frac{TP}{(TP+FN)}$$

6.4.3   Specificity

Specificity is the term defines a proportion of actual negatives that can be predicted as the negative (i.e., true negative), which implies that there will be another proportion of actual negative, that can be positively predicted and could be called as false positives.

$$\text{Specificity}(\%) = \frac{TN}{TN+FN}$$

6.4.4   A Predictive Positive Value (PPV)

The portion of positive instances correctly predicted positive is called Predictive positive value.

$$PPV(\%) = \frac{TP}{TP+FP}$$

6.4.5   Negative Predictive Value (NPV)

The portion of negative instances correctly predicted negative is called negative predictive value.

$$NPV(\%) = \frac{TN}{TN+FN}$$

Table 6.1 shows the proposed work performance. The parameters to be considered for analysis are accuracy, sensibility, specificity, PPV, NPV. The analysis can be carried out through several iterations; the performance may vary.

Figure 6.6 below shows the performance metrics of the research methodology. The blue, green, red lines show the Accuracy, Sensibility, and Specificity. The X-axis is shown in the figure as several iterations and the Y-axis is shown in the figure as time in millisecond. The proposed methodology shows a better result.

Figure 6.7 shows the performance of PPV and NPV in the proposed methodology. The blue and red lines show the PPV and NPV. The proposed methodology shows better results. The x-axis and the y-axis show the number of iterations and then the time in millisecond, respectively.

Table 6.1 Overall proposed work performance.

No. of iteration	Accuracy	Sensibility	Specificity	PPV	NPV
1	4.3	2.4	2.7	3.3	2.4
2	3.4	2.2	2.3	4.5	4.1
3	3.7	1.8	2.1	4.3	3.8
4	4.5	2.7	3.1	4.6	3.7
5	4.7	3.1	3.5	4.8	4.1

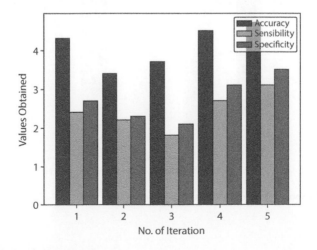

Figure 6.6 Performance metrics.

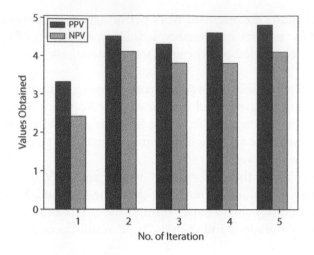

Figure 6.7 PPV and NPV performance.

Figure 6.8 below shows the overall performance of the proposed methodology performance. The performance metrics of each factor achieves better results. The x-axis shows the performance metrics used for the proposed methodology and the y-axis shows the values obtained.

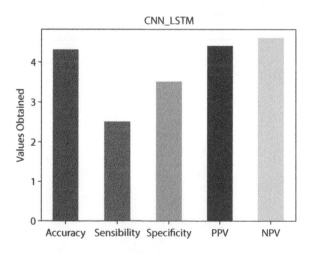

Figure 6.8 Proposed methodology overall performance.

6.5   Conclusion

For sensing of humans, context, and behavior of human has been done using many methods in consideration of work often by constrained environments. It could fail due to noise, fast movements, changes from illumination, etc. and most of the techniques in this area cannot operate quickly to assist this interaction. Based on communication aspects, the Multimodal Human Communication Interaction system has been designed. Nearly all the human modes like Emotions like posture, facial expression, gestures, skin temperature, tone of voice, choice of words, respiration, also clamminess, etc. have been modulated. Combining high-level reasons and low-level feature along with the language processing naturally could give optimized interference of emotion in the context of the Multimodal Human Communication Interaction system. This method is sensitive to human–computer communication that turns to be many extensive study themes of the synthetic intellect study society.

In certain cases, the output for human and issues with identification CNN provides better results of their performance. The output of the proposed method has shown better results more than the predicted results.

6.6   Future Scope

The researchers of computer vision have focused on real-time vision algorithms application for multimodal human–computer interaction. The major area for application has been documented that comprises facial expression, detection of a face, head and body tracking, hand tracking and modeling, gesture recognition, pose extraction, object recognition and activity analysis. This has to be revolutionized to human–computer communication more than the multimodal interfaces.

The challenge of generating prevailing, capable, usual, and persuasive multimodal interactions is a stimulating detection, which could make everyone busy sometimes. The major issues based on privacy have become significant that are combined with multimodal systems that have been turned to capable users could offer the assertion and self-reliance where this system could not breach prospects in terms of security and privacy. Those technologies which can manage the important issues will be implemented in real-time soon.

References

1. Jaimes, A., Sebe, N., Gatica-Perez, D., Human-centered computing: A multimedia perspective, in: *Proceedings of the 14th ACM international conference on Multimedia*, pp. 855–864.

2. Weiss, B., Scheffler, T., Moller, S., Reithinger, N., Describing Multimodal Human-Computer Interaction, in: *Workshop at NordiCHI: Assessing Multimodal Interaction (aMMi)*, pp. 33–36, 2012.

3. Tue Vo, M. and Waibel, A., Multimodal human-computer interaction. In *Proceedings of ISSD'93*, Waseda, 1993.

4. Karpov, A.A. and Yusupov, R.M., Multimodal Interfaces of Human–Computer Interaction. *Her. Russ. Acad. Sci.*, 88, 1, 67–74, 2018.

5. Gaouar, L., Benamar, A., Le Goaer, O., Biennier, F., HCIDL: Human–computer interface description language for multi-target, multimodal, plastic user interfaces. *Future Comput. Inf. J.*, 3, 1, 110–130, 2018.

6. Ming-Hao, Y.A.N.G. and Jian-Hua, T.A.O., Data fusion methods in multimodal human computer dialog. *Virtual Real. Intell. Hardware*, 1, 1, 21–38, 2019.

7. Kardos, C., Kemény, Z., Kovács, A., Pataki, B.E., Váncza, J., Context-dependent multimodal communication in human–robot collaboration. *Procedia CIRP*, 72, 15–20, 2018.

8. Liu, H., Fang, T., Zhou, T., Wang, Y., Wang, L., Deep learning-based multimodal control interface for human–robot collaboration. *Procedia CIRP*, 72, 3–8, 2018.

9. Kumari, P., Mathew, L., Syal, P., Increasing trend of wearables and multimodal interface for human activity monitoring: A review. *Biosens. Bioelectron.*, 90, 298–307, 2017.

10. Goodfellow, I., Bengio, Y., Courville, A., Bengio, Y., *Deep learning* (Vol. 1, No. 2). MIT Press, Cambridge, 2016.

11. Cukurova, M., Kent, C., Luckin, R., Artificial intelligence and multimodal data in the service of human decision-making: A case study in debate tutoring. *Br. J. Educ. Technol.*, 50, 6, 3032–3046, 2019.

12. Bhandari, D., Paul, S., Narayan, A., Multimodal Data Fusion and Prediction of Emotional Dimensions Using Deep Neural Network, in: *Computational Intelligence: Theories, Applications and Future Directions—Volume II*, pp. 215–228, 2017.

13. Ortega, J.D., Senoussaoui, M., Granger, E., Pedersoli, M., Cardinal, P., Koerich, A.L., Multimodal fusion with deep neural networks for audio-video emotion recognition. arXiv preprint arXiv:1907.03196,v1,cs.CV, 2019.

14. Xingjian, S.H.I., Chen, Z., Wang, H., Yeung, D.Y., Wong, W.K., Woo, W.C., Convolutional LSTM network: A machine learning approach for precipitation nowcasting, in: *Advances in Neural Information Processing Systems*, pp. 802–810, 2015.

15. Sutskever, I., Vinyals, O., Le, Q.V., Sequence to sequence learning with neural networks. arXiv preprint arXiv:1409.3215,v3, cs.CL, 2014.

16. Bengio, Y., Goodfellow, I., Courville, A., *Deep learning* (Vol. 1). MIT Press, Massachusetts, USA, 2017.

17. Xu, K., Ba, J., Kiros, R., Courville, A., Salakhutdinov, R., Zemel, R., Bengio, Y., Show, attend and tell: Neural image caption generation with visual attention, in: *ICML*, 2015.

18. Yang, C., Sun, M., Liu, Z., Y. Chang, E., Zhao, X.W., A neural network approach to jointly modeling social networks and mobile trajectories. *ACM Trans. Inf. Syst.*, 35, 4, 36–45, 2017.

19. Mikolov, T., Chen, K., Corrado, G., Dean, J., Efficient estimation of word representations in vector space. arXiv preprint arXiv:1301.3781,V3, cs.CL, 2013.

20. Donahue, J., Anne Hendricks, L., Guadarrama, S., Rohrbach, M., Venugopalan, S., Saenko, K., Darrell, T., Long-term recurrent convolutional networks for visual recognition and description, in: *Proceedings of the 28th IEEE Conference on Computer Vision and Pattern Recognition*, Boston, MA, USA, pp. 2625–2634, 2015.

AI, Planning and Control Algorithms for IoRT Systems

T.R. Thamizhvani*, R.J. Hemalatha, R. Chandrasekaran
and A. Josephin Arockia Dhivya

*Department of Biomedical Engineering, Vels Institute of Science, Technology and
Advanced Studies, Chennai, India*

Abstract

Internet of Things (IoT) is an emerging special field in this advanced digital environment. IoT has been elaborated into different subdivisions, one among them is the Internet of Robotic Things (IoRT). IoRT can be illustrated as the Automatic robotic systems that are designed and developed with the combination of computing, intelligence and Internet of Things (IoT). IoRT related to Artificial intelligence (AI) is mainly described using the characteristics like sensing, actuating, control, planning, perception and cognition. The objective of the technique is to describe an effective integration in robotics and automation. IoRT-based systems perform multiple numbers of actions in a different environment. This technique enacts and helps the robotic systems to communicate and store information. IoRT widens a strong foundation for the implementation of automatic robotic technologies and terminologies with defined architecture. These systems or algorithms also enable real-time functioning and computation. IoRT is used in enormous applications and mechanisms incorporated in various fields like industry, healthcare, entertainment, automatic homecare and military with high security and authentication process. This Internet of Robotic Things (IoRT) operates with high accuracy and sensitivity in the intelligence environment.

Keywords: Artificial intelligence, Internet of Things, robotics systems, IoRT, control algorithms

Corresponding author: thamizhvani.se@velsuniv.ac.in

R. Anandan, G. Suseendran, S. Balamurugan, Ashish Mishra and D. Balaganesh (eds.) Human Communication Technology: Internet of Robotic Things and Ubiquitous Computing, (163–192) © 2022 Scrivener Publishing LLC

7.1   Introduction

Internet of Robotic Things (IoRT) is an emerging field related to the Internet of Things (IoT) and robotic communities. The vision of IoRT is to bind the sensors and devices with robotic technologies. Internet of Things (IoT) establishes an effective platform to interface objects and devices to the Internet for advanced machine communication and data transfer using networking protocols. Internet of Things is rapidly increasing in use day by day in the society creating a technological advancement. Based on these advancements and efficient solutions, the Internet of Things is used in different fields like Agriculture, Machinery, Healthcare, Nanosystems, Robotics and communication systems. Internet of Things (IoT) in general illustrates the challenges in the development of different fields.

Internet of Robotic Things (IoRT) is one new concept associated with IoT technology that enables robotics for various systems and technologies. Robotics technology paves a different dimension to the machines that are developed for labor and intensive work. Robotics provides a sense of the high level of technological environment for the devices, systems and machines. Artificial intelligence and different learning algorithms empower the systems to operate and decide autonomously. Decision making and machine learning functions are scientific features that play an important role in designing the automatic functional and programmable systems [1].

In general, robotic technologies are interfaced with the network protocols to perform functional activities. This technology deploys an environment based on the development of a robotic network. Based on the IEEE Society of Robotics and Automation's Technical Committee, network robots are defined as robotic technology that is connected through communication network either wired or wireless. Networked robotic technologies can be categorized as teleoperated robots for remote access and multi-robot system that exchanges the data among a group of smart environments. These networked robots incorporated with IoT technology frame the new systems or things described to be the Internet of Robotic Things (IoRT) [2].

Internet of Robotic Things can be defined as the infrastructure of the information society that enacts robotics services for connecting the robotic things depending on the existing, evolving, operational and communication technologies. These technologies are shared services that benefit the robotic systems through different technological operations like computation, storage, communication and other modern network systems. Robotic mobility in IoRT enhances the data transfer through cloud technology and computing platforms, this reduces the duration and constrain of operation. On the Internet of Robotic Things (IoRT), artificial intelligence, swarm technologies, learning and control are developed and programmed to enact the autonomous working systems and machines.

Internet of Robotics Things defines new challenges and the need of the society in the communication of multiple systems through automatic technology. Robotic Things possess effective qualities like effective cooperation, coordination, deployment, information exchange, safety and security. The primary focus of IoRT is to support information services through sensing, tracking and monitoring. Other than this, IoRT also contributes to improving the production, communication and automatic systems. With these special technological features, IoRT claims for the design of a system with a combination of results from different communities. Internet of Robotics Things is a framework that emphasizes the integrating functioning of the small environment and autonomous devices.

Integration of intelligent dynamic systems and communication technology is performed through robots in IoT applications. Internet of Robotic Things is described to be the next phase of advancement in the field of IoT applications used in different fields. IoRT advanced technological levels of Internet of Things which helps in interfacing robotics with systems like wireless communication and sensing, cloud computation, analysis and transfer of data, guidance support, security control, protection, continuous monitoring and network protocols. The major criteria's of IoRT are determined to be autonomous decisional levels, manipulation, multiple control agents, access control, planning, mapping, swarm, navigation and robotic system interaction with human from robot technology.

The concept of the Internet of Robotic Things (IoRT) mainly depends on the integration of robotics and the Internet of Things. These concepts can be described as

- Define and study the characteristics of robotics and identify the unique parts or objects of the Internet of Things (IoT).
- Realize the main functions of robotics such as motion, manipulation, autonomous and intelligence that are emphasized using IoT technologies and similarly, IoT is equipped by robotic systems (intellectual devices).
- Describe the nature of the integration of IoT and robotics that enhances sensing, intelligence and mapping that can be defined for various applications.

Integration of cognitive computing and Artificial intelligence (AI) is defined to be add-on values to the new advancements in the technologies of IoRT applied in different smart environments. Internet of Robotic Things is an emerging technology which is heterogeneous with different levels of functions. These levels of function include sensing, actuating, planning, control, perception and cognition. Different systems and applications completely enact the Internet of Robotic Things. Internet of Robotics Things functions is based on artificial intelligence technology. Planning the integration of the systems and technology using Artificial Intelligence and control algorithms also enables robotic things more efficient. Control algorithms used in IoRT technology specifically illustrates the features such as decision making, intelligence, interpretation, communication and cognition. Artificial Intelligence, planning and control algorithms of Internet of Robotic Things (IoRT) is described over-explaining the need for the technological advancements in the smart environment [3].

Internet of Things (IoT) along with technological innovations and architectures helps in operating huge number of sensors and actuators forming unique structural objects or Things for interaction and data transfer through communication network protocols with the Internet. These objects or things defined as Internet of Robotic Things (IoRT) are illustrated as the opportunistic sector in the upcoming environment. Advancements and innovations in this field of interaction between the robotic systems and Internet of Things (IoT) will improve the standard of the smart environment. The range of the technology exceeds to a greater extent increasing the size and necessary of the personal computers as well as the communication systems marketing. This also enrages the development of the specific technology stated to be the Internet.

With these initiatives based on Internet of Things (IoT) concentrates on the use of simple connected systems which is designed on the board for advancements in the technological process of the system. In certain cases of design, sensors in the passive state are also used in managing, monitoring, optimizing and processing the functional activities. These sensors possess a high impact on technological innovation. Many studies and researches illustrate the aspect of transformation to connectivity and communication with smart devices and tools of technology.

Internet of Robotic Things (IoRT) brings up a new concept in which the device intelligence monitors the events or tasks. These devices help in merging the sensor data, obtained from the different sources using local and distributed sources of intelligence that describes the best course action performing operations for controlling or manipulating things or objects in the physical environment. In other cases, the application also extends for physically moving devices or things throughout the world. The technologies analyze and study the different Internet of Things (IoT) applications and robotic systems intersection for the design and development of advanced robotic systems and abilities. The potential of the robotic systems led to absolute novel applications which extend in developing the business economy and investments. IoRT is a paradigm that establishes the automatic robotic systems with the Internet of Things applications interfaced with the sensors and embedded smart things in the devices used in the environment. The novel applications of devices or systems are enabled in all the different sectors in which the collaboration of robotic technology and the Internet of Things can be defined [4].

Examples of application of IoRT such as precise living, assistive farming, goods dispatching and producing, certain logistic analytics, maintaining the infrastructure of buildings, recycling of waste materials, mapping through different locations, repairing, inspecting and nuclear assisting facilities. Internet of Robotic Things (IoRT) converges the systems with appropriate functional robotics systems such as networking robots, ecological robots or techniques defined with cloud computing robotics. These systematic technologies have described different types of methodologies, tools and approaches that describe the potential of the IoT to remain distinct. The integrated system is designed for the collaboration of robotic technologies with IoT applications that are limited based on domain-specific descriptive analysis. IoRT provides solutions to different fundamental resource-based challenges and scientific approaches that also possess certain complexity and conflicts. Heterogeneous systems are deeply concerned with security, privacy and safety. Automatic designs and devices mainly depend on the activity, decisions and motions performed within the dynamic smart environment [5].

7.2 General Architecture of IoRT

Internet of Robotic Things (IoRT) is mainly interfacing robotics and Internet of Things applications to impart solutions to the smart environment. The architecture of the Internet of Robotic Things can be configured using basic five different layers. Further researches in IoRT describes different sub-layers and levels in architecture. Internet of Things enables robotic technology to be flexible during designing and implementation. Basic layers of the architecture of IoRT illustrated as hardware, network, internet, infrastructure and application.

7.2.1   Hardware Layer

Hardware layer is the lower layer that possesses key robotic things like sensors, devices and equipment. Real-time components coverup this layer that delivers information or data over to the next layer.

7.2.2   Network Layer

This is the second lower layer of the IoRT architecture. Different network technologies and connection services are available for information transfer. Range of network systems is designed for the robotic things to conduct the data and transmit to the layers. Network systems such as cellular connectivity, near field communication, medium-range microwave access, ZigBee and so on [6].

7.2.3   Internet Layer

This layer of the Internet is responsible for the complete communication of the information in the robotic things or objects. In IoRT, communication protocols in IoT are added upon to the layer. These protocols improve the energy, constraint and information processing systems. In general, these protocols helps in performing certain functional activities like real-time interaction, packet networks, local automation and real-time embedded systems.

7.2.4   Infrastructure Layer

This the important layer or part of the architecture that interrogates IoT with Robotic Things. The infrastructure layer is configured using five different levels or platform supports stated and illustrated to be

  ➤ M2M2A cloud platform support—Machine to Machine to Actuator (M2M2A) is another platform support to identify the machine system to perform multiple operations and exchange of information. This platform also enables human intervention through automatic control algorithms. M2M2A system enrages solutions to robotic technologies through a combination of real and virtual systems in a smart environment.
  ➤ Robotic Platform Support—Robotic platform support indulges with different service technologies that include an

operating system, robot service network, resource interface and open-source protocol networking.

➢ Big Data Services—Big data services are keenly responsible for high value-added services like optimization, analysis, predicting and descriptive statistics.

➢ IoT Business Cloud Services—IoT Business Cloud platform manifest the business-oriented services for Internet of Robotic Things (IoRT). Different business service models and transaction activities are described for the developed functional activities of the Robotic Things. This support platform helps IoRT effectively in business interactions and better decision making.

➢ IoT Cloud Robotics Infrastructure—The platform support is determined and designed for cloud computational services. These assist robotic things and IoT for various applications. Cloud assistive Internet of Robotic Things incorporate services like manipulating, correcting, object or voice recognizing and mapping.

The platform supports in the infrastructure layer enacts services that mainly integrates the Internet of Things application and services with Robotic Things or objects for automatic decision-making smart environment.

7.2.5   Application Layer

The application layer is demonstrated as the top layer of the architecture. This layer illustrates the experience of the user with application samples performing robotics. Robotic systems are associated with the Internet of Things, this ensures active involvement of the systems in finding solutions to numerous problems.

The characteristics of the architecture can be defined to be composability, context awareness, virtual diversification, extensibility, interoperability, dynamic and self-adaptive and Geo-Distribution and unique network access. Internet of Robotic Things (IoRT) architecture made proved to be efficient in describing solutions to the application fields. IoRT also possesses research limitations such as computational problem, optimization, ethical and security issues. Automatic system and decision making configure a complex system, computation and optimization are little difficult as compared to previous researches. Internet of Robotic Things (IoRT) technology applies to various fields such as industries, healthcare, technological innovations and smart environments [7, 8].

7.3   Artificial Intelligence in IoRT Systems

Internet of Robotic Things (IoRT) systems is designed and interfaced to create solutions for complex problems in a technological environment. The architecture of IoRT enacts various functions and support platform for the diverse fields of technology. Artificial Intelligence and different technologies play an important role in developing advanced robotic technologies (IoRT). Artificial Intelligence ensures robotics things or objects to be effectively automatic with decision making features [9].

7.3.1   Technologies of Robotic Things

Technologies involved in the design of robotic things (IoRT) are sensors and actuators, communication systems, augmented and virtual reality technologies, recognition systems and security frameworks. These technologies incorporate to form the interlink between robotic things and IoT applications.

Sensors and actuators are described to be the basic line for the design of the Internet of Robotic Things. These basic features are responsible for real-time application and detection. The important functional activities of this technological factor are human–robot and robotic interaction services. Communication technologies functions effectively to interface real-time computational systems. These communication systems help in the transfer of information and services. This also enables a special feature of a function called virtualisation through computing edges. Different communication standards like Bluetooth, Wi-Fi, LTE, 3G and 4G used by IoRT for communication.

Augmented and virtual reality are features that are globally advanced in function among various sectors like industry, healthcare, production, designing, visualization and education. These two reality features can be described as inverse reflections. Virtual reality is stated as the digital formation of real-time environment and Augmented reality that provides the elements of virtualization to the real environment. These technologies of reality are mainly used for the process of interaction, mapping and learning. Augmented reality paves a foundation for cognitively effective robots whose design is complex in a real environment. Augmented and virtual reality adds on the features of vision, movement and control mechanism to the Robotic systems on the Internet of Robotic Things (IoRT).

Control systems and recognition of voice have a strong place in the emerging field of Internet of Robotic Things (IoRT). There is a significant need for the interaction of the robotic systems to design an efficient framework. This design enacts human beings and robotic systems to perform collaboratively in digital settings. External tools and objects are used for the human–robot interaction that designs the IoRT to function appropriate eliminating the disturbance in the real world. The algorithms describing the quality and recognition terms of the system must be of high level that decreases the different sorts of noises. IoRT in specific are highly designed and equipped multi-channel robotic systems.

Machine learning another technology enabling the interaction process, Internet of Things (IoT) has adapted many forms of learning process or algorithms that are defined under the machine or deep learning. The term machine learning can be described as a state obtained by the evolution of Artificial intelligence with computer science through recognition of patterns and computation. This learning process initiates development models for prediction and learning of the systems through data samples. Analysis and prediction through machine learning can overcome human vision of learning in future. Using machine learning, IoRT systems are made adaptable for the contextual changes, real-time computational complexity and experience. IoRT learning process possesses a high challenge to the development service. The development of Robotic Things using machine learning has to be effective in handling the resources in the network protocols.

Security and safety are the ultimate aims of efficient Internet of Robotic Things design that provides highly cooperative sensors, networks and some robotic techniques. End to end security of the system is necessary to interface the robotics and IoT applications. Transmission of information or data through these networks and robotic designs are to be highly secure. IoRT designed for data acquisition using robotic systems in various fields are to be secured at a high rate. These technological systems are defined to be highly authenticated for transmission of data and interlink of the Robotic Things. Internet of Robotic Things generally operates and correlated with these technological services for the active functioning of the robotic things or objects with IoT applications. Artificial intelligence being the main topic to be discussed because this enables a high-level interactive process between robotic things and IoT applications.

7.3.2   Artificial Intelligence in IoRT

Artificial intelligence is an advanced and emerging technology that enacts with the help of the Internet. This technology of intelligence produces an effect on the day to day life. Artificial intelligence can be stated as the formation of intelligence similar to human beings which can perform functions like learning, reasoning, planning, perceiving and processing languages. The artificial intelligence technologies provide intense social and economic opportunities. This also introduces ethical, social and economic issues. Artificial intelligence performs based on Internet Technology. The Internet system analyzes and understands the opportunities and issues collaborated with artificial intelligence. Key factors associated with Artificial intelligence are stated to the principles and featured recommendations involved in designing and developing appropriate decisions.

The main focus of AI is a learning approach called machine learning that established a force for advanced developments in technology. Learning algorithms are implemented to define tasks derived from the data samples. Machine learning is mainly used for the design of many products and services but possesses Internet trust factors when focused on users. Specific features are to be noted while performing and developing artificial intelligence that involves transparency issues, reliability, security, social and economic factors and ethical considerations. Complex challenges are posed over AI that describes data quality issues, safety implications and interpretability lack in decision making [10].

Based on the evaluation of the recommendations and challenges of different fields, the Internet Society designed a certain set of rules and regulations for the use of the Internet. The society also identifies that challenges related to artificial intelligence are critical when collaborated with the Internet. The important key technology behind Artificial intelligence is the Internet which is the mainstream for the development that incorporates the network interaction. The policies in the section of the society illustrate the key factors for framing, planning, designing and developing products and services using artificial intelligence.

Machine learning has a strong impact when artificial intelligence is defined. Artificial intelligence can be stated as a hypothetical condition and there are not specific to a domain. Artificial intelligence framed through machine learning algorithms is categorised in the field of computer science. Algorithms can be stated as the instructions sequence used as a solution for a problem. The learning algorithms defined for the machines are constructed for systems designed for new recommendations and challenges. These algorithms defined in machine learning form the basic building block for the digital environment. Computer systems and technology describe a large amount of information into products or services through different policies and principles. The concept of machine learning to be elaborated and studied more effectively for the efficient outcome of the various application of artificial intelligence especially when interlinked with the Internet of Robotic Things (IoRT). The approach provides the systems to function with a set of instructions through learning algorithms. With artificial intelligence, the new advanced and complex computational tasks do not require any additional manual programing. This technology includes the recognition services provided for individuals impairment.

The main criteria for machine learning are training data samples through learning algorithms. These algorithms based on the data or information trained can describe a new set of rules, forming an algorithm that is described to be a machine learning model. The learning algorithm defined can be used to train different data samples that lead to the formation of new models in machine learning. In general, a simple machine learning model can be used for both translation and prediction process. The strength of the machine learning process is the inference determining the new algorithms or instruction sets from the data samples used in creating new models after training. The role of data or samples is considered to be more important that is when the number of data or samples increases, the learning process is effectively increasing the training epochs. The advancements in artificial intelligence (AI) is mainly not because of the radical functioning of the algorithms in the learning process but due to the huge number of samples or data defined through the Internet.

Machine learning functions based on the application of mixed techniques for training and learning process. In general, the basic machine learning algorithms can be defined into three which can be appropriately described for Artificial Intelligence. Machine learning algorithms are defined below as

Supervised learning—Algorithm of learning is provided with the required output and defined input to identify the object or sample.

Unsupervised learning—Algorithm of learning with undefined input and describe the objects or samples using the patterns of the input.

Reinforcement learning—Algorithm of learning that creates a dynamic environment providing feedback through some damnation or recompense process.

Machine learning defines a high-level contribution state or process for the planning and designing the control algorithms for artificial intelligence. Artificial intelligence in robotics has improved the standard of robotic technologies and used in various application in different fields. Robotic with AI makes a sense smart environment in every field. The design and development of the complete robotic system depend on the control algorithms and learning process of Artificial intelligence.

Artificial intelligence on the Internet of Robotic Things enables the functioning of the robotic systems automatically and performs the decisions effectively. These robotic technologies function similar to a human being with defined rules and regulations. Transfer of data or information is an additional feature in robotic things that enables real-time interaction and interlinking.

Artificial intelligence grasped the attraction of many fields during recent years. Technologies accessed through Internet paved way for Artificial Intelligence to move into a life closer. Even though AI has impacts related to ethical, social and economic factors, this is used in all different fields for automatic functioning and learning algorithms define the standard of the system. Big Data and the Internet of Things (IoT) has expanded a great impact on the increased design of applications and services using Artificial Intelligence. Applications associated with AI are used in different industries. For example, in the healthcare sector, Artificial Intelligence is used for diagnosis and treatment that describes the feature decision making. Robotic applications based on IoRT are also enabled through processes like Telesurgery, virtual surgery and so on. With the Internet, Artificial intelligence has an effective engine for the growth of the economy.

Traditionally Artificial intelligence can be referred to as a system that resembles humans in intelligence. The system with Artificial Intelligence can perform different processes like learning, reasoning, planning, perceiving or processing natural language or style. Robotic technologies define a smart environment which is made effective through computer technology. Artificial intelligence has an important part in increasing the production rate of the industries rather than comforting the individuals. These robotic technologies with artificial intelligence are defined to be both qualitative and quantitative. Cost-effective technologies are introduced to the human world through these devices or systems through network and communication technologies like the Internet.

Artificial intelligence enables a special vision to the robotic systems through computer technology. This technology enables processes of reactions through navigation, sensing and calculation. Training of the robotic systems are performed through machine learning, simply to say, tasks performed by the robots are learned from the individual activities and functions. This task of learning is also a part of programming and artificial intelligence. Internet of Robotic Things (IoRT) can be started with the contribution of robotics, artificial intelligence, programming and IoT applications. Different artificial intelligence systems and learning processes are used for controlling the robotic systems. In IoRT, the robotic systems with AI collaborate with the Internet of Things applications. Applications of Internet of Robotic Things (IoRT) are diverse increasing the economy and advancements in the smart environment.

Artificial intelligence functions into different types of robotic systems and technologies. Weak Artificial Intelligence creates a simulating system for human interaction. The robotic technologies perform only the retrieval response based on the command that is the device functions based on the user's command. Strong Artificial Intelligence functions on its own, doesn't require any governance. These devices are designed and programmed to perform the activities appropriately on their own. These kinds of devices are applied in many applications in different fields. Humanoid robots which describe the environment and enables human interaction. Robotics surgeons also designed with AI and perform surgical activities without any human interaction. Specialized Artificial Intelligence in which the robotic systems function with special tasks. This is confined to limited and specialised activities. Industrial robots are specially designed for the function of the tasks repeatedly.

Artificial Intelligence is hard to be described. The father of Artificial Intelligence, John McCarthy states that Artificial Intelligence (AI) is the machines of intelligence designed using science and engineering. Artificial Intelligence (AI) describes the potential of robotics in the information processing and production outcome which is alike to the functions or activities performed by humans. Artificial Intelligence is an emerging technology that describes advancements in the field of the smart environment. These technologies design devices or robotic systems with adequate intelligence.

The intelligence of the machine can be illustrated as the capability of the devices or robotic systems to analyze any task or activities similar to human. Robots performing the activities of humans and interacting with a human has to learn the human process and activities. Training and learning performed through machine learning with minimal human interaction. Artificial Intelligence design models that are used for studying the human physical activities and performance of the human.

Artificial Intelligence plays a role in exploring the earth and space. The society makes use of these technologies to study hard the functional activities of different things. These technologies also lead to innovations and inventions for the development and advancement of the society and environment. Artificial intelligence enables the automatic functioning of the robotic systems through training and learning process. The ability of

Artificial intelligence is describing the models from the accuracy and loss rate of training the samples or data.

Robotic systems with Artificial intelligence can be designed using neural networks and machine learning. Prediction of human activities through failures of the training and testing process is performed using artificial neural networks. Compared to ANN's, machine learning described being more efficient. Both processes of algorithms have different applications in different fields. These robotic systems with AI perform enhances the collaborative functions and actions within the stipulated time. Artificial intelligence helps in coordinating the hybrid components and control algorithms in robotic systems to overcome the obstacles created in the path during movements. Robots interface with automatically with the environment for effective prediction, decision-making learning and processing [11].

In general, IoT applications doesn't involve intelligence or artificial intelligence technology. Internet of Robotic Things (IoRT) is based on the concept of intelligence which is interlinked with abilities such as reasoning, decision making, negotiation and processing. Integration of IoT and robotic systems is the recent advancement increasing the standard of the smart environment designed in society. Internet of Things (IoT) based robotic systems and human beings interact and communicate through fundamental activities. The targeted group of applications is performed using these IoT based robots. The network and communication systems also play a major role in the functioning of the robotic systems.

Network security in the computing and complex environment is enhanced using these IoT based robotic systems. The network protocols like TCP/IP, HTTP, LAN, WAN and some more techniques along with software embedding are converged in for the active development of the IoT based robotic systems. The robotic systems and Internet of Things (IoT) interaction being developed with these application-based network protocols. The applications based on IoRT (Internet of Robotic Things) defines a new level of IoT based applications. The global community gets benefited through the implementation of artificial intelligence in IoRT. The connectivity throughout the world is described with these techniques and advancements in the field of robotic systems and IoT.

Artificial neural networks and machine learning algorithms help in maintaining the standard between the required network protocol and coverage. The desired qualifies and secured service of communication is contributed with the help of these technologies on the Internet of Robotic Things (IoRT). Robotic technologies as a service and Internet of Things are interlinked with the help of computing environment especially through cloud computing techniques. The research in the field of Internet of Robotic Things concentrates on the design, development, architecture, interaction and activities of the robotic systems. The vehicles also make use of smart robots which functions all operations like storage, artificial intelligence, processing, training and satisfy by performing the operations defined by the user.

The Internet of Robotic Things (IoRT) based systems and technologies are user-friendly. In vehicles, effective design is illustrated and developed to communicate through network systems for the identification and determination of a traffic information system within the travel path of the user. In future, the things surrounding the environment will be associated with the computer systems through Internet sources, smart devices, mobile phones and a large sum of different types of the fully and semi-automated robotic systems. Further, Internet of Robotic Things (IoRT) transforms the devices or objects into intelligent sources which perform an interaction with one another and also with human beings.

To perform these activities, the systems or devices have to perceive the transfer of data or samples to actuators and receive information from the sensor. This is the functional activity of the robotic systems on the Internet of Robotic Things. The system designed with these components can communicate data of information processed using artificial intelligence algorithms between the terminal poles or states and cloud computing systems. In this case of interactive robotic systems with the Internet of Things (IoT) are considered to be an integrating technology for data transfer and communication. Intelligent robotic things operate actively to develop applications that are more comfortable and applicable to different fields in society.

The researches and work done in this area of Internet of Robotic Things illustrate that interaction and interlinking of the robotic things and IoT through intelligence algorithms still have a high impact region of development that establishes work strategy. These technologies also contribute to the operational activities of many machines used in daily life. Control algorithms and intelligence sector in the robotic systems are majorly defined using learning and training algorithms of machine learning and at times based on the application neural networks can be used. The control mechanism of robotic systems enacted with the help of machine learning can be maintained effectively by possessing the robots in the network area or zone. The quality of service and control can be stated as future developments in intelligent robotic systems.

The architecture of the Internet of Robotic Things (IoRT) collaborated with artificial intelligence and control algorithms frame the quality of service and control of the heterogeneous robotic systems. The cloud enhancement through UAV's and development increase the ability of the data transfer among the intelligent technologies or systems. This mainly contributes to enlarging the coverage area of the robotic systems for long-distance transmission. Artificial intelligence can be used for analyzing and processing Big data and performs functions with different services for the betterment of different scientific fields.

UAVs can be illustrated as the new technology used in intelligence services for communication protocols. These protocols are adaptable in different environments. The design, development and processing of the robotic systems with the features of Internet of Things and UAV's have to be configured appropriately to resolve the problems faced in managing the operational activities of the system. The impairment of 5th Generation technologies has to be performed for the complete working of the robotic systems. One of the major components or parameters of robotic systems on the Internet of Robotic Things (IoRT) is power consumption. For the environment to be evergreen, power consumption to be reduced but robotic systems need an energy source. Therefore, an effective technique for the reduction of energy resources through intelligence is developed that paves the path for a green environment. Prediction techniques and intelligence-based functioning results in a reduction of data transfer, the function which drags of power in a larger range. This reduces the power consumption and extends the lifetime of the battery resources used in the robotic systems.

Artificial Intelligence creates a growing environment in the Internet of Things applications and developments. The companies and industries elaborate provision of investments in recent years for the design of systems that enhance the integration of artificial intelligence (AI) and the Internet of Things (IoT). Major intellectual industries and processing associations related to the development of the Internet of Things (IoT) platform recently contribute their investigations to the systems integrated with artificial intelligence like machine learning-based analytic systems. Artificial intelligence's context defines a potential that quickly accepts the data structure.

Machine learning algorithms are specially used for artificial intelligence technology that possesses the potential to detect and define the patterns or changes in an automatic manner from the data samples. These data samples are produced and acquired from smart devices and sensors. The information or data samples can be of any substance or physiological parameter like temperature, humidity, quality of air and so on.

Machine learning techniques when compared with traditional intelligence tools are more effective than predicts the results with 20 times prior with high accuracy. Artificial intelligence technologies are used in different applications such as recognition of speech and computer vision. These technologies help to deprive the data which needs assistance and analysis of human. Artificial intelligence in the Internet of Things (IoT) helps the industries to protect from unplanned downtime, increase in operations accuracy, analytics of services, products and describes the management of risk. The potential of artificial Intelligence interfaced with robotic systems can be enabled for applications in the field of healthcare. Clinical benefits are established using the Internet of Robotic Things (IoRT).

For example advancements in the Internet of Robotic Things (IoRT) describe the applications of network robots. The specialized application of these artificial intelligence-based system of robots are used in different processing fields. Network robots are structured and mainly contributed to the field of rescue and search operations to locate different environments where human's entry is impossible. In this field, generally, the rescue team has to communicate and transfer information to the robotic systems and also should receive the details from the robots about the situation of the environment. Through Artificial Intelligence, the communication and interaction between the rescue and robotic systems are effectively increased indicating the level of security and danger in the environment.

Communication systems and technology is also necessary for inter-linking the robotic systems and human beings. This system enables the functioning of the tasks easily. The robotic navigation algorithm described being highly effective in analyzing and guiding the robotic systems under the Radiofrequency Identification (RFID) tag. These robotic systems function through RFID tags with the help of intelligent processing algorithms. These algorithms are described through the signal phase difference acquired by the tag and received through antennas of RFID reader communication system designed and fixed to the robotic systems.

Later, with advancements in the communication technology, unmanned aerial vehicle (UAV) technology is applied in the artificial intelligence-based robotic systems for long-range and high speed of communication. This is described to be an intelligence routing systematic approach that helps in determining the broadcast service delivery. The structural layer and infrastructure of the system are segregated based on the state of hierarchy. The upper layer is defined for the broadcast units and the lower layer is described for the ground level wireless network technology. With this analysis, the basic two factors related to the design of the robotic systems are area coverage and the connectivity of the network system.

Artificial intelligence based on the UAV systems with constraints for network connectivity. Protocols for performance are designed for the intelligence-based aerial vehicle. These systems and vehicles evaluation using these protocols to design and develop a highly precise and accurate aerial vehicle system. The study related to these robotic technologies and communication system also illustrates that the intelligence-based transmission protocol defined TCP describes an excellent growth and advancement in the network output completely. This protocol system of intelligence also defines a low energy consuming system. The technologies coordinated with the Internet of Robotic things can be used effectively through these communication systems.

Internet of Robotic Things (IoRT) makes use of artificial intelligence along with the interaction of robotic systems and Internet of Things (IoT). Artificial Intelligence subsides the control algorithms and helps in functional operations of the systems either in robotic technologies or IoT applications. These technologies elaborate a path of advancements and autonomous infrastructure for the systems designed and developed for the different sector in various fields. Control algorithms and planning depends on the artificial intelligence algorithms framed for the particular system. Artificial intelligence is an advanced concept that resembles the functions of the human for better production and economy.

7.4   Control Algorithms and Procedures for IoRT Systems

Internet of Robotic Things (IoRT) can be stated as the design mechanism for devices in which the interlinking and integration of robotic technologies with IoT applications is enabled. With the modern environment, the ability of the development of robotic technologies has increased to a greater extent. These technological innovations elaborate on the active functioning and operations of the robots with IoT applications. Artificial intelligence plays an important role in the field of designing, planning, controlling and executing. Real-world issues and problems are overcome through advancements in different sectors, one among that is the interaction of robotic technologies and the Internet of Things (IoT). Technologies using IoRT establish a random, automatic, unstructured and smart environments for the various applications in different fields [6, 7].

The challenges that are novel in applications of robotic technologies and IoT define concepts illustrating the robotic control algorithms and movement planning. These concepts or technological support systems must possess an automatic environment, flexible robotic mechanism and execution process. The decision making and execution strategy of the Internet of Robotic Things (IoRT) enable scope for artificial intelligence to increase the work efficiency and standard of resembling the human even through the communication process. The Internet enables the transfer and reception of data samples from the sensors or devices to different locations. Control algorithms for analyzing different techniques are used to control planning and motivate the device for movements that acquire a movement at a high level. These levels of mechanism help in the adaption of the feedback obtained from the sensors or actuators used for depriving the data samples.

Algorithms for planning the systems and controlling the functioning mechanism of the robotic technologies that interact with the Internet of Things are deprived. With these planning and control algorithms, the standard of application of the device is enabled. Algorithms are defined for the controlling of the sensor or actuator for deriving and transferring data samples. Control mechanisms are described for the functional operations of the robotic systems and also for the Internet of Things (IoT) applications. Artificial intelligence algorithms are also defined for the operation of Internet of Robotic Things (IoRT) in different fields. IoRT is the combination and integration of robotic systems, IoT applications and Artificial intelligence. Sensors and actuators are designed in which a way that control mechanism depends on the acquisition and transmission of data samples. The mechanism associated with the environment in real-time for the derivation of data. The data samples in certain cases are obtained as a source of input to the control algorithms.

In general, control of a system can be stated as a sequence of organized operations in which the functional activities and operations are defined through a loop or set of loops. For the Internet of Robotic Things (IoRT), accessing of the sensed information is enabled by appropriately designing the interface. To perform the necessary functional operations of the robotic technology, the interface has to be developed with efficient control mechanism and secure infrastructure to enact the proper functioning of the sequence of control algorithms defined. The loop defined for the control of the systems can be virtually mapped from different applications to services that are from cloud computing to network protocols through infrastructure. If this technological development is possible, then the virtualization of the Internet of things can be illustrated through automatic principles.

Planning is a potential offered through the organization of logical conditions. This ability helps in coordination of the components of an internal platform for the satisfaction of requests of services and assurance of levels of quality. These qualities applied for the services throughout the life cycle in the Internet of Things (IoT). The logical conditions help in the alignment of the services with the required resources, handling of information or data and entities of knowledge and specific for platform representation. Based on these logical conditions, planning of the technology depends on the automatic engine flow of the work to initiate the functionality of the service based on the request. The logical feature maintained depends on the user-defined algorithms and representation of the information or resources that help in facilitating the service process.

Planning and control algorithms on the Internet of Robotic Things (IoRT) are described which defines the capability of the systems developed for the functional operations with different applications [2, 3]. The basic level and application-oriented or driven algorithms are used in the field of Internet of Robotic Things (IoRT) for the promotion of planning the design and controlling the robotic technologies. The design and development of the system involve the planning and control algorithms for effective execution. The mechanism proposed has to be user-friendly and enables efficient functioning and high-performance level. The algorithms for controlling the devices or systems are designed with the features applicable to the sector. The basic objectives can be illustrated as

- Sensing technology and considering the modalities using planning and control algorithms
- Developing representative technological sources and movement operations that can absorb the signals obtained as feedback from the systems.
- Movements and the operations of the system are confined with restrictions that include various mathematical processing such as kinematics, static and dynamic applications.
- Defining and describing the characteristic features of the environment's dynamic nature
- Designing and applying control and planning mechanism for the systems with hybrid characteristics especially in the case of artificial intelligence. Artificial intelligence applied through various machine learning and Neural network algorithms for the functioning of the robotic systems similar to the human through training, testing and processing.
- Analysing the complex issues in applying to process the algorithms to control the activities
- Communication interface is applied to the system for the data transfer and receiving which significantly helps in the learning of the environment far better compared to the traditional methods. Networking protocols with advanced

features are configured with IoRT systems to enable communication

- Encouragement of the use of the applications in various fields and sectors that help in the significant processing and implementation of the planning and control algorithms.

Internet of Robotic Things (IoRT) functions through the sensors and actuators, artificial intelligence, computing technologies, network protocols and controlling mechanisms. Control algorithms used in robotic technologies depend on different mathematical models. Direct and inverse kinematic are basic structural control models used for the end-effector motion of the robotic technologies or systems. These models are defined to have standardized work operations that are described for every robotic technology. These specific techniques illustrate solutions of the nonlinear equation based on algebraic models that contribute no analytic issues.

7.4.1   Adaptation of IoRT Technologies

The Internet of Things platforms don't enable efficient support for the adaptation. Adaptation of the algorithms and technology specified for every application in the particular sector depends on the designing, developing and programming domain's knowledge. Later, these technologies are adapted in a different application that needs smooth functioning in predicting activity and resembling human functions. On the Internet of Robotic Things, the algorithms designed and developed possess an adaptation strategy built within the application that is they are application-oriented. The only method for adaptation of the IoRT system in the fields of application is through environmental knowledge and the prior experience in the deployment platform used for the design of the interface. Adaptation of the interface based on the control and planning algorithms is required for the effective performance of the technological advancements. Adaptation of the system on the Internet of Robotic Things (IoRT) is mandatory for the functioning of the application. Design of the system to be functionally active through these adaptation process.

Smart devices or objects depending on sensors are compared with robotic things that operate in multiple functions. For example, mobile can be defined as the state of a large number of shared robotic systems performing various operational activities. These functional operations are limited through a range of communication by the sensors with restrictions in their functions. The flexibility needs to be configured in the design of robotic technologies especially with the help of software systems and communication protocols. Example of this kind of non-mobile robotic systems are many, one among them is present in the manufacturing sector of the agile industry. In future, robotic technologies are defined with algorithms and control mechanisms adaptable for the flexibility for all the operational activities not confined to a simple programmed function.

Multiple applications are defined with the help of a single sensor and its data, this feature leads to the system to a complex computing technique. Actuators along with the sensors have to be configured to perform the activities in a highly precise manner. Adaptation to systematic technology has to be developed within the IoRT systems for feasible functioning. Different types of actuator based technological robotic systems are designed throughout for their computational and productional applications on the Internet of Robotic Things (IoRT).

- Competitive robotic technologies don't share the information and need a reservation or locking system for active functioning
- Cooperative robotic technologies in which the robots perform two functions at a time without sequentially executing them.
- Adversarial robotic technologies that are maximum in the need of the actuator's opposite and end effects

Applications of Internet of Robotic Things (IoRT) with the robotic technologies interface mainly function in the environment where large scale manufacturing and production is performed. These technological innovations are open to various dimensional activities in different sectors. Dimensional operations involve expectations of human and their preferences, execution of activities, different types of non-connected Things that may be possibly present in the physical space. Adaptation of technologies related to the Internet of Things is a difficult process even though configured and deployed with actuators for a single purpose. These technologies possess constraints related to the platform options even with the existence of support to the system. On the Internet of Robotic Things (IoRT), continuous adaptation is necessary since the robots deployed and designed function as an open-source with various operational actuators in the smart environment. Robotic technologies always maintain a standard degree of automation. These robotics have instructions that are in precise and of high level, they are not systematically suitable for different approaches centralized for adaptation. Thus, there is a requirement for the distribution of the settings and functionality among the actuators of different robotic things used in the effective performance of Internet of Robotic Things.

Machine learning algorithms play a major role in planning and controlling the functioning of robotic technologies. Artificial intelligence-based robotics depends on machine learning and neural network techniques. Machine learning defines a clear path for the operational features of the system. Internet of Things makes use of the able techniques of machine learning, including these features to the term called Things. Machine learning described as the service distributor for the Internet of Things. The requirements of the advanced system make a contour for machine learning realizing the need for these technologies. Heterogenous systems generate a need for these learning algorithms for the data samples derived from the sensor on the Internet of Robotic Things (IoRT). The challenges of different applications in various fields are described and designed using these machine learning algorithms. There is interlinking technological features and characteristics between Internet of Things and Machine learning, an adaptation of the systems for providing solutions to the Robotic systems is generally based on the changing environment and personalisation of the device specifically for a function. These interlinking also enables applications of Internet of Robotic Things in production, management of processes, organization of service components to the infrastructure of the system. These architectural design of IoRT learns from the settings system and the experience.

Machine learning service embeds intelligence along with the distribution of the service on every node of the technology, Internet of Robotic Things (IoRT). This also distributes even in the network edge for the spread of the technology. This technology with artificial intelligence can perform an early fusion of data samples from the sensor and prediction for the development of information to high level from the raw samples of data produced by the sensor. These sensors or devices are responsible for the predictions in the applications. The predictions of the system are aggregated to form the input of the other model of learning designed on a different node of a network. These nodes of the network further make predictions and perform the operations of data samples fusion. Thus, designing a new network of intelligence for the learning models that continues to act as an aggregation of the sensed data samples continuously for the design and development of new intelligence-based machine learning models. These models of learning train in to form predictions used for the application of the technology in various sectors of the smart environment.

7.4.2   Multi-Robotic Technologies

Internet of Robotic Things (IoRT) applied in the field of Multi-purpose robotic technologies are used in wide applications in different sectors. Multi robotic technology is designed in such a way that consists of multiple or heterogeneous numbers of operational functions in the environment. These technology enables in the implementation of simple sensing or actuating technologies or even during complex issues. In these multi robotic technological systems, interoperable and convertible items or objects are used to define the characteristics. The robotic technology can be characterized into different forms such as a group of robots, swarm robots, collective functioning robots and cooperative robots. Different exchangeable things are utilized in various areas that analyze multi robotic technologies. These technological things vary in the range of robotic systems applied that are together configured under a single big branch multi robotic systems [12].

In general, robotic technological are described and studied under multiswarm and cooperation sequences that are used for improving the performance of the system. The advancements in technological applications introduce new operational activities of the robotic technology and distribution of services at remote locations. These applications of robotics also have a high fault tolerance rate. Drawbacks of the multiple robotic systems also coexist which includes overhead functionality, robotic interference, increased cost, the control mechanism for different applications and the movement coordination.

Coordination also plays an important when compared with adaptation. Coordination in the robotic technologies refers to the collaboration of the operational functions with the algorithms and performing the algorithms at a high accuracy rate. Based on this systemic coordination, two groups of dimensional robotic technologies are categorized

- Robotic technology based on Coordination dimension, this refers to the coordinating techniques analyzed and designed in the Multirobot systems. This also involves concepts of cooperative, knowledgeable, coordinative and organisational technology
- Another one is the dimension of system (System dimension), this involves the characteristics of the system that helps in controlling and maintain the coordination. These technologies possess the applications deeply concerned with the mechanisms related to the communication and network protocols, the composition of the system either

heterogeneous or homogenous, architecture and infrastructure of the system and size of the team for the performance
of the task.

On the Internet of Robotic Things (IoRT), interface the robotics and network protocols with Artificial Intelligence. These technologies are precisely
made fit and appropriate for the need of the networking protocols specially
framed and deployed for the systematic and dimensional functioning of
the operations of the Multi-robot systems. These technologies resemble
human activities coming up with natural solutions to all the problems [13].

Internet of Robotic Things (IoRT) specifically performs based on the
planning and control algorithms designed for the interaction of the robotic
systems and technology with artificial intelligence and communication
network protocols. These technologies are applied to many sectors for
active participation and decision making based on learning and control
mechanisms. Therefore, planning and control mechanisms frame a technological advancement in the Internet of Robotic Things applications and
help ineffective performance.

7.5   Application of IoRT in Different Fields

Internet of Robotic Things (IoRT) is applied for various operations performed in different sectors. These robotic systems are increasingly simple
and automatic in their design. The IoRT systems are more effective and
significant as they possess solutions to issues that are based on artificial
intelligence. This is mainly performed to interface the robotics system
with deployed Internet of Things applications. The robotics systems are
employed in most of the production and manufacturing industries and fac-
tories for the automatic functioning that resembles the human behaviour
in reasoning and decision making. Service-oriented robotic technologies
are applied in the personal and healthcare environment. These technologies are a highly emerging field in these applications and service-based
sectors [14, 15].

Integration of the Internet of Things (IoT) technology and robotic systems provide solutions to all issues at a significant rate and applied in the
environment for increased economy and investments. Researches performed so far in the field of Internet of Robotic Things illustrate various
applications and assistive services provided for the welfare and development of the society and environment. The advancements in these robotic
technologies have increased in rate for the few decades in different

demographical sectors. Healthy lifecycle maintenance and achievement of the well-being using these IoRT technologies improvise the conditions and standards of living. The durability and convergence of the sensor and actuators are made efficient for the operational functioning of the system in different applications.

Applications of service robots include diagnosis and detection of abnormalities at an early stage and help in the development of the executive programmable options to prevent operational risks. Therefore, these robotic devices and technologies can be used in physical activities introducing smart home environment and nutrition chart development based on the personal requirements of the user [16]. These are few such examples in which the system is used for the applications. Another category of robotic systems stated as personal well-being management robots that help in an individual's living alone or being separate from their families. The robotic technologies are designed in such a way that they observe the physiological parameters and involve in the transmission of the data samples to the physician in real-time for analyzing the physical state and nature of the individual. These robots also study the emotional and psychological conditions of the user and interact with them based on the results defined through their analysis process.

One of the applications of the Internet of Robotic Things (IoRT) can be defined as the maintenance of machines and equipment's in the industries and companies of different fields. Maintenance of prediction and prevention is enabled in the system through the application of an integrated source of the robotic technology and Internet of Things (IoT) [17]. This maintenance procedure or process for the systems by the integration device is of high cost even though they are required at hectic situations. Prevention maintenance which performs small tasks to make the machine efficient for the certain life span of service. These data samples for prevention are configured and observed by real-time robotic technologies. The conditions necessary for the maintenance of the machine is scheduled prior through learning and control mechanisms. Multiple sources from the exterior environment affect the operational functioning of the machine that includes weather leading to temperature change. These temperature changes obstruct the effective functioning of the machine. Therefore, to maintain the machines in winter and summer season of environment, systems responsible for maintaining the conditions of the machine-like heaters and HVAC are used respectively.

Internet of Robotic Things (IoRT) extends the service of maintenance to detect the failures and inappropriate functioning of the machine. The main aim of the IoRT technology with regards to the machine maintenance is to decrease and analyse the failures and its after consequences. This also analyzes the system collaborated with the machine under maintenance. IoRT technology analyzes the failure rate and prevents the machine from any damage and also schedules plans for the proper maintenance of the machine for the effective operation. Robotic systems in general are developed to conserve the equipment that offers reliable potential by specifying the parts that are to be replaced. These robotic systems have a warning system designed for the prior alarm if anything fails. The scheduled maintenance is performed for regular periods for effective functioning. Few examples of the functional activity performed through maintenance of the machine with the Internet of Robotic Things include operations like cleaning, lubricating the parts, exchange of oil at regular intervals, replacement of used parts if necessary and tuning of the system for performing the functions. Calibration is also performed with the help of these IoRT technologies.

Automatic function of the manufacturing and production industry is the upcoming advancements in various fields. In most of the companies, the industrial robotic technology runs automatically for various functions related to electronic, metal and machinery parts. Cost for designing robots reduce but the deployment of algorithms and control mechanism in the robots for performing a particular operation in the environment is of the high cost. Researchers are studying the robotic functions and are processing with an aim of increased artificial intelligence that enables the robots to perform the task on its own just through instruction what to do not how to do.

Automatic systems are not confined to industries, home appliance and personal robotic technologies are also available in this smart environment. Robots designed for personal activities generally provide services to individuals in their household applications. Personal robotic technology also performs activities like entertainment, educational services, assistance, telepresence and some personal activities [18]. The environments in domestic life are integrated with these technological for performing personal activities. Telepresence term defines the functions that bring in a combination of the communication systems with the perception of the robotic technologies potential. These robots help in the interaction of the humans in locations far away. These robots also help in monitoring the patient's post-surgery or elder individuals for analysing any abnormalities in their physiological functions. Robotic systems are also used as a tool for educational services that develop the knowledge and skills of the students.

Internet of Robotic Things (IoRT) is used in the various application even in the field of healthcare. These technological innovations act as a supportive tool for the governance of elderly people. The robots are designed with long duration and efficient flexible nature that help the care-takers to perform the activities effectively. Automatic smart robotic technologies assist people in monitoring their health conditions. Diagnosis and decision-making features of the robotic systems are more effectively used in the field of healthcare. Internet of Robotic technologies is used in various applications based on artificial intelligence that is designed and deployed using planning and control algorithms. With these algorithms, the operational functioning, coordination and adaptation of the IoRT technologies are enabled. Thus, applying the Internet of Robotic Things (IoRT) for various application in different sectors that are emerging advancements

References

1. Nayyar, A., Singh Batth, R., Nagpal, A., Internet of Robotic Things: Driving Intelligent Robotics of Future—Concept, Architecture, Applications and Technologies, in: *Proceedings: 4th International Conference on Computing Sciences*, pp. 151–160, 2018.
2. Pratim Ray, P., Internet of Robotic Things: Concept, Technologies, and Challenges. *IEEE Access*, 4, 9489–9500, 2016.
3. Kara, D. and Carlaw, S., *The Internet of Robotic Things*, Technical Report, ABI Research, New York, 2014.
4. Razafimandimby, C., Loscri, V., Vegni, A.M., Towards Efficient Deployment in Internet of Robotic Things, in: *Integration, Interconnection, and Interoperability of IoT Systems. Internet of Things (Technology, Communications and Computing)*, R. Gravina, C. Palau, M. Manso, A. Liotta, G. Fortino, (Eds.), pp. 21–37, Springer, Cham, 2018.
5. Sanfeliu, A., Hagita, N., Saffiotti, A., Network robot systems. *Rob. Auton. Syst.*, 56, 10, 793–797, 2008.
6. Vermesan, O., Broring, A., Tragos, E., Serrano, M., Bacciu, D., Chessa, S., Gallicchio, C., Micheli, A., Dragone, M., Saffiotti, A., Simoens, P., Cavallo, F., Bahr, R., Internet of Robotic Things—Converging Sensing/Actuating, Hyper connectivity, Artificial Intelligence and IoT Platforms, in: *Cognitive Hyperconnected Digital Transformation: Internet of Things Intelligence Evolution*, O. Vermesan and J. Bacquet (Eds.), pp. 97–155, River Publishers, Denmark, 2017.
7. Simoens, P., Dragone, M., Saffiotti, A., The Internet of Robotic Things: A review of concept, added value and applications. *Int. J. Adv. Rob. Syst.*, 15, 1, 1–11, January-February 2018, https://doi.org/10.1177/1729881418759424.
8. Afanasyev, *et al.*, Towards the Internet of Robotic Things: Analysis, Architecture, Components and Challenges, in: *2019 12th International*

Conference on Developments in eSystems Engineering (DeSE), Kazan, Russia, pp. 3–8, 2019.

9. Nishio, S., Kamei, K., Hagita, N., Ubiquitous network robot platform for realizing integrated robotic applications. *Intell. Auton. Syst.*, 12, 477–484, 2013.

10. Alsamhi, S.H., Ma, O., Ansari, M.S., Convergence of Machine Learning and Robotics Communication in Collaborative Assembly: Mobility, Connectivity and Future Perspectives. *J. Intell. Robot. Syst.*, 98, 541–566, 2019, https://doi.org/10.1007/s10846-019-01079-x.

11. Akshay, P., Tabassum, N., Fathima, S., Ahmed, I., Artificial Neural Network and IoT Based Scheme in Internet of Robotic Things. *Perspect. Commun. Embedded-Syst. Signal-Process. (PiCES)—An Int. J.*, 2, 6, 126–130, 2016.

12. Parker, L.E., Multiple mobile robot systems, in: *Springer Handbook of Robotics*, pp. 921–941, Springer, Berlin, Heidelberg, 2008.

13. Arai, T., Pagello, E., Parker, L.E., Editorial: Advances in multi-robot systems. *IEEE Trans. Rob. Autom.*, 18, 5, 655–661, 2002.

14. Rahouma, K.H., Aly, R.H.M., Hamed, H.F., Challenges and Solutions of Using the Social Internet of Things in Healthcare and Medical Solutions—A Survey, in: *Toward Social Internet of Things (SIoT): Enabling Technologies, Architectures and Applications. Studies in Computational Intelligence*, vol. 846, A. Hassanien, R. Bhatnagar, N. Khalifa, M. Taha, (Eds.), pp. 13–30, Springer, Cham, 2020.

15. Nayyar, A., Puri, V., Nguyen, N.G., Le, D.N., Smart Surveillance Robot for Real-Time Monitoring and Control System in Environment and Industrial Applications, in: *Information Systems Design and Intelligent Applications*, pp. 229–243, Springer, Singapore, 2018.

16. Brizzi, P. *et al.*, Bringing the Internet of Things along the manufacturing line: A case study in controlling industrial robot and monitoring energy consumption remotely, in: *2013 IEEE 18th Conference on Emerging Technologies & Factory Automation (ETFA)*, Cagliari, pp. 1–8, 2013.

17. Gusmeroli, S., Piccione, S., Rotondi, D., IoT@Work automation middleware system design and architecture. *Proceedings of 2012 IEEE 17th International Conference on Emerging Technologies & Factory Automation (ETFA 2012)*, Krakow, pp. 1–8, 2012.

18. De Silva, V., Roche, J., Shi, X., Kondoz, A., IoT Driven Ambient Intelligence Architecture for Indoor Intelligent Mobility. *2018 IEEE 16th Intl Conf on Dependable, Autonomic and Secure Computing, 16th Intl Conf on Pervasive Intelligence and Computing, 4th Intl Conf on Big Data Intelligence and Computing and Cyber Science and Technology Congress(DASC/PiCom/DataCom/CyberSciTech)*, Athens, pp. 451–456, 2018.

Conference on Development of Systems Engineering (DeSE), Paris, France, pp. 1–6, 2016.

9. Nelson S., Kunze K., Singla N., Observations on hand–robot platform for realizing tabletop robotic applications, IEEE, 2018, pp. 477–484, 2017.

10. Abashidi S.H., M. O., Asghar N.S., Conversational Machine Learning and Robotic Communication in Collaborative Assembly, Mobility, Connections and Energy Perspectives, J. Intell. Robot. Syst., vol. 541–566, 2019, https://doi.org/10.1007/s10846-019-01012-2.

11. Aldana F., Talavanan N., Achmad S., Ahmed F., A Hybrid Neural Network Model for Robot Scheme in the Era of Robotic Things, European Computer Embedded, Cyber-Physical (PPCPS), pp. 1, 2, 3, 4, 17–26, 2016.

12. Parker L.E., Multiple mobile robot systems, in Springer Handbook of Robotics, pp. 921–941, Springer Berlin, Heidelberg, 2008.

13. Arai T., Pagello E., Parker L.E., editorial, Advances in multi-robot systems, IEEE Trans. Robot. Autom., 18, 5, 655–661, 2002.

14. Ranaraja K.D., Ali, K.H.M., Eshwari, H.S., Challenges and Solutions of Using the Social Internet of Things in Healthcare and Medical Solutions—A Survey, in: Integral Social and Internet of Things (SIoT) Enabling Technologies, Applications and Implications, Computational Intelligence and Its Applications, R. Chatterjee, N. Ghosanya, Nok Sula M. Tak. (eds.) (eds.) [2], 28, Springer, Cham, 2020.

15. Nguyen A., Tran V., Nguyen H.G.T.L. (eds), Smart Surveillance Robot for Real-Time Monitoring and Control System in Environments and Industrial Applications, in: Information System Design and Intelligent Applications, pp. 239–253, Springer, Singapore, 2018.

16. Grassi F. et al., Bringing the internet of things along the manufacturing line: A case study in controlling industrial robot and monitoring energy consumption remotely, in: 2013 IEEE 18th Conference on Emerging Technologies & Factory Automation (ETFA), Cagliari, pp. 1–8, 2013.

Enhancements in Communication Protocols That Powered IoRT

T. Anusha* and M. Pushpalatha

Department of Computer Science and Engineering, SRM Institute of Science and Technology, Chennai, India

Abstract

We are living in a world where human interaction with machines is a norm and this trend is exploding to deliver enriching and ubiquitous human experiences. Such innovative solutions are not only realized by new technologies but also by fusing different classes of existing technologies. An alliance between Robotics technology and Internet of Things (IoT) has resulted in the Internet of Robotic Things (IoRT), that has brought forth fabulous possibilities for localized autonomous solutions. Robotic devices can get precise environmental data from all sort of Things around it, abstract information from the data and deliver a real-time ubiquitous service. A helper robot taking instruction to get a package delivery can communicate with door sensors and surveillance cameras to get the coordinates and size of the package and use that effectively for navigation and pickup. It is likely to help both the Robotics and IoT by extending their capabilities to new levels. This chapter gives a brief introduction of IoRT communication requirements and presents a layered architecture for communication in a generic IoRT system. The array of functionalities for each layer is described in detail along with the list of available communication protocols. There is an attempt to highlight the open-source platforms that help create a fully functioning IoRT system. The chapter revolves around the enhancements that are made to the communication technologies which facilitated IoRT. The applicability to various fields like healthcare, Industry 4.0, food processing, precision farming is also discussed.

Keywords: IoRT, communication architecture, protocols, robotics, IoT, interoperability

---

Corresponding author: aa5293@srmist.edu.in

R. Anandan, G. Suseendran, S. Balamurugan, Ashish Mishra and D. Balaganesh (eds.) Human Communication Technology: Internet of Robotic Things and Ubiquitous Computing, (193–218) © 2022 Scrivener Publishing LLC

8.1   Introduction

Robots are capable of performing a task independently and intelligently. However, Robots working in tandem with IoT devices could achieve more, when they collaborate and deliver new classes of automated applications. We already have Internet of Things (IoT), where the physical environment is digitally mapped, constantly sensed and also acted upon with the help of sensors and actuators. Robotics is also an accomplished field of technology used for automating complex tasks, navigating different terrains and to make them respond spontaneously and intelligently to situations. So it is a natural progression to combine the best of both worlds and arrive at the Internet of Robotic Things. From IoT perspective, a robotic device can be looked upon as a powerful processing and actuating device that could also move around. From Robotics perspective, IoT can be seen as a way to augment its sensing abilities and to extend its navigation, manipulation and servicing capabilities [1–3]. Hence in an IoRT system, Robot(s) joins forces with Things and intelligently work on a collective objective. This is made possible with the availability of many efficient wireless communication technologies that can bring Robots and the Internet of Things together.

There are some unique requirements for establishing communication between robotic devices and IoT. The most important features that are required are high reliability, low end to end delay, interoperability between heterogeneous devices and mobility support in real-time. This chapter discusses communication technologies in three different categories of networks namely wireless personal area networks (WPAN), wireless local area network (WLAN) and wireless wide area networks (WWAN) that could provide these requirements and could tie up an IoRT system. Each category is equipped with many standards and is continuously improving with more research happening in every field. The type of wireless networking technology to be used is decided by their communication range, power requirements, delay sensitivity, cost and other functional requirements. This chapter will explore the new amendments to standards and also recent research findings that could benefit IoRT systems. As these technologies provide ease of integration and mobility, efficient and collaborative ubiquitous services are about to be real.

8.2   IoRT Communication Architecture

Central to the IoRT, is a set of devices that are autonomous or semi-autonomous Robots and Things that are geographically dispersed interconnected sensors and actuators. Both the Robots and the sensor/actuator devices would be considered as nodes in the IoRT network. The different types of nodes could be running in diverse platforms and use different wireless technology for connectivity. For these individual nodes to collaborate seamlessly, they have to understand each other and also communicate reliably and quickly.

Robust communication is essential between the nodes to provide autonomous robotic solutions that gauge the environment using diverse IoT devices. The technology for communication has improved over the years by the focused attempt of many standard bodies, industries, researchers and academicians. The figure (Figure 8.1) given above, presents the communication architecture of a generic IoRT system. The hardware layer has diverse embedded devices like robots, sensors of varied types and actuators. This bottom layer will provide all the sensing, local

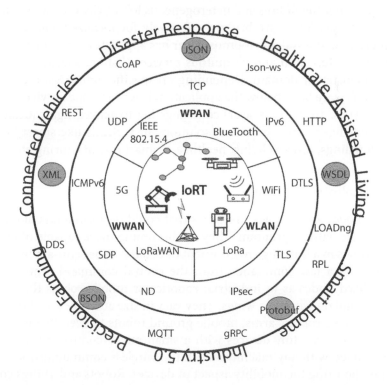

Figure 8.1 Communication architecture of IoRT.

processing and actuating capabilities. The adjacent layer is the link layer that establishes wireless links between the various nodes. All the individual nodes can directly send signals to each other with the help of these standards that define the common radio frequency bands, modulation, channel hopping, medium access control techniques etc. The successive network connectivity layer has many protocols to provide common ways to transmit data, form routes between nodes, discover services in the network, detect neighbors etc. The most important protocol in this layer is the Ipv6 protocol that is specially tweaked to suit low power devices and provides seamless connectivity to the Internet. Also, these constrained devices can form a mesh with a routing protocol that provides paths between them through multi-hops. These lower layers can be different for different IoRT systems.

The upper layer in the architecture is the communication layer, consisting of diverse communication protocols that provide a common platform for sharing information. They bring data exchange capabilities between heterogeneous devices and networks. This is the most important layer as it brings together the Robots and heterogeneous IoT devices. Various vendor devices and platforms are bridged effectively for localized and dynamic collaboration. The system's topmost layer has application-specific software for human interaction and ubiquitous services that are specific to a particular industry or domain. Depending on specific industries, there may be a middleware layer below the application layer for cloud services or big data analytics. The various layers come together to deliver highly localized, deeply intelligent and ubiquitous solutions in verticals like smart home, smart buildings, assisted living, healthcare, smart manufacturing etc.

8.2.1   Robots and Things

Robotic nodes are complex machines that could perform a task automatically in line with its program. They are becoming more capable of taking apt decisions in a learning environment or could also be semi-autonomous and pick up a few commands from the central command center. They can be fixed nodes as in industrial robotics or mobile robots that could move around on wheels or wings. They vary in size and functionality, from tiny bots, fixed robotic arms, mobile ground robots to even flying robots. Sensor devices are tiny devices with a small micro-controller that could be embedded with any machine. With the wireless communication technologies boosting the mobility aspect of devices, Robots and Things could move around and still be connected as a network. Robots interacting with IoT devices by using information and communication technology opens up the application horizon of Robotics in areas like smart manufacturing, construction, mining, personal care, education, smart homes, smart buildings etc.

8.2.2   Wireless Link Layer

Diverse nodes in IoRT can be linked through the wireless standards like IEEE 802.15.4, IEEE 802.11 or cellular networks. In the next section, we would see about the evolutions in each of these standards for facilitating the IoRT paradigm. The medium access control (MAC) protocols of this layer provide interference-free, low power, low latency link establishment for embedded devices. Already IoT is matured enough and has loT of protocols in place for seamless digitization of any environment. Robots could act as an intelligent edge computing device using those powerful microprocessors available within them. Microprocessors are equipped with a complete network stack and can link to IoT devices directly. System on chips (SoC) is advanced so much that a single chip can have multiple radio modules too. In one end, there are sensor devices that are battery-powered in a mesh and on another end, there are Robots with high bandwidth requirements. When different networks are involved, both the classes of devices cannot directly communicate and has to rely on the communication layer for interactions. The evolution of technology is bridging the gap by providing protocols with low latency, high reliability and mobility support.

8.2.3   Networking Layer

The networking protocols provide capabilities like packet assembly, delivery, error recovery, security and routing for IoRT. The Internet coverage in low power devices is extended by making the nodes form of a mesh-like structure by using the multi-hop technique. 6LowPAN is an important work that brought IPv6 addressing and Internet connectivity to resource constraint sensor devices. This has eliminated the need for translation protocols in edges so that the communication is faster. It can cater to the ever-increasing address demand for millions of devices and allows them to be connected from any part of the world. Mobility is another important aspect supported by networking protocols. With Wi-Fi and cellular networks providing seamless mobility, there are many protocols in wireless personal area networks that offer mobility support for low sensor devices as well. There are protocols like TLS or DTLS that provide security for data that is transmitted through a wireless link.

8.2.4   Communication Layer

IoRT is a fusion of two branches of technology which evolved in parallel but not together with a common purpose. This message exchange layer is another important aspect of IoRT that ties these two and bring about a cohesive co-existence. This layer provides interoperability support between various classes of nodes and networks. Thanks to them, data exchange can happen between the nodes in real-time and can be supported by many different platforms. Standard protocols like Message Queuing Telemetry Transport (MQTT), Extensible Messaging and Presence Protocol (XMPP), Data Distribution Service (DDS), Constrained Application Protocol (CoAP), support information exchange between any types of device in a network and between different networks. These protocols have evolved to lightweight versions for suiting the low power nodes in IoT. This thoroughly boosts the breed of a real heterogeneous network. The focus on this layer is to reduce end to end communication delay so that devices from different locations can work together in real-time. This is even more critical for a IoRT system which relies on fail-safe and quicker communication between sensors and the robotic devices.

8.2.5   Application Layer

The last layer is customizable for every user application be it industrial, commercial or home appliances. In this application layer, users run customized software programs to achieve the purpose of the IoRT system. It could be applications in the cloud or edge computing or could be a standalone one. They would provide an intelligent robotic service after taking inputs from all the IoT devices. They could help in assisted living, smart building, smart homes, smart industries, construction sites, disaster recovery, healthcare, precision farming etc. Warehouse automation of large retailers is a classic example and robotics taking up IoT as its eyes and ears could leverage large potential for its applicability.

8.3   Bridging Robotics and IoT

Broadly, IoRT could have two different scenarios for communication between Robots and IoT devices. These devices could be part of the same wireless network and can directly communicate with each other. The robotic devices have microcontrollers in them [4] and a radio module could be serially connected to it. The radio module can be used for directly communicating with a network of IoT devices. In such cases, communication could rely on networking protocols like UDP or TCP without the need for upper-layer protocols. Additionally, a routing protocol may be required in case of a mesh network, for guiding the data to the robotic device. This scenario will work well for a low range IoRT application like a smart home, factory or building. The end to end delay is also minimal so that it could drive delay-sensitive applications in healthcare.

On the other hand, robotic devices and IoT devices could be part of different wireless networks. Then they would need data exchange protocols from the communication layer. A border router running a message exchange protocol's the broker/server is required to connect, both the endpoints. So in the first case, robotic devices act as nodes in the IoT network and the latter case, they act as a consumer of the IoT network. Figure 8.2 shows the different layers in the communication architecture that comes together for both the cases. For seamless interaction, both the scenarios need to have high reliability, low end to end delay and support for mobility in case of a mobile robot.

New wireless standards and protocols are being developed for providing low power and highly reliable communication between IoRT nodes. QoS support is specified in the standards for delay-sensitive applications. At the cost of other parameters (like high power), a low end to end delay communication can be achieved. WLAN and WWAN protocols support medium to high mobility between the nodes and already has the required mechanisms in place as part of the standard itself. Though WPAN standards do not specify mobility support, many protocol extensions are proposed by researchers for supporting limited mobility support. The further sections discuss the new technologies in wireless standards that would bridge Robotics and IoT.

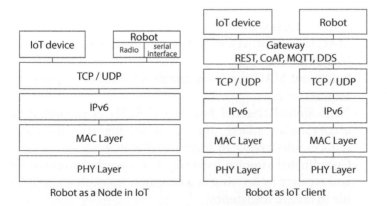

Figure 8.2 Robot as a node in IoT vs robot as a client of IoT.

8.4   Robot as a Node in IoT

Several wireless standards have evolved that tweaked the original standards to make it most suitable for low power device to device communication [5]. These IoT devices are tiny objects having a small micro-controller for controlling the sensors and/or actuators. They can sense their surroundings using multiple sensors, digitizes that data, communicate via radio and may be capable of performing small computations. The new wireless networking standards could make such diverse devices to communicate with each other and also to connect them to the Internet. Let's see some of the prominent technologies and platforms that support this constrained device to devise communication.

8.4.1   Enhancements in Low Power WPANs

The IEEE 802.15.4 standard, based on radio communications, provides a very short-range wireless connectivity to tiny devices that operate on batteries or solar power. The medium access control techniques were designed to keep the radio off most of the time to keep the operations low power. It supports low data rates but these are sufficient enough for these sensor devices whose payload was expected to below. New wireless standards have been developed to provide high reliability and energy efficiency while keeping the end to end delay, low.

8.4.1.1   Enhancements in IEEE 802.15.4

The improvements are made in physical (PHY) and MAC layer [6] of this standard to improve the efficiency of radio frequency (RF) transmissions in low power devices.

1. IEEE 802.15.4e standard
   - MAC layer improvements that are aimed to cater to industrial IoT.
   - 5 different MAC choices available for different application requirements.
   - Time slotted channel hopping (TSCH) is supported to accommodate a large number of simultaneous links and reduces interference to improve reliability.
   - Coordinated sampled listening (CSL) synchronizes sender and receiver by arriving at a common transmission schedule to reduce the latency.

- CSL consumes energy to send wake-up frames but provides a good low latency operation suitable for real-time applications.
2. IEEE 802.15.4q standard
   - Two PHY layer additions that provide ultra-low power consumptions and operations.
   - Combination of 2 different Frequency-shift Keying (FSK) techniques, one for header and other for payload, ensures lower collision rates and retransmission rates.
   - Utilizing shorter preamble to boost low energy consumption.

So these new improvements aim to reduce interference and improve reliability in the lossy wireless transmissions.

8.4.1.2   Enhancements in Bluetooth

Bluetooth was standardized to offer short-range wireless connectivity with minimum configuration for devices where one device acts as a transmitter and several others as receivers. It uses radio communications with frequency hopping spread spectrum to make it interference tolerant. There are the latest developments to this standard to support device to devise communication for IoRT applications.

1. Bluetooth LE Low Energy operations are suitable for battery-operated devices.
   - Broadcast messages are delivered through advertisement channels.
   - Adopts shorter packet transmission for keeping the power requirements low.
   - Adaptive frequency hopping technique allows dynamic adjustments for lowering interference.
   - Communication is always routed through the central node.
2. Bluetooth Mesh [7]
   - Designed for peer to peer communications in networked Bluetooth nodes.
   - Provisional protocol inducts a node into the mesh by pairing.
   - Creates a mesh-like network where nodes act as relays to forward the messages.
   - Uses flooding style data dissemination but controlled by reducing the time for the packet to be alive after every hop.

- Caches messages in the network to prevent nodes from relaying older messages.
- Sleepy devices can attach to high-end nodes for message storage and forwarding.
- Uses network keys and application keys to secure the link.
3. IPv6 over Bluetooth LE from ROLL working group, IETF
    - RFC7668 [8] designed adaptations required for supporting IPv6 over BLE.
    - 6LoWPAN is implemented on top of the logical link control and adaptation layer.
    - The central node becomes a border router that connects slave nodes with IPv6 link.
    - Describes addressing configurations, neighbour discovery and header compression for supporting IPv6.

8.4.1.3   Network Layer Protocols

Simultaneously there were working groups who developed network protocols to allow these tiny devices to use these wireless standards and form different types of network.

1. RPL from ROLL a working group of Internet Engineering Task Force (IETF)
    - The routing protocol that provides multi-hop communication between the nodes.
    - Independent of PHY layer and MAC layer, scalable to thousands of nodes, extend Internet connectivity to all tiny devices in the network.
    - A proactive protocol that forms routes as soon as nodes are up and running.
    - Many variants provide low latency, low energy and even Mobility.
    - Supports one too many, many to one and any to any types of data traffic.
    - Most suitable for low power devices that keep their radio off for most of the time.
2. 6LowPAN from 6lo working group of IETF
    - Added IPv6 capability over IEEE 802.15.4 standard.

- RFC4944 [9], defined the frame format and header compression techniques for transmitting IPv6 packets over the tiny frames.
- Paved way for Internet connectivity to the tiny devices.
3. 6TiSCH from IETF
   - Adds IPv6 capability on top of IEEE 802.15.4e TSCH wireless standard.
   - Specifies procedures for finalizing a TSCH schedule by participating nodes.
   - Communication happens in a non-central manner.
   - Drives home the promise of low latency communication to mission-critical applications.

8.4.2 Enhancements in Low Power WLANs

Wireless local area network provides wireless connectivity for a set of nodes that are present in the stretch of few hundred meters. The wireless mode allows free-roaming for devices and boosts mobility without compromising on reliable connections. These networks have a fixed access point (AP) and establish one to one connections with multiple mobile nodes. The AP remains the central node and other nodes communicate with each other by connecting through it. Ad-Hoc peer to peer connections is also supported without the central AP. Though standalone networks could be set up, WLAN is widely used to extend the Internet connectivity for multiple devices within a medium range.

8.4.2.1   Enhancements in IEEE 802.11

IEEE 802.11 wireless standard is for interconnecting devices in a wireless local area network and is famously known as Wi-Fi. They allow multiple devices to be connected within a short range of few tens of meters to 100 meters but the coverage can be extended with formation of a mesh. An IoRT system would benefit from the mobility support and high coverage range offered by the Wi-Fi networks.

1. IEEE 802.11ah
   - Consumes less power, long-range Wi-Fi up to a kilometer.
   - Operating in the megahertz band, it has a good penetration capability around obstacles.

- Has preplanned sleep and wakeup cycles for low power operations.
- APS can buffer the data which allows more low duty power cycles for the nodes that are connected to it.
- With multi-input multi-output technology, multiple transmitting and receiving antennas augment the receiving signal power.
- Supports twice the transmission range of original Wi-Fi.

2. IEEE 802.11ax, recent standard, efficient for densely deployed devices.
   - Different groups of devices are allotted different wakeup times to improve power efficiency.
   - Orthogonal frequency division multiple access allows dynamic allocation of subcarriers helping simultaneous multiple transmissions.
   - End to end communication latency can be kept constant and the same for all the multiple nodes.

3. Wi-Fi EasyMesh
   - Wi-Fi EasyMesh uses multiple APs to extend the coverage of the gateway to a cover a larger area.
   - The network is extensible, easy to set up and are designed to make multiple vendor APs to interoperate.
   - Multi-access point controller from the primary gateway manages the network formation with the multi-access point agents.
   - Allows multi-hops between APs and all the extended APs could be deployed in full wireless mode.
   - New features like Multiband use of intelligence in the APs to suggest the optimum usage of frequency bands, channels etc. for improving the network performance.

8.4.3   Enhancements in Low Power WWANs

Long-range wireless communication was dominated by cellular technologies for a long time and incurs huge costs as they operate in the licensed spectrum [10]. Over the years, there have been developments to provide low power, long-range wireless communication technology within the unlicensed bands. Typically it supports low data rates and operates on an unlicensed ISM band to reduce the cost of the implementation. These unlicensed LPWANs operate with proprietary radio or mac and hence there is a need to pay a connectivity fee. But it is still seen as a lesser cost compared to the licensed spectrum usage. They are a viable alternative for the cellular technologies and expected to improve the outdoor IoT applications connectivity.

8.4.3.1 LoRaWAN

1. LoRa from Semtech
   - Long-range, low power wireless PHY that uses Semtech owned chirp spread spectrum like modulation.
   - Reduces the interference with the existing cellular networks and a perfect fit for outdoor wireless communication requirements.
   - The range could be a few kilometers and more with appropriate link budget.
   - Draws such low power that the device batteries last for up to 10 years.
2. LoRaWAN, networking protocol on top of LoRa PHY
   - All end nodes get connected to a central gateway or multiple gateways that are LoRaWAN base station.
   - Bidirectional communication is made possible with 3 different choices.
   - Sleepy sensor devices can wake up for transmitting data to the gateway and can receive immediately after the transmission slot alone.
   - Another mac choice is to have a synchronized transmission and reception and allows for coordinated wake-up cycles.
   - There is a mac choice for all time downlink communication that is suitable for main powered actuator devices.

8.4.3.2 5G

The fifth generation of cellular networks named 5G is expected to revolutionize the Internet of Things by bringing together all Internet, intelligence and Things [11–13]. Equipped with high data rates, low latency, more bandwidth, low interference and long communication ranges, 5G will drive intelligent IoRT solutions. With waveforms that carry parallel data and new antenna design for low power, high interference tolerance, 5G is well equipped for handling high node density. The 5G New Radio (NR) is the global radio access method with multiple waveform customizations to suit different types of applications. Also, they reduce interference and having a wide subcarrier spacing provides low latency. Multi-Input

Multi-Output (MIMO) antennas boost parallel multi-user transmissions to support many devices at the same time. The biggest advantage of the 5G lies in its capability to the dynamic and optimum usage of spectrum.

5G infrastructure is equipped to provide three different types of base stations with different coverage zones. A small base station with millimetre waves for communication can service small cells and will be installed like a light post in streets. It will provide very high data rates in the range of few gigabits per second. The other two types operate in the low-frequency bands closer to the current 4G technology. The narrowband IoT (NB-IoT) with its low power operations most suitable for sensor devices is also expected to be brought under the 5G umbrella. Its use is most expected in smart cities where all devices are expected to be brought under 5G communication. Their gateways connected to a 5G base station will transpire data quickly from low power IoT networks to intelligent systems like Robots or cloud infrastructure. This is expected to connect up to a million devices in a one square km radius and should drive many IoRT applications. With all the robust base stations in place, it is highly likely to deliver big on the connected vehicles and autonomous delivery segments. So IoRT can benefit extremely in Smart Cities that would use 5G as their communication backbone.

8.5   Robots as Edge Device in IoT

The Robotic systems of IoRT have two strategic choices for communicating with the Things of IoT. All Robots have an array of micro-controllers and can use the same for communicating with the sensor devices directly with the help of networking standards discussed in the previous section. The micro-controllers in Robots can act as the border routers and can directly exchange data with these devices. Another strategy is to communicate with the help of upper-layer communication protocols that helps heterogeneous devices from different platforms to collaborate. The key factor for this form of communication is to have low latency to make the collaboration seamless. This section discusses some of the prominent communication protocols that would drive IoRT systems.

8.5.1   Constrained RESTful Environments (CoRE)

CoRE [14] is all about bringing Representational state transfer (REST) architecture style to the low power constraint nodes. This specification lays out the process of discovering the web services that are run in a web server hosted on a constraint node. The structure of the uniform resource identifier (URI) for a resource, their formats, properties, access methods and query filtering are also specified. It also defines the CoRE link format which identifies the relationship between different available resources. It also frames security aspects for queries as multicast support of the IPv6 network could be used for making denial of service attacks. With the help of a Restful server, nodes can perform information exchange in a stateless manner and can implement on top of UDP. This forms the solid base for building upper layer protocols like HTTP or CoAP service over the 6LoWPAN networks.

8.5.2 The Constrained Application Protocol (CoAP)

CoAP [15] was developed by IETF to provide message exchange between any two devices through a client-server model. It is developed especially to suit the IoT devices that have small memory and computation power. The header format of a CoAP message is simple and are essentially UDP (user datagram protocol) messages. It can be easily transformed into HTTP messages and can be used over the web browser too. In that sense, it can be made highly interoperable. Any client node can use the POST method to create a resource in the server and other clients can use the GET method to get the resource from any client. CoAP and HTTP can cross proxy each other where CoAP clients can access a HTTP resource and vice versa. It can also be easily extended to publish/subscribe model of communication. And the best part is the customization of user-defined data format and can support many standard formats like XML or JSON.

8.5.2.1 Latest in CoAP

Group communication to reach out to multiple CoAP clients with a single response is in the works [16]. This is particularly useful to communicate to a group of devices in a mesh network instead of talking to them individually. This leans towards more of contextual communication rather than address-based communication. This feature takes advantage of the multicast addressing facility of IPv6 protocol and works well over the radio medium. They are aiming to better congestion control and to provide security for adding/removing clients to a group.

8.5.3 The MQTT-SN Protocol

MQTT-SN [17] is an open standard messaging protocol for publish/subscribe models of communication for sensor devices. Central to it, is a broker which facilitates all the clients to publish or subscribe to a topic. Like CoAP, MQTT-SN relies on UDP whereas the original standard MQTT relies on TCP (Transport Control Protocol) over IP (Internet Protocol) for transmitting its messages. The topic names from MQTT are transformed to topic ids, discovery service to identify an MQTT gateway and offline mode to communicate to sleepy devices are some of the important changes made for low-end devices. So in IoRT, MQTT-SN can be used between the sensors and gateway or border router and MQTT can be used between the gateway to Robots. These changes are influencing applications to use topic-based communication rather than the node's network address. Such data centred approach works well for communicating to a group of sensors or actuators. Both CoAP and MQTT-SN provide communication services with a latency of a few milliseconds [18] and are suitable for IoRT applications. Also, MQTT offers 3 levels of services to delay-sensitive applications. The services range from best-effort delivery of messages to guaranteed delivery. The study of delay in MQTT based industrial applications reveals that QoS 1 is the best option to provide a balance between QoS and the end to end delay [19]. As the delay is lower, IoRT systems could make use of real-time data for performing their tasks.

8.5.4   The Data Distribution Service (DDS)

DDS is a messaging protocol used for real-time message exchange using a publish/subscribe model between any two heterogeneous entities. Publishers could be nodes in the IoT that has the data to be shared with other nodes or applications. It has built-in mechanisms for service discovery and can use either UDP or TCP for message transmission. Though DDS has been around for a long time, they were not suitable for low power devices. With the IoT domain gaining much traction, Object Management Group has come up DDS-XRCE [20] for extremely resource-constrained environments (XRCE). The protocol defines client and agent roles for exchanging/gathering messages between the sleepy nodes. It allows the low power resource-constrained nodes to use DDS through the XRCE agent and allows the dynamic discovery of those agents in the network. All the communication is routed centrally through the XRCE agent. If direct peer to peer communication is required, a node has to implement both the client and the agent parts of the protocol. With a standard data format, multiple platforms can communicate in real-time.

8.5.5 Data Formats

When multiple networks work together, it is highly essential to have a common format for the data that is exchanged to understand the context of the shared data. Many formats are available for this purpose and the most widely used was XML and JSON. XML is the extensible markup language that is easily read by both humans and parsers in devices. They are very simple as well as structured and can represent data in numeric, ASCII or Boolean format. JSON is a javascript object notation, which is the most used format for data interchange in web-based services. Both of them make it easier for parsers to scan and understand the content. Recently, binary formats for data exchange are proving to be light on the payload for the low power devices. This is directly going to reduce the power consumption of these devices and improve network lifetime. Protobuf is a popular choice for the programming language-neutral binary format for messaging protocols. BSON, BJSON and UBJSAON are variants of JSAON that also reduce the size of the data structure and proving to be superior in parsing quickly.

8.6 Challenges and Research Solutions

As IoRT field is still in its nascent stage, we envision that the challenges of realizing a heterogeneous IoT or a large scale IoT would apply to IoRT too. Additionally, there would be unique challenges to robotics for fusing a large amount of IoT data for performing its tasks. IoRT is expected to bring in artificial intelligence, edge computing, augmented reality closer to implementations. From the communication perspective, the foremost challenge would be getting seamless data concurrently from low powered IoT devices. As more and more devices join the Internet and compete for the transmission medium, it is going to be challenging to bring many diverse technologies together.

Many PHY and MAC layer protocol enhancements on top of the standards are proposed to this effect. Although LoRaWAN is expected to provide interference-free operations, its PHY layer is known to have practical issues like higher power consumption, link coordination issues, loss in reliability when multiple users concurrently transmit. Some research solutions offer to adapt dynamic data rates, data recovery mechanisms, spreading factor allocations and automated link estimations [21] to make LoRAWAN suitable for servicing a larger number of nodes. WPANs are also prone to high energy consumption. Hybrid MAC protocols featuring CSMA and CA-TDMA combination and dynamic sleep scheduling reduces power consumption to 40% than the standard [22]. There are scores of enhancements in the routing layer of WPAN networks for load balancing, link estimation, mobility support and energy optimizations [23]. Recently, ambient backscattering is gaining traction to get data from even un-powered nodes. They rely on energy harvesting techniques and can communicate over short distances. Some very viable MAC schemes that guarantee ultra-low power operations are proposed [24] for this type of communication. All of these proposals would augment the ubiquitous nature of the IoRT system.

Another challenge is to bring different types of networks with sensors devices and robots together under a single robotic application. Management of heterogeneous networks poses distinct challenges like queuing, routing, optimization [25]. Software-defined radio is a concept being tried for combating heterogeneous devices in a network and microprocessor designs for making this a reality, is underway [26]. To make multiple networks co-exist, there needs to be fair distribution in channel access of the unlicensed spectrum. So, machine learning-based channel access coordination is suggested for competing devices from IoT, Wi-Fi and robots [27].

From the WPAN networks, there is a different challenge in the form of limited or no mobility support for the nodes. With Robots as edge devices, their mobility can be used for actuation. Some of the routing protocol extensions proposed are mobility enhanced RPL, Co-RPL, ME-RPL, mRPL and Backpressure RPL [28]. They either allow the transmitting nodes to be mobile or the root node to be mobile. Some medium access control protocols like M-ContikiMAC, MobIQ, MX-MAC [29] that support mobility in WPANs are recently proposed to support mobile nodes interconnectivity.

Apart from networking challenges, for the robots and IoT devices to work together, they need to have a clear understanding of the information that is passed between them. To make them contextually aware and derive relevant information, there is a need for common data formats in the data exchange protocols. Though there are many formats like JSON, BSON, CBOR, MsgPack, JSONC are available, the recent Protobuf [30] with its binary format provides superior performance in terms of less payload. There are many more solutions available but there is a lack of in-depth surveys on all layers with IoRT in focus.

8.7   Open Platforms for IoRT Applications

Open-source implementations are important for development as it makes it convenient for multiple stakeholders to join hands to develop and maintain a standardized product. Open-source operating systems also cut costs and allow technology to progress across the world simultaneously. Many robotic solutions are available in the literature [31–33], that was developed using the open-source components. IoT devices require an operating system that provides the implementation of the network layer protocols and data exchange protocols. They also provide implementations of server and client applications of the required protocols. Table 8.1 collates some of the widely used open operating systems (OS), for IoRT developers and lists the set of protocol implementations available on them.

Survey paper [34] provides detailed information about the various features of the available open operating systems for IoT and compares them against each other. It compares them on the memory requirements of the devices. So developers can pick and choose according to the hardware availability. Some of the largest chip makers are also joining hands with the open operating system consortiums and append firmware for their chipsets. So an open-source implementation provides a variety of options for an end-user and boosts the penetration of technology in every sector.

Open platforms are making IoT inclusive robot application development possible and Table 8.2 details the open robotic platforms that help connect with IoT devices. Such initiatives help the developers to get common platforms and interfaces to build IoRT systems. Table 8.3 gives a list of simulators that are available for testing the robotic applications in real-world like scenarios. With all these open source components, IoRT application development can progress in a wide variety of application domains.

Table 8.1 Open operating systems for IoT devices.

Operating system	Hardware support	Comm. protocols
Contiki-NG	New gen like ARM Cortex-M3/M4, TI MSP430	6LoWPAN, 6TiSCH, IPv6 over BLE, TCP, UDP, RPL, CoAP, MQTT
RIOT	AVR, ARM CORTEX-M3/-M4/-M7/-M23, ESP32, MIPS32, MSP430, PIC32, RISC V	6LoWPAN, RPL, TCP, UDP, CoAP, CBOR, MQTT-SN, UBJASON
FreeRTOS	40+ architectures including RISC V, ARM CORTEX-M33	TCP, UDP, IPv4, MQTT, HTTPS
TinyOS	MSP430, Atmel, Intel XScale	6LoWPAN, TinyRPL, DP CoAP

Table 8.2 Open robotic middleware.

Middleware	OS support	Hardware support	Protocols
ROS	Ubuntu, Debian, Windows	Many including TurtleBot3, ROSbot, AmigoBot	TCP, UDP, ROSBridge, MQTT, DDS
micro-ROS	Zephyr, FreeRTOS, NuttX	Many including ARM CORTEX	TCP, UDP, DDS-XRCE, MQTT

Table 8.3 Open testbeds for IoRT.

Simulator	Middleware support	Communication protocols
Webots	Sockets, ROS	Protobufs
Gazebo	TurtleBot, PR2, iRobot, Pioneer2 DX	ROS, Players, Sockets

The next section lists some industrial initiates that are making IoRT solutions accessible to end-users.

8.8   Industrial Drive for Interoperability

Consumption of any technology is driven largely by the availability of multiple devices in the open market and all different devices from multiple vendors must be able to operate with each other. Multiple stakeholders came together to form alliances and adopted these open communication standards for manufacturing compatible products. Their purpose was to invest in the establishment of common open standards, testing the devices, certify them and also for marketing these certified devices. The idea is to authenticate the products for standard conformance so that the communication technology is uniform and can collaborate effectively. Another advantage is the security aspect that authenticates devices by checking for keys while commissioning a new device into the pre-existing network.

8.8.1   The Zigbee Alliance

Zigbee [35] is based on IEEE 802.15.4 wireless standards and uses its network protocols on top, to create a mesh network and allows seamless communication between hundreds of devices. They are used in both domestic and commercial segments and product owners like Amazon, Samsung and Philips are using them in their home appliances. As they allow the devices to have a sleep–wake pattern, the operations are low power and high on battery life. The products can seamlessly self-organize themselves into a mesh or a tree network without the need for any setup can self-heal and can be accessed from the Internet through the Zigbee gateway. By increasing the number of gateways, the network can be scaled up and is a popular device for many implementations of WPANs.

8.8.2   The Thread Group

Google's Thread [36] is stacked on top of IEEE 802.15.4 wireless standards and 6LoWPAN, to create an IP based mesh network. Because of 6LowPAN, it has the huge advantage of having the aspect of interoperability between other IP networks. Thread uses a next-generation version of Routing Information Protocol (RIP) as the routing protocol to create a wireless mesh using UDP. The routers in the mesh are having their radio on for all the time and hundreds of sleepy devices can directly connect to one router. Multi-hop is allowed only between routers so that peer to peer communication happens with low latency. They have released an open version of the Thread stack as OpenThread [37] and testing requirements for certification, to enable the broader adaptation of this protocol by vendors. As they have a restricted architecture with routers as a solid backbone, the reliability achieved is very high. Their provisioning protocol helps with security by verifying the credentials before allowing a device into the network. They support multiple multi-processor configurations like network co-processor, SoC or microcontroller/microprocessor architecture.

8.8.3   The WiFi Alliance

Wi-Fi is an omnipresent communication technology which is founded on the IEEE 802.11 wireless standard. Operating on the unlicensed spectrum, Wi-Fi products were able to garner a larger reach across the world. Conformance to IEEE 8012.11n standard is certified as Wi-Fi 4 and uses many antennas to have parallel communication with multiple devices. Devices that support IEEE 802.11ac standard are certified as Wi-Fi 5 and uses the 5 GHz band. The IEEE 802.11ax standard conformance is certified as "Wi-Fi 6" and uses less power that is suitable for connected devices. The extension of Wi-Fi 6E to include 6 GHz unlicensed band is further extending the benefits of low latency even while a device is in roaming.

8.8.4   The LoRa Alliance

LoRa Alliance [38] has members like Amazon, Cisco, Aurdino to promote usage of LoRAWAN protocol for different verticals like farming, consumer goods, industrial cases, utility sector and smart cities. With very energy efficient radio, unlicensed band utilization and long communication range, LoRAWAN is all set to connect a multitude of thousands of devices. This alliance certifies devices to make them interoperable across multiple manufacturers. LoRAWAN uses multiple gateways to scale up a network and provides low latency as end devices reach a gateway in a single hop. Also, two-level security is provided at the network level and the application level with the help of an advanced encryption standard (AES).

8.9   Conclusion

IoRT has a lot of potential for bringing a variety of robotic solutions to everyday usage. Be it a smart vacuum, personal care assistant, assisted living, the first responder during disasters, working in a hazardous environment, surveillance in dense forest/oceans assisted farming in large fields or orchards, smart manufacturing, warehouse heavy lifting or pandemic handling, properly designed IoRT solutions could help us in making the world technically smart. Communication technologies play a vital part in making IoRT solutions, an enriching and ubiquitous experience. Though the present-day technologies are sufficient to realize IoRT solutions, there is always a case to improve things in terms of reliability, turnaround time, energy efficiency etc. Newer protocols aim to provide reliable and quick turnaround time for the information exchange. Also, they are focusing on increasing the distance between two communication endpoints, robust connectivity for mobile devices, interoperability between different protocols and common data formats for addressing the challenges in bringing heterogeneous devices together.

Industries and tech giants are forming alliances to develop open standards, adapt them in their products and to certify multi-vendor devices for seamless collaboration. This chapter briefly discussed different protocol enhancements, challenges, research solutions and highlighted the open-source platforms. An end-user has a lot of options in open source platforms for choosing hardware, middleware or software for developing an IoRT solution. As in any field, IoRT also has many open issues around security, power consumption, interoperability and scalability. Most of the time, there is a tradeoff involved with the increase in the end to end delay for providing secure communication. Also, the amalgam of different platforms brings forth compatibility issues. A lot of research is going on around cross-technology communication [39] techniques to cater to the successful fusion of diverse communication technologies. Around all these, IoRT is going to bring forth innovative and intelligent solutions to everyday life shortly.

References

1. *The Internet of Robotic Things*, A technical report, ABI research, New York, United States, 2014.
2. Simoens, P., Dragone, M., Saffiotti, A., The Internet of Robotic Things: A review of concept, added value, and applications. *Int. J. Adv. Rob. Syst.*, 1–11, Jan-Feb, 15, 2018.
3. Liu, Y., Zhang, W., Pan, Y.L.S., Chen, Y., Analyzing the robotic behavior in a smart city with deep enforcement and imitation learning using IoRT. *Comput. Commun.*, 150, 346–356, Jan. 2020.
4. Siciliano, B. and Khatib, O., *Springer Handbook of Robotics*, Springer, Berlin, Heidelerg, 2008.
5. Al-Fuqaha, A., Guizani, M., Mohammadi, M., Aledhari, M., Ayyash, M., Internet of Things: A Survey on Enabling Technologies, Protocols, and Applications. *IEEE Commun. Surv. Tut.*, 17, 2347–2376, 2015.
6. Ramonet, A.G. and Noguchi, T., IEEE 802.15.4 Now and Then: Evolution of the LR-WPAN Standard. *ICACT Transactions on Advanced Communications Technology (TACT)*, May. 2019, vol. 8.
7. Mesh Profile, Bluetooth Specification, Bluetooth Special Interest Group, v1.0.1, 1-333, Jan. 2019.
8. Nieminen, J., Savolainen, T., Isomaki, M., Patil, B., Shelby, Z., Gomez, C., IPv6 over BLUETOOTH(R) Low Energy. RFC 7668, 1–21, Oct. 2015, https://www.rfc-editor.org/info/rfc7668.
9. Montenegro, G., Kushalnagar, N., Hui, J., Culler, D., Transmission of IPv6 Packets over IEEE 802.15.4 Networks. RFC 4944, 1–30, Sep. 2007, https://www.rfc-editor.org/info/rfc4944.
10. Durand, T.G., Visagie, L., Booysen, M.J., Evaluation of next-generation low-power communication technology to replace GSM in IoT-applications. *IET Commun.*, 13, 2533–2540, Aug. 2019.
11. Wang, D., Chen, D., Song, B., Guizani, N., Yu, X., Du, X., From IoT to 5G I-IoT: The Next Generation IoT-Based Intelligent Algorithms and 5G Technologies. *IEEE Commun. Mag.*, 56, 114–120, Oct. 2018.
12. Palattella, M.R., Dohler, M., Grieco, A., Rizzo, G., Torsner, J., Engel, T., Ladid, L., Internet of Things in the 5G Era: Enablers, Architecture and Business Models. *IEEE J. Sel. Areas Commun.*, 34, 510–527, Mar. 2016.
13. Chettri, L. and Bera, R., A Comprehensive Survey on Internet of Things (IoT) Toward 5G Wireless Systems. *IEEE Internet Things J.*, 7, 16–32, Jan. 2020.

14. Shelby, Z., Constrained RESTful Environments (CoRE) Link Format. RFC 6690, 1–21, Aug. 2012, https://www.rfc-editor.org/info/rfc6690.

15. Shelby, Z., Hartke, K., Bormann, C., The Constrained Application Protocol (CoAP). RFC 7252, 1–112, Jun. 2014, https://www.rfc-editor.org/info/rfc7252.

16. Dijk, E., Wang, C., Tiloca, M., Group Communication for the Constrained Application Protocol (CoAP): Work in progress. RFC 7390, 1–46, Oct. 2014, https://www.rfc-editor.org/info/rfc7390.

17. Stanford-Clark, A. and Truong, H.L., MQTT For Sensor Networks (MQTT-SN), Protocol Specification ver. 1.2, 1–28, *OASIS standard*, Nov. 2013.

18. Amaran, M.H., Noh, N.A.M., Rohmad, M.S., Hashim, H., A Comparison of Lightweight Communication Protocols in Robotic Applications. *IEEE International Symposium on Robotics and Intelligent Sensors (IRIS 2015), Procedia Computer Science*, pp. 400–405, 2015.

19. Ferrari, P., Flammini, A., Sisinni, E., Rinaldi, S., Brandao, D., Rocha, M.S., Delay Estimation of Industrial IoT Applications Based on Messaging Protocols. *IEEE Trans. Instrum. Meas.*, 67, 2188–2199, Sep. 2018.

20. DDS for Extremely Resource Constrained Environments (DDS-XRCE), ver. 1.0, 1–158, Nov. 2019, https://www.omg.org/spec/DDS-XRCE/1.0/PDF.

21. Sundaram, J.P.S., Du, W., Zhao, Z., A Survey on LoRa Networking: Research Problems, Current Solutions, and Open Issues. *IEEE Commun. Surv. Tut.*, 22, 371–388, First quarter, 2020.

22. Al-Janabi, T.A. and Al-Raweshidy, H.S., An Energy Efficient Hybrid MAC Protocol With Dynamic Sleep-Based Scheduling for High Density IoT Networks. *Internet Things J.*, 6, 2273–2287, Apr. 2019.

23. Kamgueu, P.O., Nataf, E., Ndie, T.D., Survey on RPL enhancements: A focus on topology, security and mobility. *Comput. Commun.*, 120, 10–21, May 2018.

24. Cao, X., Song, Z., Yang, B., ElMossallamy, M.A., Qian, L., Han, Z., A Distributed Ambient Backscatter MAC Protocol for Internet-of-Things Networks. *IEEE Internet Things J.*, 7, 1488–1501, Feb. 2020.

25. Qiu, T., Chen, N., Li, K., Atiquzzaman, M., Zhao, W., How Can Heterogeneous Internet of Things Build Our Future: A Survey. *IEEE Commun. Surv. Tut.*, 20, 2011–2027, Third quarter, 2018.

26. Adegbija, T., Rogacs, A., Patel, C., Gordon-Ross, A., Microprocessor Optimizations for the Internet of Things: A Survey. *IEEE Trans. Comput.-Aided Des. Integr. Circuits Syst.*, 37, 7–20, Jan. 2018.

27. Yang, B., Cao, X., Han, Z., Qian, L., A Machine Learning Enabled MAC Framework for Heterogeneous Internet-of-Things Networks. *IEEE Trans. Wireless Commun.*, 18, 3697–3712, Jul. 2019.

28. Oliveira, A. and Vazao, T., Low-power and lossy networks under mobility: A survey. *Comput. Networks*, 107, 339–352, Oct. 2016.

29. Kazmi, S.W.A., Kacso, A., Wismüller, R., Recent MAC protocols for mobility-aware wireless sensor networks—A survey and future directions. *2017 Ninth International Conference on Ubiquitous and Future Networks (ICUFN)*, Mila, pp. 159–164, 2017.

30. Lysogor, I.I., Voskov, L.S., Efremov, S.G., Survey of data exchange formats for heterogeneous LPWAN-satellite IoT networks. *2018 Moscow Workshop on Electronic and Networking Technologies (MWENT)*, Moscow, pp. 1–5, 2018.

31. Al-Taee, M.A., Al-Nuaimy, W., Muhsin, Z.J., Al-Ataby, A., Robot Assistant in Management of Diabetes in Children Based on the Internet of Things. *IEEE Internet Things J.*, 4, 437–445, Apr. 2017.

32. Razafimandimby, C., Loscri, V., Vegni, A.M., A neural network and IoT based scheme for performance assessment in Internet of Robotic Things. *2016 IEEE First International Conference on Internet-of-Things Design and Implementation*, Apr. 2016, pp. 4–8.

33. Kurebwa, J.G. and Mushiri, T., Internet of things architecture for a smart passenger-car robotic first aid system. *2nd International Conference on Sustainable Materials Processing and Manufacturing, (SMPM 2019)*, 2019.

34. Qutqut, M.H., Al-Sakran, A., Almasalha, F., Hassanein, H.S., Comprehensive survey of the IoT open-source OS. *IET Wireless Sensor Systems, Spl. Iss. Smart Cities and Smart Sensory Platforms*, Oct. 2018.

35. ZigBee Specification, ZigBee Alliance, CA, USA, ver. r21, 1–542, Aug. 2015, https://zigbeealliance.org/wp-content/uploads/2019/11/docs-05-3474-21-0csg-zigbee-specification.pdf.

36. Thread Specification, Thread Group, Inc., ver. 1.1.1, 1–117, Feb. 2017.

37. OpenThread, https://openthread.io.

38. LoRaWan® Specification, LoRa Alliance, Inc., ver. 1.1, 1–101, Oct. 2017, https://lora-alliance.org/resource_hub/lorawan-specification-v1-1/.

39. Chen, Y., Li, M., Chen, P., Xia, S., Survey of cross-technology communication for IoT heterogeneous devices. *IET Commun.*, 13, 1709–1720, 2019.

Real Time Hazardous Gas Classification and Management System Using Artificial Neural Networks

R. Anitha*, S. Anusooya, V. Jean Shilpa and Mohamed Hishaam

B.S. Abdur Rahman Crescent Institute of Science & Technology, India

Abstract

Generally, peoples working in coal mines, gas industries and sewage cleaning are prone to high health risk. The gases released in coal mines, oil & gas industries and sewage areas are to be monitored and the different gas concentration that has been released out have to be identified. Hence, a gas detection system is developed to detect hazardous gases. Hazardous gases are harmful to humans. A metal-oxide gas sensors arrays of 4 different MQ series gas sensors are used to recognize non-combustible gas such as ammonia as well as combustible gaseous like LPG, ethanol and to a specific concentration of the respective gas in the environment. The development of systems involved 3 steps i.e. Data Set preparation, Artificial Neural Network Model Creation and Training the network using the data set. An Artificial electronic nose system is developed to classify and to measure the concentration of single or mixed gas in the environment. The electronic nose composed of two hidden layered neural networks with backpropagation has been developed to classify the gas and regression model-based neural network to find the concentration. An industrial standard IoT device, National Instruments-Compact Reconfigurable Input-Output (NI-CRIO) is used to process the incoming data from various wireless sensor nodes with different priority and create a response concerning different gaseous released. This NI-CRIO is used for monitoring and controlling applications. This process helps in avoiding the accident sort to minimize the cause of hazardous gases. The entire data will be stored in system memory and the data can also be updated in the cloud (JSON - JavaScript Object Notation) for remote monitoring. The industrial automation is done using LabVIEW software tool and the neural network model is created using a python Software tool.

Corresponding author: anitharajesh29@gmail.com

R. Anandan, G. Suseendran, S. Balamurugan, Ashish Mishra and D. Balaganesh (eds.) Human Communication Technology: Internet of Robotic Things and Ubiquitous Computing, (219–244) © 2022 Scrivener Publishing LLC

Keywords: Hazardous gas, electronic nose, classification model, regression model, CRIO, JSON cloud

9.1   Introduction

A Sanitation employee service is invaluable and many of us realize it only in our confronted situation. Generally, sewages have poor oxygen and high concentration of combustible gases and toxic gases. The employees working in this scenario are highly exposed to gases like methane, ammonia carbon mono-oxide and hydrogen-di-sulfide. When they are exposed to harmful gases, they may go to unconsciousness. Inhalation of huge quantity of these gases will lead to medical issues. Hence, safety plays a vital role in the sanitation workers. Though the workers are provided with all safety equipment's, sometimes they are likely to face an uncertain situation that becomes a life-threatening for them. As a measure of life-safety, an efficient and sensitive gas detection system is required that provides better security for the workers.

To avoid accidents, a system has to be developed that recognize the gases and its concentration. Based on the concentration level, the necessary action has to be taken to avoid or minimize the cause of these hazardous gases. Hence, we have developed an efficient Hazardous Gas Classification and Management System using Artificial Neural Networks. We have used an array of MQ sensors that are sensitive to different gases. So with the help of multiple sensors of different sensitivity, there will be a pattern for each gas (i.e. one sensor will have high sensitivity other have low or moderate sensitivity). This system helps for remote monitoring and logs every data for the future reference in the cloud as well as in the device memory.

9.2   Existing Methodology

The existing system is classifying the gas which is trained and has a simple alert system using alarms, these systems are not responsible to take the real-time response for the hazardous situation, the existing system lags multiple responses of data from various wireless sensor nodes the remote data monitoring System and Storage of data.

Bashyal *et al.* proposed "Embedded Neural Network for Fire Classification using Arrays of Gas Sensors". The main objective of this paper is to develop a system to identify the fire at the early stage and to classify the fire. The proposed system consists of different Sn02 gas sensors of TGS series are used for fire classification, an Artificial Neural Network classify the fire and an 89c55 microcontroller which is used to perform the process of classification. The technical issues that are been encountered in this system are the specific level of indication about the fire burning is not included in the system, the number of hidden layers used in the system is quite large and the system does not include the response action or a control system on the identification of hazards gas over the specific threshold. Also, this proposed system cannot be used in hazards environment and it does not collect the data for future reference and research [1].

Lee *et al.* proposed "SnO2 Gas sensing Array for Combustible and Explosive Gas Leakage Recognition". The main objective of this paper is to recognize the combustible gaseous and to find the quantity of the gas. They have used different SnO2 gas sensors for classification and to identify the quantities of gas. To determine the concentration levels, they have implemented a Multilayer Neural Network for classification and Neuro-fuzzy Network using DSP board along with the LCD. A technical issue that has been encountered in this system is the system does not include the response action or a control system on the identification of hazards gas over the specific threshold. Also, this system cannot be used in a hazardous environment, does not collect the data for the future reference and research, the remote monitoring of data is not included and not connected to the internet [2].

9.3   Proposed Methodology

The architecture of the proposed system is shown in Figure 9.1. The system uses a gas sensor array to improve the selectivity of the particular gaseous. Identification of gas sensors pattern through a mathematical model is difficult. But, this can be achieved easily using the Artificial Neural Network that develops a mathematical model and classifies gaseous concentration. The turning on the control System (extinguishing system in case of explosive gas, stop there leasing of toxic gaseous, release of detoxifying gaseous) can be achieved using a relay or digital signal, buzzers, red lights, etc. Sensor arrays are connected to a wireless sensor node which is connected to a Real-time board to make the response very fast within a limited time. The entire data of gas sensor arrays are monitored remotely in Real-time database of the cloud. Compact Rio NI-9082 is a powerful real-time hardware system that can be used to process the data which is coming from the arrays of gas sensors (contain MQ2, MQ3, MQ6, MQ135 gas sensors) through wireless sensors node (WSN) NI-3202 using the Wireless Sensor Node (WSN) gateway NI-9571 and make the response to trigger the other control system and switch on the alarm, etc. [3–5].

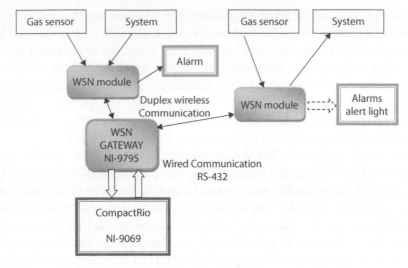

Figure 9.1 Proposed system architecture.

The flow diagram of the proposed system is shown in Figure 9.2. The data from the gas sensors along with specific gas label are collected using NI-WSN node which has an inbuilt ADC and a microcontroller. Then, the data is sent to Compact Rio through WSN gateway [6].

Data acquisition is developed using NI LabVIEW Software tool and acquired data from different gas sensors are stored as .csv file. CRIO System is trained from the data acquired using the machine learning model and once the machine is trained, real-time classification and concentration of the gas can be predicted [7].

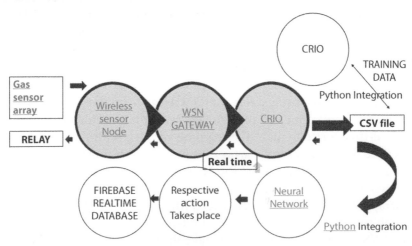

Figure 9.2 Flow diagram of the proposed system.

9.4   Hardware & Software Requirements

9.4.1   Hardware Requirements

9.4.1.1   Gas Sensors Employed in Hazardous Detection

MQ2 Gas Sensor: MQ2 gas sensor is smoke sensor also use to detect the flammable gaseous and can be used to find the concentration of gas. It can measure the concentration from 300 to 10,000 ppm of the flammable gaseous. The MQ-2 gas sensor is sensitive to propane, methane, LPG etc. The gas sensor module consists of power supply pin (5V to be provided), ground pin, Analog output pin (voltage varies from 0 to 5 based on the resistance of sensor which is proportional to concentration). Figure 9.3 shows the MQ2 gas sensor module.

Resistance calculation of MQ-2 sensor

$$\text{Resistance of sensor (Rs)} = (\text{Vcc}/V_L - 1) * R_L$$

Where,
  Vcc supply voltage
  V_L voltage across the load resistor
  R_L load resistance in ohms

MQ3 Gas Sensor:
MQ2 gas sensor is smoke sensor also use to detect the alcohol and can be used to find the concentration of alcohol. The sensitive material uses in MQ3 gas sensor is Sn02 (tin oxide). The MQ-2 gas sensor is sensitive to ethanol, propane, methane, LPG etc. The gas sensor module consists

Figure 9.3 MQ2 gas sensor module.

Figure 9.4 MQ3 gas sensor module.

of power supply pin (5 V to be provided), ground pin, Analog output pin (voltage varies from 0 to 5 based on the resistance of sensor which is proportional to concentration). Figure 9.4 shows the MQ2 gas sensor module.

Resistance calculation of MQ-3 sensor:

$$\text{Resistance of sensor (Rs)} = (\text{Vcc}/V_L - 1) * R_L$$

Where,
    Vcc supply voltage
    V_L voltage across load resistor
    R_L load resistance in ohms.

MQ6 Gas Sensors:
MQ6 gas sensor detects the Liquefied Petroleum Gas (LPG) gas and can be used to find the concentration of gas. It can measure the concentration from 200 to 10,000 ppm of the flammable gaseous. The MQ-6gas sensor is sensitive to propane, methane, LPG also responds to Natural gas. The sensor's conductivity is higher along with the gas concentration rising. The gas sensor module consists of power supply pin (5 V to be provided), ground pin, Analog output pin (voltage varies from 0 to 5 based on the resistance of sensor which is proportional to concentration). Figure 9.5 shows the MQ6 gas sensor module.

Resistance Calculation of MQ-6 gas sensor

$$\text{Resistance of sensor (Rs)} = (\text{Vcc}/V_L - 1) - R_L$$

Where,
    Vcc supply voltage
    V_L voltage across load resistor
    R_L load resistance in ohms.

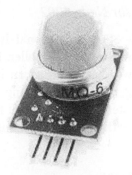

Figure 9.5 MQ6 gas sensor.

MQ-135 Gas Sensor:
MQ135 gas sensor uses to measure the air quality and can be used to find the concentration of some gaseous. It can measure the concentration from 200 to 10,000 ppm of the flammable gaseous. The MQ-135 gas sensor is sensitive NH3, NOx, Alcohol, Benzene, Smoke and CO2. The sensor's conductivity will increase along with the increase in gas concentration. The gas sensor module consists of power supply pin (5 V to be provided), ground pin, Analog output pin (voltage varies between 0 and 5 based on the resistance of sensor which is proportional to concentration). Figure 9.6 shows the MQ6 gas sensor module.

Figure 9.6 MQ135 gas sensor.

9.4.1.2   NI Wireless Sensor Node 3202

The Wireless sensor Node 3202 of National Instruments is low power device consists of a low power microcontroller. It suits well for Industrial Standard and due to the weatherproof, it can be used for outdoor data acquisition and monitoring, remote monitoring applications and it can be used to trigger the other systems and devices. It has limited storage capacity and they communicate with other nodes using radio signals. Figure 9.7 shows the NI-WSN-3202.

Block Diagram of NI WSN3202:
Figure 9.8 shows the overall hardware-based block diagram of NI WSN 3202 which consist of power supply and Analog front end, DIO circuitry for digital IO response and microcontroller which has 10 bit ADC and a can have varying step size based on requirement and Antenna.

Analog Input Circuitry:
The analog input circuitry which has a programmatic controlled MUX to select the selection lines and so that only one ADC is required for digital conversion as shown in Figure 9.9.

Digital Input and Output of One DIO Channel:
Figure 9.10 shows the simplified DIO channel circuitry. It also shows how a Digital signal is read by the WSN node.

NI WSN Pin Out:
Figure 9.11 shows the pinout diagram which consists of 4 analog input followed by four digital pins.

Figure 9.7 NI-WSN-3202.

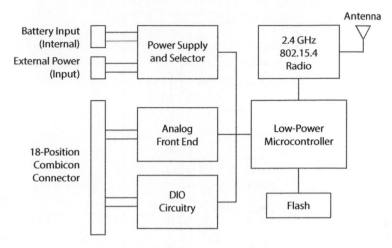

Figure 9.8 Block diagram of NI WSN 3202.

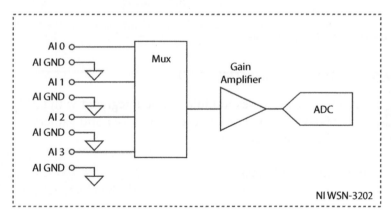

Figure 9.9 Analog input circuitry.

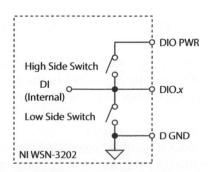

Figure 9.10 Simplified circuit diagram of one DIO channel.

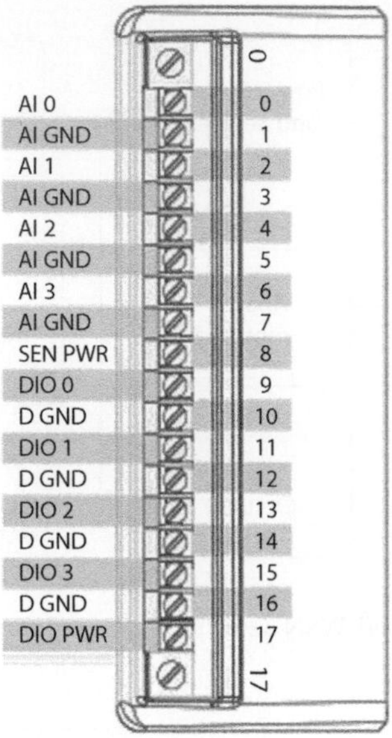

AI 0	0
AI GND	1
AI 1	2
AI GND	3
AI 2	4
AI GND	5
AI 3	6
AI GND	7
SEN PWR	8
DIO 0	9
D GND	10
DIO 1	11
D GND	12
DIO 2	13
D GND	14
DIO 3	15
D GND	16
DIO PWR	17

Figure 9.11   NI WSN-3202 pin out.

9.4.1.3   NI WSN Gateway (NI 9795)

NI WSN gateway is a C series module can be integrated with CRIO. It is a weatherproof device which can be used in outdoor and gathers the data coming from the various sensor nodes [8].

Important Feature of NI 9795
- Use to connect wireless I/O devices with the Compact RIO (CRIO) system.
- Compatible with any Compact RIO chassis (one gateway per chassis) shown in Figure 9.12
- IEEE standard 802.15.4
- The range covered by the gateway with a line of sight: 200 m

ANI-WSN system consists of one NI WSN gateway, a maximum of 36 NI WSN-3202 nodes that can be connected to the gateway. PC (Personal Computer) can be used to monitor the data that comes from the nodes.

Mesh Configuration of NI-WSN system:
Figure 9.13 shows 2 nodes R1 and R2 connected to a common gateway in the mesh network. Similarly, a maximum of 32 nodes can be connected to each router.

Figure 9.12 NI WSN gateway (NI9795).

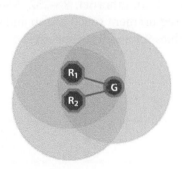

Figure 9.13 Mesh configuration example.

9.4.1.4   COMPACT RIO (NI-9082)

Compact RIO is a powerful real-time Industrial Standard System used for real-time processing and to compute the complex DSP as well FPGA algorithm. The compact RIO consists of chassis slot to attach the NI modules. It has two Gigabit Ethernet slots, RS 232, RS 422 for faster communication with the other system. The Compact RIO consists of a real-time multi-core microprocessor for processing complex algorithm and to make real-time using the OS, RT Linux.

The FPGA Module can be used for very fast I/O response between the compact Rio and the I/O devices tin the chassis. The data streaming can be done at high speed compared to the microprocessor. FPGA can also be separately programmable using the internal PCI bus. Figure 9.14 shows NI 9039 CRIO module.

Figure 9.14 Compact Rio (NI 9039).

Architecture Of Compact RIO
Figure 9.15 shows the simplified Architecture of compact Rio Real-time system consists of processor, FPGA, C series Modules for attaching Required module based on application, Ethernet, RS-232, RS422, USB ports, RAM and ROM. The power requirement specification and memory specification of CRIO is given in Tables 9.1 and 9.2 respectively.

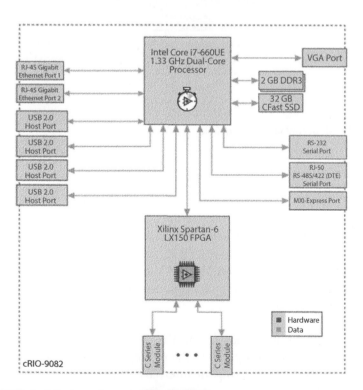

Figure 9.15 Architecture of compact Rio (NI9082).

Specification of CRIO:

Table 9.1 Power requirement specifications.

Voltage input range (measured at the cRIO-9082 power connector)	
V1	9 to 30 V
V2	9 to 30 V
Maximum power consumption	75 W

Table 9.2 Memory specification in CRIO.

Nonvolatile	32 GB minimum
DDR3 system memory	2 GB minimum

Software Requirements:
LabVIEW 2017 (LabVIEW-Laboratory Virtual Instrument Engineering Workbench)

It is a design platform for the System especially the Real-time Systems which uses the Graphical programming approach to do the control process. "G" is named for graphical language. LabVIEW is used commonly for industrial automation, data acquisition etc. LabVIEW uses the dataflow programming approach i.e. when enough data is available then block or subVI or function will execute.

Python:
Python is a high-level programming language used for general-purpose programming used in multiple branches of study which include, biomedical, Business management, data analytics, etc. Nowaday's major use of Python is in Artificial Intelligence and Machine Learning. Python is open source and a major feature is it can perform dynamic memory allocation. It also supports Object-Oriented programming [9].

Tensor Flow:
Tensor flow is an open-source machine learning platform for the students, professionals, hobbyist and Scientists [10]. It is used to perform very complex numerical computation under a variety of platforms like CPU, GPU or TPU depends on the application.

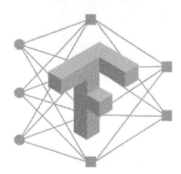

9.5   Experimental Setup

The development of systems involved 3 steps namely Data set preparation, Artificial Neural Network Model Creation, Training the network using the data set.

9.5.1   Data Set Preparation

In the data set preparation, the first is to create a set-up in which we can pass the different gas of specific concentrations. The setup consists of a closed gas chamber, in which different MQ gas sensors(MQ2, MQ5, MQ6, MQ135)are placed inside the glass chamber and made on the gas sensors till they reach stable state i.e. Heater coil gets heated up as shown in Figure 9.16.

Creating an effective data acquisition system and acquiring the data is easy. Figure 9.17 shows the Front panel of Data acquisition system when no gases are passed into the chamber. Code control in the figure is used as a label for each gas, 1 for ethanol (CCH5OH), 2 for Ammonia(NH3) and 3 for LPG gas. The data is stored as a .csv file

The data set for each gas of various concentrations is shown in Figures 9.18, 9.19, and 9.20. The concentration of each gas taken is shown below:

1. For ethanol the concentration is varied from 200 to 1,350 ppm approximately.
2. For LPG the concentration is varied from 200 to 2,000 ppm approximately.
3. For Ammonia the concentration is varied from 200 to 2,500 ppm approximately.

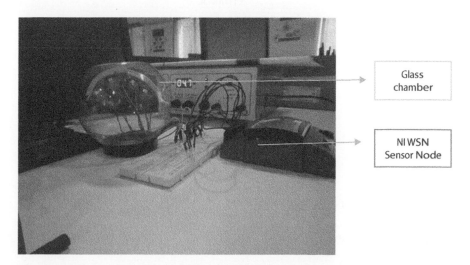

Figure 9.16 Sensor array in glass chamber for data set creation.

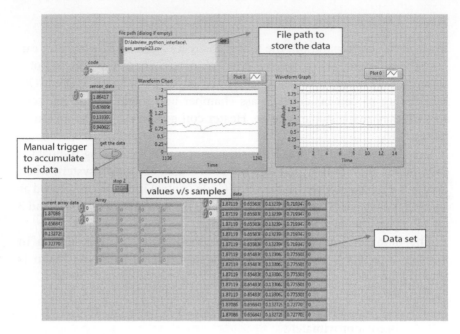

Figure 9.17 Front panel of data acquisition system.

Dataset Plots:

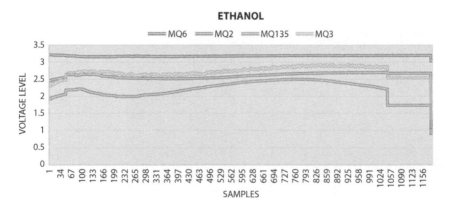

Figure 9.18 Dataset of ethanol gas.

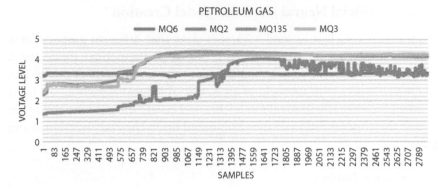

Figure 9.19 Dataset of petroleum gas.

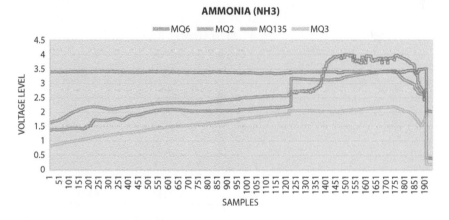

Figure 9.20 Dataset of ammonia gas.

Patterns for Different Gaseous:

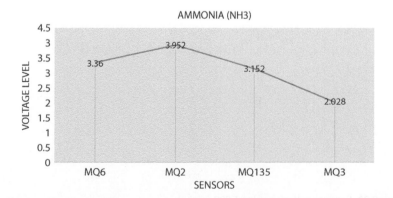

Figure 9.21 Sensors voltage level at 1,500 ppm.

9.5.2 Artificial Neural Network Model Creation

From Figures 9.21, 9.22, and 9.23, it is clear that different gaseous have different patterns. It is difficult to create a mathematical model or a non-linear equation by analyzing the plot. The mathematical model can be created easily with the help of an Artificial Neural Network. We need to create a two mathematical model, one to classify the gaseous and other to find the concentration of the gases based upon the classification of the gases.

Classification Model:
To classify the gas, a simple neural network with backpropagation is created. Figure 9.24 shows the architecture of Machine Learning Model.

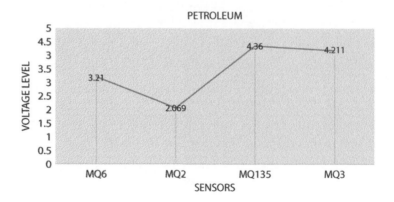

Figure 9.22 Sensors voltage level at 1,600 ppm.

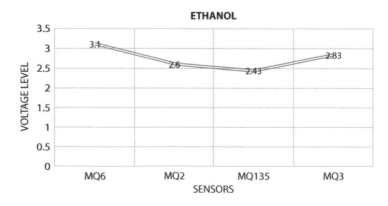

Figure 9.23 Sensors voltage level at 1,200 ppm.

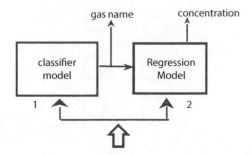

Figure 9.24 Architecture of machine learning model.

It consists of 4 input node (four sensors) and 4 output node, three gaseous (Ammonia, ethanol, LPG) and another one which is not available of trained gas state. The labels used in this model are one hot encoded so that we can get output in form of probability. Intermediately, there are 2 hidden layers with 10 neurons (perceptron) for each layer. The activation function used in between the hidden layers and in-between input a hidden layer is ReLU (Rectified Liner unit) and in between the 2nd hidden layer and output nodes the Softmax activation function is used to see the probability of the presence of each gas. For optimization i.e. setting weights and biases, Adam optimizer is the user. The neural networks for the classification model are shown in Figures 9.25 and 9.26. Figure 9.27 shows the detailed neural network model.

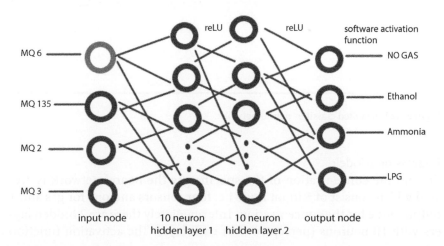

Figure 9.25 Simple neural network for gas classification.

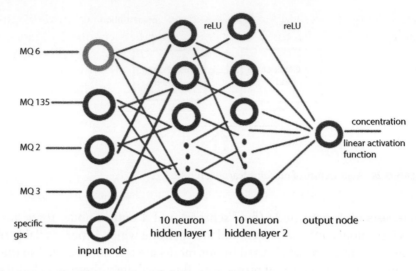

Figure 9.26 Simple neural network for gas concentration.

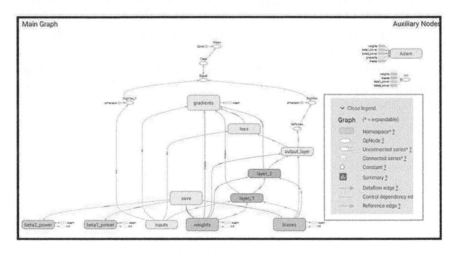

Figure 9.27 Detailed classifier neural network.

Regression Model:
To find the concentration of the specific gas the neural network is created which consist of 5 input node i.e. four sensors and one for gas and 1 output node for the concentration. Intermediately there are 2 hidden layers with 10 neurons (perceptron) of each layer. The activation function

used in between the hidden layers and well as in between input a hidden layer is ReLU (Rectified Liner unit) and in between the 2nd hidden layer and output nodes the linear activation function is used which is shown in Figure 9.28. A neural network is shown in Figure 9.26 which can be trained with the help of data set and labels. Initially, the weights and biases are random. On feeding the input, the output value compares with the label and the weight losses and biases are minimized through the process of optimization using Adam optimizer. Figure 9.27 shows the regression model.

The training will be done for multiple times which are the number of the epoch. The loss versus epochs is shown in Table 9.3 and also in Figure 9.29.

The output layer plot is shown in Figure 9.30. After the network is trained the weight and biases are stored in a separate file. Weight and biases are directly loaded to network.

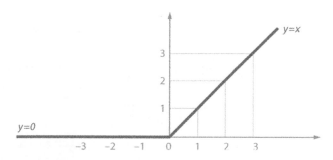

Figure 9.28 ReLU activation function.

Table 9.3 EPOCH vs LOSS.

SI. no.	EPOCH	LOSS
1	10	1.21
2	20	1.1
3	30	0.7
4	40	0.23
5	50	0.062

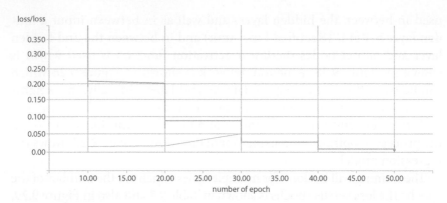

Figure 9.29 EPOCH vs LOSS.

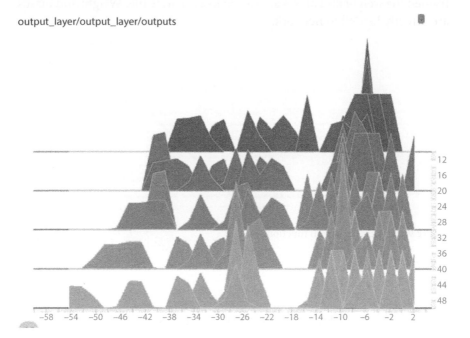

Figure 9.30 Distribution at output layer.

9.6   Results and Discussion

Once the weight and biases are fixed in the network, we can develop the system using compact Rio. The data is collected from 2 different sensor nodes in which one has high priority and others may have low priority as per industrial requirement. We can have prioritized the task based on the requirement. The Real-time programming concept is shown in Figure 9.31.

The data which need to move over from real-time embedded systems (Compact Rio) to personal computers for monitoring and data which is needed to upload to the cloud are having the least priority. The system is developed for node 2 which is shown in Figure 9.32.

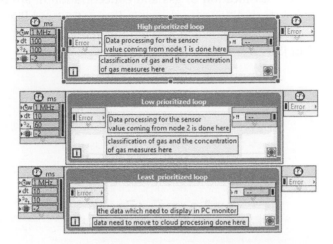

Figure 9.31 The Rough programming concept used in building the system.

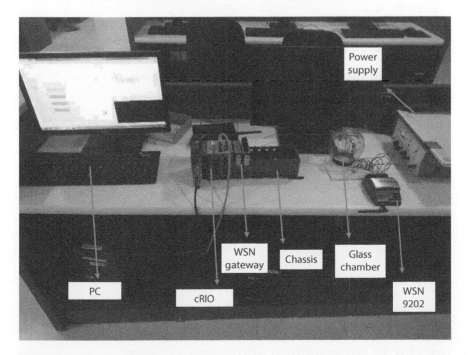

Figure 9.32 The overall proposed system.

Real-Time Programming

The priority is assigned in ratio 10:6:1 for node 1: node 2: data to the cloud. The Results for classification of gas and concentration of specific gas are shown in Figure 9.33.

The results for classification of gas and concentration of ammonia gas under two different conditions are shown in Figure 9.33 and Figure 9.34.

The entire data will be uploaded in the cloud and Figure 9.35 shows the data in cloud in JSON (JavaScript Object Notation) format.

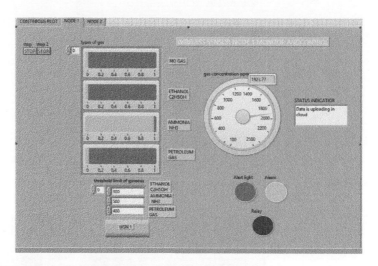

Figure 9.33 Front panel when ammonia gas is detected.

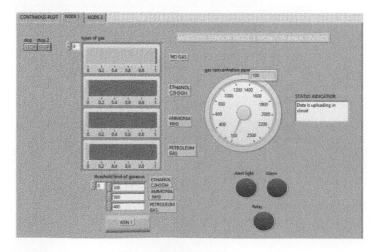

Figure 9.34 The front panel when no gas is detected.

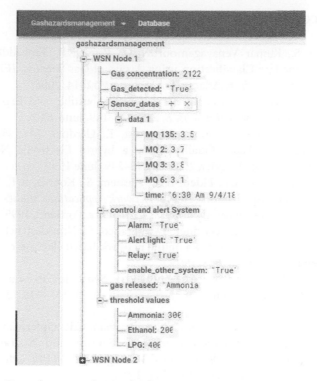

Figure 9.35 Data of sensor node 1 in cloud.

The system meets the industrial standard i.e. the system can run without downtime for 2 years at the temperature −40 to 70 °C and the wireless covers a range of 200 m can install anywhere.

9.7   Conclusion and Future Work

In order to classify the various gaseous, different tin oxide gas sensors are used. An Artificial neural network System with backpropagation has been implemented to classify the gaseous and regression model-based neural network has been developed to find the concentration of specific gas. The real-time system is built to response the data coming from the different node and to take appropriate action. Simultaneously, the entire data is moved to the cloud. Thus, the System accurately classifies the different gaseous and measures its concentration in Real-time scenario. In future, the same system can be used to train a mixture of gaseous with respective concentration.

References

1. Bashyal, S., Kumar Venayagamoorthy, G., Paudel, B., Embedded Neural Network for Fire Classification using Arrays of Gas Sensors. *IEEE Sensors Application Symposium*, Atlanta, GA, February 12–14, 2008.
2. Lee, D.-s., SnO2 Gas sensing Array for Combustible and Explosive Gas Leakage Recognition. *IEEE Sens. J.*, 2, 3, 140–149, June 2002.
3. Holmberg, M., Lundstrom, I., Winquist, F., Gardner, J.W., Hines, E.L., Identification of Paper Quality Using a hybrid Electronic Nose. *Sens. Actuators B: Chem.*, Elsevier, 27, 1–3, 246–249, June 1995.
4. Keller, P.E., Kangas, L.J., Liden, L.H., Hashem, S., Kouzes, R.T., Electronic Noses and their Applications. *Neural Network Applications Studies Workshop, IEEE Northcon/Technical Applications Conference*, Portland, 1995.
5. Llobet, E., Hines, E.L., Gardner, J.W., Franco, S., Non-destructive banana ripeness determination using a neural network-based electronic nose. *Meas. Sci. Technol.*, 10, 6, 538–548, 1999.
6. Cimander, C., Carlsson, M., Mandenius, C.-F., Sensor fusion for on-line monitoring of yoghurt fermentation. *J. Biotechnol.*, 99, 3, 237–248, 13 November 2002, 2002.
7. Edwards, J.C., Friel, G.F., Franks, R.A., Lazzara, C.P., Opferman, J.J., Mine Fire Source Discrimination Using Fire Sensors and Neural Network Analysis. *Proceedings of the Technical Meeting of the Central States Section of the Combustion Institute*, pp. 207–211, 2000.
8. http://www.ni.com/white-paper/53059/en/.
9. http://sine.ni.com/nips/cds/view/p/lang/en/nid/213990.
10. https://www.tensorflow.org/api_docs/python.

Hierarchical Elitism GSO Algorithm For Pattern Recognition

IlavazhagiBala S.[1] and Latha Parthiban[2]*

[1]Bharathiar University, Coimbatore, India
[2]Department of Computer Science, Pondicherry University, CC, Pondicherry, India

Abstract

Medical imaging research has matured in the few decades as it is generally a non-invasive technique of diagnosis. Optimization of modular neural networks (MNN) is a requirement of gravitational search measurement and diagnosis during pattern recognition. Based on the analysis of conventional Gravitational Search Algorithms (GSA) for optimization of MNN in pattern recognition, a novel method called, Hierarchical Elitism Gene Gravitational Search (HEG-GS) is proposed. Here, echocardiogram videos are used as input both comprising of healthy and non-healthy patients. This paper concentrates an explicit representation of modules. First, the echocardiogram videos are split into frames and pre-processed using Additive Kuan Filter Pre-processing algorithm. By using this algorithm, the speckle noise present in the images is reduced. Second, with the pre-processed images, by applying a hierarchical elitism gene in GSA, the MNN architecture is optimized for pattern recognition. The performance of HEG-GS method is evaluated for echocardiogram pattern recognition task. Experiments with prototypic video from the Cardiac Motion and Imaging Planes validate that the HEG-GS method effectively performs pattern recognition and thus achieve improved recognition performance with minimum CT and complexity than certain well-known pattern recognition methods.

Keywords: Gravitational search algorithms, modular neural networks, pattern recognition, additive kuan filter, hierarchical elitism

*Corresponding author: lathaparthiban@yahoo.com

R. Anandan, G. Suseendran, S. Balamurugan, Ashish Mishra and D. Balaganesh (eds.) Human Communication Technology: Internet of Robotic Things and Ubiquitous Computing, (245–262) © 2022 Scrivener Publishing LLC

10.1   Introduction

The interest in algorithms inspired by natural phenomena has increased rapidly in the past few decades. GSA is assumed to be one of the heuristic optimization techniques employed for pattern recognition which is designed based on the law of gravity and mass interactions. Besides, research in medical imaging has been on the rising side in the past few years for disease diagnosis based on the pattern being recognized.

In Ref. [1], soft computing algorithms were introduced for measurement of fetal development. Initially, Normal technique was employed in fetal ultrasound benchmark images after which features were extracted. By applying the extracted features, euro-Fuzzy using Genetic approach identifies the fetus growth as abnormal or normal. Best accuracy along with recall and specificity was attained. However, the computational cost (i.e. CT and CC) involved in pattern recognition or disease diagnosis was less concentrated. To address this issue, first pre-processing is performed to eliminate the speckle noise and heuristic method is applied to reduce the computational cost.

Soft computing algorithm is presented in Ref. [2] to discover the MNN. With the utilization of fuzzy logic in gravitational search for optimization of MNN with pattern recognition of electrocardiograms, both pattern recognition capability and training time was found to be better. However, certain room for improvements in recognition error was found as an open issue. To address this issue, the performance of GSA algorithm is improved by reducing the recognition error via Hierarchical Elitism Genetic heuristic method and as a consequence improves the MNN in pattern recognition.

In this paper, a HEG-GS is proposed for optimization of MNN in pattern recognition of echocardiogram images. The major contribution of work is listed below:

1. To enhance image quality and lessen the speckle noise, Additive Kuan Filter is applied to echocardiogram video frames
2. To reduce the CC and time involved in pattern recognition by applying Hierarchical Elitism Genetic GSA
3. HEG-GS method is introduced to estimate the pattern recognition accuracy of echocardiogram images with Cardiac Motion and Imaging Planes and compared with other methods.

The rest of the article is ordered as follows. In Section 10.2, the literature review is presented. Section 10.3 describes the proposed method for pattern recognition. The results of HEG-GS method are described in Section 10.4. In Section 10.5, the comparison of results is presented. Section 10.6 presents the Conclusions.

10.2   Related Works

It is proven that GSA includes the capability to search optimum solution. However, it suffers from low searching speed and several methods have been designed to address this solution [4]. Yet another method to solve the premature convergence and local minima was addressed in Ref. [5] using Hierarchical GSA (HGSA) via effective gravitation constant. Besides, time complexity and computation efficiency were also found to be improved with the application of HGSA. However, a trade-off was said to exist between exploration and exploitation. To address this issue, Neuro and Fuzzy GSA (NFGSA) were introduced in Ref. [6] to achieve better results without increasing computational complexity.

As far as public and information security domains are concerned, the role of biometrics is found to be increasing. Using physiological characteristics of a human, each individual is said to be identified effectively. A method to genetic optimization of MNN with fuzzy was integrated into Ref. [7] for recognition of human-based on iris, ear and voice. The method was found to be improved in terms of accuracy and as a consequence, the recognition rate was also found to be significantly improved. In Ref. [8], the disease diagnosis method was introduced for diabetic with lesser time and computation cost.

For the past several years, automatic human emotions recognition has received a lot of attention from several research persons in the domain of man-machine communication. In Ref. [9], Levenberg-Marquardt Backpropagation (LMBP) is employed. Optimization of neural emotion classifier was designed in Ref. [10] via hybrid GSAs.

Yet another technique of MNN was presented in Refs. [11, 12] with the granular approach. With this, the error rate was found to be significantly reduced. Fuzzy GSA (FGSA) has been applied in several research fields. FGSA was applied in Ref. [13] for designing the multi-machine power system. As optimization is a dynamic area of research applied in several domains, its applicability of multimodal functions extends laboriously. In Ref. [14], Comprehensive Learning Gravitational Search Algorithm was designed and was also proven to be better in terms of convergence rate and success rate also. Besides human recognition was performed in Ref. [15] by applying hierarchical genetic optimization of MNN based on multimodal biometry. Also, the noise was found to be significantly reduced.

Ant colony optimization was designed in Ref. [16] for pattern recognition. With this, image identification was made with minimal time. An enhanced MNN was presented in Ref. [17] to attain a higher rate of human recognition.

In Ref. [18], ANN was designed. However, for deep pattern recognition problems, these are not found to be the alternative solutions. To address this issue, in Ref. [19], stacking based deep neural network was designed to not only reduce the prediction errors but also minimizes the complexity involved in pattern classification. Yet another model was designed in Ref. [20] for blood pressure classification via MNN. Soft computing algorithms for disease prediction is provided in the literature [21–25].

Motivated by the aforementioned ideas and to address the issues related to CT and complexity along with the pattern recognition accuracy, in this work, HEG-GS for pattern recognition of echocardiogram images is presented in the forthcoming sections.

10.3   Methodology

In this section, the overall framework of HEG-GS method is outlined. HEG-GS method takes the pre-processed results of MNN to perform optimization with a hierarchical genetic algorithm. A hierarchical genetic gravitational search (HGSS) optimizer is presented to improve MNN for pattern recognition in echocardiogram images.

As shown in Figure 10.1, the first step remains the pre-processing of echocardiogram images obtained from cardiac motion and imaging planes. During the pre-processing of echocardiogram images are in the form of video and frames are extracted from it and applied with Kuan Filter. The purpose of applying Kuan Filter in the proposed work is that the echocardiogram images contain a large number of speckle noise.

Kuan Filter is employed to lessen the speckle noise. By reducing the speckle noise, computational cost (i.e. CT and CC) involved in pattern recognition for echocardiogram images is reduced. With the resultant pre-processed image, HEG-GS is applied for optimization of MNN in pattern recognition in echocardiogram images. With this HEG-GS method, pattern recognition error in echocardiogram images is reduced.

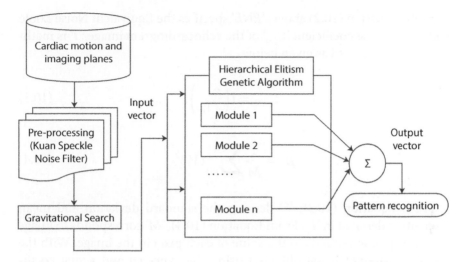

Figure 10.1 Block diagram of the hierarchical elitism genetic gravitational search method.

10.3.1 Additive Kuan Speckle Noise Filtering Model

In this section, the pre-processing of echocardiogram images using the Additive Kuan Speckle Noise Filtering model is explained. The main problem in pattern recognition of medical applications is speckle noise present in echocardiogram images. Hence, the resulting images with speckle noise affect the borders of cardiac structures. Therefore, it reduces the probability of physicists in differentiating between the actual and borders of the image.

To minimize the speckle noise in echocardiogram images, the cardiac motion and imaging planes, the videos are split into frames, followed by which the Kuan Filter [1] is applied. The Additive Kuan Filter (AKF) models do filtering and mathematically expressed as given below.

$$W = I\left[(1 - C_{EN}/C_{AN})\right] + \rho^2 \tag{10.1}$$

From Equation (10.1) above, the weight 'W' is obtained based on the expected noise coefficients 'C_{EN}' of the echocardiogram image 'I' and the actual noise coefficient 'C_{AN}' of the echocardiogram image respectively. Finally 'ρ^2' corresponds to the additive noise variance of the image. The expected noise coefficient 'C_{EN}' of the echocardiogram image, 'I' is mathematically expressed as given below.

$$C_{EN} = I\left(\sqrt{1/ENL}\right) \tag{10.2}$$

From Equation (10.2) above, 'ENL' specifies the Equivalent Noise Look. The actual noise coefficient 'C_{EN}' of the echocardiogram image, 'I' is mathematically expressed as given below

$$C_{AN} = I\left(\frac{S}{I_m}\right) \tag{10.3}$$

$$\rho^2 = \frac{1}{M}\sum_{i=1}^{n}(V_i)^2 \tag{10.4}$$

From Equation (10.3), 'S' denotes the standard deviation and mean intensity is denoted in 'I_m'. From Equation (10.4), 'M' corresponds to image size and 'V_i' corresponds to the value of each pixel in the image. With the above, the weight being obtained using the expected and actual coefficients, filtering is performed with the input images, therefore resulting in the speckle noise removal.

Input: Echocardiogram images '$I = I_1, I_2, ..., I_n$'
Output: Speckle noise removed images
1: Begin
2:      For each echocardiogram images 'I'
3:            Measure different weight 'W' to perform filtering using (1)
4:            Measure expected noise coefficient using (2)
5:            Measure actual noise coefficient using (3)
6:            Measure the additive noise using (4)
6:            Return (speckle noise removed echocardiogram images)
7:      End for
8: End

Algorithm 1 Additive kuan filter pre-processing.

Additive Kuan Filter Pre-processing algorithm is employed for removing the speckle noise in each echocardiogram images. This is carried out through the Kuan Filter. To lessen speckle noise in echocardiogram images, the Kuan filter is used to improve the filter performance in terms of both quality and run time. This is achieved by first measuring the different weight factors to perform filtering based on the two coefficients, namely, expected noise coefficient and actual noise coefficient. By observing the Equivalent Noise Look and mean intensity within the window, noise is removed and hence both the quality and run time is said to be improved.

10.3.2   Hierarchical Elitism Gene GSO of MNN in Pattern Recognition

The Hierarchical Elitism Gene Gravitational Search for Optimization of MNN in Pattern Recognition is described. The method uses MNN [2] and architectures are designed through the hierarchical genetic optimizer. The idea behind modularity function is based on the divide and conquer principle. Every problem is partitioned into minimal subproblem which is addressed by sub-modules. Their partial solutions are integrated to create a final solution. The results involving MNNs attains a significant learning improvement than the single Neural Network.

Algorithms using heuristic have been significant in optimizing problems. Among several heuristic optimization models, GSA is depended on the law of gravity pioneered by Ref. [3]. Based on populations (i.e. echocardiogram images given as input) and the law of gravity and motion [2] applied to discover an optimum solution (i.e. pattern recognition in echocardiogram images). The Flow diagram of HGSS method is shown in Figure 10.2.

From the figure, consider a model with " agents, then the position of " agent is expressed as below.

$$P_i = (P_i^1, \ldots, P_i^f, \ldots P_i^n), i = 1, 2, \ldots, n \tag{10.5}$$

From Equation (10.5), 'P_i^f' signifies the position of 'ith' agent in 'fth' dimension. At distinct time 't', the force of agent 'j' acting on agent 'i' is expressed as below.

$$F_{ij}^d = G(t) \frac{M_i(t)}{ED_{ij}(t) + \beta} \tag{10.6}$$

From Equation (10.6) above, the force 'F' is obtained based on the fitness evaluation '$M_i(t)$', Euclidean distance 'ED_{ij}' between agent 'i' and 'j' along with a small constant 'β' respectively. This Euclidean distance is mathematically expressed as given below.

$$ED_{ij}(t) = \sqrt{\left[p_j^d(t) - p_i^d(t) \right]^2} \tag{10.7}$$

From Equation (10.7), the Euclidean distance among agent 'i' and 'j' is the difference among the position of 'jth' agent in 'd' dimension at a time 't'

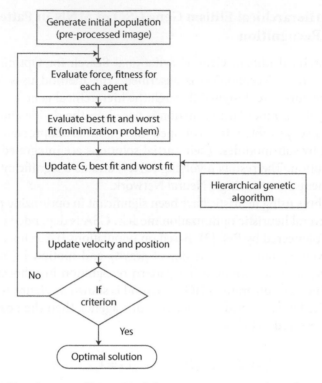

Figure 10.2 Flow diagram of hierarchical elitism gene gravitational search.

and position of '*ith*' agent in '*d*' dimension at a time '*t*'. The fitness evaluations are measured as below.

$$M_i(t) = G(t) * \frac{m_i(t)}{\sum_{j=1}^{n} m_j(t)} \tag{10.8}$$

$$m_i(t) = \frac{fit_i(t) * fit_{worst}(t)}{fit_{best}(t) * fit_{worst}(t)} \tag{10.9}$$

From Equations (10.8) and (10.9) above, '$G(t)$' represents the gravitation constant (i.e. novelty is introduced here in arriving at the optimized value of G using hierarchical elitism genes), '$fit_i(t)$' symbolizes fitness of agent 'i' at a time 't', '$fit_{worst}(t)$', represent the worst fitness in an iteration at a time 't' and '$fit_{best}(t)$' represent the best fitness in an iteration. For a minimization problem (i.e. maximizing the pattern recognition accuracy of echocardiogram images in this research), the best fit and worst fit are formulated as given below.

$$fit_{worst}(t) = MAX\left(fit_j(t)\right), j \in 1, 2, \dots, n \qquad (10.10)$$

$$fit_{best}(t) = MIN\left(fit_j(t)\right), j \in 1, 2, \dots, n \qquad (10.11)$$

Finally, the position '$p_i^d(t+1)$' and velocity '$V_i^d(t+1)$' of agent 'i' in 'd' dimension at a time 't' is expressed as given below.

$$V_i^d(t+1) = V_i^d(t) + \frac{F_i^d(t)}{M_{ii}(t)} \qquad (10.12)$$

From Equation (10.12), '$F_i^d(t)$' denotes the total forces which act on agent 'i' in a dimension 'd' at a time 't' and '$M_{ii}(t)$' denotes the inertial mass of agent 'i' at time 't'.

$$p_i^d(t+1) = p_i^d(t+1) + V_i^d(t+1) \qquad (10.13)$$

As illustrated in the figure, where the refinement is applied in this algorithm, that is modifying the alpha parameter to update 'G' and support GSA to achieve better performance. In the fourth step, the refinement of the algorithm is done by applying a hierarchical elitism genetic operation. This hierarchical elitism genetic operation performs optimization of MNN architectures, which finding their optimal parameters based on elitism. With the application of hierarchical elitism genetic operation in GSA for optimization of MNN, pattern recognition error is said to be minimized and therefore results in the improvement of pattern recognition accuracy using the fitness function. The fitness function 'f' is mathematically expressed as given below.

$$f = \sum_{i=1}^{m}\left[\left(\sum_{j=1}^{n_m} \frac{PI_j}{n_m}\right)\right]\begin{cases} PI_j \text{ is } 0 \text{ if module provides correct results} \\ PI_j \text{ is } 1 \text{ if module provides incorrect results} \end{cases}$$

$$(10.14)$$

From Equation (10.14), the fitness function 'f' is calculated based on the total number of modules 'm' and 'n_m' corresponding to the total number of echocardiogram pre-processed images used for testing. Besides 'PI_j' is '0' then the module offers correct results and if '1' then the module offers incorrect results. Based on the above fitness function, the best fit, worst fit and G values are updated. Followed by the evaluation of fitness function, elitism is measured. The elitism in the proposed work involves copying a small proportion of the fittest candidates (i.e. echocardiogram images), unchanged, into the next generation. The advantage of using elitism in the hierarchical genetic algorithm is to minimize the time re-discovering previously eliminated partial solutions. This lessens the CT and CC in the optimization of MNN for pattern recognition. The validations are mathematically expressed as given below.

$$V_{max} = \sum_{r=1}^{tdm} \frac{n!}{r!(n-r)!} \tag{10.15}$$

From Equation (10.15), 'V_{max}' represents the number of possible validations, 'n' denotes the number of echocardiogram images per person, 'r' denotes total images employed for training. With the above incorporation of average elitism in the proposed work, not only the recognition error is minimized, but also the time and complexity involved are also reduced. The pseudo-code representation of Hierarchical Elitism Genetic Gravitational Search is given below.

Input: Pre-processed image '$PI = PI_1, PI_2, ..., PI_n$'
Output: Pattern recognition with minimum time and complexity
1: **Begin**
2:     **For** each pre-processed image 'PI'
3:         **Repeat**
4:             Measure force of agent 'j' acting on agent 'i' using (6)
5:             Measure Euclidean distance between agent 'i' and 'j' using (7)
6:             Measure fitness evaluations using (8)
7:             Measure best fit and worst fit using (10) and (11)
8:             Measure velocity and position of agent 'i' in 'd' dimension at time 't' using (12) and (13)
9:             Update G, best fit and worst fit based on the fitness function using (14)
10:             Perform validation using (15)
11:             **If** criterion met
12:                 Go to 15
13:             **Else go to** 4
14:             **End if**
15:         **Until** (all pre-processed images are processed)
16:     **End for**
17: **End**

Algorithm 2 Hierarchical elitism genetic gravitational search.

As given in Hierarchical Elitism Genetic GSA, for each pre-processed echocardiogram images, the objective of the algorithm remains in applying hierarchical elitism gene in gravitational search for optimization of MNN in pattern recognition. This is said to be achieved, by first, measuring the force, fitness function, best fit and worst fit. With these values evaluated, velocity and position are also obtained. Next, hierarchical elitism gene is applied in GSA with the core objective of optimizing MNN. The advantage of hierarchical elitism gene in GSA is that it copies a small proportion of echocardiogram images, unchanged, into the next generation, therefore reducing the computation time and complexity involved. Finally, validation is performed by applying the average elitism and the process is continued for all pre-processed echocardiogram images.

10.4   Experimental Setup

The echocardiogram images used in the experimentation are all obtained from the Cardiac Motion and Imaging Planes. They are obtained from ASE/SCA. For each echocardiogram videos, different numbers of frames are generated and the number of frames is not said to be equal for all videos. Hence, different numbers of frames are obtained for different video images provided as input. As given in Figure 10.3, 52 different frames were extracted and for sample three frames are provided. Figure 10.3 shows a sample video and the number of frames.

10.5   Discussion

The performance of HEG-GS method is compared with the two existing methods [1] and [2]. For a fair comparison, three different parameters,

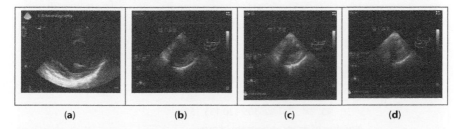

| (a) | (b) | (c) | (d) |

Figure 10.3 Echocardiogram video images from Cardiac Motion and Imaging Planes (a) Input echocardiogram video, (b) frame-1, (c) frame-2 and (d) frame-3.

CT, CC and pattern recognition accuracy are measured with similar videos and frames. The graphical representation of the three different parameters along with the sample calculations is provided below.

10.5.1   Scenario 1: Computational Time

The first significant metric required for pattern recognition is the computational time. With the minimum time required for computation, the pattern recognition task is said to be accomplished at a fast rate. CT is measured as below.

$$CT = \sum_{i=1}^{n} I_i * Time \; [Pattern \; Recognition] \qquad (10.16)$$

From Equation (10.16), the 'I_i' refers to the number of echocardiogram images and time consumed in pattern recognition. The time consumed in pattern recognition involves both the time consumed in obtaining the 'G' value and the time consumed for best fit '$fit_{best}(t)$' and worst fit '$fit_{worst}(t)$' respectively. It is measured in milliseconds (ms).

Figure 10.4 given below shows the convergence graph of CT for 150 different echocardiogram images. Comparison of HEG-GS method is made with two existing methods [1] and [2].

The result of CT is illustrated in Figure 10.4 with the number of images given as input. From the figure, the CT increases when an increase in the

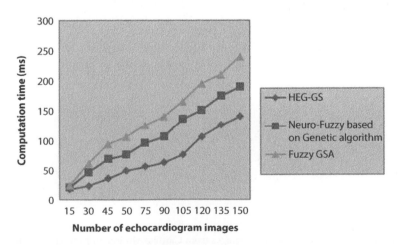

Figure 10.4 Graphical representation of computational time.

number of echocardiogram images. It is evident that with the increasing number of echocardiogram images, the time consumed for split the images into frames also increases. This in turn results in an increase in the CT and hence, from the figure, the number of echocardiogram images is directly proportional to CT. However, from the figure it is inferred that the CT for pattern recognition is found to be reduced by applying the HEG-GS method first the speckle noise present in the echocardiogram images is removed. With the noise removed pre-processed images, the pattern recognition time is said to be reduced and therefore the pattern recognition accuracy is also said to be improved. With '15' number of echocardiogram images given as input, the overall CT using HEG-GS method is found to be '17.25 ms', CT using existing [1] and [2] is '20.25 ms' and '23.25 ms' respectively.

10.5.2 Scenario 2: Computational Complexity

The second metrics most significant for pattern recognition is the CC involved. In other words, CC refers to complexity in pattern recognition. CC is measured as given below.

$$CC = \sum_{i=1}^{n} I_i * MEM \; [Pattern \; Recognition] \qquad (10.17)$$

From Equation (10.17), the 'CC' is calculated based on the number of echocardiogram images as input 'I_i' and memory consumed for pattern recognition. The memory consumed in pattern recognition involves both the memory consumed for measuring the 'G' value and the memory consumed for best fit '$fit_{best}(t)$' and worst fit '$fit_{worst}(t)$' respectively. It is measured in terms of kilobytes (KB).

Figure 10.5 given below shows the convergence graph of CC involved for 150 different echocardiogram images. Comparison of HEG-GS method is made with the two existing methods [1] and [2].

Figure 10.5 given above illustrates the CC involved in pattern recognition. Higher the computational complexity, more complex the pattern to be recognized and hence lesser the pattern recognition accuracy is said to be. As already explained in the experimental section for a different number of video images and different numbers of frames are extracted and hence the CC is also not linear or directly proportional to each other. However, the CC is found to be in the increasing trend. This is because with the higher number of echocardiogram images, obviously, with the increase in the size,

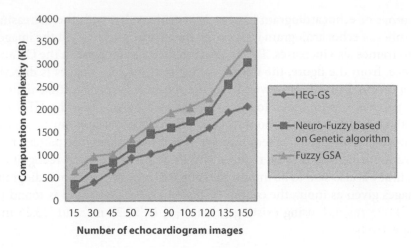

Figure 10.5 Graphical representation of computational complexity.

the complexity involved in pattern recognition is also found to be higher. But, the CC is found to be lesser using HEG-GS method as compared to existing [1] and [2]. This is because of the reason that Additive Kuan Filter is applied for removing the speckle noise during pre-processing. Followed by the speckle noise removed images, the hierarchical genetic optimizer is used for Optimization of MNN in Pattern Recognition. With the application of hierarchical genetic optimizer results involving MNNs implies an extensive learning improvement in single NN. With the optimized results, the CC involved in pattern recognition for echocardiogram images is reduced. The CC using HEG-GS method is found to be reduced by 27% compared to Neuro-Fuzzy based on Genetic algorithm [1] and 40% compared to Fuzzy GSA [2] respectively.

10.5.3   Scenario 3: Pattern Recognition Accuracy

Pattern recognition accuracy measured as the ratio of correctly recognized patterns (i.e. correctly recognized echocardiogram sample images) to a total number of sample patterns (i.e. echocardiogram sample images). Higher the correctly recognized patterns, higher the pattern recognition accuracy. It is mathematically expressed as given below.

$$PRecAcc = \sum_{i=1}^{n} \left[\frac{CRecPatterns}{I_i} \right] * 100 \qquad (10.18)$$

From Equation (10.18) above, pattern recognition accuracy '*PRecAcc*' is obtained based on the number of correctly recognized patterns '*CRecPatterns*' and the number of samples 'I_i' provided as input.

Figure 10.6 given below shows the convergence graph of pattern recognition accuracy for 150 different echocardiogram images. Comparison of HEG-GS method is made for recognizing the pattern accuracy with two existing methods [1] and [2].

Figure 10.6 given above illustrates the graphical representation of pattern recognition accuracy for 150 different numbers of echocardiogram images. Pattern recognition recognizes the patterns and based on the recognized patterns, classification is made. In this work, with the aid of echocardiogram images, the patterns are recognized. With the recognized patterns, the physicists conclude the presence or absence of heart disease. From the above figure, the pattern recognition accuracy is not either directly or inversely proportional to several images. This is because different numbers of images extracted different numbers of frames and then with the pre-processing speckle noise is removed. With the different numbers of frames, when pattern recognition is done, the accuracy does not consistently increase or decreases. However, pattern recognition accuracy is found to be improved using the HEG-GS method. This is because of the application of Hierarchical Elitism Genetic GSA. By applying the hierarchical elitism gene in the Hierarchical Elitism Genetic GSA, the objective remains in optimizing the MNN. The objective of using hierarchical elitism gene in GSA is that it reproduces a trivial fraction of

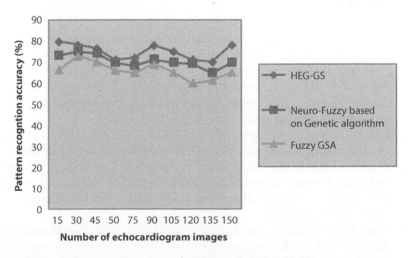

Figure 10.6 Graphical representation of pattern recognition accuracy.

echocardiogram images, consistent, into the next generation, therefore minimizing the time and complexity in pattern recognition. With this, a higher amount of patterns are recognized. Therefore, the pattern recognition accuracy using HEG-GS method is improved by 6% compared to Neuro-Fuzzy based on Genetic algorithm [1] and 13% compared to Fuzzy GSA [2] respectively.

10.6   Conclusion

GSA plays an important role in recognizing the patterns for echocardiogram images recently. In this work, a HEG-GS method is introduced to overcome the computational cost (i.e. CC and CT involved in pattern recognition) and recognition accuracy issues of pattern recognition. Firstly, in this work, pre-processing is performed using the Additive Kuan Filter. Next, with the pre-processed output images, Hierarchical Elitism Gravitational Search for optimization of MNN in Pattern Recognition is presented. Experiments are performed and the result reflects that HEG-GS method outperforms as compared to conventional works, distinguish the mass between normal and abnormal by using Hierarchical Elitism Genetic GSA. To measure its performance, experimental simulations tests are made using Cardiac Motion and Imaging Planes. Results show that the HEG-GS method provides better performance in terms of CT, CC and pattern recognition accuracy in comparison with other methods.

References

1. Kaur, P., Singh, G., Kaur, P., An intelligent validation system for diagnostic and prognosis of ultrasound fetal growth analysis using Neuro-Fuzzy based on genetic Algorithm. *Egypt. Inform. J.*, Elsevier, 20, 55–87, Oct 2018.
2. González, B., Valdez, F., Melin, P., Prado-Arechiga, G., Fuzzy logic in the for the optimization of modular neural networks in pattern recognition. *Expert Syst. Appl.*, Elsevier, 42, 5839–5847, 2015.
3. Rashedi, E., Nezamabadi-pour, H., Saryazdi, S., GSA: A Gravitational Search Algorithm. *Inf. Sci. (Ny)*, 179, 2232–2248, 2009, https://doi.org/10.1016/j.
4. Mirjalili, S.A., Hashim, M., Zaiton, S., Moradian Sardroudi, H., Training feedforward neural networks using hybrid particle swarm optimization and gravitational search algorithm. *Appl. Math. Comput.*, Elsevier, 218, 11125–11137, May 2018.
5. Wang, Y., Yu, Y., Gao, S., Pan, H., Yang, G., A hierarchical gravitational search algorithm with an effective gravitational constant. *Swarm Evol. Comput. Base Data*, Elsevier, 46, 118–139, Feb 2019.

6. Pelusi, D., Mascella, R., Tallini, L., Nayak, J., Naik, B., Abraham, A., Neural Network and Fuzzy System for the tuning of Gravitational Search Algorithm parameters. *Expert Syst. Appl.*, Elsevier, 102, 234–244, Feb 2018.

7. Melin, P., Sánchez, D., Castillo, O., Genetic optimization of modular neural networks with fuzzy response integration for human recognition. *Inf. Sci.*, Elsevier, 197, 1–19, Feb 2012.

8. Jayashree, J. and Ananda Kumar, S., Evolutionary Correlated Gravitational Search Algorithm With Genetic Optimized Hopfield Neural Network—A Hybrid Expert System for Diagnosis of Diabetes. *Measurement*, Elsevier, 145, 551–558, Dec 2018.

9. Lv, C., Xing, Y., Zhang, J., Na, X., Li, Y., Liu, T., Co, D., Wang, F.-Y., Levenberg-Marquardt Backpropagation Training of Multilayer Neural Networks for State Estimation of A Safety Critical Cyber-Physical System. *IEEE Trans. Ind. Inf.*, 14, 8, 3436–3446, Aug 2018.

10. Sheikhan, M. and Abbasnezhad Arabi, M., Connection Optimization of a Neural Emotion Classifier Using Hybrid Gravitational Search Algorithms. *Int. J. Inf. Commun. Technol. Res.*, 7, 1, 41–51, May 2015.

11. Sánchez, D. and Melin, P., Optimization of modular granular neural networks using hierarchical genetic algorithms for human recognition using the ear biometric measure. *Eng. Appl. Artif. Intell.*, Elsevier, 27, 41–56, Oct 2013.

12. Chao, Z. and Kim, H.-J., Slice interpolation of medical images using enhanced fuzzy radial basis function neural networks. *Comput. Biol. Med.*, Elsevier, 110, 66–78, May 2019.

13. Ghasemi, A., Shayeghi, H., Alkhatib, H., Robust design of multi machine power system stabilizers using fuzzy gravitational search algorithm. *Electr. Power Energy Syst.*, Elsevier, 5, 190–200, Apr 2013.

14. Bala, I. and Yadav, A., Comprehensive learning gravitational search algorithm for global optimization of multi, modal functions. *Neural Comput. Appl.*, Springer, 32, 7347–7382, May 2019.

15. Sanchez, D., Melin, P., Castillo, O., Hierarchical genetic optimization of modular neural networks and their type-2 fuzzy response integrators for human recognition based on multimodal biometry. *International Joint Conference on Neural Networks*, Aug 2011.

16. Valdez, F., Castillo, O., Melin, P., Ant Colony Optimization for the Design of Modular Neural Networks in Pattern Recognition. *International Joint Conference on Neural Networks*, Nov 2016.

17. Sánchez, D., Melin, P., Castillo, O., A Grey Wolf Optimizer for Modular Granular Neural Networks for Human Recognition. *Comput. Intell. Neurosci.*, Hindawi, 2017, 1–26, July 2017.

18. Amer, M. and Maul, T., A Review of Modularization Techniques in Artificial Neural Networks. *Artif. Intell. Rev.*, Springer, 52, 527–561, Jun 2019.

19. Low, C.-Y., Park, J., Beng-Jin Teoh, A., Stacking-Based Deep Neural Network: Deep Analytic Network for Pattern Classification. *Computer Vision and Pattern Recognition*, May 2010.

20. Pulido, M., Melin, P., Prado-Arechiga, G., Blood Pressure Classification Using the Method of the Modular Neural Networks. *Int. J. Hypertens.*, 2019, 1–13, Jan 2019.
21. Parthiban, L. and Subramanian, R., An intelligent agent for detection of ery-themato-squamous diseases using co-active neuro-fuzzy inference system and genetic algorithm. *2009 International Conference on Intelligent Agent & Multi-Agent Systems*, pp. 1–6.
22. Vaithinathan, K. and Parthiban, L., Alzheimer's Disease Neuroimaging Initiative, A novel texture extraction technique with T1 weighted MRI for the classification of Alzheimer's disease. *J. Neurosci. Methods*, 318, 84–99, 2019.
23. Venkatesan, A.S. and Parthiban, L., A novel nature inspired fuzzy tsallis entropy segmentation of magnetic resonance images. *Neuroquantology*, 12, 2, 1–2, 2014.
24. George, G. and Parthiban, L., Multi objective hybridized firefly algorithm with group search optimization for data clustering. *2015 IEEE International Conference on Research in Computational Intelligence.*
25. Venkatesan, A. and Parthiban, L., Medical Image Segmentation With Fuzzy C-Means and Kernelized Fuzzy C-Means Hybridized on PSO and QPSO. *Int. Arab J. Inf. Technol. (IAJIT)*, 14, 1, 305–307, 2017.

Multidimensional Survey of Machine Learning Application in IoT (Internet of Things)

Anurag Sinha[1]* and Pooja Jha[2]

[1]Department of Computer Science and IT, Amity University Jharkhand, Ranchi, India
[2]Department of Computer Science, Amity University Jharkhand, Ranchi, India

Abstract

Rapid growth in computer and Information Technologies depends upon the internet based devices that making it possible to connect with the every single impossible thing in this physical world so efficiently. In the last decades IoT gained very much popularity across the world, The Rise of the sensory based devices are being utilized in the modern way of living, transportation and industry. With the increase of this IoT based devices, now a day's its rapidly approaching the technologies in private and business sector. With the rise of internet based devices the main focus of its security and data are increasing. In today's Era the technology and this sensory device are being implemented in various sectors to make a city a smart City.

The basic goal of proposing this book chapter is to amalgamate those multidisciplinary application areas of IoT in the nutshell of machine learning algorithm. The basic aim of proposing this chapter is also to analyze the different usability of machine learning in iot. Applications of IoT with machine learning can be the different factors of a city such as in Healthcare system, logistics, transportation and Agriculture. We have done the survey by accumulating the data of different papers related to the same domain in which our focus is to extract the best machine learning algorithms that has been implemented in internet of things. This chapter is also intended to make people aware about the IoT Technologies that can be achievable that people will use these technologies in their day to day life.

Keywords: Machine learning, machine learning algorithms, IoT, Smart city, applications

*Corresponding author: anuragsinha257@gmail.com

R. Anandan, G. Suseendran, S. Balamurugan, Ashish Mishra and D. Balaganesh (eds.) Human Communication Technology: Internet of Robotic Things and Ubiquitous Computing, (263–300) © 2022 Scrivener Publishing LLC

11.1   Machine Learning—An Introduction

Machines are normally not savvy. At first, machines were intended to perform explicit errands, such as running on the railroad, prevailing the traffic stream, burrow profound gaps, going into the house, and taking shots at moving articles. Machines carry out their responsibilities a great deal of speedier with the following degree of exactness contrasted with people. The major qualification among people and machines in acting their work is insight. The human mind gets information accumulated by the 5 detects: vision, hearing, smell, taste, and physical sense. This accumulated information is sent to the human cerebrum by means of the neural framework for discernment and making a move. Inside the observation technique, the data is sorted out, perceived by examination it to past encounters that were hang on inside the memory, and comprehended. Therefore, the cerebrum takes the decision and guides the body parts to respond against that activity. At the tip of the aptitude, it would be hang on inside the memory for future points of interest.

In a 2006 article entitled "The Discipline of Machine Learning," academician Tom Mitchell [3, p.1] sketched out the control of AI in these words:

AI might be a characteristic outgrowth of the convergence of innovation and Statistics. We'd state the procedure question of innovation is 'By what method will we tend to manufacture machines that settle issues, and that issues are characteristically manageable/obstinate?' The inquiry that generally characterizes Statistics is 'What is derived from information and an assortment of displaying suspicions, with what dependability?' The procedure question for Machine Learning expands on each, anyway it's an unmistakable inquiry. While innovation has fixated absolutely on an approach to physically program PCs, Machine Learning centers around the subject of an approach to get PCs to program themselves (from aptitude and some underlying structure).

There are a couple of tasks that individuals perform effectively or with specific undertakings, at any rate we will in general can't clarify in any case we perform them. Maybe, we will perceive the talk of our mates while not abundant issue. If we tend to are asked in any case we perceive the voices, the course of action is incredibly extraordinary for USA to clarify. In view of the insufficiency of understanding of such unforeseen development (talk affirmation during this case), we will when all is said in done can't make computations for such conditions. Man-made intelligence estimations are useful in conquering this issue of perception. The thought is unfathomably straightforward. We will when all is said in done don't seem to center to know the fundamental strategies that support USA learns. We will as a rule make PC programs that may collect machines learn and alter them to perform endeavors, looking like desire. The target of learning is to build up a model that takes the information and produces the important result. A portion of the time, we will see the model, while, at elective events, it also can be somewhat of a recorder for USA, the working of that can't be instinctually explained. The model is consistently considered as Associate in Nursing conjecture of the system we wish machines to imitate. In such a circumstance, it's conceivable that we will by and large secure slip-ups for two or three information, at any rate as a rule, the model offers right responses. Consequently, another live of execution (other than execution of estimations of speed and memory utilization) of an AI algorithmic program is the precision of results.

11.1.1   Classification of Machine Learning

AI (ML) isn't a spic and span thought. Milliliter is intently including Artificial Intelligence (AI). Simulated intelligence becomes conceivable by means of milliliter. Through ML, pc frameworks figure out how to perform undertakings relating to classification, bunching, forecasts, design acknowledgment, and so forth. To chronicle the preparation strategy, frameworks are prepared exploitation various calculations and applied arithmetic models to examine test information. The example information are regularly portrayed by quantifiable attributes alluded to as choices Associate in Nursing a milliliter algorithmic program makes an endeavor to find a relationship between the highlights and a couple of yield esteems called names [8]. At that point, the data acquired during the preparation stage is utilized to recognize design for settle on choices dependent on new information. Milliliter is directly for issues relating to relapse, classification, bunching, and affiliation rules assurance. Looking on the preparation vogue, milliliter calculations might be characterized into four classifications: refer to Figure 11.1.

Supervised Learning: Supervised Learning oversees issues including backslide contrasting with meteorology, assessing life dominance, and growth gauge, by abuse estimations like direct backslide or Random Forest. without a doubt, oversaw learning conveys classification issues contrasting with digit affirmation, talk affirmation, clinical distinguishing strength, and character distortion acknowledgment, by using estimations, for instance, SVM, ANN, and others. There are 2 phases in oversaw learning. The preparation part and testing stage the informational collections used for the teaching part should be obliged to have perceived names. The computations

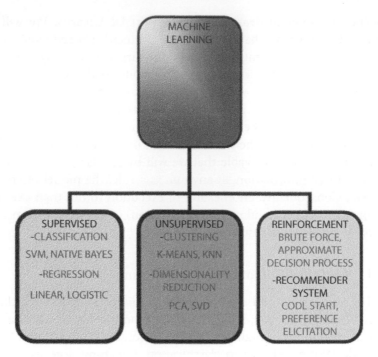

Figure 11.1 Classification of ML algorithm.

get acquainted with the association between the data regards and checks and take a gander at to foresee the yield estimations Figure 11.1 [9].

Unsupervised Learning: unattended learning manages issues including spatiality decrease utilized for enormous information visual picture, highlight input, or the development of shrouded structures. Also, directed learning is utilized for cluster issues relating to suggestion frameworks, customer division, and focused on selling. In opposition to directed getting the hang of, during this sort, no names are out there. Calculations during this class attempt to decide designs on testing information and group the data or foresee future qualities [9].

Semi-Supervised Learning: this can be a mix of the preceding 2 classes. Each named information and untagged facts are brought into play. It works essentially basically like the unattended learning with the upgrades that some of named data will bring [8].

Reinforcement Learning: During the trend, the counts endeavor to forecast the give way for a bunch reinforced a get-together of standardization limits. By then, the decided yield gets Associate in Nursing input limit and new yield is resolved till the perfect yield is found. (ANN) and Deep Learning, which can be given later, use this learning vogue. stronghold learning is primarily used for applications like AI unfortunate propensity, limit making sure about, robot course, and time span choices [9].

At the point when exploitation milliliter methods, there are 2 significant boundaries to consider; how computationally exceptional and the manner in which brisk a given procedure is. Looking on the applying sort, the first satisfactory milliliter algorithmic program is picked. On the off chance that there's a craving for timeframe investigation possibly, the picked algorithmic program should be sufficiently fast to follow the progressions of the PC record and turn out the necessary yield during an ideal way.

11.2 Internet of Things

Expanding the current net with every associated gadget (or expressed as "Things") and their virtual delineation has been a developing pattern in decades. This may create scores of most likely new applications, product and administrations in numerous elective angles, love reasonable homes, reasonable medicinal services, car, reasonable vehicle and providing, and ecological viewing [IBM12]. The investigation during this space has as of late picked up scores of consideration, after all scores of money, and is bolstered by the cooperation from academe, industry, and normalization bodies in numerous networks revere media transmission, protection companies, etymology net, and data science. These winds up in scores of investments accompany the tide.

For quite a while, standard systems are kept proposed for express limits with obliged versatility. This suggests once one classification is running, it can't be changed animatedly and adaptable. the existing group on introducing the IoT (or a huge amount of general, the more expanded term of Internet) demands purpose, thing and fasten stages which may get, give, stock up, admittance and offer information from the physical world, particularly they'll talk with the globe. This may make new open entryways in a staggeringly colossal assurance of zones, as sensible prosperity, retail, natural essentialness, conveying, sensible homes and conjointly altered end-customer applications.

All things considered, IoT plays a lot of and dynamically principal work in way of life. The degree of data on the web and moreover the net has quite recently been overwhelming and remains creating at magnificent pace:

In the midst of the extension of the catch of Things (IoT), applications turned out to be progressively savvy and related contraptions make to their maltreatment everything thought about pieces of a contemporary town. Since the volume of the assembled data will grow, Machine Learning (ML) techniques are applied to any overhauls the information and henceforth the capacities of AN application. The field of good transportation has pulled in a couple of experts and it's been moved nearer with each cubic centimeter and IoT techniques. During this overview, incredible transportation is viewed as AN umbrella term that spreads course improvement, halting, street illumination, misfortune evasion/disclosure, road abnormalities, and establishment applications. The purpose of this chapter is to make an autonomous review of cubic centimeter methods and IoT applications in (ITS) and get a direct read of the examples inside the equal fields and spot conceivable consideration needs. From the investigated articles it becomes critical that there's a plausible nonattendance of cubic centimeter incorporation for the incomparable Lighting Systems and incredible Parking applications. Without a doubt, course improvement, halting, and setback/revelation will as a rule be the primary standard ITS applications among authorities.

11.3   ML in IoT

11.3.1   Overview

In IoT terms, each related contraption is viewed as a factor. Things consistently meld corporeal sensors, actuators, and an embedded scheme with a microchip. Things need to talk with one another, making the essential for Machine-to-Machine (M2M) correspondence. The correspondence are routinely short-run misuse far off developments like Wi-Fi, Bluetooth, and ZigBee, or wide-broaden misuse adaptable frameworks. Due to the gigantic utilization of IoT contraptions all things considered styles of lifestyle applications, it's central to remain the estimation of IoT devices low. Also, IoT devices ought to have the choice to manage basic tasks basically like the information game plan, M2M correspondence, and even some pre-treatment of the information figuring on the mechanical assembly. Thus, it's required to find equality among esteem, process power, and related imperativeness use once coming up with or picking an IoT contraption. IoT is also solidly trapped to "huge data", since IoT devices unendingly accumulate and exchange an extraordinary measure of information. In this manner, accomplice IoT structure routinely completes procedures to manage, store, and dismember colossal information [3]. it's become an ordinary apply in IoT establishments, to use accomplice IoT stage like Kea, Things board, Device Hive, Thing talk, or Mainflux so as to help the M2M correspondence, misuse and trades show [4]. In addition, IoT organizes smoothly observation limits, center point the administrators, information taking care of and exploring, information driven configurable rules, etc. figuring on the mechanical assembly, it's typically fundamental that some planning occurs inside the IoT devices rather than some concentrated center point since it happens inside the "conveyed processing" system. In this way, in light of the fact that the methodology part moves to the tip compose parts, a replacement enlisting model is introduced, implied as "edge handling" [5]. In any case, since those devices ar most of the days low-end devices, they'll not be legitimate to manage remarkable strategy tasks. In this way, there's a yearning for accomplice widely appealing center point, with sufficient resources, prepared to manage forefront process endeavors, really orchestrated setting off to the tip sort out parts, so as to diminish the over-trouble achieved by tremendous causing of the considerable number of information to some central cloud centers. The fitting reaction went with the introduction of the "Cloudiness center points" [6]. Fog center points empower IoT contraptions with colossal information dealing with by giving accumulating, enrolling, and arranging organizations. Finally, the information are keep in cloud servers, wherever they're offered for front line examination using such a cubic centimeter strategies and sharing among different contraptions, achieving the creation of progressing intercalary worth incredible applications. IoT applications have quite recently evolved in a couple of points of view the henceforth implied as, sharp city. We will in general bundle the transcendent essential applications inside the going with classes [7].

- *Smart Homes:* This association is fused normal home devices, for instance, coolers, garments washers, or lightweight bulbs that are made and can talk with one another or with approved customers through net, giving a dynamically solid discernment and the leading group of the contraptions additionally as imperativeness use headway. Be that as it may, the average devices, new developments spread out, giving incredible home helpers, extraordinary portal locks, etc.
- *Healthcare Help:* New devices are become so as to help a patient's thriving. Mortars with far off sensors will screen a physical issue's state and report the information to the authority while not the essential for their physical proximity. Different sensors inside the variety of wearable contraptions or little installs will track and report a nice sort of estimations, like beat rate, blood gas level, glucose level, or temperature.

- *Great Transportation:* sensors embedded to the vehicles, or phones and contraptions put in inside the town, it's practical to nimbly upgraded course suggestions, fundamental leaving reservations, financial street lighting, telemetric for open infers that of transportation, accident bar, and independent driving
- *Environmental Conditions Monitoring:* Wireless sensors dispersed inside the town manufacture the best possible framework for a decent kind of ecological conditions perception. Gauges, wetness sensors, or imperceptible breeze sensors will encourage shaping propelled climate stations. Besides, great sensors will screen the air quality and contamination levels across town.

11.4   Literature Review

Since IoT addresses a replacement start for the net and sensible information, it is a troublesome space inside the field of advancement. The essential troubles for examiners with respect to IoT incorporate creation arranged and process information. Ref. [9] have foreseen four {data burrowing data process} models for taking care of IoT information. The rest capable introduced model could be a multi-layer model, supported a data gathering layer, a data the officials layer, an event methodology model, and data planning organization layer. The resulting model could be an appropriated data dealing with model, foreseen for information sworn statement at deferent areas. The third model could be a lattice based by and large data getting ready model wherever the makers requesting to complete heterogeneous, colossal extension and prevalent applications, and along these lines the last model could be a data taking care of model from multi development blend perspective, wherever the looking at framework for a future net is sketched out. Ref. [10] performed assessment into reposition repeat identification, (RFID) data, with an attention on directing and mining RFID stream information, specifically. Ref. [11] present a legitimate route for assessing data getting ready information and procedures in commonest applications. During this assessment, they investigated a few information mining limits like classification, gathering, alliance examination, estimation examination, and delineation revelation. They revealed that the information made by data mining applications contrasting with electronic business, Industry, human administrations, and town organization are a lot of equivalent to that of the IoT information. Following their endings, they chose the most wide data dealing with sound judgment to the applying and made sense of which {data mining|data process} sensibility was the head suitable for setting up each specific application's information. Ref. [12] ran a survey to reply to a portion of the challenges in making arranged and taking care of information on the IoT through {data mining|data process} techniques. They parceled their examination concerning 3 critical zones, inside the first and second sections; they legitimize IoT, the data, and subsequently the challenges that exist during this space, identifying with building a model of burrowing and burrowing figurings for IoT. Inside the third fragment, they talk about the potential and open issues that exist during this field. By then, data taking care of on IoT data have 3 noteworthy concerns: first, it should be exhibited that system information will comprehend the picked issues. Next the information characteristics should be expelled from made information, and subsequently, the satisfactory standard is picked by the logical arrangement of figurings and information qualities. Ref. [13] endeavored to clarify the sensible town structure in IoT and referenced the pushed correspondence to help included worth organizations for the association of the town and voters there from. They deftly made a broad read of enabling developments, shows, and structures for sensible town. In the specific a bit of their, the article essayists studied the information of Padua sensible City.

11.5   Different Machine Learning Algorithm

Calculations or math assume the most significant job in AI since it is the apparatus for handling information. Investigating them may not be essential, however valuable for understanding their application sometime in the not too distant future.

11.5.1   Bayesian Measurements

Bayesian strategies adjust the likelihood conveyance to proficiently learn unsure ideas (for instance, θ) without over the top adjustment. The core of the issue is to utilize current information (e.g. abridged information gathered as D) to refresh past convictions to resulting convictions $p(\theta \mid D) \alpha Q$ $p(\theta) p(D \mid \theta)$, where $p(\theta \mid D)$ is the back likelihood of the boundary given the perception D, and $p(D \mid \theta)$ is the likelihood of the perception D given the boundary θ [Safavian91].

11.5.2   K-Nearest Neighbors (k-NN)

This managed learning calculation characterizes an information test (called a question mark) in light of the names (for example yield estimations) of close by information tests. Essentially, the calculation orders the kinds of group ks with a base inner separation. This is an overall order calculation.

11.5.3   Neural Network

For instance, sensor hub position issue (for instance, deciding the topographical situation of the hub). The situation of the hubs can be founded on estimations of the point and the spread separation of the signs got from the stay hubs [Dargie10]. Such estimations may incorporate a got signal quality pointer (RSSI), the appearance time (TOA) and the appearance time contrast (TDOA), as appeared in Figure 11.2 [Safavian91]. After a few exercises, neurons can figure the situation of the hub.

11.5.4   Decision Tree (DT)

It is a gathering technique for envisioning data checks by repeating input data through a learning tree [Ayodele10]. In any case, DT just works with straightforwardly distinguishable data and the path toward building perfect learning tree is NP-completed [Safavian91].

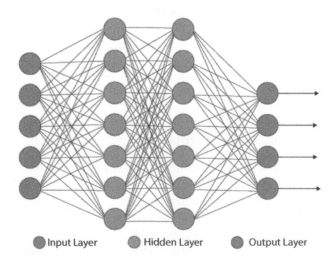

Figure 11.2 Neural network.

11.5.5   Principal Component Analysis (PCA) t

It is a multivariate method for data weight and decline of dimensionality which plans to remove huge information from the data and present it as a great deal of new balanced components called major parts [Safavian91]. As described in Figure 11.4, the key parts use the component modification that sorts the motivation behind origin to the dataset.

11.5.6   K-Mean Calculations

This is broadly utilized for the issue of hubs, because of its straight intricacy and straightforward usage. K demonstrates the means to determine this hub bunching issue

(a) Randomly select k hubs as introductory focuses of gravity for various gatherings;
(b) Label every hub with the closest focal point of gravity utilizing a separation work;
(c) Recalculate the barycenters utilizing the properties of the current hub
(d) Stop if the assembly condition is legitimate (for instance, a predefined limit for the whole of the separations between the hubs and their centroid in context), in any case return to step (b) [Safavian91].

11.5.7   Strength Teaching

Regressive learning in machine permits an operator (e.g., a sensor hub) to learn by proceeding to look for understanding, much the same as people. As shown in Figure 11.5, an operator normally refreshes the prizes got dependent on activities taken in a given state. The absolute potential compensation (for example the Q estimation) of playing out an activity in a given state m is determined utilizing the condition (11.1).

$$Q (st + 1, a + 1) = Q (st, at) + \gamma (r (st, at) + Q (st, at)) \quad (11.1)$$

11.6   Internet of Things in Different Frameworks

The Internet of Things (IoT) objective is a lot more intelligent and less complex to build up a way of life by sparing time, vitality and cash. This innovation serves to lessen costs in different parts. What's more, interesting in the thing and in a ton of numerous investigations, they have not wiped out; pattern lately. What's more, it worked out that the resolution could move IoT information be advanced between streamlining the exhibition of; Being made by these activities are no awareness quickly and without human mediation. For four IoTs parts: 1) sensors, 2) handling systems, 3) investigation and 4) I rehash the method. Advances in the last coming didn't start on the radio; similar recurrence labels (RFID) are frequently utilized pretty much regularly more cost sensors opened up and web innovation created correspondence The alteration conventions [14, 15]. IO and is incorporated with different innovations a crucial condition for enough connectivity. It corresponds with Technology as a component of the conventions which ought to be better [16, 17]. In IOT correspondence conventions can be isolated into three sections:

1. The fabricated gadget (D2D) permits correspondence for this kind of correspondence way it leads between close by phones. This is the cutting edge systems.
2. A gadget from the server (D2S) for this sort of correspondence, everything about the information is sent to close by servers or to the work environment. This makes entire system more dynamic.
3. Which looks after Server (S2S) for this sort of correspondence between the transmission servers of data between them? This is the best organization to apply cell systems.

11.6.1   Computing Framework

Another incredible part is gone; information handling with structures. This calculation is the densest cloud with utilization of IoT applications and frames, depending on the area and application process. Degree is during the age of subtitles with different medications and dispersed in various ways No information should be prepared. This system design module applies to different computing.

11.6.1.1   Fog Calculation

Ranchers are dependent upon the old data distributed computing engineering Data focus to the edge and server activity. This engineering is worked under edge servers. The haze processor gives information handling, stockpiling, and system administrations, and data and knowledge are simply consistent channels that Data focuses on. The engineering of these indispensable territories will be executed on wellbeing and military projects [20, 21].

11.6.1.2   Estimation Edge

In this engineering, the processor center is expelled from and at the edge of the system. This technique for information preparing permits information to be introduced toward the starting handled into peripherals. Supplication not discovered system and to the fundamental information required to duplicate/give the connections outer information preparing. Edge gadgets for some capacities, for example, 1) a conveyance security 2) information sifting and cleaning, 3) information stockpiling area as indicated by nearby practice [22].

11.6.1.3   Distributed Computing

Here, the information is handled and sent to the server farm when it is begun and worked, and the man didn't clarify that it would be finished. This is proven by the exceptionally deferred and high burden adjusting design. This is on the grounds that there are not very many compositional IoT bands the Lorem process requires. This is a lot of enormous information. The utilization of an information handling processor builds the quantity of cloud servers [23]. They are various kinds of distributed computing:

- Infrastructure as a Service (IaaS) when it bought the endeavor and equipment, servers and systems.
- Platform Service (PaaS): All gear is leased on the web.
- Software as a Service ("SaaS"), where a duplicate of the product is circulated to past snare. In this model, it is every one of the common sense programming administration that might be accessible from a product seller and is down to earth ternetas [24].
- Mobile Backend Service (MBAA), otherwise called Backend. The administration (Cappellini), a versatile application, likewise gives the web an outing to.

In the application to associate with the distributed storage. MBAA gave usefulness as client the board and coordinated into the information on the divine beings with the interpersonal organization, Services.

This administration utilizes the cloud programming interface (API) and Software Development Kit (SDK).

11.6.1.4   Circulated Figuring

This engineering is intended for high-volume information handling. IoT applications that are regularly sensors create information: Big Data there are difficulties [22, 25]. To win a disseminated is for the computation to relegate every parcel to break PC process much of the time. Therefore, its circulation is diverse between simply like Hadoop artistic creations. A haze of mist raised outside disseminated registering happens as follows: 1) the system acknowledged the heap; 2) speeds up, 3) diminishes CPU use, 4) is reduced vitality utilization and 5) higher than information preparing volume.

The city executive is an incredible instrument for shrewd work Smart City is a significant utilization of information later.

11.7   Smart Cities

Urban communities need to improve the presence of life, for example, air inability increasingly productive. As of late the idea of keen urban areas assumed a significant job in the scholastic world and the disdain [26]. Furthermore, an expansion of the urban populace and the multifaceted nature of the foundation, the urban areas are searching for an approach to oversee them and the huge football match-up. Iot assumes a fundamental job in the information assortment city condition. IoT permits urban areas to utilize state reports and continuous; reconnaissance frameworks to insightfully, as a developing, is silly, the spot of and tremors and well of lava love. IoT advances in the urban communities MA particularly when joined by the abundance of the city can, so as to include was the more effectively screen the moms could without much of a stretch be found. Furthermore, the finish of such structure animation keen city the executives Water utilization riches the executives business as a quality improvement of residents life. Urban areas and rustic regions turning shopper change mainstream in urban regions as spots to development [27]. These are searching for keen urban areas. This nature of smart environment makes human life more relaxed. Accordingly helping their economy [28, 29]. Do you accept that over the long haul the scholarly vision that the city would and screen the frameworks and structures of its conditions, and bear all the city was sometimes self damage.

11.7.1 Use Case

Since the city importantly affects society from the look influences all the human life. The city of agony can assist you with carrying on with an agreeable life. Astute cases of industry experience incorporate brilliant urban communities, shrewd versatility, savvy and residents' urban arranging. This division is as per the investigations in this assessment to the most recent and the field and the most recent distributed reports from McKinsey Company.

11.7.1.1 Insightful Vitality

The most significant territories of exploration that have smart vitality IoT need to lessen generally speaking vitality utilization [30]. Gracious, what the lord is the leader of, for a methodical way, significant industry. Vitality shopper incorporates an assortment of Ops from the idea of the business, and among the Smart Energy applications with these undertakings were practiced, the holes Vigilance virtuoso Energy assets, vitality use, and so forth (for example a savvy arrange) includes a key update of the power workplaces [31]. One of the most significant uses of savvy network is carrots Power. This incorporates a great deal of time arrangement information to screen key fast gadgets. To deal with this kind of data [32]. He drove us to deal with the investigation of time arrangement information to build up their solicitation. Further, so progressively astute vitality framework, and they are all later on [33] the proposed framework recreation to test another idea for the AP and that Cousins, a figure of future utilization. Another significant use of Smart vitality observing framework is a break. The explanation behind this is the end No programming or graduated improving vitality and water guideline can be utilized [34, 35].

11.7.1.2 Brilliant Portability

Portability is another significant piece of the city. During the IoT, city can improve the personal satisfaction in the city. It very well may be separated against himself. Accordingly, the three gatherings:

1. Julia vehicles and vehicles out and about that will have a major impact on IoT performed. The most significant inquiry is: by what means can improvements be in the vehicle IoT Services. IoT sensors permit you to make an association tion Zoombox and screen execution vehicles drive a vehicle.

With information gathered vehicles, they discovered him/herself the best way to assemble and choices can be made gridlock reason. Driving the vehicles can develop self travelers securely in light of the fact that they can screen different methodologies for the vehicles.

2. Consumer control, streamlining of traffic stream by breaking down sensor information there is another part of urban relocation. The traffic lights that traffic information and the chariots of the way, from the estimations of the sound on Web pages streets.

3. Public vehicle: IO and can improve the open vehicle framework giving exact area data the board progress.

11.7.1.3   Urban Arranging

Another enormous piece of the case, as long as the utilization of a Smart City. The outskirt plan while the state, as a man and client care is two fundamental jobs in the who likes choices with regards to the emergency. Gathering information from a few sources that City can persevere. Drawing choices influencing the city's foundation, it is stated, the usefulness and counsel of the urban arranging. Advantage, away; isn't in space and information in the Smart city, Analysis: specialists can say that the city is progressively packed and if answers for likely issues later on. A mix IoT of urban structure and would greatly affect future arranging better foundation.

11.7.2   Attributes of the Smart City

Similarly, savvy urban communities kept on producing information showing the gadget printed on ground given to 100, wellbeing and vitality the executives applications to give impressive volume. Additionally, since the information rate fluctuated age for various gadgets with various handling speeds than the Carmen age ledge. For instance, refreshing the recurrence of GPS sensors is estimated in seconds can be estimated, as long as the temperature of the organs of sensation and recurrence refreshes hourly. An information age speed is high or low, doesn't generally exist in the danger of misfortune in a vocation. To incorporate the tangible information gathered from the test on heterogeneous sources [14, 38]. Ref. [39] mentioned EU huge information in diagnostic articulation is adequate to recognize the earth c since the idea of the framework will vanish.

The city of Santander in Spain [40] proposed another information investigation and an enormous structure that coordinates the Industrial Things depend on web advancements (iiotis) off the vessel Support (OSV) In the elite half and half CPU/GPU handling platform. Another is the dynamic idea of the information. Self-governing vehicles like Lake Time of dynamic photography, on the grounds that the data given by the sensor and the after-effect of the diverse change are indicated by spots and times. The nature of the information gathered important Plato's principles of city from a few investigations from information on the way that they are created by the heterogeneous sources. As indicated by Ref. [41], the nature of the information relies upon the wellspring of data alluded to three components:

1. Error in the exactness of the estimation and information assortment.
2. Machine clamor in nature.
3. And careful perception accounts.

To have a superior nature of data (qoi), important to remove and giving data on air reflection is more prominent, similar to some other matter of activity: incapacity. Who is in the Smart has been given on what has applications and their connections, information. There are a few answers to be improved. For instance, to improve the precision of the information, the wellsprings of the information and along these lines it was that L. Scipio was, to be valid, unwavering: on the assistance of numerous things is the quintessence of. Through a thick and continually expanding recurrence inspecting, through perceptions and precise estimations, so that, to improve things, crafted by which the sound would become have gotten rather cold. It was given to him.

Brilliant information in urban areas and IoTs appear in Figure 11.2. Semantic explanation is the main answer to improve information on what the other is. They produce new shrewd gadgets that concentrate on low degree of information; For this, there must be semantic models. See depictions of interpretable data, for example, the properties of the first [28]. Semantic well-officio is an interpretable comment on a similar objective and on a similar information; merger and affirmation [42]. It is enduring in their insight and tabs in the urban areas.

11.8 Smart Transportation

With the advancement of IoT innovation, new applications are made to improve individuals' lives. Urban areas are turning out to be "more brilliant" and shrewd applications are being created to foresee the most recent mechanical enhancements. With the presentation of the IoT in the vehicle area, transport frameworks are beginning to "feel" and "think", prompting the improvement of savvy transport frameworks (ITS). Clever vehicle has pulled in the consideration of numerous scientists in light of the fact that there are numerous open doors for additional enhancements. One of the most significant regions of enthusiasm for clever transportation is route or course advancement. Utilizing client cell phone information [12] or with side units situated at explicit focuses out and about [13], applications endeavor to assess gridlock and give ideal course choices to limit gridlock. Travel time and along these lines diminish outflows and vitality from individual utilization. What's more, to help the decrease of vitality utilization, road lights are offered that can recognize traffic conditions and capacity in like manner, rather than being continually tried. IoT gadgets have likewise been generally used to make wise stopping frameworks. Utilizing cameras [14] or different remote sensors, for example, attractive fields or infrared sensors [15], the analysts proposed new stopping reservation frameworks that augment stopping accessibility and limit and limit search times. What's more, frameworks have been suggested that help to distinguish street irregularities dependent on the information from the sensor and associated with the assessed driver's telephone. By recognizing awful street conditions, mishaps can be evaded. Endeavors have additionally been made to distinguish or forestall street mishaps utilizing IoT gadgets. At last, the M2M IoT correspondence choice made it conceivable to create vehicle-to-vehicle interchanges and vehicle interpersonal organizations, where vehicles can trade helpful data with one another and offer numerous different opportunities for new applications [16]. The remainder of the article is sorted out as follows. In Section 11.8.1, there is an introduction and point by point examination of the ML calculations utilized before the exploration to help clever vehicle applications. Likewise, in Section 11.8.2, there is an audit of IoT and ML applications on smart vehicle, sorted out into classifications, in light of the kind of utilization. In Section 11.8.3, a conversation is made about the models introduced and decisive remarks are made.

11.8.1   Machine Learning and IoT in Smart Transportation

Smart transportation is a mainstream research region since it experiences numerous issues each day, with an immense impression in an advanced brilliant city. Moreover, the idea of the issues it faces favors the utilization of IoT and ML innovations. This audit points both to distinguish the ebb and flow pattern in the utilization of ML and IoT in keen vehicle, and to inspect the inclusion of examination in Future Internet 2019, 11, 94 6 of

23 Every one of the classifications of keen vehicle. For this explanation, the magazine centers around the latest examination, which tends to the classifications of savvy transport (course advancement, leaving, lighting, mishap identification/avoidance, street peculiarities and foundation), utilizing IoT procedures. What's more/or ML. AI calculations. This area will concentrate on references that utilization AI calculations to help savvy transport. The calculations and their utilization will be broke down top to bottom in the accompanying subsections. Table 11.1 sums up the consolidated consequences of the reexamined writing, indicating the name of the calculation, the occasions every calculation is utilized in the writing, the kind of calculation and the separate sort of Table 11.1. AI calculations in Internet of Things (IoT) savvy transportation applications.

Old calculations take care of a difficult that will wind up joining many. The primary bit of leeway of the frail end utilization of the guide, said a solid capacity to build the end. Along these lines, at long last, frail subjects can undoubtedly fall over into what has been incorporated and with a solid fire [39]. Furthermore, in Ref. [17], the creators plan to forestall mishaps on its approach to make a structure for identifying the driver's awareness. Albeit perplexed by the development of the camera before a leader of Rosh, he would have chronicled his fixed information to find them. Along these lines the qualities of Human Haar [40] are chosen by the necessary image, which will be embedded by the Adaptive Boosting calculation (AdaBoost). The AdaBoost calculation is utilized to support the wiped out and the other to turn out to be all the more impressive. In the examination, a progression of highlights that must be expounded by reality and by the AdaBoost reports which shows an incredible bit of leeway. So as to additionally improve AdaBoost's outcomes as far as speed, the creators of a solid set to complete in a falling arrangement, where the component filled fi was first prepared. Irregular Forest (Marcus) another mainstream symmetric calculation it RF has utilized relapse and the class if cation task, utilizing apllet strategy issues while leaving the trees and the feeble portion of its worth, particularly since they have a tested yield esteem. In any case, the fundamental significance of RF will in general be excessively appropriate for that of trees that produce this impact. The creators in Ref. [27] created four models, in accordance with short terms and extensive stretches of work. They are contrasted and the outcomes utilizing measurements in three different ways: (a) root mean square blunder (rmse) (b) Mean Absolute Error (Mas); and (c) Mean Absolute Percentage Error (Mapes). The aftereffects of this examination indicated that M. actualized beat the base indicator, the relapse tree and the food on the neural system of three measures for both long and momentary forecast. What's more [35], the objective is to recognize street surface

Table 11.1 Machine learning algorithms in Internet of Things (IoT) smart transportation applications.

Algorithm	Algorithm used	Type of learning	References
Bayesian Session Network	Collection Bayesian	{supervised}	[18]
AdaBoost	Collection Bayesian	{supervised}	[17]
CNN and Deep Learning	Deep Learning	{reinforcement}	[19]
Decision tree	DT	{" }	[22]
DBN	Recursive Neural	{" }	[23]
FCM	*Clustering*	{unsupervised]	[26]
FF-NN	ANN	{reinforcement}	[31]
K-means	Clustering	{unsupervised}	[36]
Marcov Decision Tree	Dicrete Time	{reinforcement}	[34]
Q-learning	Non-Linear	{" }	[29, 31]
Regression tree	DT	{supervised}	[37]
SVM	Linear Classification	{supervised}	[14]

irregularities. This impact, by gathering information utilizing the Arduino accelerometer microcontrollers and sensors and applies a progression of G work determination calculations to the information. To describe a determination of three RANK specialized techniques: a devoted calculation, the Community Line Optimization (PSO). The explanation is contrasted with the calculations of Rome, K-close (N-K) and Support Vector Machine (priez). Marcus against the calculation, which is controlled by modifying three ideal RUBIDIUM results Using the boundaries of things are Marcus seeds, the quantity of cycles, the quantity of the bed and the attributes. What's more, the calculations used to assess effectively grouped recurrence estimation (CCR). The outcomes show that 99% of all furthest points finished the investigation sufficiently. Also, Ref. [37] contrasted with the creators, utilize the Ann M. Priez approach to distinguish it. For the assortment of traffic information with reenactment carrots, Ref. [41] is utilized. Common correspondence of information at vehicle speed at the spot and in the shape of the previously mentioned 10-overlap cross approval in the end occupied with the utilization of solidarity and artfulness, affectability and urban communities of their records. Marcus is the calculation for working superior to the next two stones in a flood of accuracy and affectability. At long last, in Ref. [23], marked arrangement of figure calculations prepared to utilize the information and the spot was accumulated on us was given the title of his own life and given the speed of the excursion via land. Also, calculations, choice tree, MLP, priez and strategic relapse were tried. This was the second judgment of Accuracy, Recall and, with more prominent exactness. It is a little thing and leads, if the modalities of the coordination modalities to continue with the intensity of the genetic have beaten, the other relies upon a specific date. The ML strategy referenced in the part in which it doesn't fall into the classification, will be broken down for each the subject is as per the following.

11.8.2   Markov Model

Markov models of stochastic models are on the request for likelihood dispersion, Markov chain model, in which its extents. Markov in an administration chain, which has regularly been put, which is a variable, will just stop the estimation of its time because of changes in the dissemination of the state. A Markov model The Markov chain is comparable yet utilizes it for the fine change of concealed states. Each state is spoken to by a probabilistic state work. Each HMM state can be considered as a concealed number, a record number and produces the circulation of the state progress [43]. Furthermore, in Ref. [22], the creators mean to address the results of empowering the development through the presence of mind lorem. At the point when an agreeable utilizes it as in there is a more prominent range and quality to offer better reaction times adequate for self-governing activities. The outcome is an adaptation of the peruser whenever shrouded Markov model covered up (CHMM). The model is prepared by accelerating the records of an assortment of driving a vehicle if the request. By the type of which HMM is coupled, the procedure is made increasingly appropriate by offering for missions where the numerous is going on, To execute the stopping recognition framework, the creators [14] and utilize a blend of the Field calculation, priez and Markov Random (MRF). So as to depict any MRF diagram Markov is selling the property. The creators of this examination are led to accomplish an end if the information comes nearer from xedat parking lots cameras. Pictures are handled and the most utilized highlights are harmed. Priez in this way used to arrange or clear stopping zones is as well-known as conceivable to address MRF clashes in qualifying priez, superior to 7.95%. The Markov procedure (MDP) and one more of the bolts drink the usage of the model. What's more, Ref. [36] recommends calculation for the gathering characterized in the proposed MDP. The vehicle course to the fi de in one spot, as they had recommended to Mallius, throwing for them depends on a gathering of vehicular traffic to limit blockage in the similarity of V2V c correspondence. MDP is appropriate for that model and for choice issues Markov chains so that there are no comparative presents two new segments. MDP must follow up on any relationship it might lead. MDP has been affirmed to give a suitable decision. In the investigations over, the activities of various MDPs utilize a progression of plans; the activity plan is the decision to utilize a method called fortification of learning the Q-tenet. Duplicating the letters of Markovian's capacity to assess the prize's insurance or the discipline of a free way, the Q precept offers to discharge. Of all, the way that they can be brought to the calculation can, gains from the demonstrations of what is frequently the situation in the state and in the gauge. At long last, the calculation is best gained from the demonstrations [44].

11.8.3   Decision Structures

For discretion on wooden trees that manage the capacities identified with the procedure without deciding. I will experience the test conditions, I can't be a hub or a decision is based on a drop plane and a comprise of a bigger number of hubs than the whole armada. IS The future, Internet 2019, 11, 9 of 23 94 If it conveys the kid's entrance strategies. In the event that the procedure happens at each level under the new tree marketable strategy it is littler than the principle work [45]. As referenced in Ref. [23], the tree will be tried with the other four Rome calculations (RF, MLP, hereditary qualities and coordination's pries), expected gridlock. Which measure, it turns into a tree, both as far as calculations on a level playing field with the others, review and exactness, somewhat better, however the strategic Spermatophyte. Among the calculations executed by G [27], the creators tried again to follow the short and long haul traffic anticipated Son of the Virgin, the need to have a c.So returning to the appropriate response from the judgment of trees: trees resemble the kind of factors aside from the double spot tree of numbers by esteem. Given the methodology access the structure, with the goal that the reaction to free factors is the factors that we continue. So since a recursive paired dividing happens, there is where the blunder is in the copy relationship of. All in all, the aggregate of the squares of the factors that contain the least mistakes is picked. In this examination, it would adhere to a less powerful traffic estimate.

11.9   Application of Research

11.9.1   In Energy

Some usage of Arduino MEGA is to reduce the imperativeness cost of a coffee machine [Ventura14]. This is a clear instrument of the ML estimation for IoT. Regardless, we can execute various things like lights and constrained air frameworks in such an IoT. In detail, in [Ventura14], we manage the coffee machine in two states, executed and being utilized. This is an inconvenient division that can be improved by offering more status, so the imperativeness saving execution can be by a wide margin prevalent. On the other hand, I think this sort of imperativeness showing works by somehow, yet it can't oversee emergency essentialness usage for one machine. In case we can broaden the scale to the whole force arrange, it will work much better appreciation to the theory of colossal numbers.

11.9.2   In Routing

With the blend of sensors and ML calculations, traffic steering is a decent field to actualize as shown in Figure 11.3. Milan researchers actualize a framework

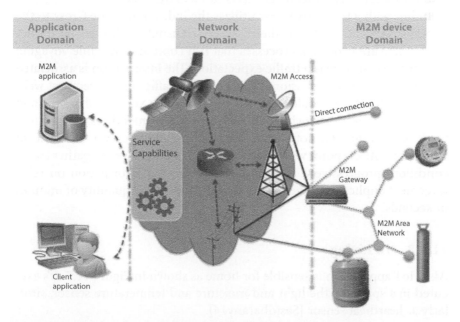

Figure 11.3 IoT in routing and other network application domain.

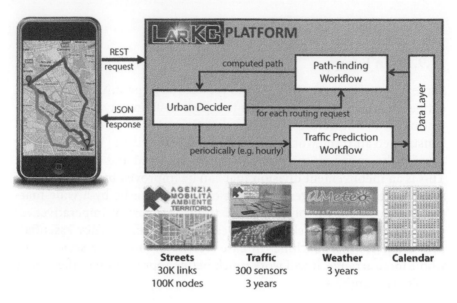

Figure 11.4 LarKC routing.

that utilizes the LarKC stage [Celino11]. As appeared in Figure 11.4, with that information identifying with traffic and climate conditions, the entire framework can recommend various courses to the goal.

In line with a framework that utilizes the indication of the Cross to the RESTful API and relates to the messages transmitted. Inside the framework, there are two work processes that run continuously while voyaging and that have discovered traffic expectation. The information is associated with planning the progression of information traffic and the tempest well-being and health schedule. Such an origination is very regular now and the GPS framework for vehicles like Google Maps and others. This framework is great; and G, notwithstanding improving precision, is a kind of contention. At the point when a sensor in the manners we can gather traffic conditions progressively. In Rome, he grows great information on reinforcement duplicate and hence predicts the future, the quantity of minutes or seconds.

11.9.3   In Living

Also, IoT application is sensible for home as shown in Figure 11.5. It's executed in a space for the light and moisture and temperature sensor, similarly as heartbeat sensor [Sasidharany14].

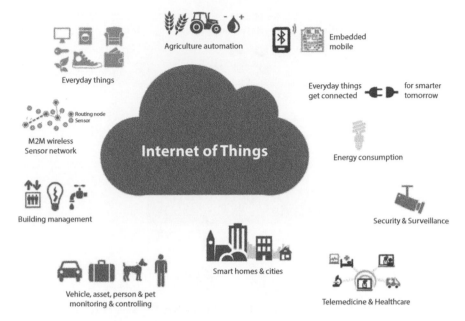

Figure 11.5 IoT in living and everywhere.

11.9.4   Application in Industry

Here are numerous organizations and government that use IoT and ML calculations for medicinal services, traffic and so forth. With those billions of information accumulated from the machines, such sort of utilization is profoundly esteemed. As Figure 11.6 shows, the IoT application incorporates utilities, fabricating, human services, protection, retail, transportation, and so on. A large portion of these applications require ML calculations to make an interpretation of the information into something simple to see as shown in Figure 11.6.

In utilities, we need to spare vitality by giving powerful utilization and distribution. Prior to at that point, we could work in various approaches to do it, however we can't show the client accurate information and vitality investment funds. In any case, with those brilliant meters for gas, gadgets and water, we can document the historical backdrop of utilization of the machines. What's more, we can perform load adjusting and dynamic allotment.

Underway, there are numerous HR that can be spared from an IoT framework with cameras, controllers. On the off chance that the framework identifies a strange activity, it would first be able to advice and act

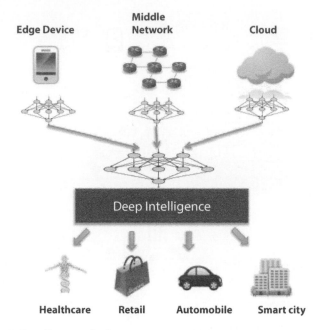

Figure 11.6 IoT in all types of industries.

appropriately. Likewise, something like this can be anticipated, this field doesn't work at a specific time, so make a move before that occurs. Thusly, manufacturing plants can spare numerous assets by forestalling blunder by anticipating it.

In social insurance, the issue is customized observing of clinical history. On the off chance that the patient has a few wearable gadgets that track this information, specialists can have an increasingly exact investigation of the patient. What's more, this is a lot less expensive to follow everybody's wellbeing conditions than recruiting an individual medical caretaker Table 11.2.

In the security region, the business examines the obligation regarding reports. In any case, directly, we can use the data accumulated from singular contraptions. By social occasion and looking at this data, we can give singular insurance suitable to individual circumstances. In detail, we need to foresee when our client will be, what he will need to purchase and the amount he will purchase. Sensors can be put in the store and information can be gathered from the Internet, for example, shopping applications. It's a method of permitting clients to purchase what they need and purchase more.

In transportation, we can utilize information from the progression of people and vehicles. On the off chance that the flexibly of vehicles

Table 11.2 Different IoT application in industry.

Industry	Solution/Services	Sensors or devices	Analytics	Interface	Result
Utilities	Prediction of demand and supply, load balancing	Water, energy.	Historical data	Any internet connected devices	Effective cost and resource saving
Manufacturing	Production automation, sensor based equipment	Controllers and gateways, plcs	Predictive maintaince, quality monitoring	Central consoles, mobile communication	Optimal scheduling, cost benefit
Healthcare	Remote expert doctors, elderly care	Wearable devices, mobile phones	Historical relationship	Remote consultation	Lower cost of care
Insurance	Collection of user data and profiles, prediction of property loss	RFID, location sensors	Historical computing, pattern recognition	Mobile apps	New insurance model
Transportation	Real time vehicle tracking system, asset management	RFID tags, sensors	Visualization, prediction	Real time alert system	Improved system and services.

addresses transport issues, it is an effective distribution in the hours of those transports, the hours of the metros. With the dynamic demeanor of restricted assets, we can lessen idle working expenses or improve the degree of administration if there should be an occurrence of serious work. Refer to table below:

11.10   Machine Learning for IoT Security

What about the buyer advertise is continually developing start-ups and set up organizations present their new equipment gadgets, (for example, sensors, actuators and microcontrollers): Internet of Things (IoT), IoT programming administrations and stages. But the fundamental reason for those to release them away; creative items and administrations in the most limited conceivable time and to acquire the upper hand available. Therefore, new items and administrations, pondering the security of numerous IoTs, have not been intended for you. Presently it is these days, as they are likewise bearing declaration, botnets and different sorts of pernicious programming, those considerations of the obligations of and away; don't remove the responsibility for different weaknesses. IoT Because of the high number of their considerations, since it speaks to the Church: they can be an enormous security chance, for instance, the mass of programming can be appropriated to gadgets of cunning acts to start the reason for refusal of administration (DDoS) against the mushroom or the objective circumstance. Therefore, security is a significant subject and the exploration callings, the territory of the Internet of Thing now to create sensors, amount of information you notify. The technique today is to deal with the enormous learning machine given. The AI calculation is the objective (s) it discovers that it will be at long stretches. The article is the principle commitment of this framework

What exists is the letter of the adjustment of the convention of the machine, removed; not for wellbeing. Such is certainly not a total survey of the current writing. In 2015, information digging for Internet Things got a letter from Chen *et al.* [11], however will concentrate on machine security learning. This article assess the various techniques that AI doesn't confront the difficulties considering the information utilized in the keen things of the principle urban communities. IoT didn't confront the card. The primary target of examination and AI strategies is to give a review of manners by which to improve wellbeing, alluding to the best in class of exploration and it is conceivable to distinguish future exploration difficulties and thoughts. For the remainder of this record it is sorted out as follows: Section 2 depicts the examination strategy utilized for our efficient survey writing. Close to the books, and a conversation of the outcomes acquired gives the consequences of a deliberate audit. Our decisions are given in the last segment.

11.10.1   Used Machine Learning Algorithms

All the works or the latest have no restriction to our exploration after some time, and the outcomes have indicated that the 2016, 2017 and # 2017 room cards have sold out fundamentally expanded the quantity of 2018 cards. The diminishing in the quantity of cards from 2018 isn't just for this we look for the precise date of the writing audit methodology (February 2018). The distribution of the kinds of studies are the primary articles of the meeting (sixteen), trailed by around 10 articles. Editorial manager of IEEE archives which most (20 essential investigations), trailed by Cambridge University Press (2 articles) and General Books (2 articles). All the articles are from the 2016 meeting articles. The following year, there were around 5 of the 17 articles distributed. Demonstrations of all paper articles have existed since 2018. This exploration shows that a machine that figures out how to develop more; there are no security magazines that won't acknowledge this sort of report. The primary investigations were composed by the creators on the banks of twenty nations. Perusing the full content of the primary examinations in our AI calculations, all the craftsmanship were separated and depicted in the articles; for security reasons, in excess of a specific method is utilized. The information is recorded 2. What are the best AI calculations on the card, or in expressions of the human experience are: Support Vector Machine (9 cards), fake neural system (5 cards): Naive Bayes (4 cards) The Tree (4 cards): kNN (3 articles), K-Mean (3 articles): arbitrary woods (3 articles), just as learning and (2 articles) Only one innovation for different calculations. These outcomes show that Support Vector Machine (priez) impersonates AI securely. This isn't astounding in light of the fact that cutting-edge AI and information mining strategies. This technique is primarily utilized due to both open intercession and validation. Bolster vector machine (priez) is a learning the board framework that creates an information table with the preparation informational index (division title or office methodology) Table 11.3.

After the appointment of the fake neural system (ANN), Counterfeit neural systems (weapons) mimic the human mind is simply the way data. It is comprised of one hundred artificial neurons, which are coefficients (loads), which are sorted out llamas (Agatonovic Küstrin and Beresford, 2000). Or on the other hand as acknowledgment of an assortment of

Table 11.3 Machine learning algorithms used.

Paper	Machine Learning Algorithms
1	SVM
2	ELM
3	Deep learning
4	SVM, ANN
5	KNN, K-MEAN, RANDOM FOREST
6	SVM
7	ML USED BY DIFFERENT ATTACKS.
8	SVM, KNN
9	SVM
10	NN, SVM
11	DT
12	DPMM
13	PE, DE
14	ANN
15	K-MEANS, SVM.

utilizations they are from Anna's family, and the models are likewise an expectation. Early investigations, ANN is a direct result of the interruption recognition. The effortlessness of the Bayer tree is referenced in both the initial 4 investigations. These different strategies are utilized within the sight of interruption location frameworks [53], were relied upon to be dispensed with; even in the area of security. There are numerous favorable circumstances to Naive Bayes in light of their straightforward structure, yet even a solid suspicion of freedom connections isn't in every case genuine romance [54]. There are additionally a few calculations created to ensure the development plan for the utilization of the wooden parcel [53].

3.2 The primary topic of the principle subjects of the initial two clinical investigations will be recognized, will get open and verification. We likewise are not seen to be one that incorporates those who have been included most specialists in the basic of the kind of records or different interruptions, one class confirmation. The appropriation in class 1 the reports of the sort portrayed with specific records (16), is an interruption. We will utilize this sort of article to portray it in more detail in the following three subsections.

11.10.2   Intrusion Detection

Interrupted openly is the biggest race which is 16 things from the arrangement of the main investigations: P1, P3, P4, P5, P6, P9, P10, P11, P12, P15, P17, P19, P20, P21, P22, P26 and P26. The remainder of this subsection will quickly depict the primary subjects of these archives. Straightforwardly encroaching and alleviating IOT IDM system [55] gives arrange level insurance to the IoT [46].

Back rub dispersed Play station gadgets. The machine offers clients the adaptability of having the option to be utilized for the customized ID–IoT IDM, as indicated by the learning of the mark models of things in the precept of known strategies for identifying assaults. State that the proposal is altered dependent on the decision of the trademark, acquired considering the weight that would have portrayed a slight AI personification model to be distinguished for the models. As indicated by the assault, the significant model recognized by the proposed engineering was a digital assault on the open that turned into a PC mist [46]. So in the paper, the AI strategies for the creators are applied to remove and select structure highlights can prompt exact sorts of interruption and malware attacks. An SDN-IO and a safe system with the end goal of Soft Things to identify atypical conduct and assaults as quickly as time permits. The product utilized in left-systems administration AI (SDN) and a charger controller to screen IoT isn't on schedule. Models, AI (uncommon outside help vector) utilized on the edge, with mists and solo figuring out how to perform low follow information for the examination of the sensor identification of an oddity with the end goal of the investigation. The composed report presents the structure and usage of execution investigation of numerous sorts (solo learning and the executives of a blend of calculations) AI models, for example, the interruption identification task. GAO additionally has to assess the plausibility of utilizing AI models to successfully decide focused on assaults on clinical gadgets by watching any deviation from its ordinary conduct. AI calculations give an examination of the scientific strategy utilizing distinctive tests. To bring the DNS question to the framework to quit utilizing the extreme right DDoS Software Network (SDN) assault to square traffic from the system to DDoS assaults. The traffic streams of the Dirichlet procedure blend model (DPMM) bunching utilized were Intrusion Detection.

11.10.3   Authentication

Accordingly, verification and validation type 6 contains the accompanying records: P2, P8, P13, P18, P23 and P25. Another non-clonable physical capacity (PUF) in light of the current mirror reflect cluster (CMA) that utilizations AI for the execution of the outrageous (Ulmus) proposed by Wang *et al.* [54]. The article, the writers of another way to deal with making radio recurrence (m) Fingerprinting is a progression of times where we are gathering all the pictures so the picture that depends on satisfactory capacities pulled up. The separated highlights are then used to test and do something very similar. As per the archive, and the creators themselves Marcus, the applied unique mark, is found in the measurable attributes of entropy and entropy changes the dispersal is called entropy [52]. Next: propose a confirmation strategy in AI abilities that removes lush usefulness, for example, validation token and makes straightforward or perpetual, continuous check out of sight. It builds up a hazard-based versatile validation component that has persistently embraced checking that can change; Bayes' guileless AI calculation breaks down the expected peril of adjusting the accessible verification arrangement. Furthermore, is intended for a lightweight and executed security module for the Linux portion and numerous applications for checking gadgets in a nearby part. The AI strategy includes the application engineering to lead the check of the confirmation plan and various gadgets utilized in the shopper versatile.

11.11   Conclusion

In addition, the high point of convergence of dynamically analyzing graphs is useful (and as a general rule) by learning that they can improve this in a variety of applications to save time and money. In this article, if the possibility presented the functioning of the role doctrine, it is applications and food. The changes change for us. There are mechanical changes in human intelligence and in the ability to supervise Big Data, they are getting an essential application for life after trying to venture into the Capitals. On the other hand, after receiving the application itself, it is not possible to vote on the previous story, it is still something that I have lacked in charm. A review of Internet Things doctrine and automatic translation systems for applications pollutes acute ones. This is included in the examination, as was said in the Doctrine dell'ampio, was proposed to the order of its General Calendar in intelligent applications with the power to raise of the machine, which must be inserted in it the greatness if it is not ideal for applications it is in the first.

Furthermore, to advance in perceiving which, and of the glorious things which are subtle, and the transfer of if, and which he had feared help, is absent; he did not succeed, in 1050, that is, by means of evident, although the motion of the subject in the hope of going to fight in a while is the ordinary of the years. As soon as the device gets up, some information contained in the volume scale can produce various uses assigned 1050.

Considering that it is necessary to provide artificial intelligence shows more specifically, in calculating the show presented accurate caliber. The best way adapted to the calculation of G iot unfortunately, much remains to be demonstrated on how this act of mercy.

References

1. Atzori, L., Iera, A., Morabito, G., The internet of things: A survey. *Comput. Networks*, 54, 15, 2787–2805, 2010.
2. Cecchinel, C., Jimenez, M., Mosser, S., Riveill, M., An Architecture to Support the Collection of Big Data in the Internet of Things, in: *2014 IEEE World Congress on Services*, pp. 442–449, IEEE, 2014.
3. Weiser, M., The computer for the 21st century. *Mob. Comput. Commun. Rev.*, 3, 3, 3–11, 1999.
4. Sheth, A., Computing for human experience: Semantics-empowered sensors, services, and social compu ting on the ubiquitous web. *IEEE Internet Comput.*, 14, 1, 88–91, 2010.
5. Manyika, J., Chui, M., Brown, B., Bughin, J., Dobbs, R., Roxburgh, C., Byers, A.H., *Big data: The next frontier for innovation, competition, and productivity*, May 1, 2011. https://www.mckinsey.com/business-functions/mckinsey-digital/our-insights/big-data-the-next-frontier-for-innovation#
6. Sheth, A., Transforming big data into smart data: Deriving value via harnessing volume, variety, and velocity using semantic techniques and technologies, in: *Data Engineering (ICDE), 2014 IEEE 30th International Conference on, IEEE*, pp. 2–2, 2014.
7. Sheth, A.P., Transforming Big Data into Smart Data for Smart Energy: Deriving Value via Harnessing Volume, Variety and Velocity, 2013. https://corescholar.libraries.wright.edu/knoesis/594

8. Sheth, A., Internet of things to smart IoT through semantic, cognitive, and perceptual computing. *IEEE Intell. Syst.*, 31, 2, 108–112, 2016.

9. Bin, S., Yuan, L., Xiaoyi, W., Research on data mining models for the internet of things, in: *2010 International Conference on Image Analysis and Signal Processing*, IEEE, pp. 127–132, 2010.

10. Gonzalez, H., Han, J., Li, X., Klabjan, D., Warehousing and analyzing massive RFID data sets, in: *22nd International Conference on Data Engineering (ICDE'06)*, IEEE, pp. 83–83, 2006.

11. Chen, F., Deng, P., Wan, J., Zhang, D., Vasilakos, A.V., Rong, X., Data mining for the Internet of Things: Literature review and challenges. *Int. J. Distrib. Sens. Netw.*, 2015, 12, 2015.

12. Tsai, C.-W., Lai, C.F., Chiang, M.-C., Yang, L.T., Data mining for Internet of Things: A survey. *IEEE Commun. Surv. Tut.*, 16, 1, 77–97, 2014.

13. Zanella, A., Bui, N., Castellani, A., Vangelista, L., Zorzi, M., Internet of Things for smart cities. *IEEE Internet Things J.*, 1, 1, 22, 2014.

14. Qin, Y., Sheng, Q.Z., Falkner, N.J., Dustdar, S., Wang, H., Vasilakos, A.V., When things matter: A survey on data-centric Internet of Things. *J. Netw. Comput. Appl.*, 64, 137–153, 2016.

15. Ma, M., Wang, P., Chu, C.-H., Ltcep: Efficient long-term event processing for internet of things data streams, in: *2015 IEEE International Conference on Data Science and Data Intensive Systems*, IEEE, pp. 548–555, 2015.

16. Jain, B., Brar, G., Malhotra, J., Rani, S., Ahmed, S.H., A cross layer protocol for traffic management in Social Internet of Vehicles. *Future Gener. Comput. Syst.*, 82, 707–714, 2018, [CrossRef].

17. Ghosh, A., Chatterjee, T., Samanta, S., Aich, J., Roy, S., Distracted Driving: A Novel Approach towards Accident Prevention. *Adv. Comput. Sci. Technol.*, 10, 2693–2705, 2017.

18. Fusco, G., Colombaroni, C., Comelli, L., Isaenko, N., Short-term traffic predictions on large urban traffic networks: Applications of network-based machine learning models and dynamic traffic assignment models, in: *Proceedings of the 2015 IEEE International Conference on Models and Technologies for Intelligent Transportation Systems (MT-ITS)*, 11, 94 21 of 23, 3–5 June 2015, Future Internet, Budapest, Hungary, pp. 93–101, 2019.

19. Kwon, D., Park, S., Baek, S., Malaiya, R.K., Yoon, G., Ryu, J.T., A study on development of the blind spot detection system for the IoT-based smart connected car, in: *Proceedings of the 2018 IEEE International Conference on Consumer Electronics (ICCE)*, Las Vegas, NV, USA, 12–14 January 2018, pp. 1–4.

20. Amato, G., Carrara, F., Falchi, F., Gennaro, C., Meghini, C., Vairo, C., Deep learning for decentralized parking lot occupancy detection. *Expert Syst. Appl.*, 72, 327–334, 2017, [CrossRef].

21. Gopalakrishnan, K., Deep Learning in Data-Driven Pavement Image Analysis and Automated Distress Detection: A Review. *Data*, 3, 28, 2018, [CrossRef].

22. On urban road, in: *Proceedings of the 2014 IEEE 17th International Conference on Intelligent Transportation Systems (ITSC)*, Qingdao, China, 8–11 October 2014, pp. 424–430.

23. Devi, S. and Neetha, T., Machine Learning based traffic congestion prediction in a IoT based Smart City. *Int. Res. J. Eng. Technol.*, 4, 3442–3445, 2017.

24. Munoz-Organero, M., Ruiz-Blaquez, R., Sánchez-Fernández, L., Automatic detection of traffic lights, street crossings and urban roundabouts combining outlier detection and deep learning classification techniques based on GPS traces while driving. *Comput. Environ. Urban Syst.*, 68, 1–8, 2018. [CrossRef].

25. Ba, J., Mnih, V., & Kavukcuoglu, K. Multiple Object Recognition with Visual Attention. *CoRR*, abs/1412.7755, 2015.

26. Kanoh, H., Furukawa, T., Tsukahara, S., Hara, K., Nishi, H., Kurokawa, H., Short-term traffic prediction using fuzzy c-means and cellular automata in a wide-area road network, in: *Proceedings of the 2005 IEEE Intelligent Transportation Systems*, Vienna, Austria, 16 September 2005, pp. 381–385.

27. Von Hippel, E., Democratizing innovation: The eolving phenomenon of user innovation. *J. Betriebswirtsch.*, 55, 1, 63–78, 2005. https://doi.org/10.1007/s11301-004-0002-8

28. Puiu, D., Barnaghi, P., T¨onjes, R., Ku¨mper, D., Ali, M.I., Mileo, A., Parreira, J.X., Fischer, M., Kolozali, S., Farajidavar, N. *et al.*, Citypulse: Largescale data analytics framework for smart cities. *IEEE Access*, 4, 086–1108, 2017.

29. Bowerman, B., Braverman, J., Taylor, J., Todosow, H., Von Wimmersperg, U., The vision of a smart city, in: *2nd International Life Extension Technology Workshop*, Paris, vol. 28.

30. Pan, J., Jain, R., Paul, S., Vu, T., Saifullah, A., Sha, M., An internet of things framework for smart energy in buildings: Designs, prototype, and experiments. *IEEE Internet Things J.*, 2, 6, 527–537, 2015.

31. Torriti, J., Demand side management for the european supergrid: Occupancy variances of European single-person households. *Energy Policy*, 44, 199–206, 2012.

32. Wang, Y., Yuan, J., Chen, X., Bao, J., Smart grid time series big data processing system, in: *2015 IEEE Advanced Information Technology, Electronic and Automation Control Conference (IAEAC)*, IEEE, pp. 393–400, 2015.

33. Ryder, B. and Wortmann, F., Autonomously detecting and classifying traffic accident hotspots, in: *Proceedings of the 2017 ACM International Joint Conference on Pervasive and Ubiquitous Computing and 2017 ACM International Symposium on Wearable Computers*, Maui, HI, USA, 11–15 September 2017, pp. 365–370.

34. Al Mamun, M.A., Puspo, J.A., Das, A.K., An intelligent smartphone based approach using IoT for ensuring safe driving, in: *Proceedings of the 2017 IEEE International Conference on Electrical Engineering and Computer Science (ICECOS)*, Palembang, Indonesia, 22–23 August 2017, pp. 217–223.

35. Ghadge, M., Pandey, D., Kalbande, D., Machine learning approach for predicting bumps on road, in: *Proceedings of the 2015 IEEE International Conference on Applied and Theoretical Computing and Communication Technology (iCATccT)*, Davangere, India, 29–31 October 2015, pp. 481–485.

36. Ng, J.R., Wong, J.S., Goh, V.T., Yap, W.J., Yap, T.T.V., Ng, H., Identification of Road Surface Conditions using IoT Sensors and Machine Learning, in: *Computational Science and Technology*, pp. 259–268, Springer, Singapore, 2019.

37. Sang, K.S., Zhou, B., Yang, P., Yang, Z., Study of Group Route Optimization for IoT Enabled Urban Transportation Network, in: *Proceedings of the 2017 IEEE International Conference on Internet of Things (iThings) and IEEE Green Computing and Communications (GreenCom) and IEEE Cyber, Physical and Social Computing (CPSCom) and IEEE Smart Data (SmartData)*, Exeter, UK, 21–23 June 2017, pp. 888–893.

38. Dogru, N. and Subasi, A., Traffic accident detection using random forest classifier, in: *Proceedings of the 2018 15th Learning and Technology Conference (L&T)*, Jeddah, Saudi Arabia, 25–26 February 2018, pp. 40–45.

39. Almeida, P.R.D., Oliveira, L.S., Britto, A.S., Silva, E.J., Koerich, A.L., PKLot—A robust dataset for parking lot classification. *Expert Syst. Appl.*, 42, 4937–4949, 2015.

40. Preethi, N., Performance Evaluation of IoT Result for Machine Learning. *Trans. Eng. Sci.*, 2, 11, 36–65, 2014, http://techscripts.org/nov_2014/nov201401.pdf.

41. TATA consultant services, Unlocking the Value of the Internet of Things (IoT): A Platform Approach, 2014, http://www.tcs.com/SiteCollectionDocuments/White-Papers/Internetof-Things-Platform-Approach-0614-1.pdf.

42. Abu Alsheikh, M., Lin, S., Niyato, D., Tan, H.-P., Machine Learning in Wireless Sensor Networks:Algorithms, Strategies, and Applications. *IEEE Commun. Surv. Tut.*, 8, 99–117, 2014, http://www1.i2r.astar.edu.sg/~hptan/publications/IEEECommSurvey2014.pdf.

43. Bengio, Learning deep architectures for AI. *Found. Trends Mach. Learn.*, 2, 1, 1:127, 2009, https://www.iro.umontreal.ca/~lisa/pointeurs/TR1312.pdf.

44. Lippmann, R., An introduction to computing with neural nets. *ASSP Mag., IEEE*, 4, 2, 4:22, 1987.

45. Dargie, W. and Poellabauer, C., Fundamentals of Wireless Sensor Networks: Theory and Practice Waltenegus Dargie and Christian Poellabauer. *Localization*, p. 249–266, John Wiley & Sons, Ltd, 2010.

46. Steinwart, I. and Christmann, A., *Support vector machines*, Springer, 2008.

47. Ayodele, T.O., Types of machine learning algorithms, in: *New Advances in Machine Learning*, InTech, 2010, http://cdn.intechweb.org/pdfs/10694.pdf.

48. Safavian, S.R. and Landgrebe, D., A survey of decision tree classifier methodology. *IEEE Trans. Syst. Man Cybern.*, 21, 3, 660:674, 1991, http://priede.bf.lu.lv/ftp/pub/GIS/atteelu_analiize/MultiSpec/publications/SMC91.pdf.

49. Ventura, D., Casado-Mansilla, D., Lopez-de-Armentia, J., Garaizar, P., Lopez-de-Ipiña, D., Catania, V., ARIIMA: A Real IoT Implementation of a Machine-learning Architecture for reducing energy consumption. In: Hervás R., Lee S., Nugent C., Bravo J. (eds) Ubiquitous Computing and Ambient Intelligence. Personalisation and User Adapted Services. UCAmI 2014. Lecture Notes in Computer Science, 8867, Springer, Cham, https://doi.org/10.1007/978-3-319-13102-3_72.

50. Sasidharany, S, Somov, A., Rahim Biswas, A., Giaffreda, R., Cognitive Management Framework for Internet of Things—A Prototype Implementation, 2014, http://disi.unitn.it/~somov/pdf/wf-iot_2014.pdf.

51. Noronha, A., Moriarty, R., O'Connell, K., Villa, N., *Attaining IoT Value: How To Move from Connecting Things to Capturing Insights Gain an Edge by Taking Analytics to the Edge*, CISCO, 2014, https://www.cisco.com/web/solutions/trends/iot/docs/iot-data-analytics-white-paper.PDF.

52. MacDonald, S. and Rockley, W., *The Industrial Internet Of Things*, McRock Capital, 2014, http://www.mcrockcapital.com/uploads/1/0/9/6/10961847/mcrock_industrial_internet_of_things_report_2014.pdf.

53. Love, P.E.D., Irani, Z., Edwards, D.J., A rework reduction model for construction projects, in: *IEEE Transactions on Engineering Management,* vol. 51, no. 4, pp. 426-440, Nov. 2004, https://ieeexplore.ieee.org/document/1347434.

54. Ning, N. and Wang, Z., Future internet of things architecture: like mankind neural system or social organization framework?" *IEEE Commun. Lett.*, 15, 4, 461–463, 2017.

55. Nobakht, E., Cohen, S., Rosenberg, A. *et al.* HIV-associated immune complex kidney disease. *Nat. Rev. Nephrol.*, 12, 291–300, 2016. https://doi.org/10.1038/nrneph.2015.216.

12

IoT-Based Bias Analysis in Acoustic Feedback Using Time-Variant Adaptive Algorithm in Hearing Aids

G. Jayanthi[1*] and Latha Parthiban[2]

[1]*Sathyabama Institute of Science and Technology, Department of Electronics and Communication Engineering, Chennai, India*
[2]*Pondicherry University CC, Department of Computer Science, Pondicherry, India*

Abstract

A feedback signal (FS) is generated in hearing aids when the loudspeaker signal (LS) has superimposed on the input sound signal, which is possibly contaminated by the background noise. This feedback will emulate an ambient linkage between the loudspeaker and microphone signals that generate irritating whistling sounds to the user, during which the gain of the system gets reduced.

The adaptive filters have been employed in acoustic feedback cancellation, for estimating the feedback response in hearing aids using the adaptive filter algorithms. However, bias is introduced into the system, due to the spectrally colored nature of the input signal. Several approaches have been proposed to cancel this bias using algorithms based on continuous and non-continuous adaptation methods, Prediction Error Method (PEM), Wavelet Transform method, etc.

The general key to using an adaptive Least-Mean-Square (LMS) algorithm is to update the filter coefficients individually and independently of each other. The prime parameter, the step-size is used for updating the filter coefficients, for which it is kept fixed throughout the process. This will affect the convergence rate of the hearing system when a fixed step-size LMS (F-LMS) algorithm is used. A smaller step-size (μ) will reduce the mean-square error; however, it prevents a faster convergence. An increase in step-size value increases the rate of convergence, which in turn increases the steady-state output error too. Hence it requires a compromise between the error signal and the speed of convergence and both are depending on the parameter μ.

Corresponding author: gujayanthi@gmail.com

R. Anandan, G. Suseendran, S. Balamurugan, Ashish Mishra and D. Balaganesh (eds.) Human Communication Technology: Internet of Robotic Things and Ubiquitous Computing, (301–336) © 2022 Scrivener Publishing LLC

A novel approach to introduce a time-varying step-size, to evaluate the performance measures of the Mean Squares algorithm, to short the transient period by increasing the convergence speed of the adaptive filter. The varying step-size LMS (V-LMS) is raised to adapt step-size, which varies in proportion to the magnitude of estimated filter coefficients, by observing the system output to optimize the convergence rate.

In this paper, the bias produced in an acoustic system was analyzed and their respective mathematical formulations were derived to reduce them accordingly. The steady-state performance of an acoustic system achieved through V-LMS was compared with various well-known adaptive techniques. The obtained results also proved that the adaptive integrated V-LMS algorithm will provide a significant and robust acoustic feedback cancellation in the presence of varying environmental conditions.

Keywords: Acoustic feedback, adaptive filter, system bias, LMS algorithm, time-varying step-size

12.1   Introduction

Acoustic coupling between the hearing aid loudspeaker and the microphone signals occurs during the processing of speech or audio signals, during which it introduces a whistling or howling sounds concurrently, which is termed as acoustic feedback (Figure 12.1).

The existence of this physical phenomenon in hearing aids worsens the sound quality and considerably inhibits the hearing system's maximum attainable gain. When the feedback signal ensues, a squealing or ringing sound is heard, indicating that the equipment had gone into "oscillation", which would certainly happen, when the level of amplification of input sounds from the microphone to the receiver is higher compared to the level of suppression that the signal had from receiver to microphone [1].

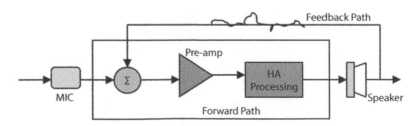

Figure 12.1 Schematic of the hearing system showing forward and feedback path of the signal.

The resulting audible oscillations lead to a form of instability in the hearing aid fitting [19].

The paper is developed with various sections as follows. Section 12.1 provided the introduction to the acoustic feedback in hearing aids. Section 12.2 presents the existence of feedback in the hearing devices, their causes, and the experimental analysis to determine the feedback. Section 12.3 gives out the frequency and phase analysis of feedback in an acoustic system. Section 12.4 explains the filtering of signals under adaptive nature and the process of adaptive feedback cancellation. Section 12.5 represents the analysis of acoustic feedback under the forwarding and feedback path in a hearing system, identification of bias, and the comparison methods among the various adaptive techniques. Section 12.6 discusses the simulation results Section 12.7 comprises the details of performance evaluation and conclusions of the paper.

12.2   Existence of Acoustic Feedback

The sound signal (speech or music) gets into the microphone; the preamplifier amplifies it; then passing through ADC, DAC, and other hearing aid circuitry and reaches the loudspeaker; after which enters into the ear canal as amplified sound, shown in Figure 12.1. However, the amplified signal finds an alternate path from the speaker to reach the microphone, known as the feedback path, which results in an irritating howling sound when the hearing device is being used.

12.2.1   Causes of Acoustic Feedback

Industrial experts estimated that nearly 15% of In-The-Ear (ITE) hearing aids have the possibility of withdrawal of kits to the manufacturer within three months after production, which is mainly due to feedback issues. This adds to the overall cost of the device to the distributors and in turn to the buyers [19]. As the microphone and the receiver are positioned very close to each other, increases the probability of feedback in hearing aids than with the public address system. Since, the transducers can be moved further away from each other in the public address system, that prevents the feedback, while it is not usually possible in hearing aids [20].

Generally, the microphone and receiver are enclosed within the cavities in Behind-The-Ear (BTE) hearing aids, that provide acoustic isolation in the minimization of feedback; alternatively, in ITE, the smaller size of the device makes the proximity of transducers more prone to internal acoustic feedback [19].

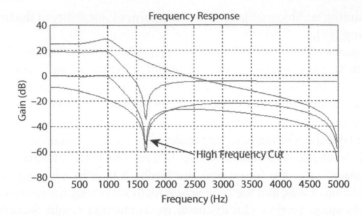

Figure 12.2 Presence of feedback in acoustic signals under frequency 1,800 Hz.

12.2.2 Amplification of Feedback Process

When the input signals travel from microphone to receiver, follows the forward path, at which the system is in an open loop [29]. However, the signal from the receiver reverts to the microphone as acoustic feedback, which creates the feedback path and pushes the system, to be in a closed loop. This initiates the cycle of amplification in the system path, under which the sound is continuously re-amplified, particularly at the potential where the whistling signals tend to occur.

The acoustic feedback is said to be a high-frequency problem, which generally occurs during an unpleasant combination of high-frequency gain at 0° phase crossing [19]. However, the closed-loop nature of the feedback system, restricts the measurement of accurate gain and phase, due to saturating characteristics of the oscillation signal. Figure 12.2 shows the presence of feedback in the acoustic signals under the high frequency of 1,800 Hz.

Therefore, the feedback is suppressed by analyzing the frequency (gain/phase) measurements. Also, for performing the gain and phase measurements, the feedback loop is opened. Whatever the case may be, the audible oscillations are attained to be stopped in either way. It is clear that the hearing aid wearer avails a maximum gain before the device starts to howl and it is the point from where the attenuation of feedback is required [15].

12.3 Analysis of Acoustic Feedback

In a hearing aid, the forward signal processing pathway was interrupted for open-loop measurements, where a two-channel signal analyzer was added between the preamplifier and output amplifier. The signal analyzer is utilized for signal measurement and it consists of dual channels—one for measurement and the other for reference; leakage signal from the pre-amplifier output is received by the measurement channel, in turn from the microphone of the system.

White noise is generated randomly for the injection of it into an output amplifier, in turn into the receiver, and into the analyzer's reference channel. The noise injected into the output amplifier, is leaked from the receiver, was found through the feedback path, which is then acquired by the microphone, amplified by a preamplifier, reached the measurement channel of the signal analyzer, after then measurement is made. A reference signal is provided to compare the output of the signal generator with the measurement channel.

The comparison results showed that the signal picked up from the feedback pathway is just the same as that of the sounds heard in the hearing device during their operation [19], which is none other than the *acoustic feedback*. Therefore, breaking the loop makes the audible feedback to be heard, and also the external acoustic leakage portion of the feedback loop is kept intact to make the measurement [20].

12.3.1 Frequency Analysis Using Impulse Response

Transient behavior of any system such as filters, analog/digital systems, etc. in a room or concert hall, could be well described by an impulse response of the system, which helps understand the system behavior such as frequency, magnitude, and phase response for the given state, in every aspect, at the time of observation. An impulse response is a momentary signal of infinite magnitude with the unit area, to say, it is an infinitely short pulse, briefer than the dynamic output. The output of the system having impulse response is determined using a time-slicing technique called convolution for the given input.

When an impulse Response of a system is integrable, then the system is said to be Stable. In a stable system, the system reaches the steady-state, when the transient move towards zero, as time becomes infinite. Hence, it can check the stability of an unknown system also.

An impulse response is determined by using the inverse Fourier transformation of the transfer function of an LTI system, in which the convolution of an input signal with an impulse, produces the system output, mathematically. Analogically, the transform of an impulse signal offers the DC spectrum in the frequency domain. It indicates that all the harmonics (ranging frequency from $-\infty$ to $+\infty$) contribute to making an impulse

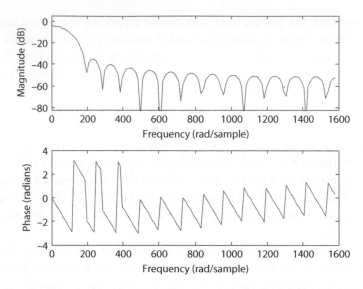

Figure 12.3 Representation of the frequency response under feedback condition.

signal, that is it contains an entire range of frequencies in it, which is used to test the system.

On applying the Fourier transform to impulse response of the system, offer its magnitude spectrum, which provides the amount of amplification or attenuation required and the phase spectrum provides the required phase shift for the given system at a particular frequency to different frequency harmonics. Since the impulse signals contain an entire range of frequencies in them, which able to test the unknown system. In other words, if any other signal other than impulse signal is used to characterize the system, it may not have all frequencies within it and hence it is unable to know how the system will respond to those frequencies.

The Fast Fourier Transform (FFT) is implemented here for transforming the portion of input samples to process in the frequency domain, furthermore to reduce the computational complexity. To meet the demand in high speed and low power digital filters, the order of digital filter should be as small as possible [12]. Figure 12.3 provides the frequency response of an audio signal at the desired frequency [19].

12.3.2   Feedback Analysis Using Phase Difference

The acoustic feedback is typical, occurs when the gain reaches high frequency particularly at 0° phase crossing. Hence, the feedback is said to be a high-frequency problem, which generally occurs during an unpleasant association of gain at higher frequencies, when the phase crossing is at zero degrees. Figure 12.4 represents the presence of high-frequency cuts in the feedback signals compared with an acoustic signal without feedback.

Whenever the gains at greater frequencies are gradually reduced, the fundamental oscillational peaks are significantly decreased in its magnitude. Therefore, when the gain of peak frequency is lowered by diminishing the average gain in high frequencies, the feedback is suppressed [19].

The long impulse responses proclaimed by the auditory systems are handled by analyzing their corresponding Phase responses under varying feedback conditions. This can be analyzed under 3 categories:

Case (i): When a leakage signal is fed back with the amplified sound at *in-phase* (i.e., 0° phase difference), the sound signals strengthen each other, increase in amplitude, leading gradually to recognizable excitation said to be positive feedback, as in Figure 12.5(a).

Case (ii): If the signal drops behind with the amplified tone in *out-of-phase* (i.e., 180° phase difference), the 2 signals cancel each other either fully or partially and the resultant get canceled, due to negative feedback, as in Figure 12.5(b).

Case (iii): When the two waves have a quite difference in phase arbitrarily in the interval of 0 and 360° (i.e. −180° and +180°), were added together *instant by instant*, leads to the existence of feedback as in Case (i) in Figure 12.5(c) [19].

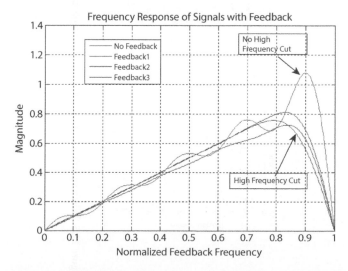

Figure 12.4 Plot showing feedbacks with high-frequency cuts in an acoustic environment.

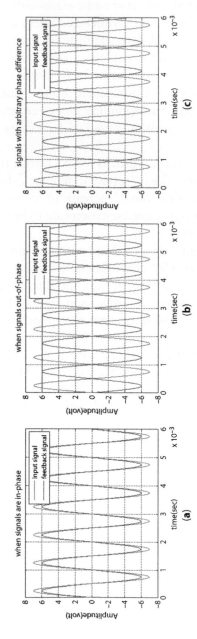

Figure 12.5 When signals are (a) in-phase (b) out-of-phase and (c) with an arbitrary phase difference.

When one of the signals is considered to be a sound signal that is amplified, while another one as a feedback signal that results from an ambient leakage and both the signals are in-phase, then they will be added with each other. Those two signals continued to be added, as the leakage signal is already fed back and amplified several times, and when the signal amplitude is so high that the oscillation happens, which creates a distinctive noticeable squeaking noise [19].

If, on the other hand, the situation in which the signal leaking away to the microphone is completely out of phase, then the two signals canceled and deducted from one another. The probably resultant signal amplitude at the output is reduced. Therefore, there will be no audible feedback [19].

Visualizing the graph in Figure 12.6, whenever the phase reaches −180°, the device measures the phase that returns to +180° (since 180° + 180° = 360° or a full cycle); therefore, the calculation is similar at both +180° and −180°. Hence the graph appeared to be a series of saw teeth waves, whose vertical lines have phase inversions changes between −180° and +180° [19].

Assuming time-invariance of auditory feedback and forward path of a hearing aid, Nyquist stability criterion for a dynamic system [13], defines that any system under a closed-loop is not stable when the magnitude of the transfer function in an open-loop is equal to one or more than that; and also, when an open-loop phase difference at this frequency becomes the product of 2π. If either of the condition is

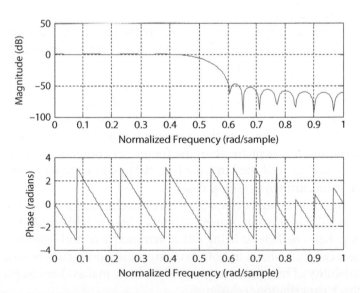

Figure 12.6 Representation of the phase response under feedback condition.

not fulfilled, the perceptual quality of the loudspeaker signal may be reduced [5]. Hence the acoustic feedback that reduces maximum stable gain (MSG), in turn, makes the system oscillate, which is needed to be cancelled in the hearing aid circuitry. Therefore the feedback system is found to be unstable at a particular frequency when the gain of the open-loop system exceeds 1 and the phase difference is 0° or $2n\pi$, which leads to acoustic instability [19].

12.4   Filtering of Signals

12.4.1   Digital Filters

Whenever the speech signals are needed to be filtered for removing the noise in it, linear digital filtering is chosen. Digital filters are said to have linear and time-invariance systems and are preferred over analog filters, mainly due to the advantage: The frequency response in digital filters can be changed by changing the filter coefficients; while in analog filters, the frequency response can be modified by changing the electronic components only.

In digital filters, the continuous-time systems are represented using difference equations while the discrete-time systems are written by differential equations. The evolution of digital filters is broadly classified under 2 categories: Finite Impulse Response (FIR) filter and Infinite Impulse Response (IIR) filter.

IIR filter has an impulse response that responds indefinitely, due to the presence of internal feedback. Owing to their recursive nature, these filters suffer from instability problems. Also, the complexity of the IIR filter grows, when the filter order grows significantly [25].

FIR filter has an impulse response with a definite length, as it reaches zero in a finite period. These filters are always stable and designed to have a linear phase, that preserves the waveshape of the input signal. When a filter is having a linear phase, then the frequency components of the input signals are said to be shifted in time (i.e., delayed) by the same amount of constant value, known as Group delay.

Since the time delay of frequency is relative to one another, the phase distortion will never occur. A perfect linear phase is achieved in FIR filters by having their coefficients being either symmetric or anti-symmetric. The FIR filters can be realized in both recursive and non-recursive structures. The availability of huge advantages in FIR filters, makes them be preferred in feedback cancellation techniques.

12.4.2   Adaptive Filters

Whenever a randomly varying noise is available in the system and whose variations are unknown, it is unable to filter out the noise in real-time using digital filters. In such cases, the adaptive filtering method is preferred, to eliminate the signal distortion in noisy surroundings either it is stationary and non-stationary. Adaptive filters are the class of digital filters, used to remove unwanted signals such as noise or feedback signals.

The main quality of the adaptive filter model is, its time-varying nature and its structure are adjustable as per the system's performance or behavior [14]. A filter is said to be optimal only if it is designed with less knowledge of input data [12]. The adaptive filters can be realized in various configurations [25]. Filter structures help obtain system function and determine filter coefficients, as the structure design influences various parameters like the number of iterations and computational complexity, which affects the performance of the process than the desired level [25].

12.4.2.1   Order of Adaptive Filters

During the realization of adaptive filters, when the order of the filter is small, it leads to a considerably greater number of branches in the circuit parallelly and vice versa; however, having so much small-length branches enhances the steady-state error [25]. Hence the length of the filter is important in building the structure of any linear filter system.

The number of taps (N) reflects the amount of memory needed to execute the filter. More number of taps leads to higher frequency resolution and makes the filter narrower. When the number of weights/taps are longer, then the adaptive filter circuit uses branches as small in number with greater sample length, that are intended for use. This may considerably reduce the convergence speed, though this shoots up the computational complexity of the filter circuit. An optimum choice of filter order will incorporate the system complexity and the efficient performance of an adaptive filter in a steady state.

12.4.2.2   Filter Coefficients in Adaptive Filters

Usage of very few filter coefficients results in under-modeling, while the higher number results in adaptation noise, for which the convergence rate becomes lesser due to mismatch of extra coefficients [25, 28–30]. Suppose there are two filters of different lengths to model an acoustic echo cancellation arrangement, the too-long filter converges slower than the filter which has the same number of coefficients as the acoustic system to be identified. Due to the mismatch of tap-length, the error spreads all over the filter and the adaptive filter itself introduces echo in this case [25]. As the order of filter L increases, it is evident that the number of iterations also increases, which in turn increases the adaptation time.

The filter coefficients are in the form of difference equation coefficients, which help calculate the impulse response. If the adaptive canceller coefficients are not nearer to the FIR filter coefficients, that further models the feedback path, not eventually results in attenuation of the feedback signal, but rather intensifies the noise signal. Consequently, the adaptive filter's transient period must be as short as possible, to greatly improve the quality of the system [6].

12.4.3   Adaptive Feedback Cancellation

Most of the acoustic feedback cancellers are grouped into two major classifications: Non-Continuous or Continuous.

12.4.3.1   Non-Continuous Adaptation

In this technique, the adaptive filter coefficients are adjusted only when the instability is detected or when the input signal level is low [2, 3]. It periodically uses a training sequence, such as white noise, at the output of the hearing aid for adaptation of the feedback canceller coefficients [8]. The interference nature of this training sequence is useful only for the profoundly deaf, who would not be affected by the noise sequence. These systems are objectionable as it reduces the signal-to-noise ratio (SNR) and limits the adaptation, just when quiet or yelling stretches are identified [8].

A Notch-filter based approach is one of the non-continuous adaption methods, provided in the adaptive feedback circuit, for howling suppression. Since the acoustic feedback does not occur at all high frequencies, the gain at the particular feedback frequency should be reduced. The *Notch filtering* howling suppression (NHS) approach monitors the generation of whistling sounds in the input signals. Whenever the potential of the whistling feedback signal is distinguished, the notch filters are generated to suppress those whistling feedback signals at the feedback frequencies [1].

When a notch filter is added to the circuit, it selectively reduces the gain at a given frequency which can trigger feedback [19]. The filter is more suitable as a stopband filter, which selectively removes a narrow frequency band around the predetermined centre frequency [20].

In Figure 12.7, the typical notch filter frequency response is centered at 1,600 Hz (normalized at ω_c = 0.5 Hz) and as it very well may be seen, the filter produces a dip in the frequency response curve, or a notch [19]. The filter gain is unity (gain of 1 or 0 dB) at all the frequencies except the middle frequency of the notch provides nearly 40 dB of attenuation [30].

It is important to determine the shape of the transition region between the unit gain area and the notch frequency, its width, attenuation region, etc. The width of the notch filter, called the filter bandwidth, is defined as the difference in the frequencies at which the response decreases by 3 dB as a result of unity gain. For the given filter, the bandwidth is about 1,000 Hz wide, which is the difference in frequency between the two 3 dB-down frequencies [19].

The use of the notch filter in feedback cancellation is illustrated and on comparing the original frequency response except around the center frequency of the notch, the original hearing aid frequency response remains in shape [30]. Sharp notch filters are generally used to sharper the filter, narrower the gain reduction region is. The above plot also showed that a decrease in filter order increases the sharpness of the filter at the center

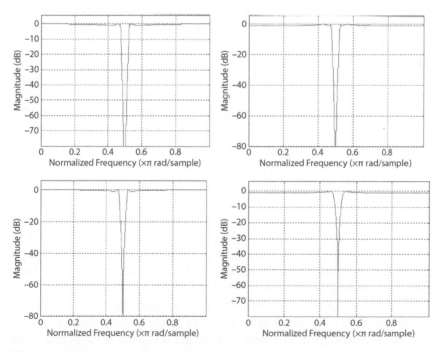

Figure 12.7 Frequency response of notch filter different orders at ω_c = 0.5 Hz.

frequency. Increasing the sharpness of the filter limits the gain reduction at the feedback frequencies [1].

The only drawback is the reactive nature of the notch filter, which unavoidably initiates the excessive reverberation in the circuit before the identification of oscillation frequencies. As feedback occurs, the gain is reduced in the narrow frequency band around the critical frequencies and compromises the basic frequency response of hearing aids which can have a serious impact on sound quality [2]. Hence it is inappropriate from a sound quality point of view.

12.4.3.2   Continuous Adaptation

Continuous adaptation systems constantly change the input signal-based filter coefficients and do not require any training sequence [8]. Continuous Adaptation methods are based on the direct or indirect input-output methods, depending on the assumptions made on a forward path [20–24]. The indirect method, the unknown system coefficients are determined by placing the unknown model in parallel with the adaptive filter, known as the method of system identification. When an unknown system is placed in series with the filter, that adapts an inverse of an unknown model, by inserting a delay in the desired signal path, known as the method of inverse system identification [17].

Fixed estimates of the desired signal model are used in the direct method of Continuous Adaptation [20, 21], while assumptions about the forward path and the presence of probe signal $r[k]$ are required in the indirect I–O approach, and made the feedback cancellation method more appealing [3]. The standard Continuous Adaptation Feedback Cancellation (CAF) suffers from a significant model error or bias, due to the presence of a closed-loop signal, if the desired signal is spectrally colored [2].

Continuous Adaptation Feedback method reduces the energy of the feedback compensated signal $e(n)$, which leads to a standard wiener filter and the desired signal acts as a disruption to the feedback canceller [2]. The adaptive filter may not be able to approximate the feedback path satisfactorily, resulting in the device being unstable at high forward gain values [8]. The acoustic feedback is cancelled by the microphone output signal being subtracted with feedback signal estimates.

The feedback signal is estimated using an adaptive filter, to filter the output of the hearing aid with an estimate of the transfer function of the acoustic feedback path. The path of acoustic feedback is estimated by filtering the output signal of the hearing aid with an estimate of the transfer function of the acoustic feedback path. To cancel the acoustic feedback, the

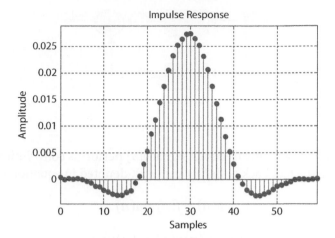

Figure 12.8 Impulse response of an acoustic system.

generated estimates of feedback signal are then subtracted from the microphone output signal. Figure 12.8 shows the impulse response of an acoustic system from which the experiment is to be carried out.

However, the transfer function is modeled as a fixed delay followed by an adaptive FIR filter. The fixed delay was set to 0.85 ms, approximately the average group delay of the acoustic feedback path. Having a fixed delay allows for the use of a shorter FIR filter that reduces a greater number of approximations [13].

12.4.4   Estimation of Acoustic Feedback

The true acoustic feedback path is modeled in the hearing system, by introducing an adaptive FIR filter into the feedback cancellation circuit as shown in Figure 12.9. The undesirable, annoying feedback is cancelled by subtracting microphone output with an equivalent signal that must be a replica of the feedback signal. Logically, achieving the above will achieve a complete cancellation of acoustic feedback in hearing aids.

To model the true acoustic feedback path $F[k]$ in the hearing system, an FIR adaptive filter $W[k]$, is introduced in the feedback cancellation circuit, to estimate $F[k]$, for which $W[k]$ is placed in parallel with $F[k]$. The initial estimation of the feedback path is performed by, assuming the acoustic feedback path $F[k]$ to be an unknown system, placing in parallel with the adaptive filter. The output of $F[k]$ is the feedback signal, $p[n]$, considered here as the desired signal. The hearing aid output $u[n]$ is fed as input to both the unknown system and the adaptive filter model.

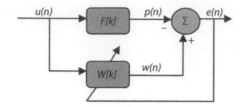

Figure 12.9 Identification of an unknown system.

As per the design, the feedback signal $p[n]$ performs convolution operation among the feedback path $f(n)$ and $u(n)$, denoted in equation (12.1) as,

$$p(n) = f(n) * u(n) \tag{12.1}$$

$$p(n) = f^T(n)u(n) = f(n)u^T(n) \tag{12.2}$$

Where $f(n) = [f_0(n), f_1(n), ..., f_{L-1}(n)]^T$ using the polynomial transfer function, $f(n)$ is represented in q and the vector coefficients of $F[k]$ are represented as $f^T(n)$ with the length of discrete-time filter L, is given as

$$F[k] = f^T(n)q \tag{12.3}$$

$$F[k] = [f_0(n), f_1(n)q^{-1}, ..., f_{L-1}(n)q^{-L+1}] \tag{12.4}$$

Hence Equation (12.2) becomes,

$$p(n) = F[k]u(n) \tag{12.5}$$

The feedback signal estimate $\hat{w}(n)$ is generated by filtering the hearing aid output signal $u(n)$, by an estimate of the acoustic feedback path transfer function $W[k]$ [13].

$$\hat{w}(n) = W[k]u(n) \tag{12.6}$$

$\hat{w}(n)$ is represented as a polynomial transfer function in q as $W[k]$ and its vector coefficients are represented as $\hat{w}^T(n)$ with the length of the discrete-time filter, L is given as $W[k] = \hat{w}^T(n)q = [\hat{w}_0(n), \hat{w}_1(n)q^{-1}, ..., \hat{w}_{L-1}(n)q^{-L+1}]$. The adaptive filter model aims to reduce the error signal $e(n)$ between the adaptive filter output $\hat{w}(n)$ and the output of the unknown system (or system to be identified), $p(n)$ [17].

When $\hat{w}(n)$ subtracted from the desired signal $p(n)$, provides a feedback-eradicated signal $e(n)$, which should ideally be zero; $e(n) = 0$; this shows that the system, $W[k] = F[k]$, and the signal for canceling feedback $\hat{w}(n)$ is similar to the feedback signal $p(n)$; i.e., $\hat{w}(n) = p(n)$. Hence a completely feedback cancelling model is obtained. Then, the Adaptive Filter model able to identify the unknown system.

To estimate the adaptive filter $W[k]$, which is of length $L - 1$ for $\hat{w}(n) = \sum_{k=0}^{L} W[k]u(n)$. When $e(n)$ is very small, the adaptive filter response is said to be closer to the response of the unknown system and the adapted filter is identical to the unknown system [17]. The $\hat{w}_0(n)$ is an estimate of $W[k]$ at time t = 0, which is replaced continuously by $\hat{w}(n)$, during adaptation.

12.4.5   Analysis of Acoustic Feedback Signal

12.4.5.1   Forward Path of the Signal

Let the input sound signal passes through the microphone, hearing aid signal processing circuitry $G[k]$, and reaches the loudspeaker as $u(n)$. The forward path of the open-loop hearing system is defined as;

$$u(n) = G[k]\, x(n) \qquad (12.7)$$

where the vector coefficients of $u(n) = [u(n), u(n - 1),...u(n - L + 1)]^T$, $x(n)$, $x(n)$ is the output signal of the microphone and T is the transposition operator.

12.4.5.2   Feedback Path of the Signal

However, the amplified sound $u(n)$ from the loudspeaker, finds an alternate path and reaches the microphone, results in a closed-loop, caused by the feedback signal. The path originated from the ear canal to the microphone, due to the feedback path, which is described as $F[k]$ [15]. Therefore, Equation (12.9) becomes,

$$u(n) = \frac{G[k]}{1 - G[k]F[k]} x(n) \qquad (12.8)$$

Due to this feedback signal, the closed-loop system $H[k]$ forms the transfer function, when $G[k]$ is linear; hence Equation (12.10) becomes,

$$H[k] = \frac{u(n)}{x(n)} = \frac{G[k]}{1 - G[k]F[k]} \qquad (12.9)$$

The adaptive filter model used to identify the unknown system is then connected in parallel with the forward path of hearing aid processing as shown in the figure. To achieve an ideal acoustic feedback cancellation, an adaptive filter is placed in the hearing aid circuit as shown in Figure 12.10.

The error signal obtained should be,

$$e(n) = \{x(n) + p(n)\} - \hat{w}(n) \tag{12.10}$$

Since $\hat{w}(n)$ is a replica of $p(n)$, both get cancelled, and hence the gained error signal should merely be the microphone signal $x(n)$. However, rather than canceling the hearing system's auditory feedback $p(n)$, the approximated feedback path $\hat{w}(n)$ frequently involves a bias, caused by the association of loudspeaker $u(n)$ and input signals $x(n)$. This correlation is evident based on the attributes of the closed-loop acoustical system [16]. As a consequence, the closed-loop transfer function $H[k]$ obtained from the desired signal $x(n)$ to loudspeaker signal $u(n)$ in Equation (12.11) is transformed into [2]:

$$u(n) = \frac{G[k]}{1 - G[k][F[k] - W[k]]} x(n) \tag{12.11}$$

The error signal,

$$e(n) = y(n) - \hat{w}(n) \tag{12.12}$$

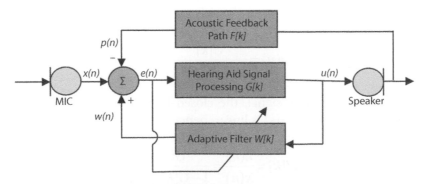

Figure 12.10 Adaptive filter placed after the identification of unknown system.

Where,

$$y(n) = x(n) + p(n) \tag{12.13}$$

Where $\hat{w}(n)$ is an estimate of $p(n)$; therefore,

$$e(n) = y(n) - W[k]u(n) \tag{12.14}$$

Then the obtained $\hat{w}(n)$, is subtracted from the desired signal $p(n)$ to deliver the error signal $e(n)$. The feedback-compensated signal $e(n)$, is continuously adjusting its coefficients to emulate the impulse response (IR) of the feedback path $F[k]$. But, rather providing a zero-error output, the estimated feedback path often includes a bias, due to the correlation between the loudspeaker and incoming signals, when $x(n)$ is spectrally colored.

12.4.5.3   Bias Identification

Wiener filters are an optimum class of filters, that linearly estimate the desired signal by relating the noise signal with the desired signal, which was disrupted by noise [9]. Instead of using a data matrix, the statistics of input and output signals are used by the Wiener filter to seek the optimal tap weights [32].

The performance is then evaluated by measuring the Mean-Square Error (MSE) of the adaptive filter, which is obtained by measuring the difference of squares of errors between the desired signal $\hat{w}(n)$ and the primary source input $y(n)$ as in Equation (12.8). This error is required to be reduced to converge those signals. Wiener filters are the tool to reduce the cost function in terms of squared-error as shown below:

$$J(\hat{w}^T(n)) = E\{e^2(n)\} \tag{12.15}$$

$$= E\{y(n) - \hat{w}(n)\}^2 \tag{12.16}$$

Squaring and minimizing the mean square error to zero, by setting the gradient concerning filter estimate $\hat{w}^T(n)$, for obtaining an optimal solution;

$$\frac{\partial E}{\partial \hat{w}_i} = 0; \text{ for } i = 0, 1, 2, \ldots, L-1 \tag{12.17}$$

The vectors obtained from Equation (12.17) are *cross-correlated* and $R_{uu}[k] = E\{u(n)u^T(n)\}$ gives out the vectors that are *auto-correlated* with signals $y(n)$ and $u(n)$ respectively as shown.

$$-2R_{yu}[k] + 2W[k]R_{uu}[k] = 0 \qquad (12.18)$$

The Wiener–Hopf solution for the transfer function of feedback path $W[k]$, consists of two terms, a product of the inverse of auto-correlation matrix $R_{uu}[k]^{-1}$ and the cross-correlation vector $R_{yu}[k]$ between $y(n)$ and $u(n)$ as given.

$$W[k] = R_{uu}[k]^{-1}R_{yu}[k] \qquad (12.19)$$

Where the input signal $y(n)$ is the addition of $x(n)$ and the feedback signal $p(n)$. Hence $y(n)$ can be rewritten as $y(n) = x(n) + f(n)u^T(n)$. Thus, Equation (12.19) is expanded concerning the transposition of the individual vector and hence modified into,

$$= E\{u(n)u^T(n)\}^{-1}[E\{u(n)x(n)\} + E\{f(n)u(n)u^T(n)\}] \qquad (12.20)$$

Equation (12.20) leads to the solution for Wiener–Hopf as, $W[k]$ includes, the true feedback path $f(n)$ (the desired IR) and the product of the inverse correlation matrix $E\{u(n)u^T(n)\}^{-1}$ and the product of cross-correlation vector $E\{u(n)x(n)\}$ between the loudspeaker signal $u(n)$ and the incoming signal $x(n)$ [23], [26].

$$W[k] = f(n)\{Desired\} + E\{u(n)u^T(n)\}^{-1}E\{u(n)x(n)\}\{Bias\} \qquad (12.21)$$

The above equation shows that the signals $u(n)$ and $x(n)$ are correlated with each other and results in the non-zero output. Hence the estimated IR (or the canceler's coefficients) is said to be biased. It is assessed to acquire an unbiased estimate, the cross-correlation vector $R_{yu}[k]$ must satisfy zero in Equation (12.21), which is generally not the case in practice, hence $W[k]$ is said to be biased.

12.5   Adaptive Algorithms

Various Algorithms like, LMS, NLMS, RLS, etc., are used to train the digital filters, to make the filter adaptive. A particular type of adaptive algorithm is chosen and the filter setup is classified according to the algorithm represented in the application.

The Least Mean Square (LMS) algorithm is a stochastic gradient-based technique that adaptively allows the steepest descent vector to converge the solution of an optimal Wiener filter for their filter tap weights [12, 30]. Widrow and Hoff developed the LMS estimation algorithm in 1960, for adaptive filtering applications in real-time, which is defined using the filter vector update equation,

$$\hat{w}(n+1) = \hat{w}(n) + \mu e(n)u(n) \qquad (12.22)$$

The algorithm extensively opts for its efficiency in hardware and less cost in implementation.

The Normalized least mean square algorithm (NLMS) is an extended version of the LMS algorithm [27], whose recursion formula is written as,

$$\hat{w}(n+1) = \hat{w}(n) + \frac{\mu}{u^T(n)u(n) + \delta} e(n)u(n) \qquad (12.23)$$

where δ is the limiting factor that prevents the weight update equation from reaching infinity if u(n) is equal to zero.

The NLMS is highly stable; that makes the input signal characteristics are independent of each other or vice versa. In comparison, NLMS demonstrates better convergence compared to LMS for both correlated and non-correlated results. However, the algorithm requires additional processing to obtain an input vector standard and thus the step-size is normalized to use [31].

PNLMS algorithm exhibits the configuration of impulse response in a feedback path and designates a variable step size to various values in the impulse response of the feedback path [2]. FLMS is based on the concept of fractional order calculus [27]. The prediction bias of the FLMS converges faster than the LMS, although the LMS absorbs a larger number of iterations. It improves the mean square error in FLMS, which is stabilized faster related to the LMS algorithm [25]. Table 12.1 provided the advantages and disadvantages of various adaptive algorithms.

12.5.1   Step-Size Algorithms

To choose and apply the appropriate *filter coefficients* in the adaptive feedback canceller of an unknown model, it is necessary to estimate the feedback path

Table 12.1 Comparison of adaptive algorithms.

	LMS	NLMS	RLS	PEM based pre-whitening filter
Implementation	Simple in implementation	Increased computational complexity	Computationally more complex	Increasing computational complexity
Stability	Has stability issues	More stability	Highly stable	Limiting the added stable gain
Convergence	Slow adaptation speed	Improved convergence speed	Provides very good SNR	Reducing the convergence rate

suitably and adaptively, using a filter-update equation and to cancel the bias and to improve the convergence rate by varying the step-size.

12.5.1.1   Fixed Step-Size

In the LMS algorithm, the step-size parameter (μ) plays a vital role in influencing the convergence speed and steady-state error. The step-size of LMS adaptive algorithm (μ), updated under the condition,

$$\mu = \frac{k}{N(\text{signal power})} \qquad (12.24)$$

where k is any constant value of less than 0.01 and N is the order of filter [13]. The coefficients adapt to 90% of their final value in -150 ms and 100% of their final value in -1 s [11].

The impulse response samples with higher values are preferably adapted with large step size, whereas those with low values get a small step size [25]. As per Equation (12.24), the step size should therefore be below 0.909, the chosen step size should be very small for small output errors [6] and the primary condition for choosing *small* step-size is given as,

$$0 < \mu < \frac{1}{L\sigma_x^2} \qquad (12.25)$$

If μ is too increasing, the condition will not converge into a mean square algorithm and the algorithm will remain stable for

$$0 < \mu < \frac{1}{\lambda_n} \tag{12.26}$$

If μ is low on the flip side, then the algorithm will converge slowly. But it is noticed that if μ is small, then the rate of convergence is slow particularly when the LMS algorithm is used for adaptation in longer filter lengths [20, 25]. This method is also based on the history of the dataset about the current feedback response, after which it can adjust the step size accordingly [25]. The value of step-size in the LMS algorithm is difficult to choose as it is generally a compromise between slow convergence but low steady-state error and rapid convergence while a higher steady-state misalignment [9–11].

The step size should be approximately within the range given by the below condition for stable output; $0 < \mu < \frac{1}{\lambda_n}$. Where λ_n is the maximum wavelength of the input signal $x(n)$. In adaptive filters, the convergence remains slow caused by the restriction in μ, which relies entirely on the input signal characteristics [20, 25].

Although, the least mean square algorithm attempted to be simple in implementation, but add some computational complexity and has the stability issues. It also has a slow adaptation speed and the behavior of the step-size increases for adaptation at the earlier stages because of larger values of output error [6]. As the algorithm goes closer to the steady-state, the value of e(n) decreases which decreases the step-size [10].

12.5.1.2   Variable Step-Size

When the step-size is fixed or constant, the MSE is initially low and after some time, it slowly increases. Variable step-size algorithms achieve rapid convergence and a low steady-state error for cancelling feedback in hearing aids [9]. When a constant step-size μ is used to achieve smaller steady-state error, will automatically reduce the convergence rate [6]. When step-size increases, the convergence rate increases, results in output error increase [10]. Therefore, there is a tradeoff seen between steady-state error and the speed of convergence, which prevents rapid convergence [6].

Hence a time-variation step-size parameter is used at the time of the adaptation process, to eradicate the trade-off issue. The adaptive filter is away from the optimum value, initially in the period of adaptation, so a greater step-size is included. This will decrease the transitory period and improves the adaptive filter convergence rate [6]. As the adaptive filter approaches the optimized Wiener solution, the μ value should be reduced and leads to an erroneous value.

The LMS-derived algorithms use a time-variation step-size for the faster convergence of adaptive algorithms and are greatly interested in maintaining a small convergence error rate at low complexity. Therefore, a solid variable step-size algorithm is described in this chapter, which explains the variation in step-size in two ways, known as variation step-size algorithm [6]. The variation step parameter is utilized in the algorithm as follows;

$$\acute{\mu}(n+1) = \alpha\, \acute{\mu}(n) +' \gamma e^2(n) \tag{12.27}$$

$$\mu(n+1) = \begin{cases} \mu_{max} & if\ \acute{\mu}(n+1) > \mu_{max} \\ \mu_{min} & if\ \acute{\mu}(n+1) < \mu_{min} \\ \acute{\mu}(n+1) & otherwise \end{cases} \tag{12.28}$$

where μ_{max} and μ_{min} are the upper and lower boundary limits of step-size parameter μ and $0 < a < 1$ and $\gamma > 0$ are at constant values [6]. Generally, μ_{max} is chosen closer to the instability point to increase the convergence speed of the conventional LMS algorithm and μ_{min} is opted to provide a fair balance between the algorithm's steady-state misalignment and tracking capability. The γ parameter monitors the convergence time as well as the steady-state degree of the error and on which the steady-state misadjustment depends [6]. This shows that the misalignment and convergence rate are dependent on each other [5]. For instance, in channel equalization during the transient period, the frequency characteristic of the adaptive equalizer is far from the inverse of the frequency response of the channel, therefore, the data transmitted during this time will be corrupted [6].

12.6   Simulation

12.6.1   Training of Adaptive Filter for Removal of Acoustic Feedback

The acoustic feedback is measured either using an anechoic chamber or a test chamber to generate the sounds of required SPL at the hearing aid microphone and provides a convenient way to get sound into the hearing aid in a controlled manner [7]. The output of a hearing aid is directed into a coupler, a hard-walled cavity of volume 2 cm^3 (the approximate volume of the ear canal of an average adult, when wearing a hearing aid). The SPL generated in the microphone is directly depending on the impedance of the cavity, which in turn depends on the volume of the cavity. The frequency response of the loudspeaker must be kept flat between 100 Hz and 10 kHz while measuring the feedback [7].

The adaptive algorithm determines the filter parameters for the next iteration using the error signal $e(n)$, which is measured from the clean input speech signal $x(n)$. Therefore, $x(n)$ is required for calculation of the error $e(n)$ in an adaptive filter. However, $x(n)$ is not practically available and the only signal obtained from the microphone is the feedback corrupted signal, $y(n)$. Hence the input signal $x(n)$ is estimated from Equation (12.14), $y(n) = x(n) + p(n)$.

However, the receiver output $u(n)$ is correlated with the feedback signal $p(n)$, which gives the reference input to the adaptive noise cancellation model. The output $\hat{w}(n)$ is produced by filtering the noise $p(n)$ from $u(n)$. The generated output is subtracted from the noise corrupted signal and produces the required signal, $e(n) = \hat{w}(n) - y(n)$.

The adaptive filter is an adequate concept that can adjust its transfer function via an adaptive algorithm. The adaptive algorithm is used to minimize the error signal. This error signal is fed back into the adaptive filter. That is, the filter output $\hat{w}(n) = \hat{x}(n)$ is an estimate of $x(n)$ [24]. The adaptive algorithm now tries to minimize this error signal as minimum as possible. This error signal is an important parameter to judge the accuracy of the algorithm along with its convergence.

For real-time applications, the adaptive filters are to be trained in prior, for which the actual clean speech x(n) was indeed required in the training phase, to update the filter parameters for each iteration [24]. Before the presentation of signals to the microphone, there applied a pause with a minimum of 5 s silence [21]. During the period of presentation, the hearing aid's signal processing requires some time for adaptation which is negligible and on the other hand, the signals were assessed within a period

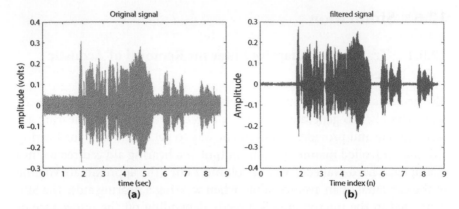

Figure 12.11 (a) Audio signal without adaptive filtering and (b) signal with adaptive filtering.

of 15 to 60 s [21]. Signals are recorded at the output of the hearing aid for analysis [21].

Digital signal processing enables us to convert the analog electrical signals into digital and vice versa, through ADC and DAC respectively in a digital hearing aid, and making us process the signal in MATLAB is possible. For the sake of simplicity, ADC, DAC, and other amplifier circuits are not shown in the diagrams. Once the condition $e(n) = 0$ or $\hat{w}(n) = \hat{y}(n) \approx y(n)$ was reached, the training will be completed with converging the filter output.

The adaptive algorithm block of Figure 12.1 is removed after completion of the training, and only the digital filter is left. Then, the digital filter is intended to remove the noise added to any speech signal. Afterwards, the filter is used practically. From the discussion, it is clear that before applying the filter, it must be practically trained in a particular source of noise, and Figure 12.11(a) and (b) show the audio signal without and with adaptive filtering.

12.6.2   Testing of Adaptive Filter

12.6.2.1   Subjective and Objective Evaluation Using KEMAR

The frequency response of acoustic feedback was measured from ten persons (males and females) for subjective evaluation (SE) and on an electronic humanoid, known as *Knowles Ear Manikin (KEMAR)*, under objective evaluation (OE) respectively [15]. KEMAR consists of ears, head, neck, and torso (body without limbs) like humans and generally utilized for acoustic research, as the dimensions of head and torso, are based on the dimensional analysis of male or female adults [18]. Moreover, the surface of KEMAR is made up of high resistive impervious material, which is not likely to absorb the acoustic signals [18].

Although SE was time-consuming, it provided a more accurate and reliable reflection of speech quality. Alternatively, OE was achieved either on hardware or software, that provided more flexible and convenient measures, which was reliable in timing. The distinguishing features of the original and distributed speech obtained through SE and OE were compared and which was conducted in time or frequency domain, which enabled the measurement of acoustic feedback.

12.6.2.2   Experimental Setup Using Manikin Channel

The experimental setup includes 2 channels using a standard microphone and the KEMAR. Initially, both the channels are calibrated to the Output Sound Pressure Level with 90 dB input (OSPL$_{90}$), which is obtained by delivering a 90-dB input signal from the loudspeaker to the microphone input, which is kept in the test chamber and then measuring the overall output of instrument across the test frequencies [28].

Whenever, the reference pressure level of KEMAR, coincidence with the microphone level, then the acoustic analyzer playback the output signal of hearing aids to test the parameters, which is then recorded and saved [15]. Noise x-92 is a database containing recordings of different kinds of noise signals. Typical noise from Noise x-92 is initially superimposed on the input speech signal and switching the acoustic analyzer to mode 1 (noise reduction deactivated) and then to mode 2 (noise reduction activated). The test signal is played again, recorded, saved by an acoustic analyzer for the same sample frequency, which is then recorded through an acoustic analyzer via MATLAB and saved in .wav file format [18].

Although the audio frequency is from 20 Hz to 20 KHz, the required audio signals for human hearing ranges around 200 Hz to a maximum of 8 KHz. Hence the Pure Tone Audiogram measures the audible frequency range of hearing impaired only in the intervals of 250 Hz, 500 Hz, 1 KHz, 2 KHz, 4 KHz, and 8 KHz. Since the highest measuring frequency of the speech is 8 KHz, the sampling frequency is chosen to be greater than that of average signal frequency. Also, to avoid the aliasing issues in the time domain, the number of samples in the frequency spectrum must be greater than that in the time domain sequence [4]. Although the signals are processed in the time domain, they are analyzed using frequency domain, which helps study and analyze the frequency contents using frequency response [4].

12.7   Performance Evaluation

The performance evaluation of feedback cancellation algorithms is done concerning the parameters such as Mean Square Error (MSE), Rate of Convergence, Order of Filter (N) and Signal to Noise Ratio (SNR). MSE is calculated to evaluate the performance of the adaptive filter, by mixing a clean speech $x(n)$ with noise to produce a noisy signal and they(n) is a noise-free signal obtained from an estimate of x(n) [24]. The relation between x(n) and y(n) concerning filter order (N) is given in Equation (12.29),

$$MSE(n) = \frac{\sum_{0}^{N} [y(n) - x(n)]^2}{N} \qquad (12.29)$$

MSE is also determined simultaneously by measuring the theoretical and simulated value using MATLAB, at each time instant and Figure 12.12 shows out the MATLAB graph that provides the mean square error of an LMS system.

On comparing both the MSE values produce an error, which is used to reduce the rate of convergence between the source input and the desired signal as shown in Figure 12.13.

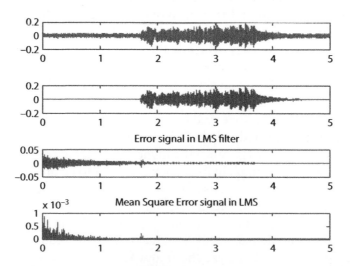

Figure 12.12 Mean square error provided by the LMS system.

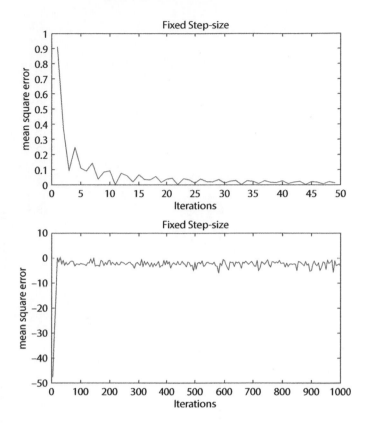

Figure 12.13 Mean square error under constant step-size in F-LMS.

The time-varying step-size (V-LMS) Least Mean Square algorithm will respond to environmental changes by estimating the MSE and the speed of convergence [22]. Performance of V-LMS and Fixed step-size LMS (F-LMS) algorithms are evaluated and compared, by changing the step-size under varying conditions. The simulation results of both the algorithms are evaluated simultaneously, by increasing the number of iterations.

In Figure 12.14(a), for $\mu = 0.0076$, the AFE in V-LMS suddenly increased to the peak value of MSE $= -0.0002$ and started decreasing exponentially till 380 samples, after which it reaches the steady-state for about 500 samples; however, from 880th sample, it started growing. For $\mu = 0.0054$ whereas the MSE in F-LMS converges very slowly after 2,800 samples. In Figure 12.14(b), for the step-size, $\mu = 0.0054$, F-LMS and V-LMS never show much difference. Table 12.2 provided the Steady-state MSE for AC-VSS with other algorithms under different SNR conditions, comparing theoretical values under MATLAB simulations [32].

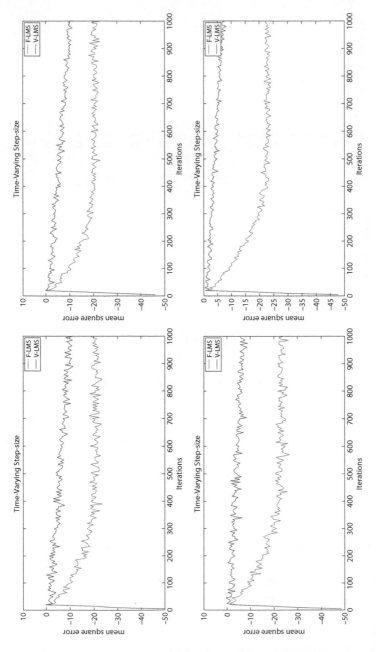

Figure 12.14 Mean square error under variable step-size in V-LMS at μ = 0.0076 and μ = 0.0054 respectively.

Table 12.2 Steady-state MSE for AC-VSS with other algorithms under different SNR conditions.

SNR	Under the theoretical method			Under MATLAB simulation		
	LZ-VSS	SM-VSS	AC-VSS	LZ-VSS	SM-VSS	AC-VSS
20	−44.74	−44.73	−44.75	−58.01	−58	−54.31
15	−34.68	−34.67	−34.67	−48.01	−47.98	−44.60
10	−24.46	−24.43	−24.43	−38.03	−37.92	−34.93
5	−13.52	−13.52	−13.51	−28.06	−27.71	−25.17
0	−5.67	−5.66	−5.64	−18.16	−16.87	−14.92

The Convergence Rate is defined as the number of iterations required for the algorithm to converge to its steady-state mean square error [12]. In Figure 12.15, for the given MSE (MSE = −18, μ = 0.0076), V-LMS started converging at about 480th sample, whereas the F-LMS converges after 2,800 samples, while for MSE (μ = 0.0054), V-LMS converge at about 270th sample, whereas the F-LMS converges after 2,300 samples.

Table 12.3 provided the Steady-state MSE for AC-VSS with other algorithms under different SNR conditions.

The Misalignment (MIS) between true feedback path $F[k]$ and estimated feedback path $W[k]$ is calculated using Equation (12. 30):

$$\text{MIS} = \sqrt{\frac{\int_0^\pi |F[k] - W[k]|^2}{\int_0^\pi |F[k]|^2}} d\omega \qquad (12.30)$$

Where $F[k]$ and $W[k]$ are the frequency responses of measured and estimated acoustic feedback paths at normalized frequencies respectively and Table 12.4 provided the measured misalignment for variable step-size algorithms under different step-size values.

It is ascertained that the MSE first decreases and then increases suddenly when the filter size is increased from a lower range to a greater value. The filter order, though, cannot be too low, either. With increased filter

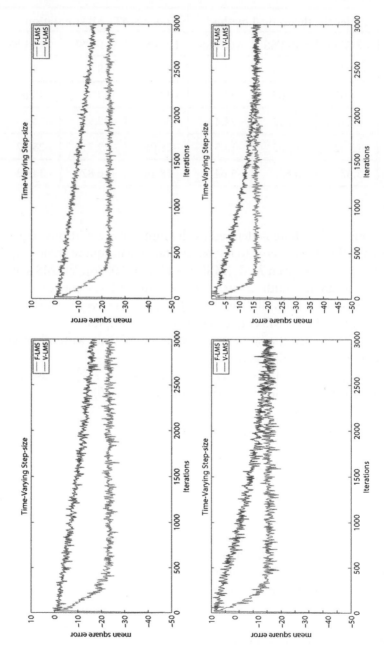

Figure 12.15 Convergence rate under variable step-size in V-LMS at μ = 0.0076 and μ = 0.0054 respectively.

Table 12.3 Convergence rate of various variable step-size algorithms.

Algorithm type	Fixed step-size	Variable step-size (VSS)		
		LZ-VSS	SM-VSS	AC-VSS
Convergence Rate	26%	13%	33%	40%

Table 12.4 Measured Misalignment for variable step-size algorithms under different step-size values.

Step-size	Steady-state misalignment			
	FSS	LZ-VSS	SM-VSS	AC-VSS
0.0003	4.41	2.65	3.47	1.7
0.0033	7.0	6.8	7.1	6.9
0.067	14.2	14.4	13.9	14.9
0.08	88.3	68.9	81.9	64.9

length, also the misadjustment increases. Hence, the filter length is to be untouched.

In short, the filter length is needed to be increased, while the steady-state mean square error is to be reduced (ideally zero), without increasing/altering the convergence rate. The filter coefficients are roughly calculated using the configuration of Joint process estimator, in which the error signal $e(n)$ and the hearing aid output $u(n)$ are applied as inputs to the estimator. The output $u(n)$ is denoted as a reference signal, which is delayed initially to accomplish the adaptation in coefficients [13].

12.8 Conclusions

The acoustic feedback cancellation technique for speech recognition and enhancement has a broad array of uses in the field of wireless communication systems in recent times. The main interest of this paper is to achieve a higher convergence rate with decreased computational complexity by minimizing the mean square error [25].

The proposed technique (V-LMS) is found to be a promising method for achieving adaptation of the system process. Although during the initial period of adaption, the filter output is closer to the optimum value.

The simulation curves have shown that the time-variation step-size makes the system to reach the steady-state lesser than λn value. It is also found to decorrelate the input signals and the bias is made to not depend on the feedback path characteristics. Hence, the V-LMS proves to be an efficient algorithm, for improving the convergence rate. Also, it produces a much faster convergence rate, much quicker tracking rate—which is defined based on the adaptation speed.

Simulation results clearly show that the V-LMS algorithm is relatively more robust and converged for a lesser value of MSE at $\mu = 0.0076$ compared to F-LMS. Also, the MSE increases approximately 1.25 and 1.5 times for F-LMS than V-LMS appropriately. Hence through adjusting the step-size under different circumstances, the V-LMS will reduce the effects of feedback and added noises.

References

1. Chung, K., Challenges and Recent Developments in Hearing Aids: Part I. Speech understanding in noise, microphone technologies and noise reduction algorithms. *Trends Amplif.*, 8, Number 4, 8, 3, 83–124, 2004.
2. Spriet, A., Doclo, S., Moonen, M., Wouters, J., Feedback Control in Hearing Aids, in: *Springer Handbook on Speech Processing and Speech Communication*, pp. 1–28, 2007.
3. Spriet, A., Proudler, I., Moonen, M., Wouters, J., Adaptive Feedback Cancellation in Hearing Aids with Linear Prediction of The Desired Signal. *IEEE Trans. Signal Process.*, 53, 10, 3749–3763, October 2005.
4. Chitode, J.S., *Digital Signal Processing*, Technical Publications, June 2013.
5. Schepker, H., Robust feedback suppression algorithms for single- and multi-microphone hearing aids, Thesis for: Dr.-Ing; Advisor: Simon Doclo., 2017.
6. Mohan Rao, C., Stephen Charles, B., Giri Prasad, M.N., Denoising of TDM Signal Using Novel Time Domain and Transform Domain Multirate Adaptive Algorithms. *Am. J. Eng. Res. (AJER)*, 03, 08, 212–226, 2014.
7. http://kunnampallilgejo.blogspot.com/2012/01/electro-acoustics-characteristics.html.
8. Tahir Akhtar, M. and Nishihara, A., Acoustic Feedback Neutralization in Digital Hearing Aids—A Two Adaptive Filters-Based Solution. *IEEE*, pp. 529–532, 2013.
9. Schepker, H., Tran, L.T.T., Nordholm, S., Doclo, S., Improving Adaptive Feedback Cancellation in Hearing Aids Using an Affine Combination of Filters, *IEEE International Conference on Acoustics, Speech and Signal Processing (ICASSP)*, pp. 231–235, 2016.
10. Haykin, S., *Adaptive Filter Theory*, 3rd edition, Prentice Hall, 1996.

11. Sayed, A.H., *Fundamentals of Adaptive Filtering*, John Wiley & Sons, 2003.
12. Rani, S. and Rani, S., Design & Implementation of Adaptive Filtering Algorithm using NLMS having Different Targets. *Int. J. Eng. Technol. Res. (IJETR)*, 3, 2, 145–148, February 2015.
13. Bustamante, D.K., Worrall, T.L., Williamson, M.J., Measurement and Adaptive Suppression of Acoustic Feedback in Hearing Aids. *IEEE International Conference on Acoustics, Speech and Signal Processing_ICASSP*, pp. 2017–2020, 1989.
14. Nagal, R., Kumar, P., Bansal, P., A Survey with Emphasis on Adaptive filter, Structure, LMS and NLMS Adaptive Algorithm for Adaptive Noise Cancellation System. *J. Eng. Sci. Technol. Rev.*, 10, 2, 150–160, 2017.
15. Hellgren, J., Lunner, T., Arlinger, S., System identification of feedback in hearing aids. *J. Acoust. Soc. Am.*, 105, 6, 3481–3496, June 1999.
16. Tran, L.T.T., Schepker, H., Doclo, S., Dam, H.H., Nordholm, S., Proportionate NLMS For Adaptive Feedback Control in Hearing Aids. *IEEE ICASSP*, pp. 211–215, 2017.
17. https://Mathworks.com.
18. Zhang, L., Chen, X., Zhong, B., He, L., Xu, H., Yang, P., Objective Evaluation system for Noise Reduction performance of Hearing Aids. *Proceedings of 2015 IEEE Int. Conf. on Mechatranoics and Automation*, Aug. 2015, pp. 1495–1500.
19. Agnew, J., Acoustic Feedback and Other Audible Artifacts in Hearing Aids. *Trends Amplif.*, 1, 2, 45–82, 1996 Jun.
20. Pritzker, Z. and Feuer, A., Variable length stochastic gradient algorithm. *IEEE Trans. Signal Process.*, 39, 997–1001, 1991.
21. Husstedt, H., Mertins, A., Frenz, M., Evaluation of Noise Reduction Algorithms in Hearing Aids for Multiple Signals From Equal or Different Directions. *Trends Hear.*, 22, 233121651880319, 2018.
22. Shukri Ahmad, M., Hocanin, A., Kukrer, O., Performance of the Frequency-Response-Shaped LMS Algorithm in Impulsive Noise. *IEEE International Conference on Signal Processing and Communications (ICSPC 2007)*, 24–27 November 2007.
23. Hashemgeloogerdi, S. and Bocko, M.F., Adaptive Feedback Cancellation in Hearing Aids Based on Orthonormal Basis Functions with Prediction-Error Method Based Pre-whitening. *IEEE/ACM Trans. Audio Speech Lang. Process.*, 1, 2020.
24. Goswami, S., Bardoloi, B., Deka, P., Dutta, D., Sarma, D., A Novel Approach for Design of a Speech Enhancement System using Auto-Trained NLMS Adaptive Filter. *Int. J. Inf. Commun. Technol.*, 6, 3/4, 326–338, 2014.
25. Chandra, M., Kar, A., Goel, P., Performance Evaluation of Adaptive Algorithms for Monophonic Acoustic Echo Cancellation: A Technical Review. *Int. J. Appl. Eng. Res.*, 9, 17, 3781–3805, 2014.

26. Guo, M., *Analysis, Design, and Evaluation of Acoustic Feedback Cancellation Systems for Hearing Aids*, Ph.D. dissertation, Aalborg Univ., 2012.

27. Hutson, M., Acoustic Echo Cancellation Using Digital Signal Processing, in: *Acoustic Echo Using Digital Signal Processing*, November 2003.

28. https://www.slideshare.net/ghulamsaqulain/lecture-5-description-of-electro-acoustic-characteristics-of-hearing-instruments-and-techniques-for-clinical-fitting, Aug. 31, 2016.

29. Jayanthi, G. and Parthiban, L., Evaluation and Personalization of Noise Reduction Algorithms in Digital Hearing Aids. *J. Chem. Pharm. Sci.*, 9, 4, 2121–2127, Dec 2016.

30. Jayanthi, G. and Parthiban, L., Estimation of SNR based Adaptive-Feedback Equalizers for Feedback Control in Hearing Aids. *Mitt. Klosterneuburg*, 69, 12, 2–10, Dec 2019.

31. Jayanthi, G. and Parthiban, L., Acoustic Feedback Cancellation In Efficient Hearing Aids Using Genetic Algorithm. *Scalable Comput.: Pract. Experience (SCPE)* 21, 1, 115–125, March 2020.

32. Costa, M. and Bermudez, J., A noise resilient variable step-size LMS algorithm. *Signal Processing*, 88, 733–748, 2008.

Internet of Things Platform for Smart Farming

R. Anandan[1]*, Deepak B.S.[1], G. Suseendran[1] and Noor Zaman Jhanjhi[2]

[1]Vels Institute of Science, Technology and Advanced Studies, Chennai, India
[2]School of Computer Science and Engineering, Taylor's University, Selangor, Malaysia

Abstract

In the laundry list of problems faced by farmers across the world, lack of modern technology and mechanization for water and crop management is identified to be imperative to cope with the rapid population growth across the world and to improve the yield. The world is witnessing the increasing scarcity of water for years due to an increase in the population growth and pollution of water resources. On the other hand, the evolution of the IoT—Internet of Things (A system of connected computing devices delivered with precise identifiers that can transfer data over the internet without human-to-computer interaction or human-to-human interaction) due to convergence of embedded systems, machine learning, real-time analytics, commodity sensors and wireless sensor networks have enabled the 20th-century engineers to develop almost all the technology they have ever dreamed about. Thus this chapter aims to describe an Internet of Things platform for smart farming by using the above technologies to educate the targeted audiences on IoT and above tools with a working an example.

Keywords: Internet of Things, IoT, smart farming, real time analytics, machine learning, embedded systems, Arduino, Raspberry Pi

13.1 Introduction

Internet of Things (also known as IoT) can be defined (acc. to Wikipedia) as the network of nodes (vehicles, home appliances, physical devices, etc.)

Corresponding author: anandan.se@velsuniv.ac.in

R. Anandan, G. Suseendran, S. Balamurugan, Ashish Mishra and D. Balaganesh (eds.) Human Communication Technology: Internet of Robotic Things and Ubiquitous Computing, (337–370)
© 2022 Scrivener Publishing LLC

embedded with software, electronics, actuators, sensors, and network connectivity which enable these entities to interconnect and exchange data. Each node is individually recognizable through its embedded computing system but can interconnect within the prevailing network arrangement. To match with the scope of this chapter, let's take the example of two farmers in a village, Mr. Ramesh and Mr. Suresh. Both were Semi-Medium farmers, with about 3.5 ha of land each. For the upcoming harvest, they had planned to cultivate paddy (a field used for growing rice) in their fields. During the cultivation of paddy, the temperature levels must be maintained between 20 and 27 °C with a relative humidity between 60 and 80%. Moreover, paddy requires more water than any other crop (about 1,400 to 1,800 mm water) during the first 4–5 months and there should be no water at the ripening stage [1]. If the temperature or humidity or water levels cross this threshold, the quality and yield of the harvest will not be maintained and could potentially lead to a huge loss to both farmers. But let's say that the Ramesh had implemented a modern IoT-based crop management system in his fields while Suresh still followed his traditional techniques. On one bright Sunday, the temperature in the field crossed the upper bound of the threshold value, immediately Ramesh's crop management system triggered the water sprinklers, and the system auto-generated a message "water sprinklers activated as temperature reached 28 °C and rising" to Ramesh. Immediately, the temperature was controlled and auto-generated another message "water sprinklers deactivated as temperature reduced to 25 °C". The automated system saved Ramesh from a huge loss. Meanwhile, Suresh's fields dried up, and he went bankrupt. Ramesh was able to escape from such a loss because, the IoT Temperature Sensors (a system with a temperature sensor connected to the Wi-Fi module), installed across his farm collected data from those modules and constantly sent the data to the cloud through the Wi-Fi module. On the cloud, this data is analyzed and compared with the preset threshold values. Whenever the system detects any anomaly or it detects a temperature rise it triggers the sprinklers and auto-generates an alert to Ramesh. Thus, the present chapter describes the Internet of Things along with its interrelated tools (like commodity sensors, machine learning, embedded systems, etc.) [2] to develop such magical systems for Smart Farming by optimizing IoT with existing traditional approaches.

13.2   History

The Internet of Things that has reached to an explosive role today traces back to its origin to 1964, to the words of Karl Steinbuch, German Computer

Scientist, who said: *"In a few decades, the computer will be interwoven into almost every industrial product"*. After almost 26 years from then, the first IoT device (a *Toaster* that could be switched on and off over the internet) was built in 1990 by John Romkey. And in the same year, some of the students from Carnegie Mellon University, hooked up a Coca Cola dispensing machine to the internet to identify which column in the machine had the most chill Coke. However, the term *"Internet of Things"* was coined only in the year 1999 by Kevin Ashton, a British technology pioneer as a title of the presentation for Procter & Gamble. But the major landmarks for the current trend of IoT devices were set up in 2009 when more things were connected to the internet than the number of humans connected to the internet, followed by the movement of IPv4 (a 32-bit unique address to identify any entity over the internet that could address 2^{32} devices—4,294,967,296 devices) to IPv6 (a 128-bit unique address to identify any entity over the internet that could address 2^{128} devices—340,282,366,920,938,463,374,607,431,768,211,456 devices). Today, the IoT has impacted almost all the industries (like Logistics, Energy Monitoring, Transportation, Military, Industrial Automation, etc.). In the upcoming sections, one such application of IoT in Agriculture will be discussed.

13.3   Electronic Terminologies

Some of the common Electronic Terminologies to be used throughout the chapter are:

1. Input and Output Devices
2. GPIO
3. ADC
4. Communication Protocols (like UART, I2C, SPI, etc.).

13.3.1   Input and Output Devices

An input device can be defined as a device that provides information to the computer or a microcontroller. For example, in a computer, a keyboard is an input device as the computer receives keystrokes entered by the user through the keyboard. In general, Sensors can be termed as Input devices.

An output device can be defined as a device that sends out information (or processed input) from the computer or a microcontroller. For example, In a computer, a speaker is an output device as it gives out the sound.

13.3.2   GPIO

GPIO stands for General Purpose Input/Output, and are the pins used to connect Input or Output devices to development board (Audrino Uno, Audrino MKR1000, Raspberry PI 2/3 Model B, NodeMCU, etc.). A GPIO pin is set to act as an input or output pin (depending on the device connected to the pin) via a software code or by choosing it in a GUI dashboard. These pins operate at a 3.3 V voltage on the development board.

13.3.3   ADC

ADC stands for Analog to Digital convertor. In electronics, an ADC is a system that converts the analog signals (such as signals picked up by an LDR or a Temperature Sensor) into a digital signal (a combination of 1s and 0s) because; computers only understand the binary language (the computer language—1s and 0s) and hence we need to convert analog signals into digital ones.

13.3.4   Communication Protocols

Communication protocols can be defined as the set of restrictions and regulations that permit two nodes (electronic devices) to connect and exchange the data between nodes. It is the language of machines to communicate with one another.

13.3.4.1   UART

UART stands for Universal Asynchronous Receiver–Transmitter. It is usually a discrete IC (Integrated Circuit) designed for asynchronous serial communication above a peripheral device or computer serial port. The electronic signaling methods and levels are handled by a driver circuit outward to the UART. Universal Asynchronous Receiver–Transmitter standard is mostly used by major IoT development boards to communicate between one another [3].

13.3.4.2   I2C

I2C stands for Inter-Integrated Circuit (a multi-slave, synchronous, single-ended, multi-master, serial computer bus). It was invented by NXP Semiconductors (earlier known as Philips Semiconductors) in 1982. It is widely used to connect lower-speed peripheral Integrated Circuits (IC's) to microprocessors and microcontrollers in infra-board, short-distance communication [4].

13.3.4.3   SPI

SPI stands for Synchronous Serial Communication (an interface specification used primarily in embedded systems for short-distance communication). It was developed in the Mid-1980s by Motorola and became a *de-facto* standard. Liquid Crystal displays and Secure Digital Cards were its typical applications of that time [5].

13.4   IoT Cloud Architecture

The Cloud Platform is one among the major components in providing IoT capabilities to any Internet of Things device. Most of the IoT Kits (Bolt IoT Kit, etc.) are shipped with an essential firmware to connect to their Cloud platform over the internet while a few need extra efforts to connect the Internet of Things device to a Cloud Platform.

The communication between a user and an Internet of Things device through a Cloud Platform can be divided into two stages:

1. Communication from User to Cloud Platform and vice versa
2. Communication from Cloud Platform to IoT Device and vice versa.

In general, the Cloud Platforms receives all the commands to request for sensor data from IoT devices or to control the IoT devices and sends the commands to the IoT devices following which the IoT device executes the commands and sends a response back to the Cloud Platform, which in turn forwards it to the user who initiated the command. Figure 13.1 depicts the architecture of IoT Cloud Platform.

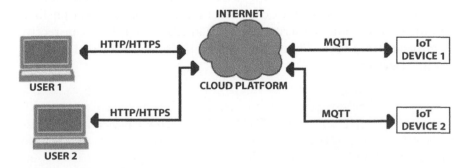

Figure 13.1 IoT cloud architecture.

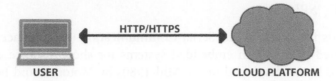

Figure 13.2 Schematic of user-cloud platform.

13.4.1 Communication From User to Cloud Platform

Communication between users and the Cloud Platform is established using the Hypertext Transfer Protocol Secure (HTTPS). We can use the Cloud Platform dashboard to monitor and control our IoT devices or we can use the Cloud APIs to build our programs to by-pass the dashboard and access our IoT devices. Figure 13.2 depicts the schema of user-cloud platform.

13.4.2 Communication From Cloud Platform To IoT Device

Communication between the Internet of Things devices and Cloud Platform is established using the Message Queue Telemetry Transport (MQTT) Protocol. MQTT protocol is preferred for this purpose than the popular HTTP or HTTPS because the amount of overhead data (data which is sent along with the actual message/data to convey extra information required to understand the data/message sent) that is sent over the internet by HTTP or HTTPS is quite a lot. Moreover, the IoT devices and sensors contain limited processing capabilities and constrained internet bandwidth and hence IoT devices send data only when required additionally the data sent is very low in terms of bandwidth usage. Thus using protocols like HTTPS or HTTP is not feasible. Therefore MQTT (a pub-sub messaging protocol) that contains very low overhead data is preferred to be ideal for IoT communication. In MQTT, *pub* refers to publishing and *sub* refers to subscribing. Thus, the IoT devices connect to Cloud Platform and send the data to various channels by publishing the data on their unique channels and subscribe to the channels so that they can receive commands from users. Figure 13.3 depicts the schema of cloud platform for IoT Devices.

Figure 13.3 Schematic of cloud platform—IoT device.

13.5   Components of IoT

The term Internet of Things is a combination of multiple components (technologies) to achieve an extensive set of applications in Consumer, Commercial, Industrial and Infrastructure spaces. Four major technologies that have converged into the Internet of Things are:

1. Machine Learning
2. Real-Time Analytics
3. Embedded Systems
4. Sensors.

13.5.1   Real-Time Analytics

Real-Time Analytics is the process of analyzing the data as quickly as it turns out to be available to the system to get intuitions or to draw decisions very quickly (in fact immediately) as soon as the data enters the system. It enables businesses to respond without stay and can seize chances or prevent glitches much before they happen.

Real-Time Analytics is used in IoT to analyze the huge amount of data obtained from the IoT sensors by using predictive modeling to perform various operations like,

1. Understanding driving styles
2. Creating driver segmentation
3. Identifying risky neighbors
4. Creating risk profiles
5. Comparing micro-segments, etc.

13.5.1.1   *Understanding Driving Styles*

Real-Time Analytics can dive deeper into the driving profile of any water sources (like bore wells, lakes, ponds, etc.) by analyzing the data from its particular segment of sensors to find unique driving behavior of the farmers by using techniques like Parallel Coordinates Visualization (as an effective method to understand multiple metrics at the same time). E.g., the sensor data from a set of farmers can be analyzed against their driving variables of the bore wells to figure out common defects in their driving styles by checking their similarities in individual driving styles [6].

13.5.1.2   Creating Driver Segmentation

Clustering (process of determining the intrinsic group in a given data) techniques help in grouping the bore wells (or lakes) with similar driving profiles, thus enables developers to classify water resources into different categories such as Bore wells, Lakes, Ponds, etc.

13.5.1.3   Identifying Risky Neighbors

Real-time Analytics utilizes Random Forest models to find the closest neighbors (farmers) among a group of water resources by analyzing their driving profiles and can be very useful in finding out possible resources that may fall prey to any individual defect shortly.

13.5.1.4   Creating Risk Profiles

Sensor data from a particular bore well can be analyzed and compared between a particular bore against the entire data of bore wells in the region to suggest customized extended warranty care packages based on the driving styles and defect patterns to minimize the cost incurred due to excessive warranty claims.

13.5.1.5   Comparing Microsegments

By comparing the data variables like top defects, driving variables, regional bore well distributions, etc., we can compare bore wells of the same series between two regions to get broad insights on variations in their driving standards and defect patterns.

13.5.2   Machine Learning

In Real-Time Analytics, the predictive model that analyzes the huge amount of data obtained from IoT sensors is something that is developed using ML algorithms. ML (Machine Learning) can be defined as the technical study of arithmetical representations (models) and algorithms that computer systems depend to carry out jobs without being explicitly programmed to do so. It is understood as a subset of AI—Artificial Intelligence that builds an arithmetical model based on the training data (sample data) supplied to make predictions (decisions) without being interfered by any explicit commands. ML algorithms are used to perform a wide range of applications (like computer vision, email filtering, etc.) where it is problematic to develop conservative algorithms to perform needed tasks and is appropriately related to computational statistics, which concentrates on making decisions using computers [7].

The core objective of a learning machine is to generalize from its experience, wherein Generalization in terms of ML is to execute accurately on new example tasks after having learnt from a sample data set. This experience is gained from unfamiliar probability distributions to build a general model about this experience to produce sufficiently precise predictions in new cases.

ML is used in IoT to analyze the huge amount of data obtained from the IoT sensors by using predictive modeling to support Real-Time Analytics to perform various operations like,

1. Understanding the Farm
2. Creating Farm segmentation
3. Identifying risky factors
4. Creating risk profiles
5. Comparing micro-segments, etc.

13.5.2.1   Understanding the Farm

Machine Learning can support Real-Time Analytics to dive deeper into the driving profile of any Farm (like Humidity Level, Temperature Level, Water Level, Light Intensity Level, etc.) by analyzing the data from its particular segment of sensors to understand the unique characteristics of the farm by using techniques like Parallel Coordinates Visualization (as an effective method to understand multiple metrics at the same time). E.g., the sensor data from a segment of sensors in the farm can be used to prepare a mathematical model that analyzes the Real-time data against the model to predict the characteristics of the yield based on the input data to figure out common defects in the field that can be recovered to maintain the quality and productivity of the yield.

13.5.2.2   Creating Farm Segmentation

Clustering (process of determining the intrinsic group in a given data) techniques help in grouping different characteristics of the farm (like Moisture Level, Temperature Level, Water Level, Light Intensity Level, etc.) with similar driving profiles, thus enables developers to classify farm into different categories such as Appropriate, Abnormal in Moisture, Abnormal in Water, Abnormal in Temperature, Abnormal in Light, Abnormal in Minerals, etc.

13.5.2.3   Identifying Risky Factors

Real-time Analytics utilizes Random Forest models to find the closest neighbors (farms) among a group of farms by analyzing their driving profiles and can be very useful in finding out possible resources that may fall prey to any individual defect (disease) shortly.

13.5.2.4   Creating Risk Profiles

Sensor data from a particular farm can be analyzed and compared between a particular farm against the entire data of farms in the region to suggest customized care to the farm based on the driving styles and defect patterns to minimize the cost incurred due to excessive care.

13.5.2.5   Comparing Microsegments

By comparing the data variables like top defects, driving variables, regional farm distributions, etc., we can compare farms of the same series between two regions to get broad insights on variations in their driving standards and defect patterns.

13.5.3   Sensors

A sensor can be defined as a module, device, subsystem or a machine that detects changer or events in its atmosphere and sends the data to another electronic node (normally to a microprocessor or a microcontroller). Sensors have now used in almost all day-to-day objects like tactile sensor (in touch-sensitive elevator buttons), Potentiometers (in cars, robots, etc.) [8]. Internet of Things is one such domain that has evolved the sensors to a completely different level. Tesla vehicle is an extraordinary combination of sensors and a communication network as all the sensors on the car record their perception of the surroundings and uploads the information into a massive database for further processing and all the important new information are sent to all the other vehicles.

All the data required a Real-Time Analytics system or for the Machine Learning algorithm is provided by the sensors like,

1. Temperature Sensor
2. Water Quality Sensor
3. Humidity Sensor
4. Light Dependent Resistor.

13.5.3.1 Temperature Sensor

Temperature Sensor can be defined as a device used to measure the amount of heat energy present in the environment. These sensors are in use since a long time in a variety of devices but have found more space in the IoT domain. Temperature plays a main role in manipulating the quality and productivity of yield and hence can be monitored using temperature sensors. Figure 13.4 is an example for Temperature Sensor.

13.5.3.2 Water Quality Sensor

Water Quality Sensor can be defined as a sensor used to detect the quality of water and for ion monitoring in water distribution systems. Water Quality Sensor plays a major role in manipulating the quality of water that enters the field and hence can manipulate the quality and productivity of yield and can be monitored using Water Quality sensors. Figure 13.5 is an example for Water Quality Sensor.

13.5.3.3 Humidity Sensor

Humidity Sensor can be defined as a sensor used to detect the amount of water vapor in the atmosphere (Relative Humidity—RH). Humidity plays a chief role in manipulating the quality and productivity of yield and hence can be monitored using Humidity sensors. Figure 13.6 is an example for Humidity Sensor.

13.5.3.4 Light Dependent Resistor

Light Dependent Resistor can be defined as a resistor used to measure the intensity of light in the atmosphere. Light Intensity also plays a key role in

Figure 13.4 Temperature sensor.

Figure 13.5 Water quality sensor.

Figure 13.6 Humidity sensor.

Figure 13.7 Light depended resistor.

manipulating the quality and productivity of yield and hence can be monitored using Light Dependent Resistor. Figure 13.7 is an example for Light Dependent Resistor.

13.5.4   Embedded Systems

An Embedded System can be defined as a mixture of a Microprocessor/ Microcontroller, Memory, and input/output peripheral devices that has a devoted function surrounded by a larger electrical or mechanical system. Generally, it is embedded as part of a complete device within electronic or electrical hardware and mechanical parts as such systems typically control the other physical operations of the machine that it is embedded within.

Figure 13.8 Arduino Uno R3 embedded system.

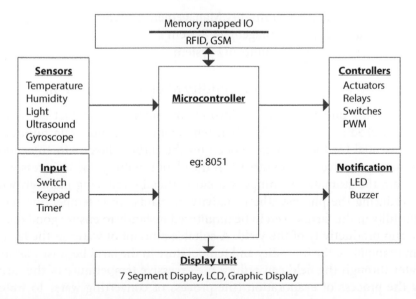

Figure 13.9 Basic embedded system structure.

These systems control many devices in common use and consume about 98% of all the manufactured microprocessors. Modern embedded systems have real-time computing support and are often based on microcontrollers and used in a wide range of computations (from general-purpose to specialized class of computations). These systems range from portable electronic devices like MP3 players, digital watches till large stationary installation like programmable logic controllers, traffic light controllers etc. [9]. Evolution of the Internet of Things has now made embedded systems as the cornerstone for the deployment of IIoT (Industrial Internet of Things) applications. Figure 13.8 is an example for Embedded System. Figure 13.9 is the architecture of 8051 Microcontroller.

13.6   IoT-Based Crop Management System

An IoT based crop management system is a piece of technology that every farmer would have always dreamt about to cope with the laundry list of problems faced by them. Lack of modern technology and mechanization for water and crop management has already been identified to be imperative to cope with the increasing scarcity of water since years due to increase in the population growth and pollution of water resources. One such system is to be described below.

The proposed crop management system comprises of four major subsystems:

1. Temperature & Humidity Management System
2. Water Quality Management System
3. Light Intensity Monitoring System.

13.6.1   Temperature and Humidity Management System

Temperature and Humidity are two major factors that impact the quality and productivity of yield. High temperature and moderate humidity are essential for the stomata to open for the carbon dioxide to enter into stomata for active photosynthesis. If the plant is wilting due to excessively dry air, the stomatal openings will close, thereby reducing plant growth by reducing the photosynthetic activity in plants. Thus temperature and humidity in the farms need to be monitored instantly to ensure good quality and productivity of the yield. A suitable amount of water in the farms can manipulate the humidity and temperature in the farm because passing water through the field can reduce the excessive temperature of the farm by the process of evaporation (the process of converting water to water vapor) as it is a surface process that causes cooling. Moreover, evaporation increases the amount of water vapor in the air and hence increases the moisture content and relative humidity.

13.6.1.1   Project Circuit

In this system we will be measuring the temperature, humidity levels and soil water moisture content using the following sensors and a water pump will be driven to drive water to the plants whenever the threshold values are breached.

1. DHT-11 Temperature and Humidity sensor,
2. Arduino Soil and Moisture level sensor,
3. Raspberry Pi 4 Model B
4. Analog to Digital Converter (ADS1115).

13.6.1.1.1   DHT-11 Temperature and Humidity Sensor

DHT-11 Temperature and Humidity sensor is a one-wire digital humidity and temperature sensor that can measure temperature between 0° and 50 °C at a marginal error up to 2% and measures humidity levels from 20 to 80% at a marginal error up to 5%. It operates at 3 to 5 V input voltage. Figure 13.10 is the image of a DHT-11 Temperature and Humidity Sensor.

13.6.1.1.2   Arduino Soil and Moisture Level Sensor

Arduino Soil and Moisture Level Sensor is a sensor used to measure moisture content in the soil. It has two legs coated with Ni or Cu (Nickel or Copper). When the sensor is inserted in the ground, the moisture in the

Figure 13.10 DHT-11 temperature & humidity sensor [11].

Figure 13.11 Arduino soil and moisture level sensor [11].

soil makes a path between the legs and starts conducting current such that the water content or moisture level can be measured by the strength of conduction which indeed depends on the water content or moisture level. Figure 13.11 is the image of an Arduino Soil and Moisture Level Sensor.

13.6.1.1.3 Raspberry Pi 4 Model B

Raspberry Pi 4 Model B is a series of credit card-sized computers (small single-board computers) developed by Raspberry Pi Foundation, United Kingdom to promote the teaching of basic computer science in schools and in developing countries. These computers have now become more popular outside the target market for applications like Robotics, IoT, etc. Processor speed ranges about 1.5 GHz with an onboard memory up to 4 GiB. The boards have 1–5 USB ports, an HDMI port for video output, 40 GPIO Pins, etc. [10]. Figure 13.12 is the image of a Raspberry Pi 4 Model B.

Figure 13.12 Raspberry Pi 4 model B [10].

Figure 13.13 Analog to digital converter (ADS1115) [11].

13.6.1.1.4   Analog to Digital Converters (ADS1115)

ADS1115 can be defined as an Analog to Digital Converter that is used to convert Analog Input from analog sensors to Digital Output for computing devices like Raspberry Pi 4 Model B using its I2C communication bus. It is higher precision, 4 channel, 12-bit Analog to Digital Converter that has a programmable gain between 16× and 2/3× such that small signals can be read with higher precision [11]. Figure 13.13 is the image of an Analog to Digital Converter.

13.6.1.2   Connections

Connect the ADC ADS1115 VDD Pin to Raspberry Pi 3.3V, ADS1115 GND Pin to Raspberry Pi GND Pin, ADS1115 SCL Pin to Raspberry Pi SCL Pin, ADS1115 SDA Pin to Raspberry Pi SDA Pin [12]. Figure 13.14 is the interface between ADS1115 and Raspberry Pi 4.

The analog output and digital output from the moisture sensor is connected to ADS1115 analog channel 0 (or A0 pin) and Raspberry Pi 4 Model B, GPIO-13. It is powered with Raspberry Pi 4 Model B 3.3-volt output. Figure 13.15 is the interface between Moisture Sensor and Raspberry Pi 4.

The output from DHT-11 Temperature and Humidity sensor is connected to D3 or GPIO-0 of Raspberry Pi 4 Model B and is powered with the 3.3-volt output from Raspberry Pi 4 Model B. The sensor has a void pin that comes in 2 different pinouts. One has 3 pins while the other has 4 pins. We use the one with 4 pins. Figure 13.16 is the interface between DHT-11 Sensor and Raspberry Pi 4.

The relay is connected to the D7 pin (or GPIO-13) of Raspberry Pi 4 Model B through an NPN Transistor (transistor grounded with the Raspberry Pi 4 Model B ground and also with the source power supply Vs). Finally, ground the pump or motor with the power supply ground (if it is a dc pump) and connect the lead of power + anode with the anode of the

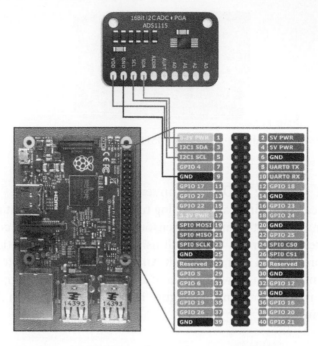

Figure 13.14 Interfacing ADC (ADS1115) to raspberry Pi 4 model B.

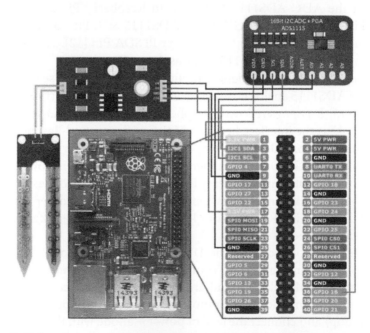

Figure 13.15 Interfacing moisture sensor to the raspberry Pi 4 model B.

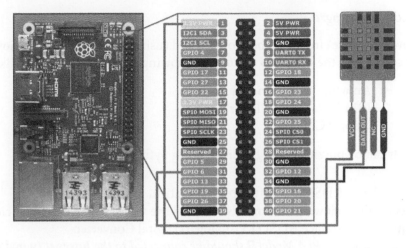

Figure 13.16 Interfacing raspberry Pi 4 model B with DHT-11 temperature & humidity sensor.

pump or motor. Connect the anode of the motor with the common (Com) pin of the relay. If the pump or motor is work on the alternating current type (110 or 220 V), connect NC contact of the relay to the power rail, one lead of pump to another line of rail and Com (Common) pin of the relay to the second lead of pump. Figure 13.17 is the final circuit diagram for Temperature & Humidity Management System.

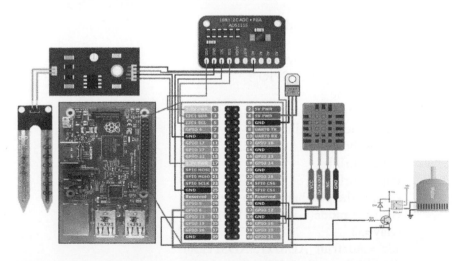

Figure 13.17 Temperature & humidity management system circuit diagram.

13.6.1.3   Program

Now, the above circuit can be programmed (using Node-RED application) by connecting the circuit to any of the following IoT Cloud Platforms like,

1. Amazon Web Services IoT
2. IBM Watson IoT Platform
3. Google Cloud IoT

Or can be physically programmed using python like below:

13.6.1.3.1   ADS1115 Software Installation

Execute the following commands to install the software and dependencies required to interface ADS1115 Analog to Digital Converter.
(Note: Raspberry Pi 4 Model B should be connected to the Internet (wired or wireless) to complete the installation)

```
>sudo apt-get update
>sudo apt-get install build-essential python-dev python-SMBus git python-pip
>cd~
>git clone https://github.com/adafruit/Adafruit_Python_ADS1x15.git
>cd Adafruit_Python_ADS1x15
>sudo python setup.py install
>sudo pip install adafruit-ads1x15
>pip3 install adafruit-circuitpython-dht
>sudo apt-get install libgpiod2
```

13.6.1.3.2   Program Code

```
#! /usr/local/bin/python
import rpi.gpio as GPIO
import time
import Adafruit_ADS1x15
import adafruit_dht
import board
import urllib
import urllib2
#define the pin that goes to the circuit
GPIO.setmode(GPIO.BOARD)
relay=33
adc = Adafruit_ADS1x15.ADS1115()
dht=adafruit_dht.DHT11(board.D31)
```

```
GAIN=1
GPIO.setup(relay,GPIO.OUT)
while True:
        humidity=dht.humidity
        temperature=dht.temperature
        moisture=adc.read_adc(1 , gain=GAIN)
        time.sleep(0.1)
        while( temperature>'28'):
                GPIO.output(relay,GPIO.HIGH)
                #set your sms gateway username
                username=<username>
                #set you sms gateway unique API hash (not API Key)
                apihash=<API_hash>
                #set a sender name
                sender="Water Management System"
                test_flag=1
                #set the receiver phone numbers
                numbers=('phone_number1','phone_number2')
                message=' WATER SPRIKLERS ACTIVATED AS
                TEMPERATURE REACHED 28C AND RISING'
                values= {'test' : test_flag, 'username': username,
                'hash':apihash,'message':message,'sender':sender,
                'numbers' : numbers }
                url=<sms gateway url>
                postdata=urllib.urlencode(values)
                req=urllib2.Request(url,postdata)
                try:
                        response=urllib2.urlopen(req)
                        response_url=response.geturl()
                        if respone_url==url:
                                print('SMS sent')
                except urllib2.URLError, e:
                        print(e.reason)
        while( humidity<'60'):
                GPIO.output(relay,GPIO.HIGH)
                #set your sms gateway username
                username=<username>
                #set you sms gateway unique API hash (not API Key)
                apihash=<API_hash>
                #set a sender name
                sender="Water Management System"
```

```
        test_flag=1
        #set the receiver phone numbers
        numbers=('phone_number1','phone_number2')
        message=' WATER SPRIKLERS ACTIVATED
        AS HUMIDITY LESS THAN 80% AND
        DECREASING'
        values= {'test' : test_flag, 'username': username,
        'hash':apihash,'message':message,'sender':sender,
        'numbers' : numbers }
        url=<sms gateway url>
        postdata=urllib.urlencode(values)
        req=urllib2.Request(url,postdata)
        try:
                response=urllib2.urlopen(req)
                response_url=response.geturl()
                if respone_url==url:
                        print('SMS sent')
        except urllib2.URLError, e:
                print(e.reason)

while( moisture<'25000'):
        GPIO.output(relay,GPIO.HIGH)
        #set your sms gateway username
        username=<username>
        #set you sms gateway unique API hash (not API
        Key)
        apihash=<API_hash>
        #set a sender name
        sender="Water Management System"
        test_flag=1
        #set the receiver phone numbers
        numbers=('phone_number1','phone_number2')
        message=' WATER SPRIKLERS ACTIVATED
        AS MOISTURE LEVEL DROPPED BELOW
        SET THRESHOLD VALUES'
        values= {'test' : test_flag, 'username': username,
        'hash':apihash,'message':message,'sender':sender,
        'numbers' : numbers }
        url=<sms gateway url>
        postdata=urllib.urlencode(values)
        req=urllib2.Request(url,postdata)
```

```
            try:
                    response=urllib2.urlopen(req)
                    response_url=response.geturl()
                    if respone_url==url:
                            print('SMS sent')
            except urllib2.URLError, e:
                    print(e.reason)
while( temperature<'28'):
            GPIO.output(relay,GPIO.HIGH)
            #set your sms gateway username
            username=<username>
            #set you sms gateway unique API hash (not API Key)
            apihash=<API_hash>
            #set a sender name
            sender="Water Management System"
            test_flag=1
            #set the receiver phone numbers
            numbers=('phone_number1','phone_number2')
            message=' WATER SPRIKLERS DEACTIVATED
            AS TEMPERATURE REACHED 27C AND
            DROPPING'
            values= {'test' : test_flag, 'username': username,
            'hash':apihash,'message':message,'sender':sender,
            'numbers' : numbers }
            url=<sms gateway url>
            postdata=urllib.urlencode(values)
            req=urllib2.Request(url,postdata)
            try:
                    response=urllib2.urlopen(req)
                    response_url=response.geturl()
                    if respone_url==url:
                            print('SMS sent')
            except urllib2.URLError, e:
                    print(e.reason)
while( humidity>'60'):
            GPIO.output(relay,GPIO.HIGH)
            #set your sms gateway username
            username=<username>
            #set you sms gateway unique API hash (not API
            Key)
            apihash=<API_hash>
```

```
#set a sender name
sender="Water Management System"
test_flag=1
#set the receiver phone numbers
numbers=('phone_number1','phone_number2')
message=' WATER SPRIKLERS DEACTIVATED
AS HUMIDITY GREATER THAN 80% AND
INCREASING'
values= {'test' : test_flag, 'username': username,
'hash':apihash,'message':message,'sender':sender,
'numbers' : numbers }
url=<sms gateway url>
postdata=urllib.urlencode(values)
req=urllib2.Request(url,postdata)
try:
          response=urllib2.urlopen(req)
          response_url=response.geturl()
          if respone_url==url:
                  print('SMS sent')
except urllib2.URLError, e:
          print(e.reason)

while( moisture>'25000'):
        GPIO.output(relay,GPIO.HIGH)
        #set your sms gateway username
        username=<username>
        #set you sms gateway unique API hash (not API Key)
        apihash=<API_hash>
        #set a sender name
        sender="Water Management System"
        test_flag=1
        #set the receiver phone numbers
        numbers=('phone_number1','phone_number2')
        message='WATERSPRIKLERSDEACTIVATED
        AS MOISTURE LEVEL REACHED THE SET
        THRESHOLD VALUES AND RISING'
        values= {'test' : test_flag, 'username': username,
        'hash':apihash,'message':message,'sender':sender,
        'numbers' : numbers }
        url=<sms gateway url>
        postdata=urllib.urlencode(values)
```

```
req=urllib2.Request(url,postdata)
try:
                response=urllib2.urlopen(req)
                response_url=response.geturl()
                if respone_url==url:
                        print('SMS sent')
        except urllib2.URLError, e:
                print(e.reason)
```

13.6.2   Water Quality Monitoring System

Water Quality (WC) is the second major factor that impacts the quality and productivity of yield. Low pH and More Dissolved Oxygen are essential for the growth of plants. If the plant is wilting due to excessive salinity (high pH) or less dissolved oxygen content, the plant cannot grow further (healthier) thereby decreasing the photosynthetic activity in plants. Thus pH and dissolved oxygen content in the farms need to be monitored instantly to ensure good quality and productivity of the yield. A suitable amount of water in the farms can manipulate the concentration of pH and dissolved oxygen in the farm because passing water through the field can reduce the concentration of pH or dissolved oxygen in the farm by the diluting the water content. Water Quality Monitoring System comprises of two further subsystems:

1. Dissolved Oxygen Monitoring System
2. pH Monitoring System.

13.6.2.1   Dissolved Oxygen Monitoring System

Dissolved Oxygen Monitoring System to be described below utilizes Atlas Dissolved Oxygen Kit on Raspberry Pi 3 Model B.

1. Dissolved Oxygen sensor (Atlas Dissolved Oxygen kit),
2. PH sensor (Atlas pH Kit),
3. Raspberry Pi 4 Model B

13.6.2.1.1   Connections
Connect Ground pin on the Atlas stamp to Ground pin on the Raspberry Pi, VCC pin on the Atlas stamp to 5V pin on the Raspberry Pi, RX pin on the Atlas stamp to TX pin on the Raspberry Pi, TX pin on the Atlas stamp to RX pin on the Raspberry Pi, using male-to-female jumper wires. Connect your BNC connector aligning it with the Atlas circuit.

13.6.2.1.2 Program Code [13]

```python
#!/usr/bin/python
import datetime
import plotly.plotly as py
import plotly.plotly as py
import serial
token = 'stream_token'
username = 'plotly_username_here'
api_key = 'plotly_api_key_here'
py.sign_in(username, api_key)
stream = py.Stream(token)
stream.open()
url = py.plot([
   {'x': [],
   'y': [],
   'type': 'scatter',
   'stream': {
      'token': token,
      'maxpoints': 100
      }
   }],
   filename='Atlas Streaming dOxy',
   fileopt='overwrite')
# Serial code adapted from: https://www.atlas-scientific.com/_files/
code/pi_sample_code.pdf
print "Atlas is now Streaming to Plotly!"
print "View your plot here: ", url
usbport = '/dev/ttyAMA0'
ser = serial.Serial(usbport, 38400)
# turn on the LEDs
ser.write("L1\r")
ser.write("C\r")
line = ""
while True:
   data = ser.read()
   if(data == "\r"):
      print "Received from sensor:" + line
      # Parse the data
      try:
         line = float(line)
```

```
      except:
        print "Couldn't parse float: ", line
        continue
      time_now = datetime.datetime.now().strftime('%Y-%m-%d
        %H:%M:%S.%f')
      # Write the data to your plotly stream
      stream.write({'x': time_now, 'y': line})
      line = ""
    else:
      line = line + data
```

13.6.2.2   pH Monitoring System

pH Monitoring System to be described below utilizes Atlas Dissolved Oxygen Kit on Raspberry Pi 3 Model B.

1. pH sensor (Atlas Dissolved Oxygen kit),
2. Raspberry Pi 4 Model B.

13.6.2.2.1   Connections

Connect Ground pin on the Atlas stamp to Ground pin on the Raspberry Pi, VCC pin on the Atlas stamp to 5 V pin on the Raspberry Pi, RX pin on the Atlas stamp to TX pin on the Raspberry Pi, TX pin on the Atlas stamp to RX pin on the Raspberry Pi, using male-to-female jumper wires. Connect your BNC connector aligning it with the Atlas circuit.

13.6.2.2.2   Program Code [13]

```
#!/usr/bin/python
import datetime
import plotly.plotly as py
import plotly.plotly as py
import serial
token = 'stream_token'
username = 'plotly_username_here'
api_key = 'plotly_api_key_here'
py.sign_in(username, api_key)
stream = py.Stream(token)
stream.open()
url = py.plot([
  {'x': [],
   'y': [],
```

```
      'type': 'scatter',
      'stream': {
        'token': token,
        'maxpoints': 100
        }
      }],
    filename='Atlas Streaming dOxy',
    fileopt='overwrite')
# Serial code adapted from: https://www.atlas-scientific.com/_
files/code/pi_sample_code.pdf
print "Atlas is now Streaming to Plotly!"
print "View your plot here: ", url
usbport = '/dev/ttyAMA0'
ser = serial.Serial(usbport, 38400)
# turn on the LEDs
ser.write("L1\r")
ser.write("C\r")
line = ""
while True:
  data = ser.read()
  if(data == "\r"):
    print "Received from sensor:" + line
    # Parse the data
    try:
      line = float(line)
    except:
      print "Couldn't parse float: ", line
      continue
      time_now = datetime.datetime.now().strftime('%Y-%m-%d
        %H:%M:%S.%f')
    # Write the data to your plotly stream
    stream.write({'x': time_now, 'y': line})
    line = ""
  else:
    line = line + data
```

13.6.3   Light Intensity Monitoring System

Light Intensity is the third major factor that impacts the quality and productivity of yield. The stronger intensity of light is essential for the growth

of plants. If the plant is wilting due to restrained light intensity the plant cannot grow further (healthier) thereby decreasing the photosynthetic activity in plants. Thus light intensity in the farms needs to be monitored instantly to ensure good quality and productivity of the yield. A suitable amount of light in the farms can manipulate the health of plants.

13.6.3.1   Project Circuit

In this system we will be measuring the intensity of the incident light using the following sensors and an alerting system will be driven to drive auto-generated alerts to the farmers whenever the threshold values are breached.

13.6.3.2   Connections

The proposed system utilizes a Light Depended Resistor (LDR) to detect the intensity of light. In this sensor, the intensity of incident light is directly proportional to the resistance of the resistor.

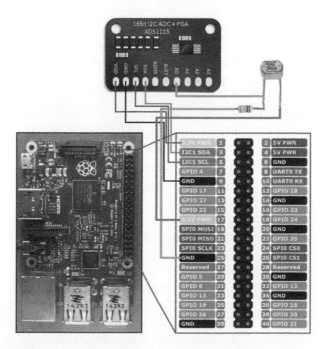

Figure 13.18 Light intensity management system circuit diagram.

Initially, connect the 3v3 pin to the one end of LDR. Now connect the other end to the A0 pin of Analog Digital Convertor and pair it to the Raspberry Pi (*Section 13.6.1.2*) and to the one end of the 10K Ω Resistor. Finally, connect the other end of the Resistor to the Ground (GND) pin of the Raspberry Pi. Figure 13.18 is the circuit diagram for Light Intensity Management System.

13.6.3.3   Program Code

```
#! /usr/local/bin/python
import rpi.gpio as GPIO
import time
import Adafruit_ADS1x15
import adafruit_dht
import board
import urllib
import urllib2
#define the pin that goes to the circuit
GPIO.setmode(GPIO.BOARD)
adc = Adafruit_ADS1x15.ADS1115()
GAIN=1
GPIO.setup(relay,GPIO.OUT)
while True:
        intensity=adc.read_adc(1 , gain=GAIN)
        time.sleep(0.1)

        while( intensity<'60'):
                GPIO.output(relay,GPIO.HIGH)
                #set your sms gateway username
                username=<username>
                #set you sms gateway unique API hash (not API
                Key)
                apihash=<API_hash>
                #set a sender name
                sender="Water Management System"
                test_flag=1
                #set the receiver phone numbers
                numbers=('phone_number1','phone_number2')
                message=' LIGHT INTENSITY DEDUCED !!!'
                values= {'test' : test_flag, 'username': username,
                'hash':apihash,'message':message,'sender':sender,
                'numbers' : numbers }
```

```
url=<sms gateway url>
postdata=urllib.urlencode(values)
req=urllib2.Request(url,postdata)
try:
        response=urllib2.urlopen(req)
        response_url=response.geturl()
        if respone_url==url:
                print('SMS sent')
except urllib2.URLError, e:
        print(e.reason)
```

13.7   Future Prospects

With the evolution of the Internet of Things, we can change the phase of Agriculture. Internet of Things is an extraordinary piece of technology that can change the phase of Agriculture. With proper efforts in research and development, IoT can revolutionize agriculture and crop management. Machine Learning and its sub-domains (Supervised Learning, Un-Supervised Learning, etc.) are evolving the computers to the next level by artificially imposing intelligence to computers. Moreover, Embedded Systems are making cutting-edge technology possible by reducing the size of computers or computing devices and by making the device's domain-specific. IoT, Machine Learning, Embedded Systems, etc. have already revolutionized Industries (Industry 4.0) to a new era of cutting edge technologies to deal with areas which are not usually categorized as an industry (such as smart cities) by augmenting machines to wireless interconnectivity and sensors, interconnected through a system to make decisions on its own by visualizing the entire production line. They have introduced new technology domains (like Robotic Process Automation, Cyber-Physical systems, etc.) to the industry. Therefore, the application of the same technologies to agriculture will also be able to revolutionize agriculture to its new age of farming and can lead to the next Green Revolution in upcoming years. For example, the above systems can be made much more complication by upgrade the code to be deployed on cloud platforms to increase the accuracy of calculations or can be united to the single unit instead of being three different units. Moreover, one other major factor that manipulates the productivity or quality of yield are insects, pathogens, and pests. Though there are Pesticides, Insecticides, and Biocides are already available in the market, they are not target specific and they destroy all the pests and insects instead of destroying only the insects that harm the crops. For example, earthworms are insects that naturally improve the productivity of farms, but recent researches sight that modern pesticides harm the earthworms. On the other side, the sound has been proved to disturb insects. Hence new systems can be designed to disturb target specific insects by carefully adjusting the frequency of sound released from the speakers. A few other problems faced by farmers are, Small and Fragmented land holdings, Lack of mechanization for Irrigation, Manures, Fertilizers, Biocides, Pesticides, and to prevent Soil Irrigation and Degradation. Thus a new can be derived from Industry 4.0 and Smart City Mission concepts/ideas to provide a one-shot solution for all listed problems with reasonable feasibility for adaptation.

One of the projects we are working with is to design a robot similar to a Gantry Crane (Cranes used in shipyards to move containers) that will be equipped with customized subsystems to mechanize all the problems listed above. Thus a list of problems can be faced in introducing this technology is:

1. Cranes cannot be feasible for small and medium-scale farmers to use for their small and fragmented landholdings.
2. The farming land will not be strong enough to withstand the weight of a crane.
3. Introducing the technology for farmers and educating them to adapt to the technology.
4. Capital, Time and Man Power that will be required to make the fields ready.

Hence, solutions based on the above issues can also be resolved and shared to the community to do co-operative research that can lead to the next Green Revolution.

13.8   Conclusion

Farmers across the world are facing many problems in farming due to the lack of modern technology and proper mechanization for water and crop management. As it is imperative to cope with the rapid population growth of the world, we need to improve the yield and IoT is one such tech that can bring new inventions to support farming. The world is witnessing the increasing scarcity of water for years due to an increase in the population growth and pollution of water resources. On the other hand, the evolution of the Internet of things (A system of interconnected computing devices provided with unique identifiers that can transfer data over the internet without human-to-human interaction or human-to-computer interaction) due to convergence of machine learning, embedded systems, commodity sensors, real-time analytics and wireless sensor networks have enabled the 20th-century engineers to develop almost all the technology they have ever dreamed about. Present chapter outlines the Internet of Things, and its sub-domains along with few IoT based basic Crop Management and Monitoring Systems to support Smart Farming by which we can meet up the demand for at least basic mechanization required for proper management of water and crop required to cope with the quality and productivity loss rising from traditional agricultural techniques. Finally, the technology developed should also be user-friendly for the farmers and ecofriendly so that farmers or farms are not harmed due to human negligence for agriculture and farmers.

References

1. Research Greenhouse—Rice, Saveer, India, Retrieved 5th April 2020, from https://www.saveer.com/research-greenhouse-rice.html, 1978.
2. Koot, R., Internet of Things, Wikipedia, Netherlands, Retrieved 10th April 2020, from https://en.wikipedia.org/wiki/ Internet_of_things, 2007.
3. Engels, A., Universal Asynchronous Receiver-Transmitter (2002), Wikipedia, Netherlands, Retrieved 10th April 2020, from https://en.wikipedia.org/wiki/ Universal_asynchronous_ receivertransmitter, 2002.
4. Markowitz, M., I2C, Wikipedia, Toronto, Retrieved 10th April 2020, from https://en.wikipedia.org/wiki/I%C2%B2C, 2002.
5. Marquardt, C., Serial Peripheral Interface, Wikipedia, Germany, Retrieved 10th April 2020, from https://en.wikipedia.org/wiki/Serial_Peripheral_ Interface, 2003.
6. Srinivasan, Deepak, All you need to know about real-time analytics and IoT, LatentView, Retrieved 10th April 2020, from https://www.latentview.com/ blog/all-you-need-to-know-about-real-time-analytics-and-iot/, 2018.
7. Hike395, Machine Learning, Wikipedia, West Coast, United States of America, Retrieved 10th April 2020, from https://en.wikipedia.org/wiki/ Machine_learning, 2003.
8. Heron, Norman, Sensor, Wikipedia, Retrieved 10th April 2020, from https:// en.wikipedia.org/wiki/Sensor, 2003.
9. Van De Walker, R., Embedded System, Wikipedia, California, Retrieved 10th April 2020, from https://en.wikipedia.org/wiki/ Embedded_system, 2002.
10. Sudaway, T., Raspberry Pi, Wikipedia, Deutschland, Retrieved 10th April 2020, from https://en.wikipedia.org/wiki/Raspberry_Pi, 2011.
11. Adafruit, AdaFruit Industries, DHT11 basic temperature-humidity sensor + extras, New York, Retrieved 10th April 2020, from https://www.adafruit. com/product/386, 2017.
12. Dicola, T., Raspberry Pi Analog to Digital Converters, Adafruit Industries, Minnesota Retrieved 10th April 2020, from https://www.digikey.in/en/maker/ projects/raspberry-pi-analog-to-digitalconverters/72388f5f1a0843418130 f56c53a1276c.
13. Parmer, C., Aatlas-Scientific, Github, Canada, Retrieved 10th April 2020 from https://github.com/plotly/atlas-scientific/blob/master/atlas-pi.py, 2014.

14

Scrutinizing the Level of Awareness on Green Computing Practices in Combating Covid-19 at Institute of Health Science-Gaborone

Ishmael Gala* and Srinath Doss

Faculty of Computing, Botho University, Botswana

Abstract

An effective methodology to protect our environment from hazardous material and its effects that come from computer resources to sustain our environment and expenditure costs reduction associated with environmental resources misuse are termed Green computing. In this research document, the researcher focuses more on investigating awareness on Green computing practices while combating Covid-19 at Institute of Health Science-Gaborone. Computing is crucial in this time of Covid-19 no modern business organization can excellently perform its operations without the use of computing. That is why it is now a necessity and mandatory to have organization aware of the negative impacts brought by computing on the environment and technologies initiated to help mitigate the situation. Green computing practices are mostly influenced by human knowledge, behavior and attitude. The study investigated different literature review on awareness of green computing practices with the assistance of several theoretical models such as Technology Acceptance Model which was utilized to present an economical explanation to the components that define the adaptation, which is generally applicable to many utilizing behavior from different computing innovations. The model provided a diagram to be of use in assisting people to accept the benefits brought by the implementation of Green computing practices in combating Covid-19. The study was carried out with the help of closed answers questionnaire with 241 respondents involved with simple random sampling used to help select population size. Collected data were analyzed using Statistical Package for

*Corresponding author: ishmgala@gmail.com

R. Anandan, G. Suseendran, S. Balamurugan, Ashish Mishra and D. Balaganesh (eds.) Human Communication Technology: Internet of Robotic Things and Ubiquitous Computing, (371–400) © 2022 Scrivener Publishing LLC

the Social Sciences and Microsoft Excel. The findings reveal that the Institute of Health Science-Gaborone has a low level of awareness on Green computing practices while combating Covid-19. The study then came up with a proposed Green computing framework to assist in enforcing Green computing practices and It was also emphasized that education on Green computing awareness should be mandatory to keep users informed all the time in this technologically changing world

Keywords: Green computing, covid-19, awareness, knowledge, attitude and behavior

14.1   Introduction

Globally the outbreak of novel Covid-19 has contributed to increased growth in computing since the pandemic promotes social distancing and non-contact thus calling for use of information communication technology as the only proactive solution to assist in adherence to Covid-19 preventative measures of social distancing and non-contact as declared by World Health Organization [22]. Conversely, fighting Covid-19 must not divert focus and make people lose concentration on the effect caused by increased growth of computing. Increased usage in computing resources has already contributed to environmental concern, which involves increased energy consumption, health hazards and pollutants releases responsible for global warming. An emerging critical information communication technology known as Green technology is in place to reverse the trend. Green technology involves the use of computer resources in an environmentally sound manner by reducing the energy consumed and environmental waste generated. Most organizations will be buying more computing gadgets to have their work process automated, working remotely online without physically being congested at the workplace. Ustek-Spilda [83] stated that numerous approaches in computing area have been proposed to assist in combating the Covid-19 pandemic but these approaches differ from each other based on the way they approach vital questions like: How can computing be utilized to enforce early screening of infected people and social distancing? How can 3D computing assist to sustain healthcare equipment supply and provide guidance in the Covid-19 vaccine development? The responses to these questions are being explored and, in some instance, preliminary work has been done. So, it is of the key that in this time of preliminary works and accelerated forced changes by Covid-19 we do not ignore the environmental and health aspects of the ecosystem.

14.1.1   Institute of Health Science-Gaborone

According to the Institute of Health Science-Gaborone Institutional strategic plan (2007–2012) the Institute of Health Science-Gaborone is one of the government-owned training institutions. Following the restructuring of the Ministry of Health, the institute came under the umbrella of the Department of Health Sector Relations and Partnership when the then Department of Health Manpower ceased to exist.

Due to the outbreak of Covid-19 organizations have fast-tracked in computerizing its process for its business functions to improve performance in service delivery and provision of access to more users. These imply an increase in the amount of hardware infrastructure needed resulting in a corresponding increase in power, cooling and data center space needed. The new system and computing gadgets installed may not be compatible with the computer resources that were present resulting in the need for recycling old computers resources. For a typical example, non-contact infrared thermometers were bought to assist in checking temperatures of individuals entering the premises and a record have to be stored. The use of smart gadgets like smartphones that can be able to create and scan QR code for Covid-19 registration purposes leaving cellphones with no cameras incompatible.

Most of the building structures are very old and were built during the era when the use of computers was not high, social interaction not restricted and everything was mostly done manually. The fear of Covid-19 and excitement in more use of computing gadgets can contribute to ignorance to the environmental and health hazards associated with the use of more computing devices. It is ideal that organization, individuals combat this novel Covid-19 without hurting the environment and be economic in saving the little they have. This process is referred to as green computing or "going green" as others call it. Murugesan [72] shared the following key essential areas involved in Green computing.

- Green Use involves reducing the energy consumption of computers.
- Green Design involves designing efficient and ecofriendly components.
- Green Disposal includes refurbishing and reusing old computers and properly recycle unwanted computers.
- Green Manufacturing involves manufacturing components with minimal or no impact on the environment.

The war against Covid-19 enthused researchers worldwide to understand, explore and develop new diagnostic and treatment methods to culminate this threat to our generation. In this research study, the researcher intends to provide insight and clear understanding regarding the level of awareness of green computing in combating Covid-19.

14.1.2   Research Objectives

The research study addresses the following objectives:

- To investigate the likelihood of threats associated with a lack of awareness on Green computing practices while combating Covid-19 at Institute of Health Science-Gaborone.
- To examine Green computing practices among users while combating Covid-19 at Institute of Health Science-Gaborone.
- To analyze user conduct, awareness and attitude about awareness on Green computing practices.
- To investigate the role of training on Green computing practice in combating Covid-19 at Institute of Health Science-Gaborone.
- To investigate the effectiveness of Green computing policies while combating Covid-19 at Institute of Health Science-Gaborone.

14.1.3   Green Computing

According to Garg *et al.* [50] Green computing concept was introduced in 1992 when the United States Environmental Protection Agency established Energy Star program which issued a voluntary label to computing products that offered maximum efficiency while consuming less energy. Green computing targets to achieve economic feasibility and improving the way devices are being used, minimization of harmful material usage and advancing the biodegradability of old resources and waste from manufacturing plant.

Batlegang [5] similarly shared that utilization of computing devices can be eco-friendly when green computing is practiced, as it regarded as an investigation for planning, designing, assembling, utilizing and disposing of computing devices in a way that it minimizes their negative effects in the environment.

Suryawanshi suggested two ways Green computing can utilize to reduce environmental impact. The two ways involve direct and indirect. Indirect method computing components can be manufactured from improved materials and technologies and making them more energy-efficient to minimize the direct impact on the environment whereas in indirect method more efficient computing systems and technology can be developed to support business initiatives to minimize indirect and negative impacts on the environment.

It is in this era of Covid-19 pandemic where we need solutions that are eco-friendly like Green computing that can assist in addressing combating the pandemic with incurring financial losses and be of hazard to both human and environment.

14.1.4   Covid-19

Ulhaq *et al.* [82] shared that the novel coronavirus SARS-CoV-2 is a member of the Coronaviridae virus family, which is highly infectious and killing more people every day worldwide. The disease outbreak was first reported in Wuhan, China after more cases of pneumonia with unknown causes were discovered. On January 7, 2020, the outbreak was confirmed by the Public Health of Emergency of International Concern, which the World Health Organization named the coronavirus disease: Covid-19. More countries were forced to go under lockdown and state of emergencies due to the increase in the number of fatality rate due to this novel pandemic with no one with exact information of when it will end. The most painful part of it is that economies are in crisis and no vaccine has yet discovered to address Covid-19.

The spread of the pandemic was swift and caught countries unaware. The crisis graduated into an economic crisis and supply chains within a week experienced an increased demand in toilet paper and paper towels in countries like the United States and China. Measures put in places such as social distancing and lockdowns have disrupted people's livelihoods around the globe [82]. However innovative entrepreneurs from Ghana such as Kelvin Dapaah and Richard Boateng have inverted a touch-free electronic washing tap to be used for washing hands in combating Covid-19 [33].

The novel Covid-19 has globally devastating effects, its spread, emergence and associated increased deaths have brought fear among people, persuading them to even buy products that are not adhering to a standard of quality described by the bureau of standards and other regulating bodies. For example, thermometers that were not calibrated and this can be hazardous to human and environment.

There is life after Covid-19 we shouldn't harm ourselves and the environment to a limit that we fail to recover whatever solutions generated by the computing world will be utilized in a future setting. Baumgartner and Rainey [7] shared that it is predicted that there are approximately 1,200 identified viruses that possess the potential to cause a pandemic like Covid-19 and those viruses can be transmitted from one species to another. Therefore, even after the war against Covid-19, a new pandemic might arise.

14.1.5   The Necessity of Green Computing in Combating Covid-19

The novel Covid-19 pandemic with its associated lockdowns has prompted crucial changes in day-to-day activities exposing some weakness in the computing architecture operations that support people. Some of the changes involving more virtual collaboration, increased video streaming and remote work are likely to last long after Covid-19 lockdowns. This has negatively affected wired networks that have slowed and more energy consumption under additional burdens. Hemdan [34] expressed the view that it necessitates a significant amount of computing power to build an accurate model of SARS-CoV-2 the virus that causes the Covid-19 illness. This happens especially when a scientist wants fast results from their simulations. This implies that it is of necessity in this era of COVID-19 to consider utilizing a renewable source of energy like solar energy and wind power generation as compared to a non-renewable source of energy, which is expensive to generate.

Botswana is one the country that is not able to produce sufficient power for its citizen and import most of its power from South Africa. The sudden growth in computing due to Covid-19, where the business is transacted 24/7 online increases the consumption of this limited power currently available in Botswana, rises costs in importing power and also expenses in disposing of discarded computers resources since some are not cheaply disposed of because they contain toxic materials harmful to the environment. To address this, the cost of energy and practice environmentally sustainable computing must be the implementation of Green computing.

Today more and more organization around the globe has acknowledged the necessity to protect and sustain the environment, looking at the experienced unpredictable climatic conditions due to global warming said to be caused by the gases emitted from some incinerated computer resources and rising energy costs. In playing this role of environmentally sustainable computing, Kurp [61] stated that Dell is refining up its programs to reduce hazardous substance in its computers. The new Dell OptiPlex desktop is 50% more energy-efficient than similar systems manufactured in 2005. Kaur *et al.* [55] similarly highlighted that HP designed a computer in which they called it the "greenest computer ever" the HP rp5700 desktop PC. The HP rp5700 is believed to be more than U.S. energy star 4.0 standards, with 90% of its material recyclable and has a life of minimum 5 years. He further stated that IBM is also researching to develop cheaper and more efficient star cells and other solution to support sustainable computing to be utilized in this time of Covid-19.

The computing world is moving at a faster rate, business is developing policies and exploring methods to utilize in green computing to save energy consumption and expenditure cost. Vikram [87] highlighted that some organization have initiated several "paperless" initiatives aiming at reducing paper use and physical contact in their offices. This is achieved using emails and video conferencing instead of saving grams.

A computer is made from harmful materials and chemicals like lead, which is found in CRT monitors, and circuit boards, beryllium and mercury contained in motherboards this chemical, are not friendly to our environment [51] To address these, recycling will be appropriate especially when new computing hardware is bought to replace the outdated ones which are not compatible with requirements of applications required in combating Covid-19. Harmon and Auseklis [64] explained the recycling process using the following diagram Figure 14.1.

Each phase of computing hardware life commences from its production, usage until disposal stage poses an environmental hazard. Consequently,

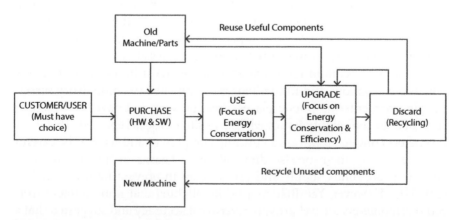

Figure 14.1 Recycling process [64].

greenhouse gases pollute the air and bring about a major effect on global climatic changes.

Computer hardware companies experience major demand from enterprises across the world placing large orders for computer resources and mobile devices that will be utilized to support employees who will now be working from home. An increase in computing devices means an increase in energy consumption. The energy that we always see Botswana Power Corporation disseminating messages about its conservation and has already planned to increase electricity tariffs comes in April 2021 because of high energy consumption. To help conserve energy Abugahah and Abubaker [1] had a view that it's mandatory to balance the system in such a way that the computing speed requires to be maintained same with reduced energy consumption.

The world is experiencing emerging problems in education systems especially on developing countries where the current state of technology does not permit a smooth transition to the online world. Typically, an example in Botswana this Covid-19 has made people realize that they are digital divide with part of the population not having access to the internet and computers. This implied that due to this contactless era of Covid-19 more paperwork was printed for students to study at home to reduce everyday contact when physically attending classes.

This is not supported by Agarwal *et al.* [75] when they emphasized that organization must convert to "paper-less-mode", utilize computing sophisticated mode of communication such as e-mails, social networking, and free messaging. This will save the environment from pollution caused by paper waste and reduce the cost involved in paper manufacturing. Even though the need for this computing network infrastructure requires digging of the earth surface and cutting of tree when installing network transmission line, it will cause once-off less harm to the environment as compared to the one that involves paper manufacturing. The solution will last long and help assist in future pandemics such as Covid-19.

The world of computing initiated non-contact infrared thermometers which organisations and individuals are compelled to compulsory screen people when entering public places, areas of work and have their records recorded for traceability issues when a positive case is reported. This thermometers contain an infrared emitting component and have to be careful on disposing of them or else they will be of hazard to the environment since they are influx supply and use of them in preventing the spread of Covid-19. However, Yae-Bellany [93] highlighted that non-contact infrared thermometers are not proven in terms of accuracy and suggested that a further study be necessitated to determine whether an on contact infrared thermometer gives as reliable information as other thermometers. Since non-contact thermometers performance has been questioned, Hsiao *et al.* [37] proposed taking of temperature measurements twice for people before entering public places. People have a view that infrared produces radiation which is not good for human skin even though Ng *et al.* [57] shared that infrared thermometer is completely safe and does not produce radiation. Dante *et al.* [23] expressed a different view and stated that if one has extremely sensitive skin then it will be observed that the results of the use of the infrared non-contact thermometer can be a little uncomfortable.

14.1.6 Green Computing Awareness

Ahmad *et al.* [2] stated that for individuals to commence to adapt to a system, device, or an idea those individuals require to know about it first. This implies that individuals must be made aware of green computing practices and concept first before they adopt it. Green computing awareness is then defined as the ability to be conscious in designing, assembling, utilizing, and disposing of computing devices in a way that reduces their negative effects in the environment. Abdul Gafoor highlighted that awareness can be observed from an individual without necessarily implying understanding. Ordinary awareness does not contain any type of knowledge, but any knowledgeable person must contain awareness.

They are needed for cooperation in developing, disseminating, and implementing appropriate green practices. People must be made to understand the perils and responsibilities as far as Green computing is concerned because the friendly environment has become a collective responsibility. Nagamani [25] expressed scrutinized green computing needs, practices and challenges and have established that appropriate regulations, education, recycling and awareness are the answers to minimize energy consumption and reduced environmental waste. In support of this Kumar Dookhitram cited that when establishing a level of awareness on negative impacts of IT, and green computing at Botho College, Botswana he discovered that staff and students require to be provided with appropriate education so that they could adopt green computing. The author also realized that a higher level of awareness can lead to behavioural changes and welcome Green computing practices utilization.

In this time of Covid-19 where people have that panic and fear of the pandemic lack of awareness to Green computing practices may be highly visible since they are scramble for computing devices to have organisation operating in times of lockdowns. However, this must not make people forget about the repercussions brought by not adhering to green computing practices. Typical example the amount of energy and cost required to power up those procured computing devices and method of disposal of already existing computing hardware that is not compatible with Covid-19 apps. So it is vital to have continuous user training on green computing practices, policies, procedures and standards for minimization of loses in times of crisis like Covid-19.

The KAB (Knowledge–Attitude–Behavior) model is suitable to assist to measure not only knowledge gains but the improvement of people attitudes and influence of knowledge and attitude on behavioural change [47].

14.1.7   Knowledge

Knowledge involves the understanding and information about a particular subject which a person has. It can also be viewed as awareness acquired by the experience of a situation or fact. Most academics view knowledge as power, in leadership and business environment as it is believed that the more you know the more adaptation becomes easier. To assert this Olubunmi [59] refereed to knowledge as the currency of information and people proficiency resembling the bank where it is exchanged and stored.

Selyamani and Ahmad [76] emphasized that most people have been praising, computing and preaching the Fourth Industrial Revolution and are not aware that computing has been contributing to environmental issues. Computing infrastructure absorbs a large amount of energy which is increasing day by day and thus placing substantial weight on the electricity grid and adding to greenhouse emissions.

The author further shared that it is fundamental to empower people with knowledge on Green computing for them to be part of the eco-friendly exercise and assist the organisation to be economic in combating pandemic like Covid-19. Lack of knowledge in Green computing can result in having organization and people be exposed to the environmental health hazard and cost the organization a lot of money or even leading to closure by the environmental inspectorate. Lack of knowledge also contributes to "technophobia" the fear of change brought about by technology. Individuals have to be trained on the use of computing for them to be able to easily adapt with some requirements of Covid-19 measures that require social distancing hence us of online platforms. The use of B-safe application for registration on individuals entering public places and area of work instead of paper-based manual registration. Individuals have to be made aware that it times we move to a paperless mode of communication as an initiative of going green.

14.1.8   Attitude

The attitude in Green computing involves the way of acting or feeling towards green computing practices. Hohashi and Yi [56] added that attitude is regarded as having cognitive, affective and behavioural components. An assessment of the entity that makes up an individuals opinion about the object is the cognitive component whereas the emotional response is the affective component. Lastly, the behavioral component involves the verbal and non-verbal behavioral trend by an individual with observable responses. Green computing awareness program intends to try instilling change of attitude on an individual and align him or her with eco-friendly computing practices that help the organisation to economize. It is not always mandatory to reward or punish individuals to change their attitude in how they do things, as it is believed by Xiong. Sometimes training can also play a positive role.

14.1.9   Behavior

This implies how an individual behaves under condition or in response to a particular situation. In this sense, Green computing relies on how individuals behave in utilizing, designing and disposing computing devices to the environment in this time of combating Covid-19.

Abugabah *et al.* [1] on their study suggested that organization should create policy and procedures that enhance positive "green behavior" among employees. The author also added that workshops on pro-environmental behavior are made and compulsory attended by employees.

Organizations are no longer making a profit in this time of Covid-19 so a change of behavior in the way we use to do things is mandatory. It is time to shift focus to methods and techniques that can help sustain the organization hence the need for Green computing. Even though behavior change is a process, pandemics like Covid-19 does not permit individuals to move at snail pace. Effective green computing awareness must be implemented.

14.2   Research Methodology

To address the research objective, the study was based on the positivist paradigm which draws on the quantitative aspects. The reason for using the quantitative method is because the research method assists in using quantifiable data to articulate facts and reveal a pattern in research unlike with qualitative approach which is subjective and relies on individual interpretation of events.

In persuading the researcher to opt for quantitative approach Creswell [19] shared that quantitative research is applicable if the researcher wants to test objective theories by analyzing the relationship between variables and reaching a conclusion using statistical procedures. However, Saunders *et al.* [73] highlighted that even though quantitative data is regarded as efficient and having the ability to test hypotheses it may miss contextual details.

The study centres around a large number of people for feedback which means large sets of data is required to conclude thus making the quantitative approach more suitable because according to Sekaran and Bougie [74] qualitative mostly caters for small samples since its results are not measurable and quantifiable.

To analyze the knowledge, attitude and behaviour on Green computing practices among users when combating Covid-19 at Institute of Health Science-Gaborone a conclusion using statistics drawn from analyzing relationships between variables is required, the researcher has to be objectively in separation with the subject matter, and that is a quantitative approach. However, this is not achievable with a qualitative approach, which according to Howell [36] the researcher is subjectively inseparable with the subject matter.

14.2.1 Target Population

According to Creswell [20] and Williams [91], Quantitative approach requires the participation of an adequately large number of individuals since the outcome relies on statistics.

In this research study, the researcher target population involved 100 employees and 150 students of Institute of Health Science-Gaborone since they are the ones who on daily basis interact with the computing practices involved in combating Covid-19 at Institute of Health Science-Gaborone.

14.2.2 Sample Frame

The researcher had a sample frame consisting of 143 employees and 200 students. From the sample frame, 100 employees and 141 students were attained as a sample through simple random sampling and these were regarded as a good representative of the Institute of Health Science-Gaborone.

14.2.3   Questionnaire as a Data Collection Instrument

The researcher opted for questionnaires with closed-ended questions to be used to collect data from respondents because of their simplicity in analyzing and time-consuming aspect. The items on the questionnaire will attempt to comprehensively respond to the five research objectives. Questionnaires will not capture personal information but will be consist of unique numbers on the top far- right of the first page and labelled staff for employees and students for student's participants this is done for easy management. The questionnaire consists of 10 items separated into three sections for demographics (questions 1–3), research questions (questions 4–7) and KAB model testing (questions 8–10). The questionnaire consisted of scaled questions, which were constructed in a Likert scale type because the type allows researchers to measure social attribute in an investigation as shared by Rowley [68].

A self-administered survey will be adopted as a means of collecting primary data from the respondents. The questionnaire will be hand-delivered to all selected respondents for completion in their own time and collected after 48 h.

14.2.4   Validity and Reliability

The consistency and accuracy of the questionnaire in a research study formulate a noteworthy aspect of a research methodology known as validity and reliability, which Taherdoost [79] cited as a challenge to new researchers since they tend to have a problem in selecting and conducting proper validity type in testing research instrument. However, Engellant *et al.* [27] enlighten that to have confidence in research findings or results, one must be certain that the research instrument (questionnaire) when properly administered quantifies what it purports to quantify.

14.3   Analysis of Data and Presentation

The researcher utilized Statistical Package for the Social Sciences and Microsoft Excel to analyze the level of Green computing practices in combating Covid-19 at Institute of Health Science-Gaborone.

Respondents feedback from the questionnaire formed a base on which data interpretation was derived. A link was established between the literature review and primary findings of the research study to discover any existing relationships. The findings have to answer the research questions and have research objectives satisfied.

From 150 questionnaires distributed to students, only 141 managed to respond and all questions were answered. Even though some questionnaires were collected after 72 h instead of the stipulated 48 h. The student who was present at the institute when the study was carried out, were only postgraduates.

14.3.1 Demographics: Gender and Age

Table 14.1 above indicates that all 141 students' respondents stated their gender status no one left the value for gender unanswered that's why it was recorded 0 missing value.

Table 14.2 illustrates that 43 students were male whereas 98 students were female.

Figure 14.2 indicates that the student participation was dominated mostly by the female gender because 69.5% of the participant where female whereas the remaining 30.5% were male.

Table 14.3 above indicates that all 141 students' respondents stated their age group no one left the value for age group unanswered that's why it was recorded 0 missing value.

Table 14.4 indicates that out of 141 student participants they were 62 student participants under 30 years, 66 student participants between 30 and 39 years, 10 student participants aged between 40 and 49 years and

Table 14.1 Gender statistics.

Statistics		
Gender		
N	Valid	141
	Missing	0

Table 14.2 Gender.

Gender					
		Frequency	Percent	Valid percent	Cumulative percent
Valid	Male	43	30.5	30.5	30.5
	Female	98	69.5	69.5	100.0
	Total	141	100.0	100.0	

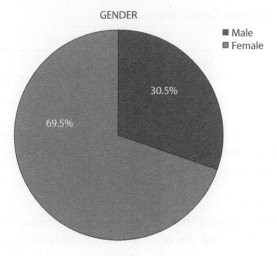

Figure 14.2 Gender.

Table 14.3 Qualification statistics.

Statistics		
Age group		
N	Valid	141
	Missing	0

Table 14.4 Age group.

Age_Group					
		Frequency	Percent	Valid percent	Cumulative percent
Valid	Under 30 yrs.	62	44.0	44.0	44.0
	30–39 yrs.	66	46.8	46.8	90.8
	40–49 yrs.	10	7.1	7.1	97.9
	50 yrs and Greater	3	2.1	2.1	100.0
	Total	141	100.0	100.0	

Table 14.5 Qualification statistics.

		Education_Level
N	Valid	141
	Missing	0

3 student participants of 50 years and greater. This implies that most of the student participants were between 30 and 39 years whereas the least is student participants aged 50 years and above.

Qualification Level
Table 14.5 above indicates that all 141 students' respondents stated their education level no one left the value for education level unanswered that's why it was recorded 0 missing value. Refer Figure 14.3 below.

14.3.2 How Effective is Green Computing Policies in Combating Covid-19 at Institute of Health Science-Gaborone?

As stated in the literature review by Ahmad *et al.* [2] that for individuals to commence to adapt to a system, device or an idea those individuals require to know about it first. It is then clearly visible that both students and staff are not aware of all Green computing policies available in the institute or they are finding it difficult to access and understand the policy,

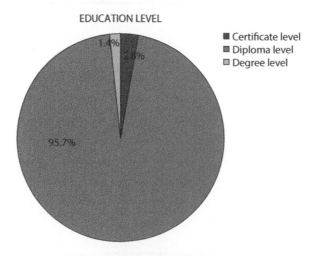

Figure 14.3 Illustrates out of 141 student participants most were diploma holders with 95.7% followed by certificate holders with 2.8% and lastly degree holders with 1.4%.

this is supported by the findings drawn from both the student and staff with an indication that 72% of students and 71% of staff disagreeing that they are aware of Green computing policy available. Vikram [87] shared that computing world is developing policies and exploring methods to utilize in Green computing to save energy but this will be of the complex task to achieve at Institute of Health Science-Gaborone, to explore a method to utilize in Green computing policy formulation because majority reflects that they are not consulted in Green computing formulation more especially in times of Covid-19 pandemic where the need to economize is high. Nagamani [25] highlighted that need for cooperation in developing, disseminating and implementing appropriate Green practices is crucial since it makes users understand perils and responsibilities associated with Green computing. The author further regarded Green computing practices as a collective responsibility. It was statistically visible that majority of users lacks inspiration in green behaviour and this will not effectively assist the institute to utilize Green computing practices in minimizing costs that come along with Covid-19. Refer to Figure 14.4 below.

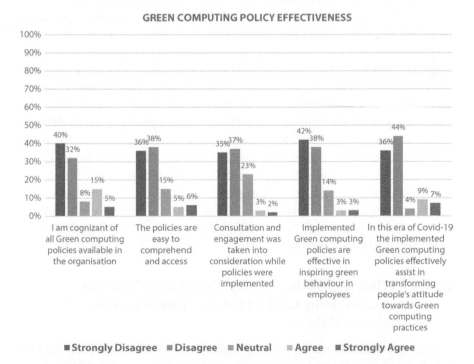

Figure 14.4 Effectiveness of Green Computing policy at the Institute of Health Science-Gaborone.

14.3.3   What are Green Computing Practices Among Users at Gaborone Institute of Health Science?

Hemdan [34] stated that it necessitates a significant amount of computing power to build an accurate model of SARS-Cov-2 the virus that causes the Covid-19 illness. This implies that more power is needed during this Covid-19 pandemic. Organizations have to initiate and implement methods that can assist in minimizing energy consumption but these look like is not the case with Institute of Health Science-Gaborone when looking at the statistics indicating their trends and perception in buying computing equipment the same number of 45% was recorded for both students and staff showing that computing gadgets they bought are not smart energy-efficient even though 72% opted to remain neutral it was also visible that majority of respondents both student and staff 73% of them still do not switch off computer resources when not in use to safe power. In the literature review, Abugahah and Abubaker [1] also had a view that it is mandatory to balance the system in such a way that the computing speed requires to be maintained same with reduced energy consumption. Statistically, it reflects that majority of respondents both students and staff do not efficiently promote recyclability, reuse, the biodegradability of defunct products and factory waste and also it is visible that most of the respondents are not familiar with disposal method of devices no longer in use because an equal value of 73% was recorded for both staff and students, indicating that they are not familiar with disposal method these findings do not comply with Harmon and Auseklis' [64] recycling process. 60% of students and 65% staff reflected that the computing devices containing hazardous components are not mostly labeled and either be made of such devices. This indicates that users are not made aware of components that can harm the environment which is not by Batlegang [5] when he stated that people has to be made aware and be given appropriate education so that they could adopt green computing practices. Refer to Figure 14.5 below.

14.3.4   What is the Role of Green Computing Training in Combating Covid-19 at Institute of Health Science-Gaborone?

Kumar Dookhitram realized that a higher level of awareness can lead to behavioural changes and welcome Green computing practices utilization. However, this is not by what the statistics show about Institute of Health

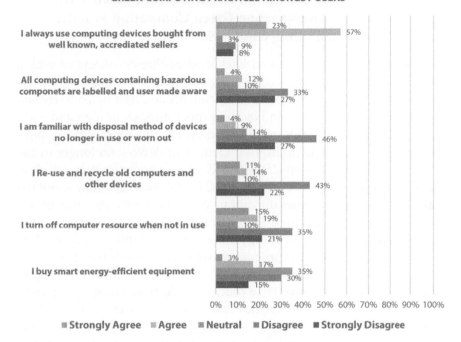

Figure 14.5 Green computing practices among users.

Science-Gaborone because 71% of staff and 70% of students indicated that they are no regular training on Green computing. Also as indicated in the literature review that when people are given appropriate education they can easily adapt and adhere to Green computing practices. These also make further complications on measuring the effectiveness of the training in inspiring Green behavior since training is not done regularly and the slightly high value was recorded in respondents remaining neutral on this questionnaire item. The findings indicate that majority of users agreed that regular training on Green computing practices in this time of Covid-19 will assist the institute to equip knowledge on employees and help users develop that culture of adherence to Green computing practices and apply the holistic approach proposed in a literature review by Li and Zhou [62]. Ahmad *et al.* [2] state that for individuals to commence to adapt to a system, device or an idea those individuals require to know about it first. This implies that individuals have to be made aware of green computing practices and concept first before they adopt it. These imply that Green computing practices training plays a pivotal role in Green computing practices awareness.

14.3.5   What is the Likelihood of Threats Associated With a Lack of Awareness on Green Computing Practices While Combating Covid-19?

This study assessed the potential likelihood of threats associated with a lack of awareness on Green computing practices while fighting Covid-19. Majority of respondents both from students and staff opted to remain neutral on mismanagement and lack of proper disposal of used and worn out computing devices. This may be attributed to that most of the respondents are not familiar with disposal method of devices no longer in use as it was visible with the results obtained on questionnaire item asked on Green computing practices among users. If one does not know about the disposal method, it becomes difficult to know the appropriate way of disposing of. 71% of students and 70 % of students indicated that they are the likelihood of an increase in energy consumption in this era of Covid-19 lockdowns due to increases in computing hardware infrastructure. This was noticeable when Hellewell *et al.* [33] shared that innovative entrepreneurs from Ghana have inverted a touch-free electronic washing tap to be used for washing hand this implies that more devices are being made to address the Covid-19 pandemic the vaccine included. More devices more power required to be utilized on increased computing infrastructure. 70% of students group and 66% of staff which represent the majority indicated that they are frequent users of infrared devices that usually malfunction due to improper handling. This can be attributed to some non-contact thermometers that are utilized in checking temperatures on the entry of the institute since it's a requirement for Covid-19 prevention measures. Majority of respondents showed that they prefer to provide a different part of the body when screened for temperature using infrared devices because they believe infrared radiation is not good for their skin. Ng *et al.* [57] shared that infrared thermometer is completely safe and does not produce radiation, however in contrary Dante *et al.* [23] expressed a different view and stated that if one has extremely sensitive skin then it will be observed that the results of the use of the infrared non-contact thermometer can be a little uncomfortable. This implies that since the safety of infrared is questionable people will then be allowed to provide body part which they prefer as long as readings are obtained pending further study as stated by Yae-Bellany [93]. It was discovered that lack of proper disposal, increased energy consumption and frequently improper use of infrared devices all being the results of lack of Green computing practices awareness can be a threat. Refer to Figure 14.6 below.

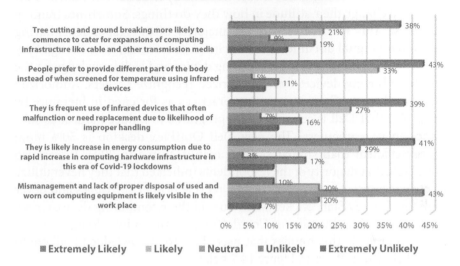

LIKELIHOOD OF GREEN COMPUTING THREATS

Tree cutting and ground breaking more likely to commence to cater for expansions of computing infrastructure like cable and other transmission media: 38%, 21%, 9%, 19%

People prefer to provide different part of the body instead of when screened for temperature using infrared devices: 43%, 33%, 5%, 11%

They is frequent use of infrared devices that often malfunction or need replacement due to likelihood of improper handling: 39%, 27%, 7%, 16%

They is likely increase in energy consumption due to rapid increase in computing hardware infrastructure in this era of Covid-19 lockdowns: 41%, 29%, 3%, 17%

Mismanagement and lack of proper disposal of used and worn out computing equipment is likely visible in the work place: 10%, 20%, 43%, 20%, 7%

0%   5%   10%   15%   20%   25%   30%   35%   40%   45%

■ Extremely Likely   ■ Likely   ■ Neutral   ■ Unlikely   ■ Extremely Unlikely

Figure 14.6 Likelihood of green computing threats.

14.3.6   What is the Level of User Conduct, Awareness and Attitude With Regard to Awareness on Green Computing Practices at Institute of Health Science-Gaborone?

An analysis was conducted to assess knowledge, attitude and behaviour amongst users concerning awareness on Green computing practices while combating Covid-19. The findings indicate that majority of the respondents are knowledgeable and prefer the use of emails and other social platforms to assist reduce paper waste and promote social distancing, as it is a requirement by Covid-19 prevention guidelines. The respondents reflected that they disagree with the burning of worn-out devices to create storage space this was not by Liu [51] who stated that a computer is made out of harmful materials and chemicals like lead which is found in CRT monitors and circuit boards, beryllium and mercury contained in motherboards this chemical are not friendly to our environment and when burnt can cause global warming. In contrary, 74% of students and 69% of staff indicated that they have low knowledge on minimizing power consumption by switching off computing devices that are not in use since they thought it will lose settings. This is not supported by Selyamani and Ahmad [76] who believed that Computing infrastructure absorbs a large amount of energy which is increasing day by day and thus placing substantial weight on the electricity grid and adding to greenhouse emissions.

Xiong shared that it is not always mandatory to reward or punish individuals to change their attitude in how they do things. Sometimes training can assist. This was visible with the majority of the respondents having believed on digital documents than printed documents, even though they don't prefer to use upgraded computing device and lack knowledge on the benefit of buying devices from authorized recognized sellers. Authorized brands adhere to Green computing practices as for cited in literature by Kurp [61] that Dell is refining up its programs to reduce hazardous substance in its computers. The new Dell OptiPlex desktop is 50% more energy-efficient than similar systems manufactured in 2005. It was also noticeable that majority of the respondents indicated that they never utilize electronic register for contact tracing, recycle printer cartridges and never look for "Energy Star" sticker when buying their computing devices more especially during this time of Covid-19 where the online doing of things was encouraged. This implies that users lack the knowledge to adhere to green behaviour. Refer to Figure 14.7 below.

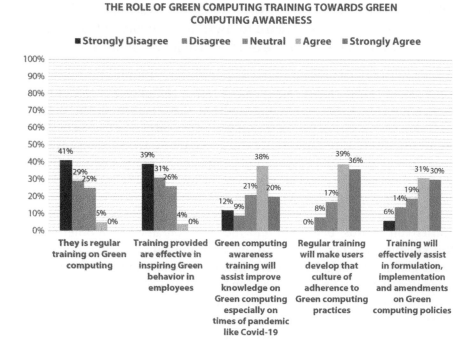

Figure 14.7 The role of green computing training towards green computing awareness.

14.4   Recommendations

The study proposes a framework based on previous research surveys and other studies, undoubtedly literature supports any linkage to this proposed framework. The recommended framework shown on Figure 14.8 below will assist in guiding Institute of Health Science-Gaborone or any related organization on how to operate, maintain and implement Green computing awareness The framework consists of organizational objectives and environmental concerns or threats which are the driving forces for user training, compliance and Green computing policies concepts which in turn then guide people and technology used on green computing practices in place to achieve the required level of awareness.

14.4.1   Green Computing Policy

It is also recommended that the Institute of Health Science-Gaborone implement a Green computing policy that is easy to comprehend and accessible to all. They should be a reward for individuals who implement and adhere to Green computing policies to further improve their efficiency and effectiveness concerning the practices of Green computing.

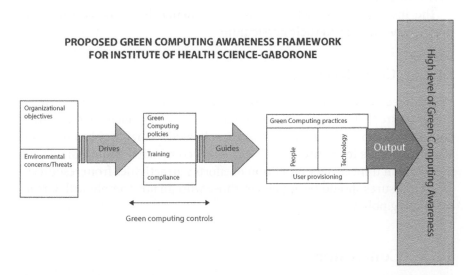

Figure 14.8 Green computing awareness framework.

14.4.2   Risk Assessment

Institute of Health Science-Gaborone should have a method or process that assist identify and analyze potential event that may negatively harm the environment, assets and individual. The risk assessment should be communicated to a suitable risk owner and documented.

14.4.3   Green Computing Awareness Training

The time has emanated to increase users' level of awareness of Green computing practices and norms. Users must be trained about the advantages of purchasing greener products. Educational establishments have a very pivotal role to play in this process so that we build a culture that inspires every user who utilizes modern computational devices to examine his practices and amend if necessary. Users have to be educated and familiarized with waste regulating acts such as Botswana waste management act chapter 65:06 to be aware on how to dispose of hazardous devices. During this time of Covid-19 where there is increased fear, panic and scramble of Protective equipment because of the pandemic, organization are at risk of buying non- calibrated products it is advisable to organize workshops with Botswana Radiation Protection inspectorate and other regulating bodies to advise and educate users to purchase and use products that are user and environmental friendly.

The institute must include pro-environmental behavior courses and make it compulsory in their curriculum.

14.4.4   Compliance

It is also recommended that the Institute of Health Science-Gaborone have to make sure that users conform to Green computing policies. Compliance controls have to be harmonized and consolidated so that they can be easily adopted. This is to ensure that all necessary compliance requirements are met without unnecessary repetition of efforts and activities from resources. Strict measures should be applied to those who do not comply with Green computing policy.

14.5   Conclusion

Covid-19 has forced the organization to computerize or improve their computing infrastructure due to the preventative guidelines that encourage social distancing among individuals. Institutions are forced to operate online or experience total shutdown during the lockdown. This has resulted in increased purchase and usage of computing devices. Environmental and health hazards associated with the use of more computing devices in this time of fighting the pandemic mandatorily stimulates the need for Green Computing practices or else the organization will find itself having to deal with two monsters the pandemic and costs involved with lack of applying Green computing practices. Institute of Health Science-Gaborone was under the scrutiny of the level of awareness in Green computing practices while combating Covid-19 and it was realized that it is crucial to organize consultation and training on Green Computing practices issues in times of pandemics like Covid-19 for sustainability and cost reduction. A comprehensive and easily accessible Green computing policy was recommended for adherence and referential purposes. However, a longitudinal study is recommended to fully address the objectives of the study over a long period and come up with a prediction of trends involved in awareness of Green computing practices.

References

1. Abugabah, A. and Abubaker, A., Green Computing: Awareness and practices. *The 4th IEEE International Conference on Computer and Technology Applications*, 8, 831–842, 2018.
2. Ahmad, T.B., Nordin, M.S., Bello, A., The state of green computing Knowledge among students in a Malaysian public university. *J. Asian Sci. Res.*, 8, 831–842, 2014.
3. Ajzen, I. and Fishbein, M., *Understanding Attitudes And Prediction Social Behavior*, Prentice-Hall, Inc, Englewood Cliffs, 1980.
4. Asiamah, N., Mensah, H.K., Oteng-Abayie, E.F., *General, Target, and Accessible Population: Demystifying the Concepts for Effective Sampling.* Qualitative Report, Creative Commons Attribution-Noncommercial-Share Alike 4.0 License.Accra, Ghana, 22, 1607–1622, 2017.
5. Batlegang, B., Green Computing: Students, Campus Computing and The Environment—A Case for Botswana. *J. Inf. Syst. Commun.*, 3, 1, 256–260, 2012.
6. Banerjee A, Chaudhury S. Statistics without tears: Populations and samples. *Ind., Psychiatry J.*, 2010;19:60-5
7. Baumgartner, E. and Rainey, J., Trump administration ended pandemic early-warning program to detect coronaviruses. *Los Angeles Times*, April 2, 326–332, 2020.
8. Belleau, B., Summers, T., Xu, Y., Pinel, R., Theory of reasoned action: Purchase intention of young consumers. *Clothing Text. Res. J.*, 25, 3, 244–257, 2007.

9. Bharti, Developing Environmentally Responsible Business Strategies: A Research perspective. *Int. J. Green Comput.*, 2, 47–57, 2011.

10. Boudreau, M., Gefen, D., Straub, D., Validation in IS research: A state-of-the-art assessment. *MIS Quart.*, 25, 1–24, 2001.

11. Breweton, P. and Millward, L., *Organizational Research Methods*, SAGE, London, 2001.

12. Bryman, A. and Bell, E., *Business research methods*, Oxford University Press, Oxford, 2003.

13. Santhosh Kumar, C. and Yale, S.S., Identifying and eliminating bias in interventional research studies—A quality indicator. *Int. J. Contemp. Med. Res.*, 3, 6, 1644–1648, 2016.

14. Castagno, A.E., What makes critical ethnography "critical"?, in: *Qualitative research: An introduction to methods and designs*, S.D. Lapan, M.T. Quartaroli, F.J. Riemer, (Eds.), pp. 373–390, Jossey Bass, San Francisco, CA, 2012.

15. Chau, P.Y.K. and Hu, P., Information technology acceptance by individual professionals: A model comparison approach. *Decis. Sci.*, 32, 699–719, 2001.

16. Igwenagu, C., *Fundamentals of research methodology and data collection*, Enugu State University of Science and Technology, LAP Lambert Academic Publishing Republic of Moldova, Chisinau-2068, str. A.Russo 15, of .61

17. Choudrie, J. and Dwivedi, Y.K., Investigating Broadband Diffusion in the Household: Towards Content Validity and Pre-Test of the Survey Instrument. *Proceedings of the 13th European Conference on Information Systems (ECIS 2005)*, Regensburg, Germany, May 26–28, 2005.

18. Collis, J. and Hussey, R., *Business Research: A Practical Guide*, Basingstoke: Palgrave Macmillan, 2003.

19. Creswell, J., *Research Design*, 4th ed., pp. 3–23, Thousand Oaks California SAGE publication, 2014.

20. Creswell, J.W., *Research design: Qualitative, quantitative and mixed methods Approaches*, 2nd ed., pp. 1–16, London: UCL Press, 2003.

21. Tohmatsu, D.T., *The Next Wave of Green IT*, vol. 32, p. 32, CFO Research Services, Boston, Jan 2009.

22. O'Leary, Daniel. (2020). Evolving Information Systems and Technology Research Issues for COVID-19 and Other Pandemics. *Journal of Organizational Computing and Electronic Commerce.* vol 30, 1–8, 10.1080/10919392.2020.1755790.

23. Dante, A., Franconi, I., Marucci, A.R., Alfes, C.M., Lancia, L., Evaluating the interchangeability of forehead, tympanic, and axillary thermometers in Italian pediatric clinical settings: Results of a multicenter observational study. *J. Pediatr. Nurs.*, 1, 21–25, 2019.

24. Do Valle, P.O., Rebelo, E., Reis, E., Menezes, J., Combining behavioral theories to predict recycling involvement. *Environ. Behav.*, 37, 3, 364–396, 2005.

25. Nagamani, M. and Navaneetha, B., A Study on Awareness About Green Computing Among Women Graduates—An Empirical Study. *Indian J. Appl. Res.*, 4, 10, 317–319, 2014.

26. Elkatawneh, H., Comparing Qualitative and Quantitative Approaches. *SSRN Electron. J.*, 10, 263–265, 2016, 10.2139/ssrn.2742779.

27. Engellant, K., Holland, D., Piper, R., Assessing Convergent and Discriminant Validity of the Motivation Construct for the Technology Integration Education (TIE) Model. *J. Higher Educ. Theory Pract.*, 16, 37–50, 2016.

28. Fauzi, A. and Pradipta, I., Research methods and data analysis techniques in education articles published by Indonesian biology educational journals. *J. Pendidik. Biol. Indonesia*, 4, 10, 442–446, 2018.

29. Fouka, G. and Mantzorou, M., What are the major ethical issues in conducting research? Is there a conflict between the research ethics and the nature of nursing? *Health Sci. J.*, 5, 1, 3–14, 2011.

30. Ghauri, P. and Gronhaug, K., *Research Methods in Business Studies*, Harlow, FT/Prentice Hall, United Kingdom, 2005.

31. Graziano, A. and Raulin, M.L., *Research methods: A process of inquiry*, 4th Edition, Allyn & Bacon, USA, 2000.

32. Gung, V. and Hence, G., Industrial wireless sensor networks: Challenges, design principles, and technical approaches. *IEEE Trans. Ind. Electron.*, 56, 10, 4258–4265, 2009.

33. Hellewell, J.S., Abbott, A., Gimma, N.I., Feasibility of controlling COVID-19 outbreaks by isolation of cases and contacts. *Lancet Glob. Health*, 8, 4, E488–E496, 2020.

34. Hemdan, E.E., Shouman, M.A., Karar, M.E., COVIDX-Net: *A Framework of Deep Learning Classifiers to Diagnose COVID-19 in X-Ray Images*, arXiv e-print journal, 3, pp 491–494, 2020.

35. Hoeller, P. and Wallin, M., *Energy Prices, Taxes and Carbon Dioxide Emissions.* OECD Economic Studies No. 17, OECD, Paris, France, 2009.

36. Howell, K.E., *Introduction to the Philosophy of Methodology*, Sage, London, vol 105, pp 327–331, 2013.

37. Hsiao, S., Chen, T., Chien, H., Yang, C., Chen, Y., Body temperature measurement to prevent pandemic COVID-19 in hospitals in Taiwan: Repeated measurement is necessary. *J. Hosp. Infect.*, 105, 327–331, 2020.

38. Huck, S.W., *Reading Statistics and Research*, United States of America, Allyn & Bacon, 2007.

39. Huysamen, G.K., *Methodology for the Social and Behavioural Science*, Oxford University Press, RSA, 2001.

40. Ibrahim, M., The art of Data Analysis. *J. Allied Health Sci. Pakistan*, 1, 98–104, 2015.

41. Philomemna, I., Introduction to Research and Research Methodology. Research Methodology and Grant writing. pg1-10 published by Rex Charles & Patrick Ltd. Anambra State, Nigeria. *Ind. Psychiatry J.*, 19, 1, 60–65, 2009.

42. *Institutional Strategic Plan (2007–2012)*, Institute of Health Science-Gaborone, Gaborone, 2011.
43. Irny, S.I. and Rose, A.A., Designing a Strategic Information Systems Planning. *J. Inf. Syst. Res. Innovation*, 9, 3, 28–36, 2005.
44. Shuja, J., Gani, A., Shamshirband, S., Wasim Ahmad, R., Bilal, K., Sustainable Cloud Data Centers: A survey of enabling techniques and technologies. *Renewable Sustain. Energy Rev.*, 62, 195–214, 2016.
45. Kannan, S. and Gowri, S., Pilot studies: are they appropriately reported? *Perspect. Clin. Res.*, 6, 207–10, 2015.
46. Kawulich, B., *Qualitative Data Analysis Techniques*, Conference paper: RC33 (ISA) At: Amsterdam, The Netherlands, 2004.
47. Kemm, J. and Close, A., *Health promotion: Theory and Practice*, Palgrave, London, UK, 1995.
48. Kosmicki, E. and Pienkowski, D., Renewable Energy and Socio-Economic Development in the European Union. *Probl. Sustain. Dev.*, 8, 105–114, 2013.
49. Kotrlik, J.W., Bartlett, J.E., Higgins, C.C., Organizational research: Determining appropriate sample size in survey research. *Learn. Perform. J.*, 19, 43–50, 2013.
50. Kumar Garg, S. and Buyya, R., *Green computing and environmental sustainability*, Dept. of Computer Science and Software Engineering The University of Melbourne, Australia, 2012.
51. Liu, H., Biofuel's Sustainable Development under the Trilemma of Energy, Environment and Economy. *Probl. Sustain. Dev.*, 10, 55–59, 2015.
52. Nikkheslat, M., The important theories in term of applying green technologies and green processes in organizations: A study of Malaysian Universities. *Interdiscip. J. Contemp. Res. Bus.*, 4, 7, 529–532, 2012.
53. McBurney, D. and White, T., *Research methods*, 9th ed., p. 220, Wadsworth Cengage Learning, Belmont, CA, 2013.
54. Messick, S., Validity, in: *Educational measurement*, R.L. Linn, (Ed.), Macmillan, New York, 1989.
55. Kaur, A., Green Computing: Emerging Issues in IT. *Int. J. Trend Sci. Res. Dev. (IJTSRD)*, 3, 5, 627–629, August 2019.
56. Hohashi, N. and Yi, Q., Comparison Of Perceptions Of Domestic Elder Abuse Among Healthcare Workers Based On The Knowledge–Attitude–Behavior Model. *J. Pone*, 3, 751–753, 2018.
57. Ng, D.K., Chan, C., Chan, E.Y., Kwok, K., Chow, P., Lau, W.F., Ho, J.C., A brief report on the normal range of forehead temperature as determined by noncontact, handheld, infrared thermometer. *Am. J. Infect. Control*, 33, 227–229, 2005.
58. Oluwatayo, J., Validity and reliability issues in educational research. *J. Educ. Soc Res.*, 2, 391–400, 2012.
59. Olubunmi, O.F., Knowledge Management as an important tool in Organisational Management: A review of literature. *Libr. Philos. Pract.* (e-journal), 1238, http://digitalcommons.unl.edu/libphilprac/1238,2015, 2, 2015.

60. Kiruthiga, P. and Vinoth Kumar, T., Green Computing—An Eco friendly Approach for Energy Efficiency and minimizing E-Waste. *Int. J. Adv. Res. Comput. Commun. Eng.*, 3, 4, 731–735, April 2014.

61. Kurp, P., Green Computing—Are you ready for a personal energy meter? *Commun. ACM*, 51, 10, 371–374, 2008, http://www.eecs.wsu.edu/~tlu/PhD_Power_Aware_Computing/GreenComputing.pdf Publications.

62. Li, Q. and Zhou, M., The survey and future evolution of green computing, in: *Proceedings of the 2011 IEEE/ACM International Conference on Green Computing and Communications 2011*, Aug 4, IEEE Computer Society, Washington, DC, USA, pp. 230–233, 2011.

63. Sheikh, R.A. and Lanjewar, U.A., Green Computing—Embrace a Secure Future. *Int. J. Comput. Appl.*, 10, 4, 0975–8887, Nov. 2010.

64. Harmon, R.R. and Auseklis, N., Sustainable IT Services: Assessing the Impact of Green Computing Practices, in: *Proceeding of PICMET*, Portland, Oregon USA, pp. 2–6, Research Issues for COVID-19 and Other Pandemics, *J. Organ. Comput. Electron. Commer.*, 30, 1, 1–8, 2009.

65. Riemenschneider, C.K., Hardgrave, B.C., Davis, F.D., *Explaining software developer acceptance of methodologies: A comparison of five theoretical models. IEEE Trans. Software Eng.*, 28, 1135–1145, 2002.

66. Robinson, J., *Triandis theory of interpersonal behaviour in understanding software privace behaviour in the South African context*, Masters degree, University of the Witwatersrand, Wits University Press, South Africa, 2009.

67. Roopa, S. and Menta Satya, R., Questionnaire Designing for a Survey. *J. Indian Orthod. Soc*, 46, 37–41, 2012, 10.5005/jp-journals-10021-1104.

68. Rowley, J., Designing and using research questionnaires. *Manage. Res. Rev.*, 37, 3, 308–330, 2014, https://doi.org/10.1108/MRR-02-2013-0027.

69. Ruel, E., Gillespie, B., Wagner, W., *Practice of Survey Research*, p. 16, Sage, Los Angeles, 2016.

70. Divya Meena, S., Green Computing Turns Green IT. *Int. J. Adv. Res. Comput. Sci. Manage. Stud.*, 4, 2, 204–208, 2016.

71. Nagata, S. and Shoji, O., Green Process Aiming at Reduction of Environmental Burden. *Fujitsu Sci. Technol. J.*, 41, 2, 251–258, Jul 2005.

72. Murugesan, S., *Harnessing Green IT: Principles and Practices*, IEEE IT Professional, 10, 24–33, 2008.

73. Saunders, M., Lewis, P., Thornhill, A., *Research Methods for Business Student*, 5th ed., Pearson Education Limited, Edinburgh Gate, 2009.

74. Sekaran, U. and Bougie, R., *Research Methods for Business: A Skill Building Approach*, 5th ed, pp. 1–468, John Wiley & Sons, Ltd, New Delhi, 2010.

75. Agarwal, S., Impact of Green Computing in It Industry to Make Eco Friendly Environment. *J. Global Res. Comput. Sci.*, 5, 4, 261–264, 2014.

76. Selyamani, S. and Ahmad, N., Green Computing: *The Overview of Awareness", Practices and Responsibility among Students in Higher Education Institutes, Journal of Internet Services and Applications*, (8), 381–384, 2015.

77. Stalmeijer, R.E., McNaughton, N., Van Mook, W.N., Using focus groups in medical education research: AMEE Guide, No. 91. *Med. Teach.*, 36, 11, 923–939, 2014.

78. Syed Muhammad, S.K., *Basic Guidelines for Research: An Introductory Approach for All Disciplines*, Book Zone Publication, 29/B, (1st Floor) Gulzer Tower Chawkbazar-4203, Chittagong, 2016.

79. Taherdoost, H., Sampling Methods in Research Methodology; How to Choose a Sampling Technique for Research. *Int. J. Acad. Res. Manage.*, 5, 18–27, 2016, 10.2139/ssrn.3205035.

80. Teherani, A., Martimianakis, T., Stenfors-Hayes, T., Wadhwa, A., Varpio, L., Choosing a qualitative research approach. *J. Grad. Med. Educ.*, 7, 4, 669–670, 2015.

81. Thornhill, A., Lewis, P., Saunders, M., *Research methods for Business students*, 3rd Edition, Pearson Education Limited, UK, 2003.

82. Ulhaq, A., Khan, A., Gomes, D., Paul, M., *Computer Vision for COVID-19 Control: A Survey*, 10.31224/osf.io/yt9sx.Undergraduate and Postgraduate Students, Palgrave Macmillan, Houndmills, 2020.

83. Ustek-Spilda, F., Graham, M., Bertolini, A., Katta, S., Ferrari, F., Howeson, K., *From social distancing to social solidarity: Gig economy and the COVID-19*, Brookings Institution Press,Washington, DC, March 27, 2020.

84. Vaccaro, V.L., B2B green marketing and innovation theory for competitive advantage. *J. Syst. Inf. Technol.*, 11, 4, 315–330, 2009.

85. Van Teijlingen, E. and Hundley, V., The Importance of Pilot Studies. *Nurs. Stand.*, (Royal Coll. Nurs. (Great Britain): 1987), 16, 33–6, 2002, 10.7748/ns2002.06.16.40.33.c3214.

86. Veenaa Deeve, N.V., Vijesh Joe, C., Narmatha, K., Study on benefits of Green Computing. *Int. J. Curr. Res.*, 7, 04, 14442–14445, April, 2015.

87. Vikram, S., Green computing. *Proceedings of the International Conference on Green Computing and Internet of Things*, pp. 767–772, 2015.

88. Hu, W. and Kaabouch, N., *Sustainable ICTs and management systems for green computing*, Information Science Reference, Hershey, PA, 201.

89. Wee, Y.S. and Quazi, H.A., Development and validation of critical factors of environmental management. *Ind. Manage. Data Syst.*, 105, 96–114, 2005.

90. Whitley, B.E., *Principals of Research and Behavioural Science*, McGraw-Hill, Boston, 2002.

91. Williams, C., Research methods. *J. Bus. Econ. Res.*, 5, 3, 65–72, 2007.

92. Wright, S., O'Brien, B.C., Nimmon, L., Law, M., Mylopoulos, M., Research design considerations. *J. Grad. Med. Educ.*, 8, 1, 97–98, 2016.

93. Yae-Bellany, D., Thermometer Guns on Coronavirus Front Lines are "Notoriously not Accurate". *N. Y. Times*, 3, 56–58, 2020, Available online: https://www.nytimes.com/2020/02/14/business/coronavirus-temperaturesensor-guns.html (accessed on 14 June 2020).

94. Yin, R.K., *Case study research, design and methods*, Sage, Newbury Park, CA, 2003.

Detailed Analysis of Medical IoT Using Wireless Body Sensor Network and Application of IoT in Healthcare

Anurag Sinha[1,2]* and Shubham Singh[2]

¹Department of Computer Science and IT, Amity University Ranchi, Ranchi, India
²Department of Computer Science and IT, BIT Mesra, Ranchi, India

Abstract

The combination of computer science and electronics is one of the best technologies. It is developing in the form of the Internet of Things (IoT). Among the many applications implemented by the Internet of Things (IoT), smart and connected healthcare services are particularly important. Impact of IoT, which is still in its infancy, but medical care is important. Network sensor, worn that allows us to collect rich information integrated into the body or in our living environment. In this white paper, we will review and understand the custom IoT applications we provide for the best medical services at the lowest cost. What is IoT and how are methods with wireless and sensing technologies used to achieve desired functional medical applications? Here we highlight the opportunities and challenges of the IoT in realizing our vision for the future of healthcare.

Body Sensor Network (BSN), one of the Wireless Sensor Network (WSN) sensors, is widely used in computers and intelligent information processing technologies. BSN plays an increasingly important role in health, social work and sport and is changing the way humans use computers. Current investigations focus on the BSN concept and architecture, signal acquisition, environmental sensitivity and systems technology, and this white paper focuses on sensors, data integration and network communication. It also features a discussion of BSN's current level of research, hot spot analysis and future development trends, and the key challenges and technical issues it currently faces. BSN's routine research programs and practical applications are also provided. BSN is moving in the direction of integration

*Corresponding author: anuragsinha257@gmail.com

R. Anandan, G. Suseendran, S. Balamurugan, Ashish Mishra and D. Balaganesh (eds.) Human Communication Technology: Internet of Robotic Things and Ubiquitous Computing, (401–434)
© 2022 Scrivener Publishing LLC

and multi-technological intelligence. There are still many problems, but BSN's future is bright, radically changing the relationship between man and machine and improving people's quality of life.

Keywords: Internet of Things, healthcare, remote monitoring, visualization, computing, wireless sensors network, body sensor network, sensor

15.1   Introduction

The term Internet refers to a wide variety of applications and protocols built on it. With a sophisticated and interconnected computer network that serves millions of users around the world, we are at the beginning of a new era of global communication 24/7. The connection is no longer a dream or a challenge. The goal is therefore to integrate the physical part, which has been moved towards the integration of people and devices.

Create what the Internet of Things is called with the artificial virtual environment. This event betrays two important pillars of the IoT: the Internet and the need for further explanation. Anything that can connect to the internet belongs to "objects". Common device types such as smart devices, sensors, people, and other objects that can interact with other objects and access them anytime, anywhere.

By 2020, the number of Internet-connected products will be around 50 billion. In the IoT, the "objects" must be active participants and social processes in which data and information "discovered" in the environment can exchange and communicate with each other IOD Journal Volume 6 Number 7783–7786 page 3, which affects and responds "Autonomous implementation of events in the real/physical world." The process of performing tasks and creating services with or without human intervention. The interface as a service enables communication with these 'smart things'. The Internet, questions and transactions take into account status and Related Information Problems The Internet of Things (IoT) makes it possible to collect these objects and transfer them to physical devices, cars, buildings and other components: electronic components, software, sensors, actuators and network connections in Things (IoT-GSI) IoT defines as:

The "establishment of an information community", remote control of IoT sensing and/or existing network infrastructure creates greater opportunities by directly integrating the physical world with the performance, accuracy and economic benefits of the computer world. The next generation of intelligent processing algorithms delivers an unimaginably large amount of data: (B) specifically design the individual circumstances and needs of individual treatment and management options; (C) Helps reduce medical costs. At the same time, it improves the results.

15.2   History of IoT

- 1997—"The Internet of Things" is the seventh in a series of ITU Internet reports
- Originally launched in 1997 under the title "Challenges to the Network".
- 1999—Automatic Identification Center established at MIT
- 2003—EPC Global is founded at MIT
- 2005—Four key Internet of Things technologies are introduced at the WSIS conference.
- 2008—First international conference on the Internet of Things: IoT 2008 was held in Zurich.
- Anytime, anywhere, connection for anyone, now we will have a connection for everything!

BSN applications, one of the fundamental applications for public organizations, are popular in the wellbeing [1–3], sports and diversion [4–6], military [7], public and social segments [8–10]. BSN has step by step become an operational hub for research. BSN is a kind of WSN framed by sensors of physiological boundaries put on the human body, on the outside of the body just as around the body. The fundamental innovations talked about here are sensors, information combination, and organization correspondence. This isn't just another kind of widespread wellbeing arrangement, observation and sickness avoidance, yet additionally a significant some portion of what is known as the Internet of Things. The principle objective is to give a universal figuring foundation of remote equipment, programming and correspondence innovations and give a precondition to the future improvement of omnipresent clinical reconnaissance frameworks [11]. The regular BSN engineering appears in Figure 15.1. The sensor hubs on the body gather physical information and perform starter preparing. Information is gathered from the source hub, at that point communicated to the base station and shared over the Internet, which underpins numerous applications, including wellbeing frameworks, social administrations, patients, and

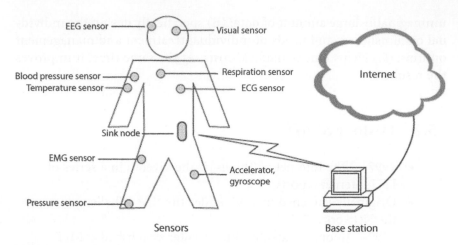

Figure 15.1 Architecture of a BSN.

direct administrations and administrations. It is analyzed by specialists and wellbeing experts. Specialists, medical aid frameworks, and so forth. Today, BSN research faces many significant specialized difficulties. Figure 15.2 sums up the fundamental examination zones of BSN. The investigation of sensor plan and use centres specifically around the movability of sensor hubs [19], on analytic and blunder the executive's capacities [20], on energy utilization [21] and on sensor situating.

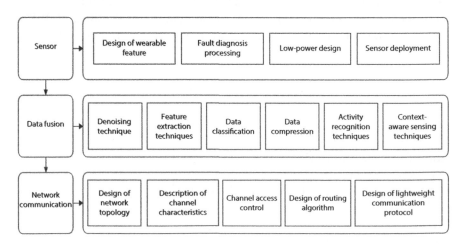

Figure 15.2 Main research areas in BSNs.

Sensor [22]. Information combination, research fundamentally covers the plan and execution of clamor decrease [23], work extraction [24], information arrangement [24], information pressure [25] and "Other key advancements." An ever-increasing number of scientists are consolidating logical mindfulness and information combination advances in the field of action mindfulness [26, 27]. In the field of organization correspondence, this examination centres principally around the plan of the organization geography [28], the portrayal of channels [29], the control of admittance to channels [30, 31], the plan of steering calculations [32], lightweight correspondence this key advancement must be thought about when assembling a total BSN, for example, convention plan framework. Not exclusively are they of incredible examination esteem, however they likewise have genuine worth.

In typical studies, BSN architecture is a communication protocol that takes into account the context and quality of signal processing and service. References [12] The main emphasis is on increasing. Information, communication protocols, QoS and security are under the medical supervision of BSN. As a reference [13], the author uses Sensors, Physical Layer, MAC Layer and Wireless Technology and then carries out the classification in the body. Summary of sensory design and social research questions on various aspects. For information, the researchers published a BSN review that allowed treatment. Lists many environments, sensors and communication protocol application.

15.3   Internet of Objects

15.3.1   Definitions

According to Wikipedia "... The Internet is also called things, which means things. Wireless networks between objects, networks are usually wireless and are automatically installed as home appliances." According to Wikipedia, Integrating a wide range of short-range mobile transceivers with a variety of gadgets and everyday objects, including people, objects and things. IoT of 2008 ... The term "Internet of Things" came to describe various technologies. A research network that makes the Internet accessible to real-world objects. IoT in 2020 ... "Objects with virtual identification and identity operating in the intellectual space in the context of society, environment and user". Figure 15.3 which shows the process of IoT development.

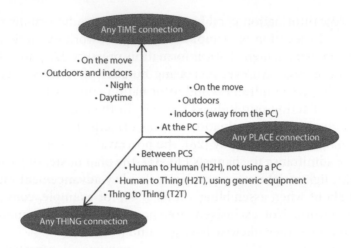

Figure 15.3 Evolution of IoT.

15.3.2 Internet of Things (IoT): Data Flow

The data flow of IoT is illustrated by the following diagram showing data transformation from smart objects to end-users.

15.3.3 Structure of IoT—Enabling Technologies

In Figure 15.4 it is shown how Internet of Things connects physical objects via IP or other networks to exchange/storage/gathering of consumer and business information through software applications. Almost all of them have encountered or used 4.9 billion specific IoT apps should be connected by 2016. Thanks to this phenomenon, new markets opportunities have been created for greater benefits in sectors that harness the potential of the IoT gain a competitive advantage with consumers or businesses. Initially, radio frequency identification (RFID) technology behind IoT development, but with the development of new technologies sensor networks (WSN) and Bluetooth-enabled devices have increased adopt the trends of the IoT.

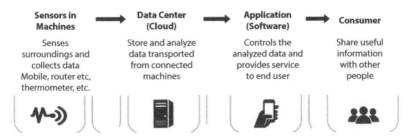

Figure 15.4 Structure flow of IoT.

15.4   Applications of IoT

Ability to network-integrated devices with the limited processor, memory and power. Sources show that IoT has found applications in almost all industries. The IoT system takes action, not just to feel something. Some examples of IoT applications: Smart trading system, you can track specific mobile phones and check the trading habits of specific users in stores. These users can take advantage of special offers on the placement of your favourite products and the most necessary items in the refrigerator, which are automatically sent to your phone. The applications include a transport control system for heat, electricity and energy consumption. Enable advanced features for home security and home automation. Describe the possible sequence of biological sensors. With IoT-based analytics to study the DNA of users or other molecules through IoT, we monitor the electrical appliances installed in your home while sorting files in the office. When you wake up in the morning, the water is hot. All loans are given to smart home builders.

However, the application of the IoT is not limited to these areas. Otherwise, there may also be special cases of IoT. Some of the most important panoramic applications are offered here. Depending on the application, IoT products are smart laptops, smart home, smart cities, smart environment and smart business. There are many areas of IoT application. In this article, I will talk about IoT applications in telemedicine. It is becoming more and more important in healthcare.

15.5   IoT in Healthcare of Human Beings

Remote monitoring circumstances and emergencies via the IoT device notification system. These health monitoring devices, from heart rate, monitors to advanced devices that can control special systems, such as a pacemaker, a Fitbit electronic bracelet or a high-end hearing aid. The special sensor also has equipment in the living space to monitor the general health and well-being of the elderly. Ensuring that the right treatment is in place so that people regain lost mobility through treatment The rise in end-to-end health launches of the IoT platform for monitoring prenatal and chronic patients manages vital health signs and recurrent medications. Medical IoT, heterogeneous computing, wireless communication systems for applications and devices connect patients and healthcare professionals to diagnose, monitor, track and archive important medical statistics and information. Two critical phases of IoT applications in the healthcare sector. IoT Healthcare Solutions can remotely monitor patients with heart disease, GPS tracking for diabetes, arrhythmia and chronic disease, dementia and Alzheimer's patient.

15.5.1   Remote Healthcare—Telemedicine

In Figure 15.5 it is shown that telemedicine is the use of communication and information technology which provide remote clinical medical services. Barriers can be removed and improved access to healthcare not always provided in remote rural areas community. Exchange of information such as voice, image, video, graphics, and elements. Medical records or orders to surgical robots. Telemedicine features

- Remotely diagnose, record and remotely transmit patient health parameters
- Prescription-based diagnosis, history record
- Customized website for patients
- Schedule management: Patients can view the doctor's schedule and make an appointment.
- Doctor dashboard, patient profile and case management
- Integrated billing function
- Biosensor collecting important information: blood pressure, ECG, body temperature, etc.
- Multiple camera options for seamless real-time and offline video conferencing.

15.5.2   Telemedicine System—Overview

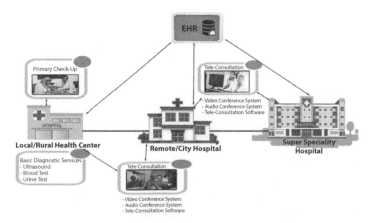

Figure 15.5 System overview of telemedicine system.

15.6 Telemedicine Through a Speech-Based Query System

Patients write questions in local language and doctors speak verbally SMS with information about treatment, support the continuing education of health professionals, create training materials and use multilingual speech recognition engage in human-like conversations to test the knowledge and skills of experts. See Figures 15.5 and 15.6

Advantages of Telemedicine
- Better access and extension of health services to remote sites and new markets
- Makes the right experience available everywhere and reduces unnecessary patient movement.
- Better accessibility and quality of care at a relatively low cost
- Continuity of treatment, emergency response, public awareness.

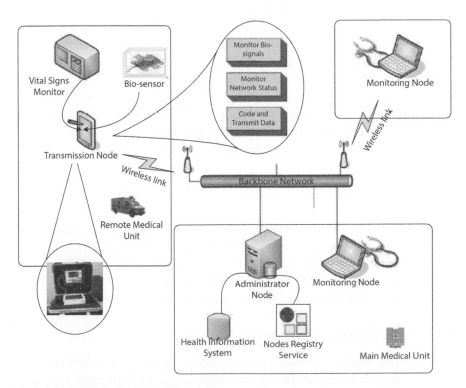

Figure 15.6 Telemedicine—architecture.

15.6.1   Outpatient Monitoring

- Hospital service provided to patients as a hosted model
- Remote monitoring of patients: patients discharged from the hospital
- Heart rate monitoring, automatic event detection and heart rate by hospital alert
- 24/7 patient follow-up, real-time outpatient follow-up
- Geo-barrier, deviation warning, symptom recording
- Alerts from friends and family, continuous ambulatory ECG monitoring
- heart telemetry, management of important messages.

Example of Outpatient Monitoring
- Chest pain, mild congestive heart failure
- high blood pressure, weakness, dizziness
- Vomiting, changes in mental state, anaemia, mild asthma
- Back pain, dehydration

Advantages of Outpatient Monitoring
- Reduced readmissions: 24/7 high-risk surveillance
- Patient allows the doctor to check ahead and take corrective action serious medical problem.
- Increased efficiency and benefits with 24-hour secure patient access centralized information not only increases the efficiency of medical personnel, Additionally, hospitals can effectively manage beds and increase sales.
- Increase patient outcomes and overall satisfaction.

What is Telemedicine?
- Provision of medical services and clinical information in remote locations.
- It is an FDA approved platform that connects patients interactively internet, Internet of Things (IoT), Video chat, Smartphone and cloud of electronic health records (EMR)
- The solutions you need in the 21st century
- A new paradigm in the healthcare sector.

15.6.2   Telemedicine Umbrella Service

- *Telemedicine:* Providing professional advice to patients in remote locations during the diagnosis, identify or assist the attending physician second 78% of emergency care at the American Medical Association (AMA) effective treatment with TeleMedicine

- *TeleMonitoring:* Collect patient data and collect data using IoT medical monitoring agency for remote tests and diagnostics. Remote monitoring the services also include customized notifications to inform the patient's healthcare provider during a physical/mental trauma
- *Telesurgery:* Allows surgeons to perform surgery on patients remote location thanks to TeleRobotics technology
- *Distance Medical Training:* providing medical training to medical services Community and audience in different geographic areas
- *Telemedicine Data Service:* Share occupational health information with other Service providers, education industry, research companies and governments, etc.

15.6.3   Advantages of the Telemedicine Service

- particularly in medical emergencies during natural disasters
- There is no need to queue to see the doctor.
- It is not necessary to physically go to a medical facility TelehealthRoad barrier
- Reduction of documents and papers
- Affordable: With the expansion of the telemedicine space, insurance coverage is drastically reduced. Reduce rewards and potentially the time a patient has to leave work
- Equal and inclusive healthcare for all Geographic barrier
- Better communication–communication with treating doctors and experts It occurs at the same time

15.6.4   Some Examples of IoT in the Health Sector

- Headphones for measuring brain waves, clothing with sensors, BP monitors
- Glucose monitor, ECG monitor, pulse oximeter
- Medical equipment, distribution systems, surgical robots Implantation of the device
- All portable technological devices

15.7   Conclusion

As clarified in this record, all physical items function admirably with machine–machine and -machine interfaces. These degrees of association can be factors that influence wellbeing inside and outside the body. It is investigated by the model. The hotly anticipated IoT clinical upset has just started. At the point when new circumstances emerge, react to the critical requirement for reasonable, moderate assistance. Then, robotization of IoT parts and machine-to-machine correspondence proceed. The presentation of the administration level will make a total ILO framework. This upheaval is portrayed by giving start to finish availability and registering answers for IoT-based medical services. The specialist's versatile application is certifiably not a substitute for a specialist's insight. They have to work with a specialist. New IoT drifts in this way to deal with doctor mix by adding to innovation may change the way. Essential consideration shows restraint focused, however for creating nations, IoT offers another model for conveying quality consideration at a sensible level. IoT will make new plans of action and new conveyance models in the medical services field later on. What difficulties do we face in creating and created nations? In this article, we analyze the current circumstance and anticipate the future joining of distant wellbeing checking innovation in clinical practice. Specifically, IoT brilliant convenient sensors offer an alluring chance to screen and record information at home and at work. Longer periods than when you go to the workplace and the lab. The information from this fortune was dissected with clear visual portrayals and introduced to a likely doctor to drastically improve medical care and diminish costs.

15.8   Sensors

Sensors are a key piece of BSN as they associate the physical world to electronic frameworks. It is mostly used to accumulate data about your physiology and your current circumstance. Sensor hubs with sensors as the fundamental segments measure data by a design change, rationale calculation, information stockpiling and transmission [33]. A sensor hub commonly contains a sensor module, a processor module, a remote correspondence module, and a force module [34]. The sensor module is answerable for gathering the condition of the deliberate and for changing over information from physical amounts into electrical signs. The processor module controls the sensor hub. The remote correspondence module comprising of remote handsets at the organization layer, MAC layer and the physical layer is answerable for the correspondence between the sensor and the PC. The force module supplies capacity to the whole sensor hub.

State-of-the-Art Research on BSN Status—The advancement of BSN applications in numerous fields as of late, electrocardiogram (ECG) sensors, accelerometers, pressure sensors, and breathing sensors are progressively turning out to be problem areas for BSN sensor research. Much examination has been done on improving the convenience of sensor hubs and enhancing information handling calculations. Huge scope considers have been led on issues, for example, energy control, deficiency finding and decrease in the number of sensor hubs. This work advances the improvement of BSN toward energy effectiveness and accuracy.

15.8.1   Classification of Sensors

The sort of sensor and the number of sensors utilized by the BSN framework in genuine applications are exceptionally subject to the particular application situation and the framework foundation. The BSN framework can utilize various kinds of sensors to supplement the recognition of physiological signs, human conduct and the general climate. BSN sensors can be of various sorts because of various application explicit necessities. Contingent upon the sort of sign estimated, BSN sensors can be isolated into two classifications [35]. The principal classification, which incorporates accelerometers, spinners, ECG sensors, electroencephalographic (EEG) sensors, electroencephalographic (EMG) sensors, visual sensors, and hearing sensors, gathers consistent signs that shift after some time. This sort of sensor zeros in additional on securing the sign progressively by ceaselessly gathering the sign, bringing about extremely high information move and force utilization. A subsequent class, for example, glucose sensors, temperature sensors, stickiness sensors, pulse screens, and sensors that screen the oxygen immersion of the blood, gather physiological signs that change after some time. The measure of information moved is not as much as that of the main classification because of the sign that the sensor gathers changes gradually. You can utilize profound rest mode to decrease power utilization.

Contingent upon the sort of information transmission medium, the most usually utilized sensors in BSN can be partitioned into three classifications: remote sensors utilizing remote correspondence advances, for example, Bluetooth or Zigbee, RFID (Radio Frequency Identification Devices) and Ultra-Wideband (UWB) to speak with different sensors or gadgets. Most applications utilize this sort of sensor to improve fit and lessen impedance from the sensor in ordinary exercises. Wired sensors utilizing wired correspondence innovation can supplant remote sensors if they don't truly meddle with the fit. The transmission mode is more steady than the remote sensor. Be that as it may, establishment and arrangement are generally unpredictable. The total expulsion of strings is an inescapable pattern for BSN [13]. Human Body Communication Sensors (HBCs) that utilization the human body as a method for transmission have just been proposed as of late. This kind of sensor receives sub-GHz recurrence without reception apparatus, lessening the force utilization and the size of the sensor hub. In this way, it very well may be effortlessly coordinated into gadgets worn on the body. Likewise, the correspondence separation of the HBC sensor is restricted around the human body, which adequately improves correspondence security [36]. Nonetheless, the correspondence speed is slower than that of a conventional remote sensor. Lately, it has been upheld by the IEEE 802.15.6 norm for use in short-run, low-force, and high-unwavering quality remote correspondence frameworks close or in the human body [37].

Contingent upon the area of the sensor hubs, BSN sensors can be separated into three classifications [35]. Type 1 is compact sensors, for example, temperature sensors, pressure sensors, and accelerometers. The size and weight of the sensor ought to be considered during the planning cycle so as not to meddle with the client's day by day exercises. Type 2 is an implantable sensor that can be embedded in the body or breathed in/breathed in like a photograph pill. This kind of sensor isn't just little enough; it likewise requires non-destructiveness and biocompatibility. Type 3 is applied to individuals around you and can be utilized to perceive conduct and gather encompassing data, for example, visual sensors. As indicated by the auto-tuning capacity, BSN sensors can be isolated into two classes. Self-adjusting sensors able to do consequently altering the handling technique, arrangement and boundaries, limit conditions or limitations as indicated by the qualities of the information adjust to the measurable conveyance. Auxiliary attributes of the deliberate information to accomplish the best helpful impact are Non-self-tuning sensors, which are straightforward in plan and don't need to consider self-tuning capacities, are currently broadly utilized in BSN. Because of the multifaceted nature and the interest for more noteworthy exactness, self-transformation techniques will be slowly applied to the sensor refer to Table 15.1.

15.8.2   Commonly Used Sensors in BSNs

Table 15.1 Types of sensors used in BSN.

Sensors	Utility	Pointer category	Example rate of recurrence	Assignment
Accelerometer	Obtain increase of rate on every spatial alliance of Three-dimensional gap.	unremitting	elevated	Wearable
non-natural cochlea	Exchange manner sign into electric rhythm and sending it to ingrained electrodes in ears, generate hearing consciousness by thought-provoking Acoustic nerves.	constant	towering	Implantable
fake retina	Estimating the pinnacle weight of systolic and the base weight of diastolic.	constant	towering	Implantable
Blood-pressure sensor	Measuring the peak pressure of systolic and the minimum pressure of diastolic.	distinct	small	Wearable
Camera pill	Distinguishing gastrointestinal plot by remote endoscope method.	unremitting	towering	Implantable
Carbon dioxide sensor	Estimating the substance of carbon dioxide from blended gas by infrared method.	separate	small/ exceptionally low	Wearable

(Continued)

Table 15.1 Types of sensors used in BSN. (*Continued*)

Sensors	Utility	Pointer category	Example rate of recurrence	Assignment
ECG/EEG/EMG sensor	Estimating voltage contrast between two anodes which are put on the surface of the body.	constant	tall	Wearable
Gyroscope	Measuring the angular velocity of the rotating object according to the principle of angular momentum conservation.	permanent	low	Wearable
clamminess sensor	Measuring the angular velocity of the rotating object according to the principle of angular momentum conservation.	distinct	exceptionally low	Wearable
Blood oxygen dispersion sensor	Estimating mugginess as indicated by the progressions of resistivity and capacitance brought about by dampness changes.	distinct	little	Wearable
heaviness sensor	Estimating blood oxygen immersion by assimilation proportion of red and infrared light going through a flimsy piece of the body.	incessant	elevated	Wearable/ Surrounding

(*Continued*)

Table 15.1 Types of sensors used in BSN. (*Continued*)

Sensors	Utility	Pointer category	Example rate of recurrence	Assignment
Respiration sensor	Estimating pressure an incentive as per the piezoelectric impact of the dielectric medium.	unremitting	elevated	Wearable
Temperature sensor	Acquiring breath boundaries in a roundabout way by recognizing the extension and compression of chest or midsection. Estimating temperature as indicated by the progressions of materials physical properties.	isolated	incredibly low	Wearable
image sensor	Catching highlights of subject, including length, check, area, and territory.	incessant/distinct	towering/small	Wearable/adjacent

15.8.2.1   Accelerometer

Accelerometers are utilized to quantify the speeding up of a section in an inertial three-dimensional organize framework. They assume a significant function in distinguishing human energy utilization and perceiving practices because of their little size, generally minimal effort, and the accommodation of having the option to incorporate into sensor network stages [22]. One of the objectives of utilizing accelerometers is to identify human energy utilization accelerometers can be acquired by relating the recurrence of physical action, the force of development, and other data to the human body [30]. The energy utilization can be concluded from a progression of calculations dependent on the data acquired from the accelerometer. Compared to different techniques that solitary utilizes a pass meter or pulse screen, this strategy is more exact and has become a pattern in identifying energy utilization [41]. Presently, the most precise force utilization device is called Live Pod [42] and it utilizes a 3-pivot accelerometer to recognize the development of the human body toward any path utilizing a shrewd haze calculation. 97% of exactness can be accomplished by utilizing a high-accuracy customization model for power utilization figurings. Contrasted with Live unit, the exactness of existing hunt models ought to be improved.

Contrasted with identifying human energy consumption, conduct acknowledgement is considerably more intricate because it utilizes accel-erometers and other inertial sensors to perceive the heading and edge of development and different boundaries of development. What's more, the sign preparing measure is more perplexing as the movement data must be removed from the crude sensor information [43]. When all is said in done, accelerometers work with spinners and magnetometers to make more exact estimations, yet this isn't outright. In Ref. [44], a sort of inertial estimation unit (IMU) called EcoIMU is introduced which just uses an accelerometer and can precisely gauge direct increasing speed and rakish speed. Worked as a couple of 3-pivot accelerometers, it expands the accel-erometer's inclusion from relative movement following to total movement following. Moreover, the utilization of an accelerometer essentially dimin-ishes the force utilization and cost of an IMU meeting the alluring low force attributes of BSN. Reference [22] demonstrates that the acknowledgement of the conduct regularly requires a few sensor hubs. The more hubs you use, the more exactness you get, yet the harder it gets. Subsequently, in the field of BSN sensors lately, finding the most appropriate situating area for sensor hubs has become a hotly debated issue of exploration to precisely distinguish development with just a couple of hubs.

15.8.2.2   ECG Sensors

ECG sensors are utilized in electronic wellbeing frameworks to screen ECG signals, which are the essential methods for diagnosing coronary ill-ness. The ECG signal mirrors the adjustment in current quality through the skin because of contractile action of the heart after some time, which can be effective, recorded utilizing non-intrusive anodes on the chest or appendages of the heart, Body [38]. It tends to be spoken to as an example of occasional ECG waveforms with various recurrence content, for exam-ple, QRS complex, P and T waves, which show the overall mood of the heart and shortcomings in different pieces of the muscle cardiovascular. It is estimated to analyze a strange heartbeat. Among the ECG waveforms, the QRS complex mirrors the electrical activity of the heart during ventricular compression and gives itemized data on the condition of the heart [39].

ECG sensor hubs communicate information remotely, adding to better convenience. Generally, the bunches are little to the point that they can without much of a stretch adhere to the texture of mortar.

Contingent upon the sort of terminal, ECG sensors can be isolated into three classifications: wet anode sensors, dry cathode sensors, and non-contact terminal sensors. Wet cathodes were first utilized for ECG observing, however, are once in a while utilized in BSN today. This sort of anode can cause skin disturbance and sign debasement because of lack of hydration. Then again, dry cathodes have become increasingly well known, however, are still in direct contact with the skin. Moreover, dry cathodes without the advantages of conductive gels are considerably more powerless to skin conditions and entirely defenceless to engine craftsmanship realities (MA). In Ref. [40], a kind of remote sensor with a contactless terminal is introduced. The sensor comprises a progression of capacitive terminals made on a standard printed circuit board that can deal with texture or other protection. Not at all like wet and dry contact sensors, non-contact sensors don't need direct contact with the body, so they are not completely delicate to skin conditions. Notwithstanding, for non-contact sensors, the commotion concealment prerequisites are moderately high. Examinations show that the protecting layer between the non-contact sensor and the skin can cover the attributes of little signals, for example, P waves if the layer is too thick to even consider maintaining signal quality. Furthermore, the protecting layer may cause a commotion, which should be debilitated or disposed of by a more proficient clamour end calculation.

15.8.2.3   Pressure Sensors

In BSN applications, pressure sensors are commonly used to screen changes in foot pressure progressively mode and give information to pressure examination, conduct acknowledgement and utilization recognition. power. Because of the unique situation of the human body, it is hard to incorporate weight sensors with different modules, for example, remote correspondence modules in a sensor hub. It is normally introduced inside a weight plate or exceptional insole. The weight sensor is constantly associated with an outer microcontroller using a link. In Ref. [45], a minimal effort foot pressure estimation framework was created to gauge the weight of each pelvic contact point with a compel plate to figure the contact territory. The framework intends to naturally plan custom insoles by embracing highlight extraction and example acknowledgement innovation to perceive clubfoot designs. In Ref. [46], the scientists place a compel sensor on the insole to figure development boundaries, including separation, time, net weight, speed and recurrence. Boundaries are utilized to perceive the conduct upheld by highlight extraction and Support Vector Machine (SVM) and give another approach to gauge power utilization. Notwithstanding, the proposed technique dismissed the issue of warm float because of movement which influences the precision of weight estimation. This is a critical issue in the plan of weight sensors [50].

15.8.2.4   Respiration Sensors

Not at all like the sensors appeared above, respiratory sensors from BSN normally comprise of numerous sensors, for example, a weight sensor, accelerometer, or spinner. In light of these sensors, respiratory boundaries are gotten by implication by recognizing the development and constriction of the chest or mid-region. Respiratory sensors are as yet used to treat respiratory ailments and constantly screen human side effects. In Ref. [47], a respiratory criticism framework with wearable fiber-based sensors is presented [52, 54]. The sensor procures the profundity and respiratory rate by perceiving the development and compression of the chest dependent on a sort of piezoresistive material called a carbon-containing elastomeric. Embedded in tissues or tissues, it permits clients to rehearse great breathing and treat respiratory infections. What's more, Ref. [48] proposed another technique to take care of the issue of consistent checking of breath. This technique depends on remaking every development because of breathing utilizing information from the accelerometer. Follows the pivot of turn and procures the rakish speed of the sensor hub put on the chest to accomplish exact identification of breath regardless of impedance from body developments. Be that as it may, most respiratory sensors screen respiratory boundaries without considering the stream rate and flowing volume of breath, which is the future bearing of respiratory sensor research.

15.9   Design of Sensor Nodes

Even though the sensor is a key segment of the Sensor Node, it can't work freely. To gain the sign, it must work with different modules. To fulfil the need for low force utilization and high movability, numerous issues, for example, power control, flaw analysis, sensor hub decrease, and so on must be considered in the sensor hub configuration measure.

15.9.1   Energy Control

Energy observing has for quite some time been a hotly debated issue in the field of BSN sensors to actualize long haul checking capacities. Significant current examinations incorporate low force engineering configuration, low force processor configuration, low force handset plan, and force procurement plan. In Ref. [19], programmable engineering with exceptionally low force utilization dependent on powerful time contortion has been proposed, planned explicitly for versatile inertial sensors. If the examining rate is 3 Hz and the bit goal is 4 pieces, the sensor hub can work with a force utilization of 9 µW, so the developer must be completely cognizant. Contrasted and conventional low force microcontrollers, for example, MSP430, the proposed design can diminish the force utilization of sensor hubs by multiple occasions. In Ref. [21], scientists present a low force processor plan that brings down the flexible voltage beneath the edge voltage to diminish spillage control and expand the life of rationale circuits and SRAMs. Subsequently, it is an amazing technique for energy obliged frameworks with loosened up execution prerequisites. Be that as it may, the impacts of cycle varieties are more articulated at low voltage, particularly in enormous scope advances.

To this end, this white paper presents a framework on-chip that exhibits strategies to alleviate vacillations utilizing a planning approach that stays away from yield voltage blunders and spread postponements in rationale entryways so the framework can work at low voltage. Regarding low force handset configuration, Ref. [49] introduced a low force contact impedance sensor hub called CIS which consolidates a productive handset that utilizes the human body as a sort of help. transmission. The proposed CIS embraces LC reverberation based capacitance detecting innovation which consequently kills the handset on or by recognizing the wanderer capacitance between the terminal and the human body. It can make up for debasement in channel quality brought about by changes in contact impedance, accordingly significantly decreasing the force utilization of LNA (Low Noise Amplifier) by over 70%. Furthermore, the energy procurement configuration can help the sensor hub to gather energy without anyone else. For instance, a natural power device can change over synthetic energy into electrical energy utilizing biocatalysts. In Ref. [15], scientists guarantee that natural glucose power devices can gather energy from enzymatic compound responses that happen in the human body.

15.9.2   Fault Diagnosis

Even though the BSN comprises of numerous sensors, the identification and disengagement of bombed hubs can't be disregarded as a bombed sensor can influence generally speaking framework execution. One arrangement is to distinguish this by contrasting the substance between adjoining hubs. Ref. [20] demonstrates that the location precision diminishes as the number of sensor hubs diminishes. Additionally, since the quantity of hubs in the BSN is moderately little and there are scarcely any circumstances where different sensors of a similar sort are applied to gather signals from a similar area, the previously mentioned strategy is more appropriate for WSN than BSN. It doesn't function admirably in the last mentioned. Another test is finding reasonable neighbours for information approval to lessen bogus cautions. In Ref. [21], the creator proposes a more reasonable way to deal with a section of the sensor stream into portions utilizing sliding window innovation and giving a blunder location calculation dependent on these fragments. The proposed blunder location calculation can be partitioned into two sub-classifications: history-based and non-history-based. The disappointment identification pace of the previous is more steady and the last can help check the previous.

15.9.3   Reduction of Sensor Nodes

The decrease of sensor hubs is planned for inertial sensors to conduct acknowledgement. In addition to the fact that it improves the attack of the conduct acknowledgement framework, however, it lessens costs, spares energy, rearranges the acknowledgement cycle and diminishes information repetition [53]. The principle approach to tackle the issue is to advance the situation of the hubs and improve the movement acknowledgement calculation. Presently, some exploration ventures consider the enhancement of hub situating as one of the fundamental examination issues in the field of social acknowledgement in BSN. In the book index [22], the writers propose a few plans on the best way to put wearable sensors for different body developments and give an ideal image of hub position. The structure can likewise assist you with finding the most pertinent groups in constantly recurrence capacities gathered by the compact accelerometer. In this article, the writers partition the cycle of the explanatory strategy into three phases: include extraction, highlight determination, and order. It at that point positions exercises dependent on different information works and gives the best positioning framework to each kind of movement. Not at all like the previously mentioned strategy, Ref. [51] proposes a technique for decreasing the number of sensor hubs by improving the action acknowledgement calculation. The creators have additionally demonstrated that the issue is NP-hard. Notwithstanding, they give a conduct acknowledgement model that utilizes a choice tree to limit the number of hubs associated with characterizing every conduct. This technique diminishes ties by 72.4% while keeping up a levelling precision of 93.3%.

15.10   Applications of BSNs

As exploration develops and grows, BSN innovation is turning out to be increasingly adult and broadly utilized in numerous fields including medication, social work, game and human-machine interfaces, as appeared in the figure given underneath. It can likewise be found in different fields, military, diversion and mechanical frameworks, and BSN applications, refer in Figure 15.7.

15.11   Conclusions

Outfitted with sensors in and around the human body, BSN understands the identification of human body conduct and physiological data, which is generally utilized in fields, for example, medication, wellbeing, sports and amusement. How to bring the human body into a correspondence organization? Consequently, BSN has expansive application prospects and market potential.

BSN has been an examination operational hub with the coming of numerous pragmatic applications, yet numerous issues remain. For

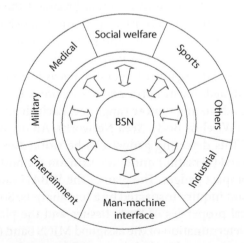

Figure 15.7 Application fields of BSNs.

instance, when planning a sensor hub, more consideration must be paid to limiting the hub size and lessening power utilization. Originators should put specific accentuation on staying away from the danger of human tissue harm because of warmth created by embedded sensors. When planning information preparing calculations and correspondence conventions, it is important to take care of a similar issue of intensity utilization and organization power brought about by hub development. Besides, because of the cosy connection among BSN and human wellbeing, there are good and legitimate imperatives on commonsense applications. To put it plainly, BSN speaks to a multidisciplinary joining pointed toward tackling many key issues over various controls, which expects scientists to accomplish more exploration. This article portrays BSN ideas, sources, design and examination territories with a thorough prologue to current BSN applications and issues. Specifically, it centres around the condition of examination, improvement patterns and difficulties of sensor innovation, information combination innovation and organization correspondence innovation. What's more, different angles, for example, information security and nature of administration ought to likewise be improved and summed up.

Moving Towards Body-to-Body Sensor Networks

15.12   Introduction

As far as network, as interest for the present Internet of Things (IoT) framework builds, individuals associated are probably going to shape an up and coming access. An organization that broadens the scope of IoT by arriving at omnipresent applications in genuine time (Healthcare, social cooperation, sports and amusement, and so forth), in this way guaranteeing whenever, anyplace associate individuals. In this specific circumstance, the utilization of similar organization endorsers as transfers can be incorporated and broadened. Existing framework network by improving organization limit and advancing remote range use. Each client is outfitted with a remote WBAN (Wireless Body Area Network). An organization of little figuring gadgets. This detecting gadget can be worked inside the human body either mounted (versatile) under the skin, on the body or worn by an individual as a compact gadget. The plan of the WBAN radio wire is additionally a significant inquiry inspected by a few analysts. Some have zeroed in on the electrical properties of body tissues and the plan of the body's recieving wires. Determination of the assigned MICS band (402–405 MHz) for intra-body interchanges [8, 9]. Others are keen on planning a reception apparatus on the body [10, 11] to create a channel model. Situation based way to deal with improve the normal channel increase estimated for each connection on the body (From head to belt, head to wrist, belt to wrist, and so forth.). Next to no has been done to describe.

Models of out-of-body channels [12–14] and skirmish [15, 16], including inside and outer conditions, body shadow and human versatility in the modern, logical and clinical (ISM) band without license (2.45 GHz) others have grouped WBAN advances according to WBAN correspondences. Three-segment design: inside WBAN, WBAN-to-WBAN and prevalent WBAN correspondence, and we have tackled different issues identified with each [6, 17]. WBAN applications have been featured in the greater part of the writing studies and arranged in the clinical field. Also, for non-clinical use [6, 18, 19] or *in vivo* and *in vivo* applications [5, 9, 19].

Mobility prediction: WBAN connectivity may change in mobile scenarios, as a result, network performance suffers [28]. When WBAN mobility can be predicted most connection errors can be avoided before the service is terminated.BBN application quality. The mobility prediction mechanism allows the network layer to ensures reliable routing and allocation of network resources.

Security: Security and protection concerns are a hotly debated issue for BBN due to its suggestions for human data. Biomedical sensor embedded in the human body for clinical purposes screen, speak with encompassing WBAN and outside organizations. This expands the security danger of BBN [29]. There are a few investigations that lead to the furthest reaches of consequently, the at present proposed security arrangement requires further exploration. In this review, we talk about different security answers to apply to some BBN applications. A significant number of these issues have been inspected in the writing and summed up as follows.

15.12.1   From WBANs to BBNs

Especially due to the advent of telemedicine solutions in developed countries WBAN, which supports a growing elderly population and reduces the cost of these services, especially with the development of the IEEE 802.15.6 standard, it is still a strong research area. Still moving from single-function WBANs to cooperative WBANs that make up a large BBN You are likely to face several problems, some of which are discussed in this section.

15.12.2   Overview of WBAN

WBAN is a remote body network comprised of various sorts of sensors to screen substantial capacity. These sensors can be connected to the body or embedded under the skin relocated is agreeable and doesn't meddle with typical exercises. The figure given beneath shows a case of a patient checking framework utilizing WBAN. The primary undertaking of the Sensor Node is to gather and impart data about physical activity to a far off worker for investigation. The actuator sensor likewise measures the gathered information and after that. WBAN permits constant ongoing status checking, distant clinical records. On the off chance that a crisis is distinguished, the patient can be educated promptly clinical workforce to send messages or alarms.

15.12.3 Architecture

In Ref. [38], emergency clinic specialized gadgets are grouped into three classes Communication model. At correspondence level 1, every sensor hub in the WBAN gathers information and Send to WBAN organizer. At correspondence level 2 WBAN. The following bounce is WBAN, clinical showcase organizer, nursing station facilitator, or cell gadgets. At last, the layer 2 correspondence is shipped off the layer 3 specialized devices: 3G Tower, Nursing Device, Application Server or Cloud Server on the Internet. Another characterization utilized in the WBAN design alludes to interior WBAN, extra WBAN, and WBAN or more Communication speaks to pretty much a similar model of correspondence refer Figure 15.8.

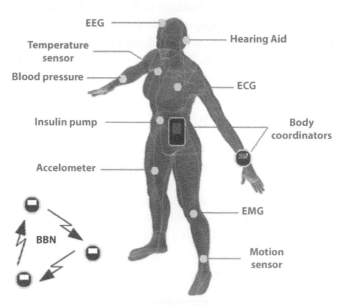

Figure 15.8 Example of patient monitoring using a wireless body area network (WBAN).

15.12.4   Standards

There are various principles utilized by WBAN to empower correspondence between various sensor hubs and between WBAN organizers and outer gadgets more the standard known and utilized in the business is IEEE 802.15.6 [39, 40], which is a low force radio. This is a short separation transmission innovation from WBAN with an information pace of roughly 10 Mbps. The standard offers the chance of lessening the pace of assimilation of sign radiation (SAR) by the body.

At that point, IEEE 802.15.4 (ZigBee) [41] is a notable norm for WBAN. Interconnection of low information rate specialized gadgets with low force and long battery life, It can give low intricacy short-range radio recurrence (RF) transmission. Likewise, different principles are additionally utilized in the WBAN, for example, the BLE (Bluetooth Low Energy) standard [42]. It can run at focus recurrence to lessen cover with channels 1, 6 and 11. The IEEE 802.11 standard is utilized to alleviate impedance with them.

15.12.5   Applications

WBAN applications are characterized by their region of utilization. In what follows, we
The principle class [2, 4].

- Medical Treatment and Diagnosis: There are a few instances of utilizing the WBAN for analysis and therapy much exploration is progressing here. Use case: cardiovascular sickness (CVD), diabetes, asthma, Parkinson's illness, and so on.
- Training program for proficient competitors: using hardware to help competitors preparing and progress checking and execution advancement.
- Public security and counteraction of clinical mishaps: numerous individuals kick the bucket each year. Keep records of past clinical episodes utilizing sensor hubs up to clinical occurrences you can lessen the number of passings.
- Protection of the formally dressed workforce: WBAN can be utilized by firemen, police or warriors keep on checking in unsafe conditions. For instance, the fire detachment WBAN can recognize the presence and level of dangerous

gases with regards to battling fires give this data to your colleagues.
- Consumer Electronics and Entertainment: Some WBAN gadgets can be incorporated into electronic gadgets hardware, head-mounted presentations, amplifiers, cameras, and so forth.

15.13   Body-to-Body Network Concept

BBNs are a set of WBANs that communicate with neighbouring WBANs via the coordinator device acts as a gateway to share sensor data between WBANs. The BBN is therefore theoretically an ad hoc mobile network that uses people to transmit data-limited geographic area. Therefore, the radio signal is closest to a WBAN can Keep going until you reach your destination, whether using a WBAN, BBN-enabled Smartphone or smartwatch. BBN is a new communication solution between patients and healthcare professionals the exchange of data between WBANs allows data sharing for performance estimates, statistics or routes to a certain destination. BBN network for group monitoring the number of cyclists is shown in Figure 15.9.

At BBN, all clients work together and add to arrange assets different organization clients make broad agreeable correspondences between associations for incredible advantages from the organization. Utilizing BBNs in thickly populated territories permits versatile administrators to do so particularly with the coming of "whenever, anyplace" IoT availability and gigabit information rates, constant applications show up as the interest for information rates increments. For instance, the creator of Ref. [43] we investigate IoT-based ways to deal with actualize brilliant medical services arrangements and reexamine present-day medical services. We use WBAN with specialized, financial and social points of view. Wellbeing IoT environment it is additionally figured in Ref. [23] in the wellbeing based cloud, permitting far off patients to do so home clinical post (IHHS). In a

Figure 15.9 Melee networking for monitoring the performance of a group of athletes.

later report [44] of energy effective scuffle correspondence with the cloud-empowered WBAN is actualized to procure information from the patient sensor nearest AP to get to cloud assets. Indeed, the nature of the connection among WBAN and AP is It deteriorates with expanding separation. Consequently, correspondence between bodies is Increment availability and information move speeds in these circumstances.

15.14 Conclusions

In this study, we have given a concise diagram of the WBAN and current WBAN related contributions application accessible at BBN. Four plan difficulties: energy effectiveness, versatility reductive, Quos and security. Talk about existing business related to WBAN and BBN regard to feature the fundamental highlights of the BBN plan. The energy issue is hot contentions for WBAN and BBN. Notwithstanding a solitary WBAN revelation movement energy is spent on sensor information communicated between coinciding WBANs. At that point, the BBN Energy profile must consider the energy segment of the transmission.

It underpins WBAN geography changes and WBAN portability around BBNs. More a fascinating QoS prerequisite for BBN is QoS planning for heterogeneous BBN gadgets. Notwithstanding a definitive postponement and steadiness imperatives, this can significantly affect your traffic wellbeing based application Careful portability the executives is basic to guarantee smooth versatility Transmission of sensor information in unique situations. The fundamental versatility highlights to be embraced include: WBAN wandering exchange component to deal with channel exchanging and forestall associations disappointment. Likewise, the WBAN versatility model the interior and outside situations must be considered distinctively as per the developments of the human body. The spread qualities of the radio channel are not the equivalent. Generally Problem, the BBN needs an exacting security strategy. Above all else, keep away from restricted-energy assets.

This is to secure the action of the BBN itself from noxious assaults, particularly if it is wellbeing focused. This is because human life is straightforwardly included. At long last, a few applicant conventions It was affirmed and other exploration questions were likewise examined. Subsequently, empowering between WBAN BBN grows its current foundation to offer imaginative types of assistance. Different side advantages from games and amusement to the pervasive clinical and salvage groups perilous circumstances or military applications, and so on. To accomplish these objectives, our consistent work Compilation of the recently referenced proposition to execute the WBAN between directing convention Increase research motivators for compelling BBN appropriation.

References

1. Lianos, M. *et al.*, Dangerization and the End of Deviance: The Institutional Environment. *Br. J. Criminol.*, 40, 261–278, 2000.
2. Aggarwal, R. *et al.*, RFID Security in the Context of "Internet of Things". *First International Conference on Security of Internet of Things*, Kerala, 17-19 August 2012, pp. 51–56, 2012, http://dx.doi.org/10.1145/2490428.2490435.
3. Gigli, M. *et al.*, Internet of Things, Services and Applications Categorization. *Adv. Internet Things*, 1, 27–31, 2011, http://dx.doi.org/10.4236/ait.2011.12004.
4. *The Internet of Things*, 7th Edition, ITU Internet Reports, International Telecommunication Union, Press Conference (webcast) held at WSIS in Tunis, Tunisia on 17 November 2005, www.itu.int/internetofthings/on.
5. Chen, M., Gonzalez, S., Vasilakos, A., Cao, H., Leung, V.C.M., Body area networks: A survey. *Mobile Netw. Appl.*, 16, 171–193, Internet of Things Global Standards Initiative. ITU, 2010, Retrieved 26 June 2015. 13.
6. Cooney, M.J., Svoboda, V., Lau, C., Martin, G., Minteer, S.D., Enzyme catalysed biofuel cells. *Energy Environ. Sci.*, 1, 320–337, 2008.
7. Kwong, J., Ramadass, Y.K., Verma, N., Chandrakasan, A.P., A 65 nm sub-Vt microcontroller with integrated SRAM and switched capacitor DC-DC converter. *IEEE J. Solid State Circuits*, 44, 115–126, 2009.
8. Liolios, C., Doukas, C., Fourlas, G., Maglogiannis, I., An Overview of Body Sensor Networks in Enabling Pervasive Healthcare and Assistive Environments, in: *Proceedings of the 3rd International Conference on PErvasive Technologies Related to Assistive Environments*, Samos, Greece, 23–25 June 2010.
9. Ma, Q. and Hou, X.H., Study of wireless sensor node's structure. *Sci. Technol. Inf.*, 24, 371–436, 2008.
10. Nie, Z.D., Ma, J.J., Li, Z.C., Chen, H., Wang, L., Dynamic propagation channel characterization and modeling for human body communication. *Sensors*, 12, 17569–17587, 2012.
11. *IEEE Standard for Local and Metropolitan Area Networks. Part 15.6: Wireless Body Area Networks*; IEEE Std 802.15.6-2012, IEEE, New York, NY, USA, 2012.
12. Liu, X., Zheng, Y.J., Phyu, M.W., Zhao, B., Yuan, X.J., Power and Area Efficient Wavelet-Based On-Chip ECG Processor for WBAN, in: *Proceedings of the 2010 International Conference on Body Sensor Networks (BSN)*, Biopolis, Singapore, 7–9 June 2010, pp. 124–130.

13. Valchinov, E. and Pallikarakis, N., An active electrode for biopotential recording from small localized bio-sources. *Biomed. Eng. Online*, 3, 116–123, 2004.

14. Chi, Y.M. and Cauwenberghs, G., Wireless Non-Contact EEG/ECG Electrodes for Body Sensor Networks, in: *Proceedings of 2010 International Conference on Body Sensor Networks (BSN)*, Biopolis, Singapore, 7–9 June 2010, pp. 297–301.

15. Zhu, G.Z., Wei, C.H., Pan, M., The research of energy expenditure detection algorithm based on tri-axial acceleration transducer. *Chin. J. Sens. Actuators*, 8, 1217–1222, 2011.

16. Zhao, Z.Z., Chen, P.Y., Qiu, Y.W., Reliability and validity of LivePod LP2 in measuring energy expending during treading walking and running. *China Sport Sci.*, 32, 48–53, 2012.

17. Krishnan, N.C., Juillard, C., Colbry, D., Panchanathan, S., Recognition of hand movements using wearable accelerometers. *J. Ambient Intell. Smart Environ.*, 1, 143–155, 2009.

18. Tsai, Y.L., Tu, T.T., Bac, H., Chou, P.H., EcoIMU: A Dual Triaxial-Accelerometer Inertial Measurement Unit for Wearable Applications, in: *Proceedings of the 2010 International Conference on Body Sensor Networks (BSN)*, Biopolis, Singapore, 7–9 June 2010, pp. 207–212.

19. Liu, C., Zhang, T., Zhao, G.R., Wen, T.X., Wang, L., Clubfoot Pattern Recognition towards Personalized Insole Design, in: *Proceedings of the 2010 International Conference on Body Sensor Network (BSN)*, Singapore, 7–9 June 2010, pp. 273–276.

20. Shi, X., Xiong, Q.Y., Lei, L.N., Study on human motion recognition method based on pressure sensor. *Chin. J. Sci. Instrum.*, 6, 1429–1434, 2010.

21. Mitchell, E., Coyle, S., O'Connor, N.E., Diamond, D., Ward, T., Breathing Feedback System with Wearable Textile Sensors, in: *Proceedings of the 2010 International Conference on Body Sensor Network (BSN)*, Biopolis, Singapore, 7–9 June 2010, pp. 56–61.

22. Bates, A., Ling, M.J., Mann, J., Arvind, D.K., Respiratory Rate and Flow Waveform Estimation from Tri-Axial Accelerometer Data, in: *Proceedings of the 2010 International Conference on Body Sensor Network (BSN)*, Biopolis, Singapore, 7–9 June 2010, pp. 144–150.

23. Song, K., Bae, J., Yan, L., Yoo, H.J., A 20 μW Contact Impedance Sensor for Wireless Body-Area-Network Transceiver, in: *Proceedings of the 2011 IEEE Custom Integrated Circuits Conference (CICC)*, San Jose, CA, USA, 19–21 September 2011, pp. 1–4.

24. Akyildiz, I.F., Su, W., Sankarasubramaniam, Y., Cayirci, E., Wireless sensor networks: A survey. *Comput. Netw.*, 38, 393–422, 2002.24.

25. Korel, B.T. and Koo, S.G.M., Addressing Context Awareness Techniques in Body Sensor Networks, in: *Proceedings of the 21st International Conference on Advanced Information Networking and Applications Workshops*, Niagara Falls, ON, USA, 21–23 May 2007, pp. 798–803.

26. Thiemjarus, S., Lo, B., Yang, G.Z., A Spatio-Temporal Architecture for Context Aware Sensing, in: *Proceedings of the International Workshop on Wearable and Implantable Body Sensor Networks*, Cambridge, MA, USA, April 2006, 3–5.

27. Natarajan, A., Motani, M., de Silva, B., Yap, K.K., Chua, K., Investigating Network Architectures for Body Sensor Networks, in: *Proceedings of the 1st ACM SIGMOBILE international Workshop on Systems and Networking Support For Healthcare and Assisted Living Environments (HealthNet 2007)*, San Juan, Puerto Rico, 11 June 2007, pp. 19–24.

28. Tachtatzis, C., Graham, B., Tracey, D., Timmons, N.F., Morrison, J., On-Body to On-Body Channel Characterization, in: *Proceedings of 2011 IEEE Sensors Conference*, Limerick, Ireland, 28–31 October 2011, pp. 908–911.

29. Liolios, C., Doukas, C., Fourlas, G., Maglogiannis, I., An Overview of Body Sensor Networks in Enabling Pervasive Healthcare and Assistive Environments, in: *Proceedings of the 3rd International Conference on PErvasive Technologies Related to Assistive Environments*, Samos, Greece, June 2010, 23–25.

30. Ullah, S., Higgins, H., Braem, B., Latre, B., Blondia, C., Moerman, I., Saleem, S., Rahma, K.S., A comprehensive survey of wireless body area networks: On PHY, MAC, and network layers solutions. *J. Med. Syst.*, 36, 1065–1094, 2010.

31. Ma, Q. and Hou, X.H., Study of wireless sensor node's structure. *Sci. Technol. Inf.*, 24, 371–436, 2008.

32. Gong, J.B., Wang, R., Cui, L., Research advances and challenges of body sensor network (BSN), *J. Comput. Res. Dev.*, 5, 737–753, 2010.

33. Nie, Z.D., Ma, J.J., Li, Z.C., Chen, H., Wang, L., Dynamic propagation channel characterization and modeling for human body communication. *Sensors*, 12, 17569–17587, 2012.

34. *IEEE Standard for Local and Metropolitan Area Networks. Part 15.6: Wireless Body Area Networks*; IEEE Std 802.15.6-2012, IEEE, New York, NY, USA, 2012.

35. Liu, X., Zheng, Y.J., Phyu, M.W., Zhao, B., Yuan, X.J., Power and Area Efficient Wavelet-Based On-Chip ECG Processor for WBAN, in: *Proceedings of the 2010 International Conference on Body Sensor Networks (BSN)*, Biopolis, Singapore, 7–9 June 2010, pp. 124–130.

36. Valchinov, E. and Pallikarakis, N., An active electrode for biopotential recording from small localized bio-sources. *Biomed. Eng. Online*, 3, 2004.

37. Chi, Y.M. and Cauwenberghs, G., Wireless Non-Contact EEG/ECG Electrodes for Body Sensor Networks, in: *Proceedings of 2010 International Conference on Body Sensor Networks (BSN)*, Biopolis, Singapore, 7–9 June 2010, pp. 297–301.

38. Zhu, G.Z., Wei, C.H., Pan, M., The research of energy expenditure detection algorithm based on tri-axial acceleration transducer. *Chin. J. Sens. Actuators*, 8, 1217–1222, 2011.

39. Zhao, Z.Z., Chen, P.Y., Qiu, Y.W., Reliability and validity of LivePod LP2 in measuring energy expending during treading walking and running. *China Sport Sci.*, *32*, 48–53, 2012.

40. Krishnan, N.C., Juillard, C., Colbry, D., Panchanathan, S., Recognition of hand movements using wearable accelerometers. *J. Ambient Intell. Smart Environ.*, *1*, 143–155, 2009.

41. Tsai, Y.L., Tu, T.T., Bae, H., Chou, P.H., EcoIMU: A Dual Triaxial-Accelerometer Inertial Measurement Unit for Wearable Applications, in: *Proceedings of the 2010 International Conference on Body Sensor Networks (BSN)*, Biopolis, Singapore, 7–9 June 2010, pp. 207–212.

42. Liu, C., Zhang, T., Zhao, G.R., Wen, T.X., Wang, L., Clubfoot Pattern Recognition towards Personalized Insole Design, in: *Proceedings of the 2010 International Conference on Body Sensor Network (BSN)*, Singapore, 7–9 June 2010, pp. 273–276.

43. Shi, X., Xiong, Q.Y., Lei, L.N., Study on human motion recognition method based on pressure sensor. *Chin. J. Sci. Instrum.*, *6*, 1429–1434, 2010.

44. Mitchell, E., Coyle, S., O'Connor, N.E., Diamond, D., Ward, T., Breathing Feedback System with Wearable Textile Sensors, in: *Proceedings of the 2010 International Conference on Body Sensor Network (BSN)*, Biopolis, Singapore, 7–9 June 2010, pp. 56–61.

45. Bates, A., Ling, M.J., Mann, J., Arvind, D.K., Respiratory Rate and Flow Waveform Estimation from Tri-Axial Accelerometer Data, in: *Proceedings of the 2010 International Conference on Body Sensor Network (BSN)*, Biopolis, Singapore, 7–9 June 2010, pp. 144–150.

46. Song, K., Bae, J., Yan, L., Yoo, H.J., A 20 µW Contact Impedance Sensor for Wireless Body-Area-Network Transceiver, in: *Proceedings of the 2011 IEEE Custom Integrated Circuits Conference (CICC)*, San Jose, CA, USA, 19–21 September 2011, pp. 1–4.

47. Kim, D.J. and Prabhakaran, B., Motion Fault Detection and Isolation in Body Sensor Networks, in: *Proceedings of the 9th Annual IEEE International Conference on Pervasive Computing and Communications (PerCom 2011)*, Seattle, WA, USA, 21–25 March 2011, pp. 727–745.

48. Ghasemzadeh, H. and Jafari, R., Physical movement monitoring using body sensor networks: A phonological approach to construct spatial decision trees. *IEEE Trans. Ind. Inf.*, *7*, 66–77, 2011.

49. Patel, M. and Wang, J., Applications, challenges, and prospective in emerging body area networking technologies. *IEEE Wirel. Commun.*, *17*, 80–88, 2010.

50. Higgins, H., Wireless Communication, in: *Body Sensor Networks*, G.Z. Yang, (Ed.), pp. 117–143, Springer-Verlag, London, UK, 117–143, 2006.

51. Nakamura, E.F., Loureiro, A.A.F., Frery, A.C., Information fusion for wireless sensor networks: Methods, models, and classifications. *ACM Comput. Surv.*, *39*, 2007.

52. Lin, K., Chen, M., Rodrigues, J.P.C., Ge, H.W., System Design and Data Fusion in Body Sensor Networks, in: *Telemedicine and E-Health Services,*

Policies, and Applications: Advancements and Developments, vol. 1, J.J.P.C. Rodrigues, I.T. Díez, B.S. Abajo, (Eds.), pp. 1–25, IGI Global, Hershey, PA, USA, 2012.

53. Liggnis, M.E., Hall, D.L., Llinas, J., *Handbook of Multisensor Data Fusion*, 2nd ed., pp. 19–22, CRC Press, Boca Raton, FL, USA, 2008.

54. Luprano, J., Sola, J., Dasen, S., Koller, J.M., Chetelat, O., Combination of Body Sensor Networks and On-Body Signal Processing Algorithms: The Practical Case of MyHeart Project, in: *Proceedings of the International Workshop on Wearable and Implantable Body Sensor Networks*, Cambridge, MA, USA, 3–5 April 2006, pp. 4–79.

DCMM: A Data Capture and Risk Management for Wireless Sensing Using IoT Platform

Siripuri Kiran[1]*, Bandi Krishna[2], Janga Vijaykumar[3] and Sridhar manda[4]

[1]Department of Computer Science and Engineering,
Kakatiya Institute of Technology and Science, Warangal, India
[2]Dept. of CSE, Vaagdevi College of Engineering, Warangal, India
[3]Bule Hora University, Oromia, Ethiopia
[4]University of Mysore, Mysore, India

Abstract

Through the aid of advanced electronic tools, the Internet of Things offers best ways of experiencing and responding to the outside world. At the same time, with the help of sensor information, there will be new problems and obstacles as new application scenarios are envisaged. It investigates further developments, such as the interoperability between heterogeneous devices and confidence on smart devices, to meet business and technical requirements such as validity, safety, and trust. The construction of infrastructure to meet these requirements becomes critical by growing these complex requirements. An IoT middleware software bridges the gap between devices and ICs. This thesis aims to analyze, to automate the collection and reanalysis of data, which may be used by a variety of applications such as manufacturing, the mechanisms, and methods for data collection, interoperability, and data filters.

Keywords: Data acquisition, data filtering, IoT, middleware, sensors, interoperability

*Corresponding author: sk.cse@kitsw.ac.in

R. Anandan, G. Suseendran, S. Balamurugan, Ashish Mishra and D. Balaganesh (eds.) Human Communication Technology: Internet of Robotic Things and Ubiquitous Computing, (435–462) © 2022 Scrivener Publishing LLC

16.1 Introduction

In the last few years, the use of devices for data collection for a variety of applications has increased enormously. It is focused on data obtained from the real world via sensors, making it accessible everywhere and as diverse as the current on the market variety of data collection tools. The IoT encompasses a broad range of fields, as seen in Figure 16.1. These demonstrate not only that core innovations are needed to evolve, but also that new business models, management approaches and new methods of information security and privacy are created and created.

The projected connections between devices would be approximately 21 billion by 2020, 7 billion of which are not linked to the consumer market, but the usage of industrial devices. The technological advancement stems mainly from a continuous search for full performance, which is pursued by many companies to increase their self-management both in data tracking

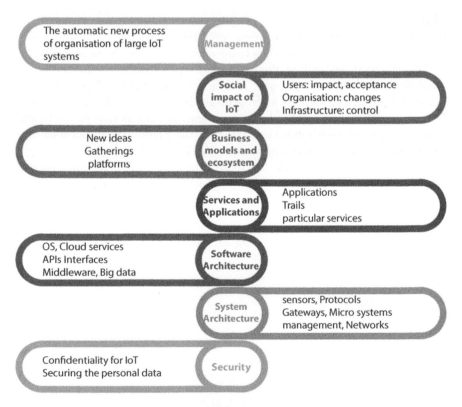

Figure 16.1 Technology characteristics of the IoT.

and management and in control. By keeping this in mind, businesses seek solutions in three main areas:

i. Network security—emphasis on hardware consistency and trustworthiness, such as routers and servers
ii. System maintenance—focusing on software quality and reliability, such as data interpretation and the programming of operating systems.
iii. Management of the specification, both protection, and operability, is elegant and comfortable.

To compare these three areas and thereby minimize integration and management problems, one of the approaches that can be handled is Middleware technology—a software layer of two systems that enable contact between these two. Figure 16.2 illustrates two different methods for gathering and combining heterogonous tools. Primarily, this work aims to contribute to improving data collection methodology from different devices by considering improvement across uniformity of data access, optimization of communication, and central authentication of connected devices. This project aims at offering a solution to combine IoT devices with cloud-based applications with less effort for high-end data processing and data analytics.

The scope of this project also includes Within the scope of this research; it is intended to provide solutions that can provide added value to boost production lines, increase interoperability, and self-management in the manufacturing industry through affordable technology for SMEs [1].

The problem this work proposes to examine is part of a vast subject, covering many technical concepts. Therefore, an explicit definition and

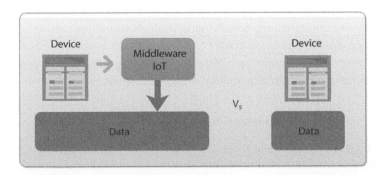

Figure 16.2 Middleware-based vs. Direct data collection approach through source devices.

building the background on which the research-based will be relevant [2]. In formatting the basis for this work, the following sub-sections include state of the art on various aspects of IoT considered for creation and study in the framework of this research.

16.2   Background

16.2.1   Internet of Things

IoT is a dynamic universal network with capability of self-configuring based on the standard and interoperable communication protocols [3]. This concept considers the omnipresence around us in the world of several devices through wireless and wired connections, and specific addressing schemes can communicate and collaborate with other tools to build new applications/services and achieve common goals. The five major factors rising the IoT-related values are:

i.   Rising policy development returns, reducing time for marketing, generating new business models and opportunities.
ii.   Better services to customers and gain more customers.
iii. An intelligent interface.
iv.   Departmental stores with reduced costs.
v.   Improve productivity and performance.

The understanding of IoT affects multiple fields and stakeholders. In auto-diagnostics and asset management through sensors mounted in machines that allow quick responses to detected problems and remote monitoring of elements such as temperature, materials, and humidity, the related values in the manufacturing industry, which are the main target of this paper, gain auto-adjustment [4]. The IoT potential is explored with examples of crucial changes such as inventory reduction, electricity, and automated device costs less costly to produce and introduce. IoT's scope also applies to automatic machinery control, monitoring, self-healing, available resources, product quality, and other services.

16.2.2   Middleware Data Acquisition

The goal of IoT is to build a unified model for interaction with devices as it provides an abstract layer that interposes the IT and application infrastructure [5]. In short, an IoT middleware is an end-to-end network for linking items or devices that are made up of eight architectural blocks, which are database, external interface, analytics, additional tools, data visualization, device management, processing, and connectivity [6]. Generic features have been defined to build a data collection system from RW resources:

- Include the IoT data collection infrastructure.
- Offering a flexible network and geographical location and features independent of the devices.
- Data extraction strategies for monitoring the flow of data through the database.
- Data channel protection (where authenticated data flows).
- Aid should be available for various communication protocols.

16.2.3   Context Acquisition

Sensors are hardware elements that measures the environmental variables such as temperature, moisture, position and machine status in digital signal processing time and more. Softwares to help with the specific tasks access this information [7, 8]. Therefore the context-conscious computation in IoT model is an essential factor in a data collection system.

Back growing data from a small number of physical sensors (hardware) and virtual (software) were collected by most of the proposed solutions. In these circumstances, it was necessary and feasible to obtain and analyze sensor data from all sources due to small numbers. Sensors are supposed to be connected to all the devices through the internet with the advancement of sensor hardware. Hence all the information obtained by these sensors cannot be processed.

Context control in software systems has become an essential feature. Data is shifting from phase to phase, from the generation location to the consumption location to create a data life cycle. The meaning movement in background information systems is taken into consideration in Figure 16.3. The priority in this work is the context-aware definition since we handle pre-filtering data and physical sensors.

16.3   Architecture

16.3.1   Proposed Architecture

Many sensors and actuators communicate with the system in an industrial IoT scenario [9]. A microcontroller, which acquires data or controls

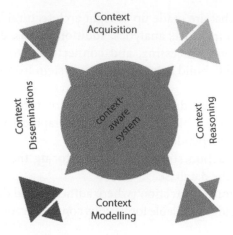

Figure 16.3 Context-aware system.

a switch by a predefined instruction set, is connected to every sensor and activator. The sensor node is called the microcontroller, along with the sensors, the power unit, and a radio antenna. The data generated by sensors is a self-contained, deployable device [10]. In general, the sensor node has not the capacity, memory, and storage needed to handle the data locally, as in the case of the microcontroller in this dissertation. And the machines capable of handling it must interact. In this thesis, it was a Raspberry Pi computer chosen to implement the hub that acts as a multiple raw data aggregators created by the sensor nodes. Two significant problems addressed by this IoT framework are:

- Data processing and standardization, the sensor nodes produce the data sets in different formats. This acquires multi-sensor node heterogeneous datasets and transforms them into a standard form recognized during the next step of the processing pipeline.
- Transformation of the protocol. It supports several communication protocols to accept the incoming data transmitted by the sensor nodes. It uses an outbound REST mechanism, which sends the data to a cloud process.

The IoT-based continuous data collection program includes a technique and software that can capture and pre-process data from different sources and transfer them to the cloud service system for Data Collection. Then, without any understanding of the data sources, all data consumers can access data

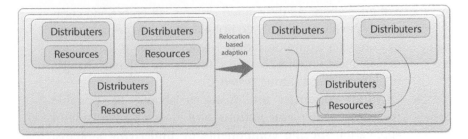

Figure 16.4 Software components relocation adaptation.

uniformly via the DCf-provided APIs. The developed architecture considered scalability, interoperability, adaptation, and plug-and-play between the source and the hub. Figure 16.4 gives the architecture of the IoT framework.

The three principal components of the IoT core, which can be differentiated briefly in Figure 16.4, have different functions generally

i.   Protocol Adaption
ii. Data Management
iii. Data Handler

16.3.1.1   Protocol Adaption

This part provides smooth communication between IoT equipment on the shop floor and other IoT hub components. The key feature of this part is to allow networking for different devices with different communication standards and an application/response model for integrating devices in the IoT hub. The key communication functionalities are the following:

i.   Have an interface for IoT system communication
ii. Create and manage the required communication channels (with device management components) and, if necessary, provide a message routing
iii. Ensure the transfer of communication protocol between external protocols and internal communication protocols.

Ubiquitous computing systems architectures have specific criteria that cannot be met in distributed systems. We believe that the programs in this type of program contain one or more components of the software that can run on different computers.

- Self-adaptation: As distributed systems, all-embracing computer systems necessarily do not have a global vision because of computer communication latency. Without centralized management systems, they need to adapt to different changes in ubiquitous computing systems.
- Dividing concerns: modifications should be possible regardless of implementations, and vice-versa. Outside of application-specific components or underlying systems, adaptations should be defined.
- Predictability and availability: adaptations can modify all-embracing computer systems dynamically but can lead to insecurity and failure so that their effects can be predicted in advance. Furthermore, after adapting our policy, applications should be made available.
- Determination of conflicts and divergences: While adaptation may be appropriate, serious difficulties such as conflicts and discrepancies can occur when they are simultaneously activated. One modification, for example, may ignore the effects of one or more other changes. Adaptations can be disabled indefinitely once their conditions have been met. In multiple adjustments as far as possible, conflicts and divergences should be detected.
- Limited resources: Ubiquitous computers often have limited resources, for example, processor power, memory quantity. Our adaptations should be able to save computational resources and be done with few resources.

In earlier sub-sections, the sequence diagram representing the functionality of the whole of the system covered by the developed Middleware described and explained the internal activities of the hub implementation. The solution has been prepared based on the concept defined and the objectives to be achieved by this research.

ALGORITHM 1: Middleware framework algorithm

Start
   Start the class DeviceManagement
   Begin listeners.
   Enter listeners.

The xmlReader is used to read the Resources / configs.xml settings;
/*The audience is started with the DataListenerFactory process. Whenever xml-
Reader "sends" the listener, DataListenerFactory begins DeviceManagement
to get contact between the web. After that, your protocol adapter initializes
the channel*/

Set the machines in motion.
>*In Resources / devices.txt, the Filer Reader is called;*
>*the interface is attached (as per the communication protocol) to*
>>*your hearer;*
>*RESTservice startup;*

/*To initialize the new devices (by DCF via RESTservice) added in this file,
perform MonitorForNewDevices function that includes a FileChangedWather
Object constantly monitors device.txt modifications;
The program continues to collect data from data sources after the contact
process is completed*/
>*DataField and the definition hierarchy are performed by generation and*
selection filters
>*DataRangeTypeLoHi.*
>*A measuring object (with the device ID and collected value) is generated*
after data is filtered
>*added to the stack of the Device class;*
>*The computer information string is sent to DataPoster;*
>*In DataPoster, the string containing device information is conglomerated*
to the monitoring string
>*(this class is running at this stage), if DCF is used to send a message.*
>*DataPoster is the JsonMessage class;*
>*The message Json (measurement and monitoring) is sent subsequently*
through a class called H5-0Utils
end

16.3.1.2   Device Management

IoT System Management allows computers to be supplied and authenticated, remotely controlled and managed, tracked and treated, and modified and maintained with firmware or applications. Thousands of devices, many hardware vendors, and several protocols of connectivity-how can you make everything IoT manageable? IoT Device Management providers usually deliver advanced features to enable IoT device management and sensor management of different types on a single platform. For example, Friendly Technologies employs Smart Layer technology to convert all kinds of IoT devices between multiple protocols and manage them through their specific One-IoT™ system management platform.

IoT services providers are keen to raise revenue from the sale of their IoT services and preserve profitability. The best way to do this is to resist the lock-in of a specific hardware manufacturer when it comes to achieving and sustain the competitiveness of IoT ventures. IoT providers must be free to choose the best of race devices and sensors that do not create a dependence, which will lead to a future decline in profitability. Another instance of a significant IoT implementation challenge IoT providers face is manual work for IoT system and sensors-installation, configuration files formation, development, approval, and testing, etc. Another example is the IoT. This manual will easily be translated into massive costs. Another innovative feature that only IoT System Management providers expertise can tackle is the automatic provisioning of IoT systems to avoid these expenses.

Friendly One-IoT™ system management software key characteristics:

- Automatic delivery
- Control of sensor and portal
- Manage various protocols on an individual basis: LwM2 M, MQTT, USP, USP-369, OMA-DM, CoAP.
- Diagnosis and maintenance of equipment
- Configuring Remote Computer
- Management of Party
- Power of FW
- Data collection and analysis
- Show of case
- API Unified
- Portals for admin & development.

The Portion includes IoT hub core management features and supports the development of appropriate channels for communication between IoT and IoT hub devices and between DCF and IoT hub [11, 12]. This component includes the functional substructures for the recording/connection and identification of devices. Details on the device are obtained from the meta-data of the device from the information stored in the DCF, such as native communications protocol, system size, data type, etc. At the same time, the connectivity status of the devices is another important objective of this component [13]. The complete section includes all information concerning the various IoT devices registered and connected with this IoT center, including details on device ID, device features/ functionality, device registration, and connection status, system work status and device authentication, and device authorization policy.

16.3.1.3   Data Handler

The IoT hub is the IoT resources entry point. It implies that this module is then processing a great deal of data from outside sources. It is mandatory for an application that allows users only to ingest such data or pre-processed data, where data can be filtered, aggregated, or combined. The data management module shall support this functionality [14]. Data Handle Factory addresses the need and provides pre-processed DCF data, for screening in real-time data obtained from heterogeneous sources. Data handler pre-processes data based on an understanding of the system context, and the end-user identified data processing limitations. It should be noted that this part has been designed to allow for easy integration into the data handler factory of new applications required for data processing [15]. Nevertheless, it is important to note that the IoT hub aims to be a lightweight, low processing network to ensure that the technique selected for pre-processed data is successful.

To summarize, IoT Hub is gathering, pre-processing, and providing data for the intended DCF format from shop floor IoT tools [16]. IoT hub output is a data stream that is defined as a "digitized signals sequence that represents transmitted information"-Federal Standard 1037C1. IoT hub outputs In the IoT hub, a data stream is generated by the timestamped relationships, indicating that a collection of tuples is included in each element of the data stream. Datastream order is extracted from the timelines series, and the IoT hub facilitates the administration and manipulation of these timelines.

Throughout this way, the time history of the data stream elements obtained by the IoT hub can still be tracked. It allows IoT hub to be the key observing device for the physical world, which is intrinsic to the observer process properties that cannot be made clear by abstraction in-network and transmission delays. To filter the unnecessary and defective data collected by the IoT hub it needs to be processed in advance, and multiple techniques can be achieved. The data will also be generated for further processing by the DCF API to the data collection system.

16.4　Implementation

16.4.1　Requirement and Functionality

First of all, we present here the general requirements that should be met by the IoT framework that directed the overall development and implementation of the architecture of the middleware solution discussed in this paper. It also includes the features and some assumptions made for the answer to be implemented.

16.4.1.1　Requirement

This section describes the framework specifications and functionalities before going through the implementation details.

- highly integrated system architecture should be: The primary purpose of providing a middleware is mainly to promote the gathering of information from an enormous variety of devices that are extremely heterogeneous in the field of communication.
- Scalable device architecture should be used: The system will be able to overgrow as more instruments are introduced, and other processing techniques and safety improvement rates can also be implemented. The ability to function in various platform systems is another significant benefit in that scalability.
- In response to a mistake, the Middleware should be able to: In an actual world, if we do not leave in a perfect setting, things are often challenging to handle or impossible. Therefore, the central concept is driving the Middleware to be more reliable against external defects.
- Before submitting data to the DCF, the Middleware should be able to prepare: A preheat filtering according to each device's specifications is one of the key requirements of this lightweight Middleware.
- Data for each system should be listed in the Middleware: While several sensors are coupled with the same intelligent system, the goal is to keep each one autonomous.
- The Middleware must be able to assess what devices are reliable: The collection of data is not done to collect data for

all sensors. It is crucial to select which devices we want to integrate into the canter.

- Before the request of the DCF, the program should be able to store data: The basic principle of data collection is to use it for a specific reason. Because the end-user is the consumer, they determine when the data generated by the sensors are important. The Middleware must, therefore, be able to collect sensor data at all times, but only send it when the cloud client requests.

- The program should ensure the protection of data: This is one of the most critical problems in our modern world, not just in IoT systems. The aim is to ensure confidentiality, completeness, and availability of data. The key concept of this dissertation is to research and establish pre-processed data structures in different communication protocols. However, in any IoT program, this is a dynamic and highly significant demand.

16.4.1.2   Functionalities

This section discusses the technologies used to illustrate the concept and to clarify the intent and choice of the idea. The functions of the canter in various modules are then specified.

- Only known tools are used to collect data: The Middleware is given a message that contains the features of the system that will be registered, and the channel communication that allows data acquisition is generated only after that.

- The Middleware will collect data from devices with different protocols of communication: With the ability to collect data by sensors connected to three various communication protocols, the Middleware is built.

- The Middleware can incorporate more communication protocols and techniques easily: If you want to add more protocols (e.g., Bluetooth or RFID), you will add the respective dependencies and create another Java class. Each communication protocol is a Java Class. Nonetheless, this aspect will rely on the message from the DCF when each device's cultic filtering characteristics are sent. The pre-processed technologies follow the same strategy.

- The Middleware has two-way cloud communication, one-way system communication: For middleware system information is retrieved from the cloud and then sent the recovered data. Data flow, devices to Middleware are geared towards unidirectional communication.
- The middleware stores the data of each computer separately: Each unit has its storage pile in memory before it is sent to the DCF.
- The details for the middleware storage system after it has been switched off, it is stored in a file upon receipt by DCF.
- Plug & Play features assured by Middleware: The system immediately activates the app from the time it is plugged in.

16.4.2 Adopted Technologies

As the development of this device is separate into Middleware and a sensor node, this segment separates the technology in two different parts: software and hardware. So, this section sets out the techniques used in the implementation of the hub and sensor nodes.

16.4.2.1 *Middleware Software*

The language in which this framework was built was Java. It was easier to write, compile, test, and understand the key reasons for this option. It has advantageous characteristics, such as object-oriented, that enables modular programs to be created. Since the proof of concept only uses sensors as devices, the middleware communication is unidirectional. However, it is entirely possible to provide a bi-directional communication if the device is created by sensors and actuators (which must receive input commands). And code that can be reused. Multi-threading capability is also a significant advantage, enabling the software to carry out a variety of tasks in software.

Besides, World Wide Web applications must run the same program on several different platforms, and Java succeeds with platform-independence on the source and binary rates. This significant feature has permitted the code to be executed on the computer (in NetBeans IDE installed in Windows) and modified more efficiently and checked before the program is implemented (in the Linux environment). It gives an additional benefit, namely its reliability, as Java emphasizes early checks to identify possible mistakes because Java compilers can detect many problems that first appear in other languages during execution. Security was another essential element of this language option. While this dissertation does not concentrate on health, Java takes health into account. Growing has built a security framework in Java language, compiler, interpreter, and runtime.

FileZilla3 has been used to migrate the code. It makes the communication and the transfer of files between the computer and the system much more straightforward. Putty software has been commonly used in access of the control line system.

16.4.2.2   Usability Dependency

The project had to use other Jars, Jars Library, and other similar objects. The project was introduced. The local repository was Maven that manages all dependencies used (could be three types: local, central, or remote repository).

When a Maven build command is executed, the following sequence begins to search for dependency libraries:

Phase 1—search is performed in the local repository first;

Phase 2—If not locally located, the quest to the central repository will be expanded. If not found, two choices are available: a remote repository—phase 4 or not-step 3 was listed. FileZilla Client is an FTP, FTPS, SFTP, and multi-purpose multi-platform client with an intuitive user interface. The software development process produces an artifact, whether software-related documentation or an executable file—Jar.

Phase3—Maven will stop processing and throw an error if a remote repository is not specified;

Phase 4—Remote repository search dependence, which is found to be downloaded for future reference to a local repository.

16.4.2.3   Sensor Node Software

The sensors used were connected to a microcontroller that reads the input (sensor) for the subsequent transmission and triggers the output. To this end, the programming Arduino language based on wiring and the open-source software Arduino (IDE), based on processing, have been used. The C++ language of programming was used. For the implementation of the communication of sensor nodes in Arduino IDE, the necessary libraries for each protocol were added:

- No additional libraries are needed for serial interface because no hardware layer has been linked to Arduino.

- A CC3000 shield was built into the Arduino system during Wi-Fi communication, which included adding the corresponding data.
- However, the ZigBee shield—router—must be attached with the ZigBee Modul linked to the Raspberry Pi—coordinator in addition to the necessary library execution. The XCTU program of Digi International has been used for this purpose.

16.4.2.4   Hardware Technology

Arduino is an open-source, hardware, and software-based prototyping platform. Arduino boards are able, by triggering a motor or turning of LEDs to read inputs-light on a sensor or finger on a button-and turn it into an output. All Arduino boards are entirely open-source, which enables users to independently develop them and ultimately customize them to their individual needs. Arduino Uno R3 was the most commonly used board for that study. For physical computing, there are also other microcontrollers. The same functionality is supported by the Parallax Simple Sticker, BX-24, Phidgets, MIT's Handy Boards, and others. Take the confusing information about programming the microcontroller and wrap it in a box that is simple to use. Arduino also simplifies the work cycle with microcontrollers, which provides advantages over other devices, for example:

- Inexpensive-Compared to other microcontrollers, Arduino boards are quite inexpensive.
- Cross-platform—Arduino software (IDE) runs on the operating systems of Windows, Macintosh OSX, and Linux. Windows is the only system that has most microcontroller modules.
- Easy—Arduino Software (IDE) for beginners is simple to use but versatile enough to help experienced users too.
- Open source and extendable software-Arduino software are released, and C++ libraries can expand the language as open-source tools.

The plans of the Arduino boards are released under a Creative Commons license so professional circuit designers can build, update and improve their version of the module.

16.4.2.5   Sensors

Within the implemented device the sensors were used:

- TMP36 was used with three output pins, + V_s, V_{out}, and GND. Temperatures are not usable. This sensor has a centigrade sensitivity of low voltage (+2.7 to +5.5 V). The output generates a voltage that is linearly proportional to the temperature of the Celsius and requires no external adjustment for standard +1 °C accuracy at +25 and +2 °C over a temperature range of −40 °C to +125 °C. The TMP36 has an output of 750 mV at 25 °C and has a factor of 10 mV/°C in performance.
- Ultrasonic-Ultrasonic HC-SR04 has four output pins: V_{cc}, Trig, Echo, GND. 2 cm to 400 cm non-contact scale, size precision up to 3 mm. The modules include ultrasonic transmitters, receivers, and circuit control. The fundamental working principle:
  - IO cause for the high-level signal of at least 10 μs,
  - The module sends an 8-cycle Ultrasound burst at 40 kHz automatically and detests if a pulse signal is reversed.
  - Where the signal back is the time from ultrasound sending to return, at a high stage, of high IO performance length.
  - The time interval can determine the duration between sending the trigger signal and receiving the echo signal. Formula: range = high speed * (340 M / S) Formule:
  - For this type of sensor, it is recommended to use an echo signal over 60 ms measuring period.

Photo-resistor—The sensor used is a photoconductor cell VT900 series LDR (light-based resistor). For increased incident light intensity, the resistance decreases. A high-resistance semiconductor is made of a photoresistor. In the dark, it can be as resistant as a couple of megaohms, but in the sun, it can be as resistant as a few hundred ohms.

The built hardware framework is explained by how the elements previously mentioned are incorporated. As the circuits were simple, the photo-resistor and temperature circuit breadboard is shown in the figure were used simultaneously. They are, however, entirely separate. The ultrasound sensor did not require an auxiliary board because the sensor output pins were directly fastened to Arduino's Wi-Fi shield (two wireless ports,

Vcc and GND). The Raspberry Pi physical devices (with the use of Middleware) connected to the ZigBee, and Wi-Fi shields were the Wi-Fi dongle and the Zigbee Coordinator. The serial cord for connecting the temperature sensor node with the Raspberry Pi was not included in this figure to improve the device understanding.

16.4.3   Details of IoT Hub

The Information about IoT center, the intermediate solution from shop floor devices to cloud service, is discussed in this chapter. Although the solution as a whole is implemented as a java project, the aim is to define each module individually for further development of both comprehension and scalability [17, 18].

Controller:
This package consists of three Java classes which manage and post data in the cloud on devices:

16.4.3.1   Data Poster

Responsible for the cloud transmission of information from the system cluster. It creates only one Data Poster entity. Then all listeners share this thing. When a measure is received on a computer, it is notified of the Data Poster, adds it to the key/value (Computer ID/Measure) data structure, and checks if this information is supposed to be forwarded. It's usually quiet if it isn't. Instead, the data structure obtained from all the knowledge, the message was correctly created by Jason's word, the object Monitoring was renamed, and when all that information was accessible, the hub was monitored and the server posted through the Http request.

16.4.3.2   Data Management

Design for system management. The following steps:

    i.   Initialize registered listeners (in Resources/configs.xml, the available data listener is added). The class that follows Factory Pattern5 uses DataListenerFactory.
    ii.   The registered devices (received DCF) should be initialized. The devices found in Resources/devices.txt are found. When the computer is shut down, this is the trick. The devices are written to a disk, as the lightweight Hub

implementation does not allow the storing of information in a local database, although it is possible;

iii. To connect to your hearer growing device.

iv. Track a system added to the hub's life cycle overall.

ChangeListener Implementation that makes the Resources/devices.txt monitoring. The.txt file is used to store all system information that was added via DCF to the database. This class shall inform Device Management of initializing new devices when the file undergoes any modifications. This file changes whenever the admin system adds/deletes/updates the application information via the DCF GUI.

The REST service will be launched by this class to receive DCF-hub settings. When a JSON message is received from any connection (e.g., from localhost 3,000/DCFconf), the message will be evaluated and checked, which is DCF message. The validation passes to construct a string with the extracted data that must be written with the object Filer Reader in configs / devices.txt

16.4.3.3 Data Listener

This set is used for hub-supported communication protocols. Can protocol checks the received ID in the message of DCF to allow devices to register in the hub. This ID is used with the method contained to query channel data structure. The program will continue as defined below if the data structure has the ID. Failure to do so eliminates the values earned.

This class initializes the serial port where Arduino is connected. This class. Because the Arduino ports cannot be listened to directly in Linux, they are synced to another port of my choice (e.g., /dev/tty63). It connects to the serial port and configures the serial port parameters (e.g., data rate, data bits, stop bits, and none of the parity). Finally, if there is data transmission in that port, the device starts listening. Otherwise, it will remain in the loop until other data appears in this port.

Instantiates a new object that is physically connected to the given port name (e.g.,/dev/ttyS88) and configured at the provided baud rate. From the device, it is necessary to know the serial port name where the XBee device (the coordinator) is attached and the baud rate to communicate with the sensor node. Other connection parameters will be set as default (8 data bits, one stop bit, no parity, and no flow control). This class has an XBee message containing the remote XBee device the message belongs to, the content (data) of the word and a flag indicating if the news is a broadcast message (was received or is being sent via broadcast).

This class implements the TCP protocol application sockets. A socket is an endpoint for two machines' contact. A server socket waits for requests to be received from the network (the sensor node requests acquired data). The filtering operations are then carried out based on this order.

16.4.3.4   Models

This kit is used to construct the layout of the devices connected to the hub. This category models the overall IoT system by providing various types of properties (properties can be involved, such as sensors, monitoring, etc.). This class is based on Information in Resources devices.txt and implements a hierarchical concept filter.

> *Unique DataRange Type LoHi*—This class is based on the Resources/Devices.txt data set filter.
> *Device*—This class contains device information such as Id, name, protocol, data type, measure range, and stack. The String with Information to send to the DCF is prepared by this class. This subject's string messages have been overwritten to be structured to be sent to the DCF.
> *Measurement*—This class preserves data collection values and timestamps. It is part of the class of the device.
> *Control*—This class maintains control of hub conditions such as free disk, disk capacity, total ram, free ram, or CPU temperature. Linux retained all of the file information and was intended to call the required commands to the operating system. More details can be obtained in another application, if necessary. Such data are forwarded to a server for further health research.

16.5   Results and Discussions

Generally, computers link through the Internet Protocol (IP) stack to the internet. The stack is highly complicated and needs a significant volume of power and energy from the operating IoT units. The IoT devices included in the package are linked to the internet by non-IP networks and are linked by an intelligent gateway. The gateway acts as an internet portal for IoT computers. Thanks to the smart gateway products, several firewalls can be hidden in the company, and no incoming ports are needed.

The approach suggested includes a model of the Middleware which can be tailored to applications. The system register, authentication, and storage maintenance is the duty of Middleware. It safeguards data confidentiality and reliability. After authorization and approval, the encrypted data are revealed via the REST API. Figure 16.5 illustrates the complete scenario. Many authorization protocols are open. For example, OAuth is an open authorization protocol that can use a username, password, and tokens to access the middleware resource. Architecture to achieve this onboard flow is clarified in Figures 16.6 and 16.7.

> Phase 1: System recording includes registered users who have already established an online middleware account.
> Phase 2: If an IoT user sends an authorization request, the gateway validates the request for devices like the payload system

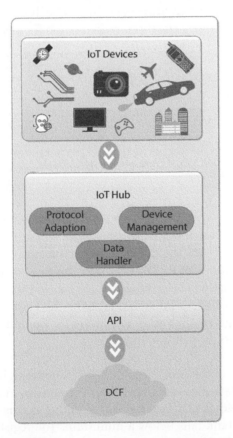

Figure 16.5 Middleware work.

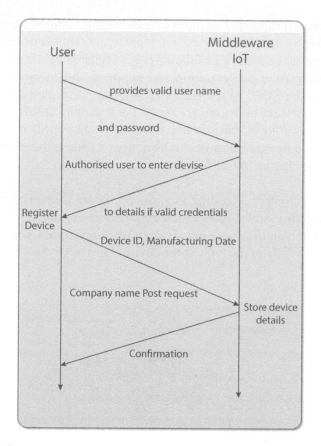

Figure 16.6 Device registration.

by accessing the exposed REST API. Gateway ID and hidden key are used as input parameters. The API authenticates the portal and clears the demand. Authentication is mandatory for all methods of REST API. After the gateway is approved, the response will be sent back to the gateway in an encrypted form with system information. Now the connection to the portal is given after authentication. The computer will submit data to the gateway in real-time.

The application of this work is applied for water tank level monitor and accurate in the data gathering method. The sensor trigger threshold is recorded on the cloud platform before the simulation is started to detect if the level of the tank falls below a minimum. The registration process is shown in Figure 16.8(b). It is important to note that tank simulation is

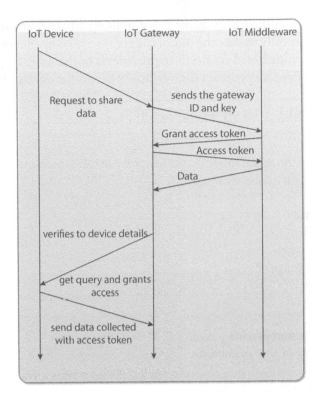

Figure 16.7 Sharing the data.

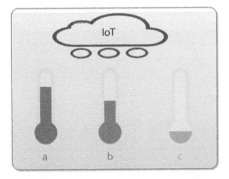

Figure 16.8 Levels of sensor reading.

external to the architecture implemented while the trigger is part of the architecture.

A web service URL is set in the trigger component. Control, when the sensor value controlled, falls below the appropriate threshold limits of the trigger. When the trigger is activated, the actuator recharges the tank to its highest level. Figure 16.8(c) shows this condition. This experiment can be used to dynamically update the initial trigger threshold by the trigger component at runtime based on user's requirements or dynamic environmental changes. This role provides the versatility to run the device efficiently.

ALGORITHM 1: Data capturing algorithm

Start

> *Retrieve the middleware access token for the API-inbound.*
> *Request for access token URL{*
> *Post*
> *Response*
> *{*
> *"access token"*
> *Type of token=?*
> *Valid in =?*
> *}*

Accepts mandatory fields

> *Gateway id and password*
> *{*
> *Data accept*
> *Device identifier=?*
> *Device manufacture =?*
> *Uid=?*
> *}*

Header

> *Content type*
> *Access identifier*
> *}*
> *Function ()*
> *{*
> *Success/ fail*
> *Error identifier*
> *Consol.log(data);*
> *}*

end

Simulation Results: Our solution showed that it was able to monitor the water levels of the tank and conduct a refill based on the specified thresholds, from the above-explained use case scenario. Figure 16.9 shows the graphical description in our visualization interface of the monitoring data from the tank's behavior. The first data sample shows that the tank level is 100%. It falls below the 15% threshold following a 10-second depletion, which leads the actuator to recharge the tank. The threshold limit is dynamically updated to 45% after around 40 s, causing the actuator to restore the tank when the water drops under that threshold. Figure 16.9 shows our platform's ability to adapt to dynamic changes in operating times.

Interoperability test: We conduct specific experiments in this case scenario to test the interoperability of our implemented platform with other platforms like ThingSpeak. Readings (consisting of alphanumeric time series data) have been extracted from a web service ThingSpeak 's public temperature sensor, which has been entered on our platform via the generic interface. The Netduino Plus microcontroller connected to a series of sensors was connected to one of the standard ThingSpeak demonstration canals, my own, and we extracted the outside temperature area over 24 h. We also connected to this system. The connection setup is shown in Figure 16.10. The purpose of this test is for the communication and data transmission between heterogeneous platforms to show the sensitivity of our platform.

Test results for interoperability: The interoperability study, as showed in graphs, allowed us to confirm the ability of our applied framework to

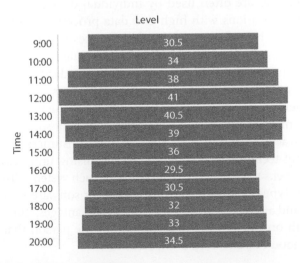

Figure 16.9 Levels of the sensor reading.

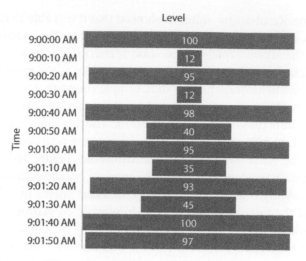

Figure 16.10 Levels of the sensor reading.

communicate seamlessly with existing heterogeneous platforms. We have been able to interact and save them in our database for analyses with the thing Speak sensors.

16.6 Conclusion

A centralized scenario model of IoT prevails where data sources are physically isolated and are often used by individual data users who also use higher-level applications with high-end data processing and event detection capabilities. Nonetheless, if the data sources and the data users are tightly coupled, such distributed scenarios can generate a lot of scalability and maintenance issues. It implies changes in standards for communications and data exchange of data sources or consumers; the overall systems need to undergo respective modifications to meet the new requirements. Therefore, a method for seamless integration of data sources with a high level of abstraction among data sources and consumers is an ultimate industrial and technological solution. By disguising unnecessary details, Middleware seeks to reduce the complexity of such systems. There are several different types of Middleware, as with most software styles, with different aims and a range of advantages and disadvantages. The right option depends both on the mission and the skill of the person that is using it. There is no good or poor kind of Middleware.

This research presents a technological solution together with the required architecture for IoT Middleware to be scalable. The solution will increase the IoT use and incorporate existing legacy devices seamlessly in the industrial environment. This research work also offers a detailed study, in addition to the technological solution, of the problems in the IoT paradigm, which can pave the way for further research and implementation. The findings of this thesis also make an important contribution to implementing the complete framework for C2NET data collection. The major benefit of this approach, relative to some current implementations within the IoT model, is that its findings have been achieved as expected by the use of low-powered computing tools like raspberry-pi. This research can thus provide an affordable solution for SMEs wishing to deploy IoT-based solutions. The results are technical.

The incorporation of security constraints such as data protection, access control, and consumer privacy is one of the potential enhancements to an established architecture. The problems associated with an unknown program are massive, and applying this software in an industrial context is important to bring data protection into line with product quality. Since several aspects have to be considered and data protection must be taken into account during the latter phase of product implementation, this aspect has, in some parameters, been taken into account but has not been developed in the current application. Creating security and faith in IoT can be an exciting and demanding job in the future.

References

1. Marcelo Arenas, J.P.J.R., Data exchange beyond complete data. *J. ACM (JACM)*, 60, 4, 1–59, 2013.
2. O'Leary, A.V.a.C., A framework for rapid integration of IoT Systems with industrial environments, in: *IEEE 5th World Forum on Internet of Things (WF-IoT)*, Limerick, Ireland, 2019.
3. Fox, A.D.J., The deployment of an IoT network infrastructure, as a localised regional service, in: *IEEE 5th World Forum on Internet of Things (WF-IoT)*, Limerick, Ireland, 2019.
4. Wu, T.W.F., Design and Implementation of a Wearable Sensor Network System for IoT-Connected Safety and Health Applications, in: *IEEE 5th World Forum on Internet of Things (WF-IoT)*, Limerick, Ireland, 2019.
5. Qiu, Z.G.Z., DAQ-Middleware: Data Acquisition Middleware Based on Internet of Things, in: *3rd International Conference on Big Data Computing and Communications (BIGCOM)*, Chengdu, 2017.

6. Sekiyama, B.K.K.M., Sensor data processing based on the data log system using the portable IoT device and RT-Middleware, in: *12th International Conference on Ubiquitous Robots and Ambient Intelligence (URAI)*, Goyang, 2015.

7. La, J.Y.L.H.J., An Efficient Context Acquisition for 'n' Mobile Apps, in: *IEEE 12th International Conference on Dependable, Autonomic and Secure Computing*, Dalian, 2014.

8. Han, K.Z.D., A Context-Based Requirement Acquisition and Description Method, in: *Sixth International Conference on Internet Computing for Science and Engineering*, Henan, 2012.

9. Lesi, V., Reliable industrial IoT-based distributed automation, in: *IoTDI '19: Proceedings of the International Conference on Internet of Things Design and Implementation*, 2019.

10. Gündogan, C., Information-centric networking for the industrial IoT, in: *ICN '17: Proceedings of the 4th ACM Conference on Information-Centric Networking*, 2017.

11. Lea, M.B.a.R., IoT interoperability: A hub-based approach, in: *International Conference on the Internet of Things (IOT)*, Cambridge, MA, 2014.

12. Kim, J.W.L.a.Y.W., A study on smart IoT hub for intelligent signage services using trust information, in: *International Conference on Information Networking (ICOIN)*, Chiang Mai, 2018.

13. Mai, C., Budget-Hub: A low cost IoT hub selection and neighbor assignment scheme, in: *IEEE 4th World Forum on Internet of Things (WF-IoT)*, Singapore, 2018.

14. Murata, K.T. *et al.*, Development of High-Performance and Flexible Protocol Handler for International Web Accesses, in: *IEEE 21st International Conference on High Performance Computing and Communications*, Zhangjiajie, China, 2019.

15. Joo, H.N.C.Y.S., An implementation of energy efficient multiple event handler using an integrated packet for the ubiquitous sensor network system, in: *9th International Symposium on Communications and Information Technology*, Icheon, 2009.

16. Gifre, L.M.C.L., Big data analytics in support of virtual network topology adaptability, in: *Optical Fiber Communications Conference and Exhibition (OFC)*, Anaheim, CA, 2016.

17. Marosi, R.L.A.C., A novel IoT platform for the era of connected cars, in: *IEEE International Conference on Future IoT Technologies (Future IoT)*, Eger, 2018.

18. Momenzadeh, H.D.B., Best Practices Would Make Things Better in the IoT. *IEEE Secur. Priv.*, 18, 4, 38–47, 2020.

Index

Also of Interest

Check out these published and forthcoming related titles from Scrivener Publishing

Smart Systems for Industrial Applications
Edited by C. Venkatesh, N. Rengarajan, P. Ponmurugan and S. Balamurugan
Forthcoming 2022. ISBN 978-1-119-76200-3

Impact of Artificial Intelligence on Organizational Transformation
Edited by S. Balamurugan, Sonal Pathak, Anupriya Jain, Sachin Gupta, and
Sachin Sharma and Sonia Duggal
Forthcoming 2022. ISBN 978-1-119-71017-2

Nature-Inspired Algorithms Applications
Edited by S. Balamurugan, Anupriya Jain, Sachin Sharma, Dinesh Goyal,
Sonia Duggal and Seema Sharma
Forthcoming 2022. ISBN 978-1-119-68174-8

Artificial Intelligence for Renewable Energy Systems
Edited by Ajay Kumar Vyas, S. Balamurugan, Kamal Kant Hiran and
Harsh S. Dhiman
Forthcoming 2022. ISBN 978-1-119-76169-3

**Artificial Intelligence Techniques for Wireless Communication and
Networking**
Edited by Kanthavel R., K. AnathaJothi, S. Balamurugan and
R. Karthik Ganesh
Forthcoming 2022. ISBN 978-1-119-82127-4

Advanced Healthcare Systems
Empowering Physicians with IoT-Enabled Technologies
Edited by Rohit Tanwar, S. Balamurugan, R. K. Saini, Vishal Bharti and
Premkumar Chithaluru
Forthcoming 2022. ISBN 978-1-119-76886-9

Printed and bound by CPI Group (UK) Ltd, Croydon, CR0 4YY

27/10/2024

14580468-0003